BROADBAND
COMMUNICATIONS

SIGNATURE SERIES

Broadband
Communications
Signature Edition

Balaji Kumar

McGraw-Hill

New York   San Francisco   Washington, D.C.   Auckland   Bogotá
Caracas   Lisbon   London   Madrid   Mexico City   Milan
Montreal   New Delhi   San Juan   Singapore
Sydney   Tokyo   Toronto

Library of Congress Cataloging-in-Publication Data

Kumar, Balaji.
   Broadband communications / Balaji Kumar.—Signature ed.
     p. cm.—(The McGraw-Hill series on computer communications)
   Includes index.
   ISBN 0-07-038293-X
   1. Broadband communication systems. I. Title. II. Series.
TK5103.4.K88 1998
004.6'6   98-2695
                                               CIP

McGraw-Hill

A Division of The **McGraw·Hill** *Companies*

  4 5 6 7 8 9 0 DOC/DOC 0 3 2 1 0

ISBN 0-07-038293-X

The sponsoring editor for this book was Steven Elliot, the editing supervisor was Frank Kotowski, Jr., and the production supervisor was Tina Cameron. It was set in Vendome ICG by McGraw-Hill's Professional Book Group composition unit, Hightstown, N.J.

Printed and bound by R. R. Donnelley & Company.

McGraw-Hill books are available at special quantity discounts to use as premiums and sales promotions, or for use in corporate training programs. For more information, please write to the Director of Special Sales, McGraw-Hill, Professional Publishing, Two Penn Plaza, New York, NY 10121-2298. Or contact your local bookstore.

 This book is printed on recycled, acid-free paper containing a minimum of 50% recycled, de-inked fiber.

To my son Anup, my wife Durga, my parents Joola and Sahasranaman, and my brother Vijay

CONTENTS

Contents

Contents

Contents

Part 3   BROADBAND ARCHITECTURE

Contents

Contents

Contents

INTRODUCTION

The 1990s have inaugurated the second revolution of telecommunications. Changes have already occurred so rapidly in the telecommunications and computer environments that it is hard to believe that more is to come. This book gives the reader a snapshot of different technologies that will drive the future of telecommunications. Welcome to the New World!

The primary objective of this book is to present a comprehensive view of one aspect of next-generation telecommunications technology—broadband communications, which encompasses multimedia applications where voice, video, and data are integrated. The reader learns the standards, technology, services, architecture, and protocols of end-to-end broadband communications. Among the different broadband technologies mentioned, the most inportant, asynchronous transfer mode, or ATM, is covered in detail. Here the different environments that ATM can effect are covered, including local area networks (LANs), wide area networks (WANs), and public networks.

The focus is in the ATM aspects of broadband communications that will be applicable in the next few years. Although ATM is capable of handling all types of traffic (voice, video, and data), data traffic will most likely be the initial target for ATM, with other traffic to follow later. Because broadband communications is a new technology and its applications are still unfolding around the world, it is not possible to cover every aspect. Within the context of data traffic, experts argue about which environment (LAN or WAN, etc.) ATM will penetrate first. The penetration will most likely depend on which vendor designs the right equipment at the right time. Some say ATM's first environment will be LAN, some say WAN, and others say public backbone (long distance). This book provides a list of web addresses for some broadband equipment vendors.

Intended Audience

This book covers the basics of broadband technologies, emphasizing the end-to-end broadband environment such as access, switching technology (ATM), transmission technology, and intelligent architecture (IN). As broadband IN area is relatively new, the book is organized in such a way to address audiences who have some understanding of communication (voice or data) as well as those in any other professional field. For those in other fields, sufficient background and history are provided. In addition, this book can be used as course material for a senior or graduate-level communications class. Every effort has been made to ensure that this book can remain useful as a reference guide for a long time.

Major Changes in the Second Edition

In spite of the fact that this book was written to be a future reference, many changes have occurred since the first edition. This is due to the rapid changes occurring in the telecommunication environment. Along with the technology and its application, it has become difficult to be up to date with the acronym list, let alone trying to understand the technology.

I have received numerous comments on what the second edition should include. With the ever-changing telecommunication environment, and trying to be, at the same time, within the objective of the book (handbook for broadband communications), we decided to update the book to provide a comprehensive story with respect to broadband communications. After careful consideration, the following changes are included in the second edition:

1. General update: The entire book has been reviewed for completeness and consistency. Hundreds of small changes have been made to keep the text up to-date. Particular emphasis is made on the standardization, and new technology and its application.

2. Chapter organization: The organization of the text has been changed in a few chapters to reflect the feedback received. Changes were done to make each chapter generally self-contained and modular. Some of the modifications are as follows:
   - CATV architecture has moved from Chap. 18 to Chap. 1 to reflect the third type of network, namely the video network, along with a voice and data network discussed in Chap. 1..
   - The future CATV architecture, the hybrid fiber coax (HFC), is now part of the new Chap. 13.
   - Chapter 7 has been removed to reflect the importance of SMDS technology and service in global environment.

- Intelligent network (IN) architecture session in Chap. 1 has moved to be with broadband IN architecture in Chap. 16.
- Additional ATM applications information have been added in Chap. 7.

3. New chapters: The changing environment motivated me to add the following chapters:

- Broadband access technologies: This chapter covers some of the new broadband access technology trends. It includes the missing pieces of providing end-to-end broadband communication.
- Broadband access network architecture: This chapter covers various public access network architecture options that take advantage of the broadband access technologies mentioned in Chap. 9. These architectures are some of the potential candidates for the public network around the world.
- Broadband intelligent network: This chapter discusses some of the limitations on the current intelligent network and some potential ATM based broadband IN architecture.

Organization of the Book

This book is organized into seven parts, with each part containing related chapters.

Part 1 provides the background of communications as a whole, including a history of telephone and computer networks and video networks. We then introduce the broadband concept and discuss possible evolution of different types of networks to potential target architecture.

Part 2 describes the different broadband technologies. Here FDDI, DQDB, frame relay, SMDS, ATM, SONET, and broadband access technologies are covered.

Part 3 provides the broadband architecture as defined by the ITU-T. Here the BISDN architecture protocol layers are covered in detail, along with other aspects of BISDN.

Part 4 covers access architectures, broadband switching, transmission, and broadband IN. The various access architecture options are discussed, in addition to the functional components of broadband switching transmission systems and intelligent networks.

Part 5 covers the different environments applicable to ATM switching. Here ATM in LAN, WAN, and public network are discussed.

Part 6 discusses how to design a broadband network from any existing network facilities. The emphasis here is not on the simulation or modeling of traffic characteristics, but on the process of designing a broadband network.

Part 7 covers topics that do not fit in any of the above categories. These chapters add value in terms of understanding ATM in the real world and the standardization process for new technology at the international level and the next step to take from the existing ATM/SONET systems. Figure I.1 illustrates the organization of the book.

—BALAJI KUMAR

Figure I.1
Organization of the book.

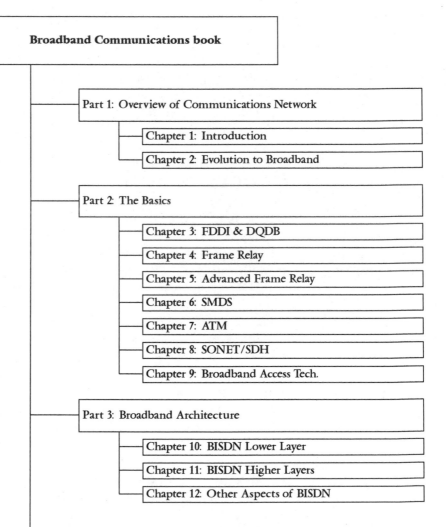

Figure I.1
(Continued)

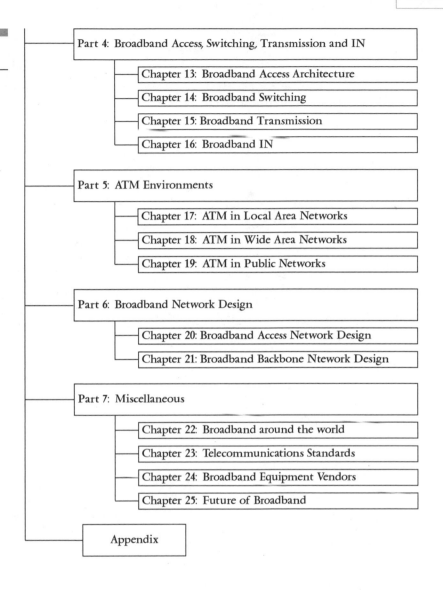

Part 4: Broadband Access, Switching, Transmission and IN

Chapter 13: Broadband Access Architecture

Chapter 14: Broadband Switching

Chapter 15: Broadband Transmission

Chapter 16: Broadband IN

Part 5: ATM Environments

Chapter 17: ATM in Local Area Networks

Chapter 18: ATM in Wide Area Networks

Chapter 19: ATM in Public Networks

Part 6: Broadband Network Design

Chapter 20: Broadband Access Network Design

Chapter 21: Broadband Backbone Ntework Design

Part 7: Miscellaneous

Chapter 22: Broadband around the world

Chapter 23: Telecommunications Standards

Chapter 24: Broadband Equipment Vendors

Chapter 25: Future of Broadband

Appendix

ACKNOWLEDGMENTS

Many people have helped me prepare the first edition of this book. During the second edition I would like to thank my friends at MCI. They provided valuable critique, information, and other services. I thank all of them. In particular, I am grateful to Ned Fairnholt, Hack Kim, Jack Wimmer, John Montgomery, Steve Jones, Tim Scheafer, Richard Kellerman, Rick McLean, Sri Nathan, Eric Chern, and Zhara Ghasamian.

In addition, I would like to mention some of my friends who have helped me in many different ways, namely Sridhar, Jey, Biswajit, Jay Ranade, Achala, Beena, and Joylyn.

ACRONYMS AND ABBREVIATIONS

AAL	ATM adaptation layer
ABR	asynchronous bit rate
ADSL	asymmetric digital subscriber line
AN	access node
ANS	advanced network and services
ANSI	American National Standards Institute
APS	automatic protection switching
ARPA	Advanced Research Projects Agency
ATM	asynchronous transfer mode
ATU	ADSL terminal unit
AU	access unit
BAGNET	Bay Area Gigabit Network
BECN	backward explicit congestion notification
BER	bit-error rate
BH	busy-hour
BISDN	broadband integrated services digital network
BOM	beginning of message
BRI	basic rate interface
BSS	broadcast satellite service
CAC	connection admission control
CAD	computer-aided design
CAE	computer-aided engineering
CAM	computer-aided manufacturing
CAP	carrierless amplitude phase
CATV	cable television *or* community antenna television
CBDS	constant bit rate data service

CBR	continuous bit rate *or* constant bit rate
CC	congestion control
CCS	hundred call seconds
CCITT	Consultative Committee on International Telegraph and Telephone
CDDI	coaxial distributed data interface
CFM	configuration management
CIR	committed information rate
CIX	commercial internet exchange
CLLM	consolidated link layer management
CLP	cell loss priority
CMISE	common management information service elements
CMT	connection management
CNET	Centre National L'Etudes des Telecommunicating
CNRI	Corporation for National Research Initiative
CO	central office
COI	community of interest
COM	continuation of message
CPE	customer premise equipment
CPN	customer premises node
CRC	cyclic redundancy check
CS	convergence sublayer
CSMA/CD	carrier sense, multiple-access high-collision detection
CSU/DSU	channel service unit/data service unit
DAS	dual attachment stations
DBS	direct broadcast satellite
DCC	data communications channels
DCE	data communications equipment
DE	discard eligibility
DLCI	data link connection identifier
DMT	discrete multitone
DOD	Department of Defense
DOJ	Department of Justice
DQDB	distributed queue dual bus

DSP	digital signal processors
DTE	data terminal equipment
DTP	data transport protocol
DTPM	data transport protocol machine
DWMT	discrete wavelet multitone
EA	extended address
EC	European Commission
ECM	coordination management
ECN	explicit congestion notification
ECSA	Exchange Carriers Standards Association
EO	end office
EOM	end of message
EST	end system identifier
ESO	European Standards Organization
FCC	Federal Communications Commission
FCS	frame check sequence
FDDI	fiber distributed data interface
FDM	frequency division multiplexing
FEC	forward error correction
FECN	forward explicit congestion notification
FEP	front-end processor
FFT	fast Fourier transform
FiFo	first-in—first-out
FIX	federal internet exchange
FR	frame relay
FRF	Frame-Relay Forum
FRI	frame-relay interface
FSK	frequency shift keying
FSAN	full-service access network
FSN	full-service network
FTAM	file transfer access and management
FTTC	fiber to the curb
FTP	file transfer protocol

FTTH	fiber to the home
GAN	global area network
GEN	global European network
GFC	generic flow control
GOS	grade of service
HDLC	high-level data link control
HDSL	high bit-rate digital subscriber line
HDT	host digital terminal
HDTV	high-definition television
HE	header extension
HEC	header error control
HFC	hybrid fiber/coaxial
HIPPI	high performance parallel interface
HOB	head of bus
HRC	hybrid ring control
HSSI	high-speed serial interface
I/O	input/output
IAO	intra-office optical interface
IC	integrated circuit
ICI	intercarrier interface
ICIP	intercarrier interface protocol
IDLC	integrated digital loop carrier
IEC	interexchange carriers
IFFT	inverse fast Fourier transform
IFRB	International Frequency Registration Board
IIME	intranetwork SMDS mapping entity
IN	intelligent network
INTUG	International Trade and User Groups
IO	international organization
IP	intelligent peripheral
IS	information systems
ISDN	integrate services digital network
ISO	International Organization for Standardization

ISP	internet service provider
ISSI	interswitching system interface
ITFS	instructional television fixed service
ITU	International Telecommunications Union
IWU	internetworking unit
IXC	interexchange carrier
JPEG	Joint Photographic Experts Group
JTCI	Joint Technical Committee on Information Technology
JTM	job transfer and manipulation
JTPC	Joint Technical Programing Committee
LAN	local area network
LANE	ATM LAN emulation
LAP-B	link access protocol-B
LATA	local-access transport area
LEA	line extender amplifier
LEC	local exchange carrier
LECS	LAN-emulation configuration server
LED	light-emitting diodes
LEN	local exchange node
LES	LAN-emulation server
LI	length indicator
LLC	logical link control
LMDS	local multipoint distribution service
LME	layer management entity
LMP	layer management protocol
LOH	line overhead
LOS	line of sight
LT	line termination
LTE	line terminating equipment
LUNI	LAN-emulation use-network interface
MAC	media access control
MAE	metropolitan area exchanges
MAGIC	Multidimensional Applications and Gigabit International Consortium

Acronyms and Abbreviations

MAN	metropolitan area network
MDS	multipoint distribution service
METRAN	managed European transmission network
MFJ	modified final judgment
MHS	message handling system
MIB	management information base
MID	message identified
MIN	multipath interconnection
MMDS	multichannel multipoint distribution service
MMF	multimode fiber
MPEG	Motion Picture Experts Group
MPOA	multiple protocol over ATM
MSO	multisystem operators
NAP	network access points
NCGN	North Carolina GigoNet
NIF	neighborhood information frame
NITT	National Information Infrastructure Test Bed
N-ISDN	narrowband ISDN
NIUF	North American ISDN User's Forum
NME	network management entity
NNI	network-network interface
NSAP	network source access point
NSF	National Science Foundation
NTIA	National Telecommunications and Information Administration
NTSC	National Television System Committee
NVOD	near video on demand
O/E	optical to electrical
OAM	operations, administration, and maintenance
OAMP	operations, administrations, management, and provisioning
OC	optical carrier
OCI	optical carrier interface
ONI	optical network interface
ONU	optical network unit

OS	operations system
OSI	open systems interconnection
OSS	operations systems
OTA	Office of Technology Assessment
PA	Prearbitrated
PAD	packet assembler and disassembler
PC	priority control
PCM	physical connection management
PCS	personal communications services
PDH	plesiochronous digital hierarchy
PDU	protocol data unit
PES	packetized elementary stream
PFM	parameter frame management
PHY	physical layer protocol
PLOAM	physical-layer OAM
PLPC	physical layer convergence protocol
PM	physical medium
PMD	physical layer medium dependent
PMF	parameter management frame
POH	path overhead
PON	passive optical network
POP	point of presence
POTS	plain old telephone service
PPL	phase-locked loop
PPV	pay-per-view
PRI	primary rate interface
PRM	protocol reference model
PS	program stream
PSTN	public-switched telephone network
PT	payload type
PTE	path terminating equipment
PTI	payload type indicator
PTM	packet transfer mode

PTT	post, telegraph, and telephone
PVC	permanent virtual circuit
QA	queued arbitrated
QAM	quadrature amplitude modulation
QOS	quality of service
QPSX	queued packed synchronous exchange
RACE	Research and Development in Advanced Communication Technologies in Europe
RADSL	rate adaptive digital subscriber loop
RARC	Regional Administrative Radio Conference
RATT	RIO22 ATM Technology test bed
RBOC	Regional Bell Operating Company
RER	residual error rate
RM	resource management
RME	routing management entity
RMN	remote multiplexer node
RMP	routing management protocol
RMT	ring management
RPOA	recognized private operating agency
SAP	service access point
SAR	segmentation and reassembly sublayer
SAS	single attachement stations
SCP	service control point
SDH	synchronous digital hierarchy
SDSL	symmetrical digital subscriber loop
SDU	service data unit
SIF	status information frame
SIO	scientific and industrial organization
SIP	SMDS interface protocol
SLC	simple line code
SMDS	switched multimegabit data service
SMF	single mode fiber
SMS	service management system
SMT	station management

SN	sequence number
SNA	system network architecture
SNI	subscriber network interface
SNMP	simple network management protocol
SNP	sequence number protection
SNR	signal-to noise ratio
SOH	section overhead
SONET	synchronous optical network
SPE	synchronous payload envelope
SPID	service profile identifer
SPM	SONET physical layer mapping
SPN	subscriber premises network
SRF	status report frame
SS7	signaling system number 7
SSP	service switching point
ST	sequence type
STAR	special telecommunication for regional development
STB	set-top box
STM	synchronous transfer mode
STP	shielded twisted pair
STS	synchronous transport signal
STV	Sprint Telecommunications Venture
SVC	switched virtual circuit *or* signaling virtual circuit
TA	trunk amplifier
TC	transmission convergence
TCB	Telecommunications Development Bureau
TCD	Technical Cooperation Department
TCP/IP	transmission control protocol/internet protocol
TDM	time division multiplexing
TDMA	time division multiple access
TEN	transit exchange node
THT	token holding timer
TNN	transport network node
TOH	transport overhead

TP	transaction processing
TR	Bellcore technical reference document
TRT	token rotation timer
TS	transport stream
TTRT	target token rotation time
TVX	valid transmission timer
UNI	user network interface
UPC	usage parameter control
UTOPIA	universal test and operation physical interface for ATM
UTP	unshielded twisted pair
vBNS	very high-speed backbone network service
VBR	variable bit rate
VCC	virtual channel connection
VCI	virtual channel-identifier
VDSL	very high-speed digital subscriber loop
VDT	video dial tone
VG	voice grade
VIP	video information provider
VOD	video on demand
VPC	virtual path connection
VPCI	virtual path connection identifier
VPI	virtual path identifier
VPN	virtual private network
VT	virtual tributary
WAN	wide area network
WARC	World Administrative Radio Conference
WATTC	World Administrative Telephone and Telegraph Conference
WCA	Wireless Cable Association
WDM	wavelength division multiplexing
XAME	exchange access SMDS mapping entity
XC	cross connect
x-DSL	x-digital subscriber loop

PART 1

Overview of Communications Networks

P art 1 of this book introduces you to some background and history of communications followed by the evolution of various communications networks. The reader learns about existing telephone, computer, and video networks with their potential technological paths to reach the target network of the future: an integrated asynchronous transfer mode/synchronous optical network (ATM/SONET)-based broadband network. Many reasons exist for the migration toward this type of integrated network, the most important being that no other existing network has the ability to handle all types of communications traffic (voice, data, and video) efficiently both in terms of utilization of resources and the cost of providing the service. Each of these networks handles traffic with different characteristics in the most optimum way possible. Also, in this part the drivers for migrating toward a broadband environment are addressed along with some of the potential broadband applications that are candidates for an integrated broadband network.

CHAPTER 1

Communication Basics

1.1 Introduction

You've just driven home from work. You get out of the car and walk up to the front door. You don't need to reach into your pocket to get your keys because your eyes open the door for you. As you enter your home and walk through the living room, you have the following dialog with your computer:

YOU: Do I have any messages?

COMPUTER: Yes, you have three new messages. Do you want to play them?

YOU: Yes, I want them on my bedroom screen (they are video messages).

The computer displays the video messages on an enormous flat screen on the bedroom wall. (Additional screens are in other rooms of the house.)

After dinner, you would like to help your child with his or her homework. The assignment is to write a paper on the pygmy tribes of Africa. Although you don't have a clue about the topic, you don't worry. First, you ask the computer to gather enough information about the pygmies to complete the paper. The computer searches all available libraries and video images to compile the data. In a matter of minutes the computer asks, "Are you ready to view the data?" Once you are ready, the computer then displays the information on the flat screen.

Now that your child is busy writing the report, you decide to relax and watch a movie. You ask the computer for a list of the latest PG-13 ones. It brings up a list, you select one, and ask the computer to play it. The computer extracts the movie from the database at a video store nearby and plays it as if it were being played from your home VCR, the only difference being that the VCR is at a remote location.

Suddenly, the computer interrupts you from viewing the movie to announce that a video call is coming in. You ask the computer to put the movie on pause and answer the video call. When you complete the call, the computer automatically switches the movie from pause to play so you can continue to view it from the point where you stopped before the video call.

The previous example illustrates the range of services available through broadband technologies. They include the following:

■ *Video voice mail:* Voice-activated remote video answering machine

■ *Interactive video phone:* Voice-activated, video-based telephone conversation

- *Video on demand:* Access of remotely located VCRs on demand
- *Data and video transfer:* Voice-activated access of information from remote text and video libraries across the country

In addition to these, numerous other applications are being provided by broadband communications. The objective of the example, however, is to illustrate the integration of voice (a video call of voice and video), data (accessing information such as text, graphics, and video from a library), and video (viewing a movie played at a remote location). A cost-effective integration like this is not possible with today's segregated communication systems.

The example is not a science fiction movie, and, yes, one day you will be living in this type of world. The technology that is going to bring you this type of service is right here. Broadband communications is made up of three components:

- Synchronous optical network (SONET)
- Asynchronous transfer mode (ATM)
- Intelligent networks (IN)

These are the transmission, switching, and intelligent network architecture of future technologies. This book provides you with a clear understanding of these and other related technologies that are the backbone of broadband communications. This chapter reviews the basics of communications from the standpoint of both the computer and telecommunications. The future of communications is an integrated communications system that can handle both voice from telephone networks and data from computer networks. As a result, the future network will not be distinguished solely by the network's applications, unlike today's telephone networks based on voice and computer networks which are based on data traffic.

Before we go into detail, let's first understand the basics of communications. The word *communication* is derived from Latin *communicare*, which means to share. Communication is a process of representing, transforming, interpreting, or processing information among persons, places, or machines. This process involves a sender, receiver, and transmission medium over which the information flows.

Figure 1.1 illustrates the simplest of all communications: a basic conversation between two people, where the person speaking transfers information by talking, thus changing the pressure of the air that impinges on the other person's eardrum.

Figure 1.1
Basic form of
communication.

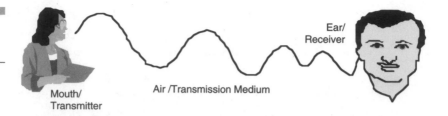

The problem with this type of communication is distance. Once the two persons move away from each other, the information carried in the air loses its strength before it reaches the other person; thus, the need for a better transmission medium arises. The earliest form of telecommunications was the telephone. To communicate, both persons need similar equipment. A basic telephone conversation uses electricity in a wire instead of air as the transmission medium, allowing the transfer of information between two persons to be carried over a longer distance. Figure 1.2 shows a simple telephone connection. This connection is not adequate if more than two people need to communicate with each other, which is where a communications network comes into existence. A communications network provides the means of linking many people efficiently using links and nodes.

1.2 What Is a Communications Network?

A *communications network* is a system of interconnected facilities designed to carry traffic from a variety of telecommunication sources. A network consists of nodes and links. Node locations include switching offices, junction pairs, or both, and links includes cable, terminating equipment, etc. Traffic is the information within the network that flows via these nodes and links. Three characteristics influence the design of a communications network:

■ Traffic carried over large geographic areas

■ Variation of traffic distribution pattern

■ Ability to exchange information with negligible delays

A communications network is a common resource shared by numerous end users that need to communicate with other users at remote locations. Not every user uses the network all the time, so it is logical to share this important resource. Sharing is where the concept of switching comes into play. Suppose no switching exists in a network. Then, in a network of m locations, you would have the following:

■ The number of links required is $m(m-1)/2$

■ The number of telephones needed is $m(m-1)$

A central switch reduces the number of links and telephones required to m. As shown in Fig. 1.3, a communications network consists of three major component categories:

■ Station equipment or customer premises equipment (CPE)

■ Switching

■ Transmission facilities or links

1.2.1 Station Equipment

Station equipment is generally located at the user's premises. Its function is to transmit and receive user information (traffic) and exchange control

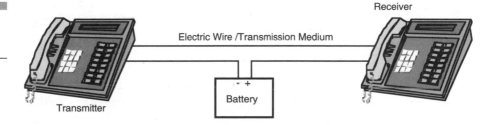

Figure 1.2
Simple telephone connection.

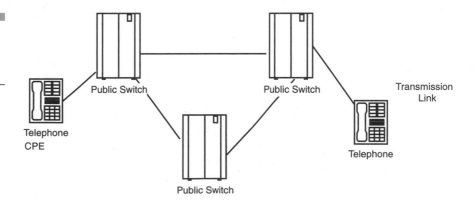

Figure 1.3
Interaction between switches, links, and CPE.

information with the network that makes it possible to place calls and gain access to the network. The information is converted into electrical signals and transmitted to the other end, where it is converted back to its original form. The CPE equipment can be a telephone, computer terminal, or fax machine.

1.2.2   Switching

Switching systems are generally called nodes. These systems interconnect the transmission facilities at various locations and route the traffic through the network. In a typical node, the number of incoming lines is greater than the number of outgoing lines (trunks) because of multiplexing, which results in improved utilization in the use of trunk facilities. Multiplexing is possible because the utilization on the incoming or access side is very low, usually less than 10 percent.

1.2.3   Transmission Facilities

Transmission facilities provide communications paths to carry the user's voice and network control information between nodes in a network. In general, transmission facilities consist of a medium such as air, copper wires, coaxial cables, or fiber-optic cables, in addition to other electronic equipment located in the path. This equipment amplifies the signal so it can be carried over a longer distance without losing its strength. The most difficult part of building a communications network is laying the transmission network because of the cost and time involved in deploying cable across the country or even around the globe.

Having explained the basis of a communications network, we can now categorize this communications network based on its dominant applications. A network used for voice communication is called *telecommunications network,* and one used for data communication among computers is called a *computer communications network* or *data communications network.* This separation does not mean that data cannot be carried over the telecommunications (voice) network or vice versa. It only means that the network is designed and optimized for its specific application, and transporting any other information results in the inefficient use of network resources.

1.3   Telecommunications Network

This section describes a voice-oriented network, starting with the history and then the specific architecture of the network.

1.3.1   Telecommunications History

Telecommunication first came into existence with the development of the telegraph in the 1830s and 1840s. For the first time, news and information could be transmitted over great distances almost instantaneously. The invention of the telephone in 1876 by Alexander Graham Bell fundamentally transformed telecommunications. The telephone system assumed its modern form with the development of dial telephone service and its spread during the middle decades of the twentieth century.

Until the 1980s the world telecommunications system had a relatively simple administrative structure. In the United States, telephone service was supplied by a regulated monopoly, American Telephone and Telegraph (AT&T). During the same period, Western Union Corporation provided telegraph service. In almost all other countries both services were the monopolies of government agencies known as PTTs (post, telephone, and telegraph).

In the United States, however, beginning in 1983, the situation became far more complex. As a result of an antitrust suit launched by the federal government, AT&T agreed in a court settlement to divest itself of the local operating companies that provided basic telephone service. They remained regulated local monopolies, grouped together into eight regional companies. AT&T now offers long-distance service in competition with a half dozen major and many minor competitors while retaining ownership of a subsidiary that produces telephone equipment, computers, and other electronic devices.

To summarize the history of telecommunications, Table 1.1 highlights the history of the telephone network in chronological order.

Historically and today, telephone traffic (voice) has been the major user of communications facilities. Over the last 25 years, however, a stable growth of facilities transmitting information other than voice from the telephone has occurred. To address those and other new services, new technologies are needed that adapt easily to the new services.

TABLE 1.1

Highlights in the
History of Telecom-
munications

Year	Event
1844	Morse sends the first public telegraph message
1876	Telephone patent issued to Alexander Graham Bell
1877	First telephone in private home
1881	First long-distance line, from Boston, Massachusetts, to Providence, Rhode Island
1889	A. B. Stowger invents telephone switch, dial telephone
1890	Undersea telephone cable, England to France
1915	First transcontinental telephone call in the United States
1929	Coaxial cable invented; Herbert Hoover becomes the first president with a phone on his desk
1947	Transistor invented
1951	Direct long-distance dialing
1956	First transatlantic-repeated telephone cable
1960	First test of electronic switch
1963	Touch-tone service introduced
1964	First trial offers for reversing telephone charges (collect call)
1970	Laser invented
1976	First digital electronic switch installed
1977	First light wave system installed
1984	Divestiture of AT&T (Ma Bell and the Baby Bells)
1988	First transatlantic optical fiber cable
1989	First fiber-optic cable to the home field trial, Cerritos, California
1990	Demonstration of 2000-km link using optical amplifiers without repeaters
1996	Telecom Act of 1996

1.3.2 Telephone Network Architecture

Before we go further, we need to understand the U.S. public telephone network architecture as the benchmark for the development of networks around the world.

The U.S. network consists primarily of local services offered by regional bell operating companies (RBOCs), which were a part of AT&T before the 1984 divestiture, and long-distance service still offered by AT&T.

A growing number of providers have sprung into being both in local and long distance service to compete against Ma Bell (AT&T) and the Baby Bells (RBOCs). In this section, we look at the architecture of the network formed by local exchange carriers (LECs) and interexchange carriers (IECs), which interact with each other to complete an inter-LATA (local-access transport area) telephone call.[1] LEC services are provided by RBOCs, whereas long-distance companies (IEC) such as AT&T, MCI, and Sprint provide long-distance services. With the new Telecom Act of 1996, this logical demarcation is disappearing very fast.

Although both routing and the specific architecture of the telephone network have evolved since the AT&T divestiture, the overall architecture can still be described with the basic components of a communications network. In a telephone network, each subscriber is connected via the local loop to a switching center known as an end office (EO) or central office (CO). Typically, an end office can support thousands of subscribers in a localized area. About 25,000 central offices exist in the United States today. Clearly, it is impractical for each CO to be connected with a direct link. If that were the case, we would need 3×10^8 links. Therefore, intermediate switching nodes are used. These intermediate nodes provide traffic aggregation and reduce the number of links required to connect the central offices together. The intermediate nodes are called access tandems. Each of these nodes in the network has an average of 10 to 15 central office switches connected to it. Thus, in the United States, about 1200 access tandem switches exist. Traffic routing in the LEC network is based on how the access tandem and central offices are connected. The switching centers are connected by links called *trunks*. These trunks are designed to carry multiple voice frequency circuits using frequency division multiplexing (FDM), synchronous time-division multiplexing (TDM), or wavelength division multiplexing (WDM) for fiber optics.

Figure 1.4 shows a segment of an LEC and IEC interconnected by a 1984 modified final judgment (MFJ) act. Without going into details about MFJ, post-MFJ telecommunication functions, service, responsibilities, and restrictions can be described by tracing an inter-LATA call via a LEC and IEC public-switched telephone network (PSTN).

In Fig. 1.4 a call originates in LATA X. If the call terminates within the same LATA, the traffic goes no further than the access tandem node. The traffic is routed to the appropriate central office and on to

---

[1] *LATAs* are logical boundaries defined by regulatory bodies in the United States to define the scope of service for local exchange carriers and long-distance carriers. This demarcation point is disappearing as the Telecom Act of 1996 is implemented. This demarcation is different in other countries.

Figure 1.4

Relationship between
IEC and LEC in the
United States.

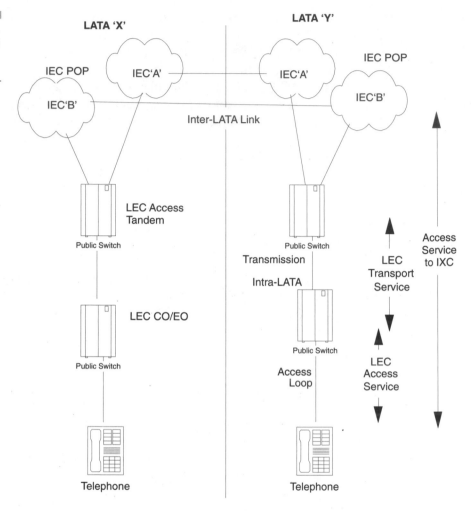

the destination phone within the same access tandem serving area. If
the call has a destination address in a different LATA (LATA Y), the call is
handed to the appropriate IEC (depending on which carrier the call originator has subscribed to), which switches the call to the appropriate
LATA. At the LATA, the call is handed to the local exchange carrier serving the destination address. This LEC then routes the call to the appropriate destination. In most countries around the world, the country's
government under post, telegraph, and telephone (PTT) authorities owns
the telecommunications network. As a result, these networks are not as
segmented as in the United States. Most countries, however, now adopt

the hierarchy mentioned here. With the privatization of PTTs around the world, competition now thrives in every segment of telecommunications, and U.S. telecommunications stands as an example for other countries. The entry of other carriers to compete against Telecom Canada in the Canadian long-distance market for example is a good starting point. The Canadians are learning from U.S. experiences in the long-distance area. In a telephone network, which primarily carries voice traffic, circuit switching is the preferred switching technology. Communication via circuit switching implies a dedicated communication path between two terminals. The path is a connected segment of links between network nodes. On each physical link, a channel is dedicated to the connection. Communication via circuit switching involves three phases:

- Circuit establishment
- Signal transfer (information transfer or data transfer)
- Circuit termination

Note that the circuit path is established before data transmission begins. Thus, the channel capacity must be reserved between each pair of nodes in the path, and each node must have sufficient internal switching capacity to handle the requested connection. The switches must be intelligent switches to make these allocations and route the call through the network. Some of the requirements for circuit switching are the following:

- Establishing/maintaining and terminating calls on subscribers' request
- Providing a transparent full-duplex signal
- Limiting acceptable delays for call setup (~0.5 s)
- Providing adequate quality for the voice connection
- Limiting blocking probability

1.4 Computer Communications Network

This section discusses the data, or computer communications network, to explain the differences between telecommunication and data communications networks.

1.4.1 Computer Network History

The unprecedented technology revolution involving computers did not begin until the later part of this century. It is now predicted that, by the turn of the century, the traffic generated from computers will dominate communications networks, compared to today's voice-dominated traffic. Early computer networks were not standardized, and were developed by companies such as Xerox, IBM, DEC, etc. These networks consist of proprietary systems, which means that a network built by one company does not communicate with a network built by another company. These networks were designed with the communication requirement of the early 1950s, which was batch-based and minimal. The processor communicated with its peripheral via input/output (I/O) devices over short distances at a very low speed. The 1960s brought the concept of time-sharing, where users were connected to computers via a dumb terminal, as shown in Fig. 1.5.

The 1970s saw the development of integrated circuits (IC) technology and the microprocessor, making it possible to bring personal computers to an individual's desk. This development drastically changed the way people viewed computers. The growth of local area networks (LANs) in the 1980s provided personal computers with the technology to communicate with each other, thus enabling the migration from centralized computing to distributed computing. Figures 1.6 and 1.7 show centralized and distributed computing, respectively.

Figure 1.5
Time-shared computer system.

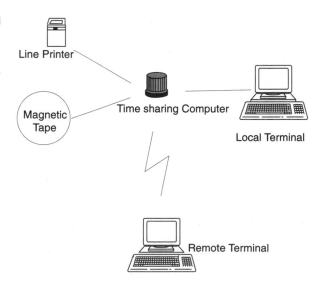

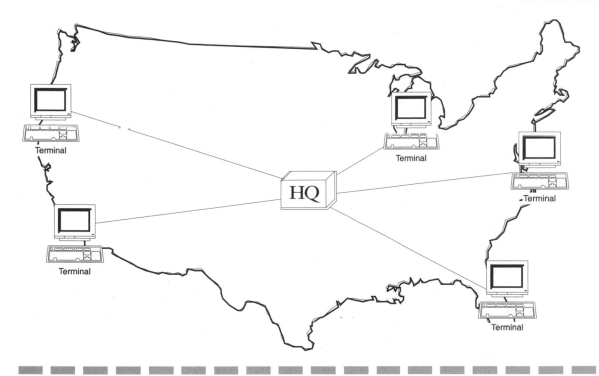

Figure 1.6
Centralized computing.

Figure 1.7
Distributed computing.

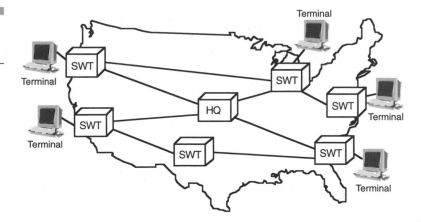

In a centralized computing environment, the main system or processor is centrally located, and all remote locations are connected via a direct link. All the information, i.e., the entire database, is located at the central system.

In a distributed computing environment, the processors, or main computers, are distributed at different locations, with each node having a complete copy or a portion of the database. The user accesses the information from the nearest processor, which keeps current by periodically updating the information in its databases. This distributed computing environment has made a real impact on today's computer network. This concept was originally developed by a project underwritten by an agency of the U.S. Department of Defense known as Advanced Research Projects Agency (ARPA). The task this agency was given was to bring about a solution to a difficult problem: allowing different computers to communicate with one another as if they were one computer. This led to a suite of protocols called TCP/IP (transmission control protocol/internet protocol) that provided the building block for today's Internet connecting millions of users around the world. With the advancement of computers, the trend toward a distributed environment is nothing but real.

1.4.2   Computer Network Reference Model

Before discussing the different types of computer networks, one must understand the basics of computer interactions, or the protocols on which all computer communications systems work. A data communications network requires a high degree of compatibility and interoperability among network elements, particularly with respect to its physical and logical interfaces and controls. So, to address such issues, the International Organization for Standardization (ISO) established a subcommittee (Technical Committee 97) in 1977 to develop a standard architecture to achieve the long-term goal of open systems interconnection (OSI). This committee established the current data communications standards.

The term OSI denotes the standards for the exchange of information among systems "open" to one another by virtue of incorporating the ISO standards. The fact that a system is open does not imply any particular system's implementation, technology, or interconnections, but refers to the system's compliance with applicable standards.

With this in mind, ISO has specified an OSI reference model that segments the communications functions into seven layers. Each layer is assigned a related subset of communications functions, which are implemented in data terminal equipment (DTE) that communicate with other DTEs. Each layer relies on the next lower layer to perform more primitive functions and in turn provides services to support the next higher layer. The layers are defined so that changes in one layer do not affect other layers.

Information exchange occurs when corresponding (peer) layers in two systems communicate using a set of rules as their protocols. *Protocols* define the syntax (arrangements, formats, and patterns of bits and bytes) and semantics (system control and information context, or the meaning of patterns of bits and bytes) of exchanged data, as well as numerous other characteristics such as data rates and timing. Defining the details of seven layers of protocols for data communications is an enormously complex task. To understand the concepts and objectives of layering, we use an example. Figure 1.8 illustrates the three layers of communications between two philosophers, one in China and one in India. The exchange

Figure 1.8
Simplified example of multilayer peer-to-peer communication.

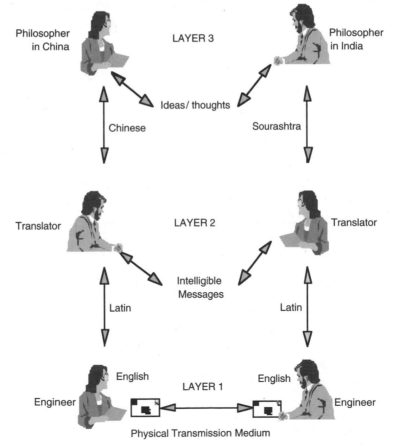

of ideas between the two philosophers represents layer 3, peer-to-peer communication. As the philosophers do not share the same language, they each engage the services of a translator. In Fig. 1.8, the exchange in Latin represents layer 2, peer-to-peer communications. Each translator must then engage the services of an engineer to transmit the ideas by letter, telegram, telephone, computer network, or other means. Just as the translators had to agree on a common language, layer 1, peer-to-peer communications requires that an agreement on the physical transmission media must be made between the two engineers.

Note that the translators could use English to speak to each other without affecting either the layer 1 or layer 3 process. Similarly, neither the message integrity at layer 3 nor the translation process of layer 2 is affected if the engineers changed layer 1 physical medium choices. Performance aspects, such as message delivery time, however, could be drastically different if the postal service were substituted for a real-time form of communications.

1.4.3 ISO Reference Model for OSI

Figure 1.9 shows the ISO reference model for OSI. The objective is to solve the problem of heterogeneous DTE and data communications equipment (DCE). The OSI model is not a product blueprint; two companies can build computers consistent with the model but may be unable to

Figure 1.9
OSI reference model.

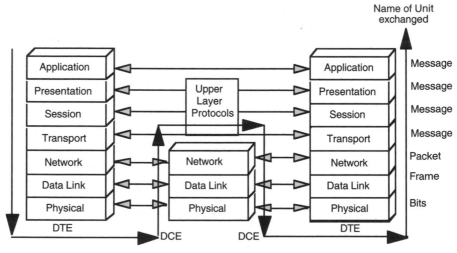

DTE: Data Terminating Equipment
DCE: Data Communications Equipment

exchange information. The model is only a framework for implementation with standards developed for each layer. Standards must define services provided by each layer, as well as the protocols between the layers. Standards do not dictate how the functions and services are implemented in hardware or software, so these can differ from system to system.

In Fig. 1.9, the protocol stacks to the left and right represent two DTEs connected by a communications subnetwork shown in the middle. Each layer has a specific name and job function. There are seven layers in the OSI model:

- Physical layer
- Data link layer
- Network layer
- Transport layer
- Session layer
- Presentation layer
- Application layer

Each layer is described in the following subsections.

1.4.3.1 Layer 1: Physical. The physical layer provides mechanical, electrical, functional, and procedural characteristics to activate, maintain, and deactivate connections for the transmission of unstructured bit streams over a physical link. The physical link can be connectors and wiring between the DTE and the DCE at a network access point and fiber-optic cable within a network. Layer 1 involves such parameters as signal levels and bit duration. X.21 is an option for layer 1 within the ITU-T X.25 (International Telecommunications Union) recommendation. In the United States, the RS-232C standard is generally used at layer 1, and bits are exchanged as data units.

1.4.3.2 Layer 2: Data Link. The data link layer provides for reliable transfer of data across the physical link. It maps data units from the next higher (network) layer to data frames to permit transmission. The data link provides necessary synchronization, error control, and flow control. Layer 2 provides for multiplexing one data link into several physical links when necessary. A single physical link can support multiple data links. An option for this layer exists in the ITU-T X.25 recommendation called link access protocol-B (LAP-B). It is a subset of the ISO-developed high-level data link control (HDLC).

1.4.3.3 Layer 3: Network. Layer 3 provides higher-level layers with independence from the routing and switching associated with establishing a network connection. Functions include addressing, end-point identification, and service selection when different services are available. An example of a layer 3 protocol is the ITU-T X.25 recommendation standard widely used around the world.

1.4.3.4 Layer 4: Transport. In conjunction with the underlying network, data link, and physical layers, the transport layer provides end-to-end (station-to-station) control of transmitted data and optimizes the use of network resources. This layer provides transparent data transfer between layer 5 session entities. In ISO terminology, an *entity* is the network processing capability (hardware, software, or both) that implements functions in a particular layer.

Transport-layer services are provided to upper layers to establish, maintain, and release transparent data connections over two-way, simultaneous data transmission paths between pairs of transport addresses. The transport protocol capabilities needed depend on the quality of the underlying layer services. When used with reliable, error-free virtual circuit network service, a minimal transport layer is required. If the lower layers provide unreliable datagram service, the transport protocol must implement error detection, recovery, and other functions.

1.4.3.5 Layer 5: Session Layer. A session is a connection between stations that allows them to communicate. For example, a host processor might need to establish multiple sessions simultaneously with remote terminals to accomplish file transfers with each station. File transfer access and management (FTAM) is an example of an ISO application-layer standard for network file transfer and remote file access.

The purpose of the session layer is to enable two presentation entities at remote stations to establish and use transport connections by organizing and synchronizing their dialog and managing the exchange of data.

1.4.3.6 Layer 6: Presentation. The presentation layer delivers information to communicating application entities to resolve syntax differences but preserve meaning. Toward this objective, layer 6 can provide data transformation (data compression and encryption), formatting, and syntax selection. Virtual terminal protocol, a layer 6 protocol, hides differences in remote terminals from application entities by making the terminals all appear as generic or virtual. When two remote host processors use virtual terminal protocols, terminals appear as locally attached to their host.

1.4.3.7 Layer 7: Application. The application layer enables the application process to access the OSI environment. It serves as the passageway between application processes that use OSI to exchange information. This layer provides all services directly used by the application process. Services include the following:

- Identifying intended communications partners
- Determining the current availability of intended partners
- Establishing the authority to communicate
- Agreeing on responsibility for error recovery
- Agreeing on procedures to maintain data integrity

Protocols currently being defined or enhanced for this layer include FTAM, transaction processing (TP), directory services (ISO 9595, ITU-T X.500), and job transfer and manipulation (JTM). The ITU-T X.400 message handling system (MHS) protocols issued in 1984 were substantially revised in 1988 as application-layer protocols.

In a communications environment, the information flow starts at the application layer at one end and terminates at the application layer at the other end. This process is shown in Fig. 1.9 by a line in the middle of the protocol stacks. At the intermediate node, the information goes up to layer 3 in the case of an X.25-based network. The protocols of the future (described in this book) will only require that the information go to layer 2 or even layer 1, rather than layer 3.

1.4.4 Types of Computer Networks

Computer networks can be classified based on their geographic scope. The four major categories are

- LANs (local area networks)
- MANs (metropolitan area networks)
- WANs (wide area networks)
- GANs (global area networks)

One can infer the geographical reach of the network from the name itself. These network *terminologies* are typically applied to corporate/business environment. Networks in public domain, however, use the network facilities.

1.4.4.1 Local Area Networks LANs are typically used to interconnect computers and PCs within a relatively small area, such as within an office, building, or campus. A LAN typically operates at speeds ranging from 10 to 100 Mbps, connecting several hundred devices over a distance of up to 5 or 10 km. LANs became popular because they allow many users to share scarce resources, such as mainframes, file servers, high-speed printers, and other expensive devices.

Figure 1.10 shows two different types of LAN connectivity. One is connected via a bus architecture, in which the physical medium is

Figure 1.10
Examples of a LAN.

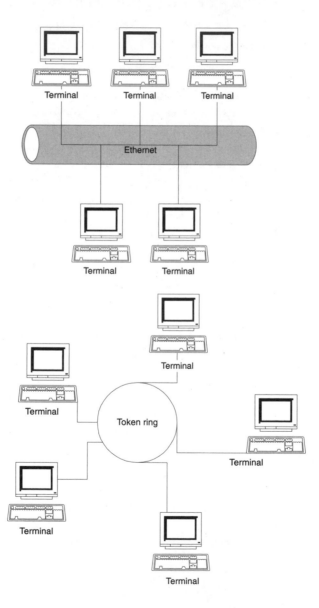

Figure 1.11
Example of a MAN.

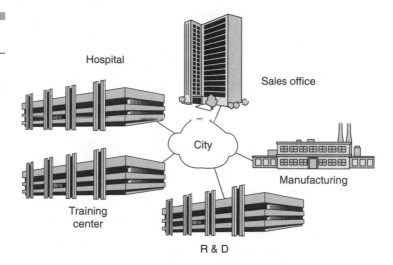

shared by users connected to the bus. A protocol called carrier sense, multiple-access high-collision detection (CSMA/CD) is used in this network. The next topology is called the ring topology, in which the token protocol is used. In the ring topology, the user who has control of the token transmits data on the ring. Technology in the LAN environment has evolved in the last few years. Some of the LAN technologies are mentioned in Chap. 17.

1.4.4.2 Metropolitan Area Networks MAN, as the name implies, is a network covering a metropolitan city. The MAN connects many LANs located at different office buildings. A MAN has a larger geographical scope compared to a LAN and can range from 10 km to a few hundred kilometers in length. A typical MAN operates at a speed of 1.5 to 150 Mbps. Figure 1.11 illustrates a MAN. One of the reasons a MAN is connected via a much lower speed than LAN technology is because of the high cost of bandwidth and because most of the traffic remains within the LAN environment. Thus, traffic management becomes a critical factor in managing the cost of the public network.

1.4.4.3 Wide Area Networks A WAN is designed to interconnect computer systems over very large geographic areas, such as from one city to another city within a country. A WAN can range from 100 to 1000 km, and the speed between the cities can vary from 1.5 Mbps to 2.4 Gbps. In a WAN, the cost of transmission is very high, and the network is usually owned and operated by a public network. Businesses lease a transmission

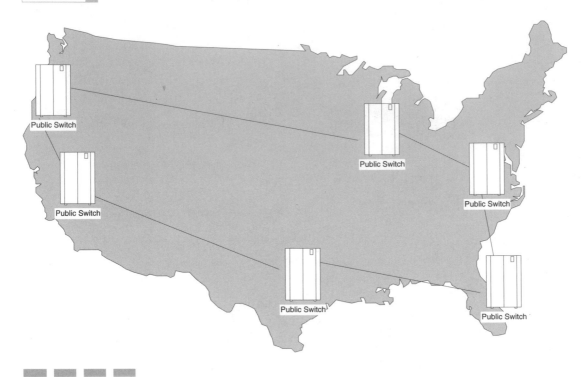

Figure 1.12
Example of a WAN.

system from the public networks to connect their geographically diverse sites. Figure 1.12 illustrates an example of a WAN. WAN terminology is also used in conjunction with a corporate network, virtual private network, or private line network. The network is designed to carry voice, data, or video or combinations of these services in an integrated or nonintegrated way.

1.4.4.4   Global Area Networks   As the name implies, GANs are network connections between countries around the globe. A good example of such a network is the Internet in the United States, which has a connection to similar networks in other countries. A GAN's speed ranges from 1.5 Mbps to 100 Gbps, and its reach is several thousands of kilometers. Figure 1.13 illustrates an example of GAN.

Figure 1.14 shows how the different types of networks interact. In this type of network, the traffic leaving the network is usually small, but this fact is changing daily. As more and more companies do business globally, the constant need to communicate within the company or with international customers is increasing drastically, thus making the GAN appear as a LAN in terms of access. The interfaces between these networks are usually via international or regional standard interfaces, enabling equipment from different vendors to be interconnected.

1.4.5 Real World Example of WAN/MAN/GAN—The Internet

The Internet is a good example of a WAN/MAN/GAN. Today, the Internet is one of the most widely used *networks* in the world. Currently it has more than 100 million users worldwide. The Internet was initially developed in the 1960s as a data network for linking computers at universities

Figure 1.13
Example of a GAN.

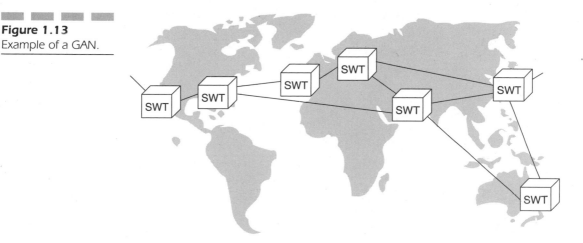

Figure 1.14
Interaction between LAN, MAN, WAN, and GAN.

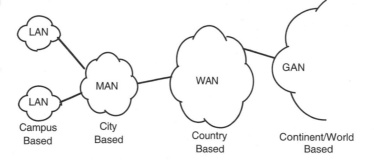

and governmental agencies around the country. It has been an obscure research tool except for three fundamental technology breakthroughs which occurred over the last three decades.

1. The development of packet data technology, which transforms large computer files into small "packets" of information, each with its own destination and return address. This created an entirely new way to move information electronically between computers over traditional telephone networks.

2. The implementation of a private, high-speed Internet "backbone" network, which links major computer centers. This network, initially financed by the federal government, enabled the "internetworking" of users around the globe over a common set of open protocols which communicated with any other computer operating system.

3. The development of the World Wide Web, which is a standard method of organizing and uniformly presenting text, image, and video information in a way that was intuitive and user friendly on virtually any computer system.

These technologies, along with the commercialization of the Internet in the business community, transformed the Internet from an academic network serving a relatively small number of researchers with text files into a widely used information network serving millions of users with text and graphical images. What is driving this tremendous growth? The drivers are the regulatory environment, technological changes, businesses (commerce), and economics of doing business on the Internet. Without question, the higher-performance computers with larger data storage and graphical software applications have outpaced the capabilities of the telecommunications infrastructure—hindering users in their efforts to access increasingly richer content.

Until recently, the perception had been that most of the growth in the Internet and online services use had come from the consumer, not the business users. This perception came about because of security concerns for business transactions, but new encryption technologies have enabled businesses to use Internet technologies aggressively. Large companies typically can afford the investment in the high-speed communications network services necessary to gain the full benefit from Internet technologies.

One of the major factors driving businesses to use Internet technology is the dramatic cost savings that are achievable. The Internet, as a communications alternative, can be as much as 100 times less expensive than other methods, including commonly used fax services. It is these compelling economics that are driving a fundamental shift from the traditional communications network to the Internet—a shift as fundamental as that from the mainframe to the PC or from the telegraph to the telephone.

The basic Internet structure includes end users, ISPs (Internet Service providers), and backbone providers, although these categories can become intermingled. End users connect to an ISP via media ranging from standard telephone service (POTS) for domestic customers to ISDN (integrated services digital network) or T1 lines for corporations. ISPs connect end users to the backbone. The backbone providers connect together and route traffic between ISPs. An additional level could be added between the backbone providers and ISPs; these would be the regional networks, which typically provide dense local networking and connect to one or more national backbone providers. These operators include JvnCnet in New Jersey, CERFnet in San Diego (see Fig. 1.15), and Colorado Supernet in Colorado.

Figure 1.15
Regional internet—
CERFnet.

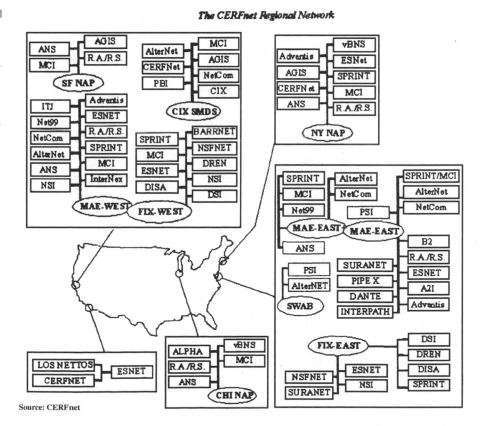

Source: CERFnet

The current structure of the Internet owes much to the later history of the system. Merit Network, IBM, MCI, and Michigan completed the NSFNet T1 (1.544-Mbps) backbone in 1988 for the National Science Foundation. It connected 13 regional networks, primarily to provide access to supercomputing sites. It is important to note that the networks already existed. The backbone's purpose was to link the networks, and this hierarchical structure has been maintained.

Other sites such as universities could connect to the regional networks, which in turn connected to the federally subsidized NSFNet backbone. The NSFNet capacity was gradually upgraded to T3 (45 Mbps). In 1990, Merit, IBM, and MCI spun off Advanced Network and Services (ANS), originally a nonprofit organization, to operate the backbone, and on April 30, 1995, the government pulled out. Alternate backbones had already begun to develop, starting with the Commercial Internet Exchange (CIX) router in Santa Clara, California.

To move from the NSFNet backbone structure, the NSF has supported development of four network access points (NAPs) in northern California, Chicago, New York, and Washington, D.C. (MAE—East), which let backbone providers exchange traffic and provide routing arbitration. To these access points, fiber-optic metropolitan connection systems called metropolitan area exchanges (MAEs) have been added by Metropolitan Fiber Systems. These provide NAP services, and are located in Los Angeles (MAE—LA), Dallas (MAE—DALLAS), San Jose (MAE—WEST), Chicago (MAE—CHICAGO), and two in Washington (MAE—EAST and MAE—EAST+). MAE—EAST/EAST+ and MAE—WEST are full-service NAPs, while the others should be considered potential full-service NAP points.

In addition to these general connection points, there are two federal internet exchange sites: FIX-EAST at the University of Maryland and FIX-WEST at the NASA Ames Research Center in California. The CIX (computer interchange exchange) router in Santa Clara is also operational, but of less importance, particularly since both UUnet and Sprint dropped out.

Sitting on top of the NAPs and MAEs are the peering networks along with the big seven (with UUnet) providers who engage in cost-free peering with each other. (Peering refers to networks that operate at the same level to each other; they perform some function. Each network has its own customer base. Networks establish a relationship to share the information among users of different networks.) These are Bolt, Beraneck & Newman (BBN), MCI Communications (see Fig. 1.16), UUnet

Figure 1.16
MCI's internet
backbone.

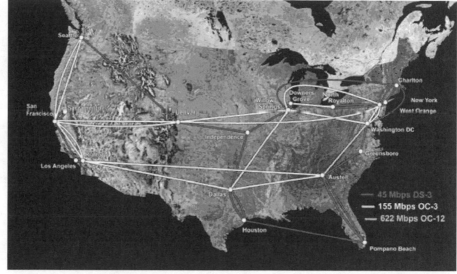

Source: MCI

Technologies, Advanced Network Services (ANS), Sprint, PSINet, and Apex Global Information Services (AGIS). Among the alliances of significance in this area, ANS and UUnet are subsidiaries of WorldCom, GTE recently acquired BBN, and MCI has been acquired by WorldCom. BBN is currently providing Internet access for AT&T customers.

The Internet infrastructure is still in the investment phase, where profits are often measured in relation to reductions in loss. However, being a backbone provider has lots of side benefits beyond carrying today's traffic. For one thing, many backbone providers also provide ISP services. Strategies for charging for these services are changing, and free peering is being limited to boost potential revenues.

After the government decided not to provide funding, private arrangements have prevailed. The largest private backbone providers have negotiated peering arrangements to exchange traffic with each other, as well as to establish exchange points. New companies have built nationwide backbones. Universities and a number of government agencies are supporting research into Internet 2, or the next generation Internet, to establish a new high-speed backbone for noncommercial uses. The NSF has also funded the vBNS (very high-speed backbone network service) project, a research backbone operating at 622 Mbps. MCI has received the grant to provide the backbone (see Fig. 1.17).

Figure 1.17
vBNS Network.

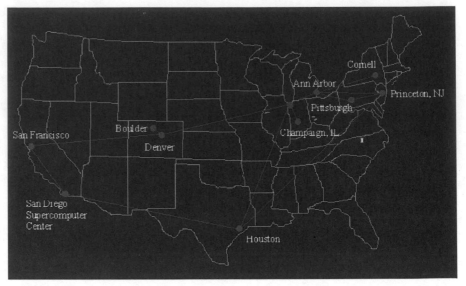

Source: MCI

1.5   Video Networks

Today's video networks are one-way broadcast video sent via coaxial cable or wireless media. In the United States, about 60 percent of homes receive video service via cable. (Wireless-based video has had a local significance with the expectation of satellite.) Recently satellite-based one-way video broadcast has gained popularity due to the availability of digital technology such as DBS (direct broadcast satellite), dish TV, etc. On the other hand, wireless is not considered a potential long-term solution for two-way broadband communication due to its scarcity of spectrum. Some potential two-way broadband wireless solutions such as MMDS (multichannel multipoint distribution service) and LMDS (local multipoint distribution service) are discussed in Chap. 13. This does not mean that wireless has no application for broadband. Wireless is considered more of a potential threat to traditional narrowband services than broadband services, as evidenced by the number of cellular and PCS (personal communications services) services available around the world.

Of all the options, CATV (cable television or community antenna television) has become very popular because of its ability to provide video entertainment services to residential subscribers with relatively better quality than wireless broadcast and at a lower cost. This is because of the coaxial cable in the access infrastructure. From the network infrastructure perspective, CATV is valuable because of the coaxial in the last mile of the network to every home. The last mile of coaxial cable accounts for 50 percent of the total network investment. Since coaxial cable has the capability to transport broadband services, the network is capable of providing a wide range of services in the future.

1.5.1 CATV Network

Different CATV architectures are used around the world today. However, the majority of the CATV architecture are the tree-and-branch architecture. The physical architecture of the tree-and-branch is capable of delivering 64 channels of one-way distributed video service, as shown in Fig. 1.18. In this network, the signals from the different sources to be delivered to the subscriber are gathered at a central head end. The head end is equivalent to a central office switch in the telephone network. Typical sources of these signals are satellite earth stations, off-air antennas, videotape playback, and super trunking, which provide delivery of signals from studios at remote locations.

At the head end, the various video sources at different radio frequencies are combined into a single broadband signal and transmitted over a

Figure 1.18
CATV tree-and-branch architecture.

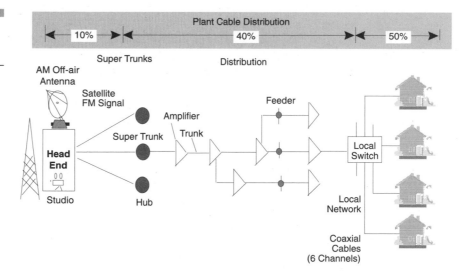

single coaxial cable. This coaxial cable undergoes branching through power splitters until it passes down each street in a community. Broadband amplifiers are required every 1000 to 2000 ft to overcome losses from cable branching and transmission. The biggest concern of the CATV system is its limited capacity and its deterioration in service quality due to noise, modulation distortion, and reliability. The current generation of analog coaxial CATV equipment consists of simple unidirectional transmission devices with limited telemetering capability for monitoring.

The electronic components in the network include the trunk and feeder amplifiers, which maintain network signals at adequate power levels to ensure signal quality, and the converter box on the subscriber's premises. The passive components include the coaxial cable connectors, signal splitters, and signal taps for the drop. The network requires that a power station be located about every 2 miles along the cable to amplify the electrical signal onto the coaxial cable. These stations drive the electronics in the trunk and feeder portions of the network, and the customer power drives the converter box. The network does not provide backup power. Hence, if commercial power fails, the cable system is inoperable, and cable services are lost.

Because every subscriber receives all channels carried by the cable system, controlling access to services such as pay-per-view becomes a key technical issue. One approach employed by roughly half the industry is to install inexpensive coaxial filters that trap signals at the drop, blocking the portion of the bandwidth occupied by the premium channels. When cable service was first offered, whenever a subscriber requested pay-per-view cable service, personnel were dispatched to the site to remove the appropriate filter. The high labor cost for service changes and the inability to provide pay-per-view services led to the use of addressable converters to control service access. These addressable converters are basically enhanced tuners that descramble the signals of premium channels when authorized by the network. In this way, the premium channels are blocked or opened for the subscriber.

CATV networks currently use analog technology and coaxial cable in the backbone. One of the main reasons for using analog technology is that today's televisions are analog and receive only analog signals. It is not possible to change the analog televisions to digital easily because there are more than 200 million televisions in the United States alone. To save additional equipment costs for converting the signals, the CATV providers will keep the analog format all across the network until televisions are equipped with digital-to-analog converters.

Some of the benefits of CATV architecture are:

- Lower up-front costs
- Transparent service to end user
- Fiber-optic cable from head end to feeder
- Multisource (switched-star is single-sourced)
- Ablility to carry all the bandwidth to the home, providing greater flexibility in the future which can be used for the expansion of channel capacity for HDTV (high-definition television), and digital hi-fi audio services.

Recent developments in tree-and-branch technology have resulted in little distinction between tree-and-branch and other architectures in terms of providing low-level interactive services, such as pay-per-view, and high-level interactive services, such as home-banking, database access, and video on demand (VOD).

1.6   What Is Broadband?

ITU defines broadband service as the following:

> A service requiring transmission channels capable of supporting rates faster than 1.5 Mbps or the primary rate in ISDN or T1 or DS1 in digital terminology. In European version it is called E1 or 2.048 Mbps.

Many other definitions exist, but we use this one for now. From the telecommunications perspective, broadband communications evolved from current integrated services digital network technology (ISDN), which is now called narrowband ISDN. The broadband communications network described in this book is known as BISDN, for broadband integrated services digital network.

As shown in Fig. 1.19, BISDN is not a technology but a platform supported by different technologies, including ATM (asynchronous transfer mode), SONET, and IN (intelligent network). We address each of these technologies in detail later in the book.

1.7   The Need for Broadband

One of the most important factors driving the need for broadband communications is the changing user needs and demands. With the

Figure 1.19
BISDN framework.

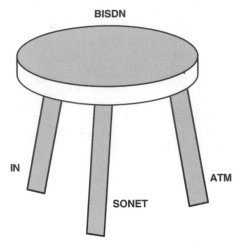

BISDN	Broadband ISDN
ATM	Asynchronous Transfer Mode
SONET	Synchronous Optical Network
IN	Intelligent Network

development of the Internet, the need for broadband communication has become clear. Prior to the late 1970s and early 1980s, public network needs were almost entirely driven by telephone (voice). Data traffic has been growing slowly until recently, thus indicating the changes of user needs and demands. In addition to the Internet, other factors led to this sudden drastic change. Several are listed here:

- Lower relative telecommunications cost because of lower cost/higher performance of integrated circuits (ICs) and microprocessors used in telecommunications switches

- Competition in the telecommunications sector with the 1996 Telecom Act

- Introduction of low-cost, reliable fiber-optics transport in the network

- Proliferation of PCs at homes and LANs that connect the PCs at the workplace. Currently 40 percent of households have PCs.

Lower cost and the increased processing power of computers enabled a number of users to access the public network, but their applications and needs are completely different. One of the most important applications is the Internet access that opens the door to the world of broadband communication and information. Some of the applications of broadband are:

- Video telephony
- Low-cost video conferencing
- Imaging
- High-definition television (HDTV)
- Hi-fi audio distribution
- LAN interconnect
- Computer-aided design/computer-aided engineering/computer-aided manufacturing (CAD/CAE/CAM)
- Visualization
- Multimedia
- Supercomputing and channel extension
- High-speed internet access

Each of these has potential application for broadband communications because each has very high bandwidth requirements. Figure 1.20 shows the bandwidth requirements for different applications, including the traditional application of voice. One can see that the applications mentioned here require very high bandwidth.

Figure 1.20
Characteristics of potential applications (*Courtesy of Rick McLean, Nortel.*)

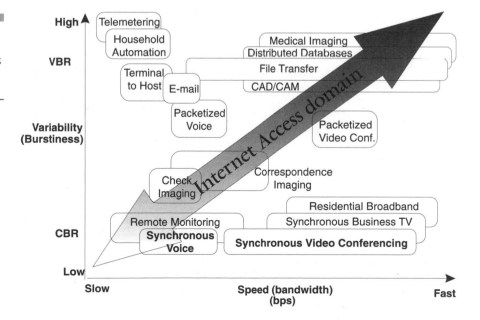

In addition to these new applications, other factors are also driving the need for broadband around the world, including the following:

■ The service demand has changed in nature. Customers want mobility (both terminal and personal), bandwidth on demand, access to management functions, flexibility in establishing connections, end-to-end connectivity, and management.

■ A competitive market generally operates more efficiently than a regulated one.

■ Equipment and components for the processing and transport of information are becoming increasingly inexpensive.

We address these trends and driving forces in detail in Chap. 2.

1.8   Overview of Broadband Technologies

In this book, we explain the technologies that drive the components of a broadband network. Before we go into any of these technologies, it is very useful to understand where and how they interact with each other. Figure 1.21 shows a broadband network that can be implemented with the technologies mentioned in this book. The information (voice, data, and video) that originates at the source node is carried to the destination through a switched network. The switched network consists of an access network and a backbone network. The origination and destination are typically LAN-based for most business customers. The fiber distributed data interface (FDDI), distributed queue dual bus (DQDB), and asynchronous transfer mode (ATM) are some of the emerging LAN protocols that coordinate information flow at the source and destination node. These protocols along with the current Ethernet and token ring will generate the traffic.

The data flows from the customer's location to the switched network via the access network. The access network uses technologies like X-DSL (X-digital subscriber loop), CAP (carrierless amplitude phase modulation), QAM (quadrature amplitude modulation), etc., over twisted pair, wireless, or coaxial to transport the traffic in the access network. This access traffic is then carried over to the backbone network. The traffic is mapped to one of the broadband technologies such as frame relay, SMDS (switched multimegabit data service), ATM/SONET, etc. All these technologies can be used together or separately, and each can use any physical transmission medium such as twisted pair, fiber, coaxial, etc., which has its own standard for implementation. In this book, we discuss a standard for fiber called synchronous optical network (SONET), which is used in the United States and Canada, and synchronous digital hierarchy (SDH), which is used in Europe and other countries. In addition, other technologies such as FR (frame relay), SMDS, ATM, X-DSL, etc., are also discussed in detail.

1.9   Summary

There are three fundamental types of networks: telecommunications, computer, and video networks. Each is designed for specific applications using the most suitable technology for the application. With the emergence of new services and the need for integrated voice, data, and video, none of the existing networks can be used to handle or provide optimum cost-effective services in the future. In recent years, new network technologies have been developed that can offer a wide variety of services, including some potential broadband applications described in Chap. 2.

Figure 1.21
Integrated Broadband Network.

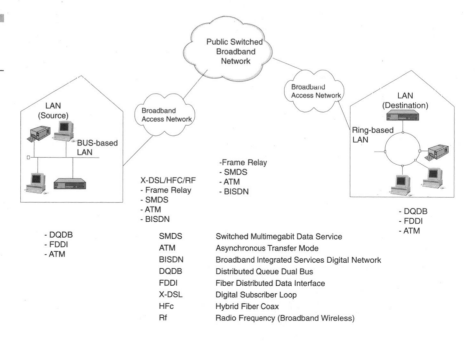

SMDS	Switched Multimegabit Data Service	
ATM	Asynchronous Transfer Mode	
BISDN	Broadband Integrated Services Digital Network	
DQDB	Distributed Queue Dual Bus	
FDDI	Fiber Distributed Data Interface	
X-DSL	Digital Subscriber Loop	
HFc	Hybrid Fiber Coax	
Rf	Radio Frequency (Broadband Wireless)	

The chapters in this book provide a better understanding of different broadband communication technologies and its environment. The reasons why ATM and SONET have become the backbone technology for broadband are explained, along with a detailed explanation of broadband's proposed framework (called BISDN). This book covers the BISDN's principles, standards, and architectures as defined by ITU, along with some real world environments.

2

Evolution toward Broadband

2.1 Overview

This chapter addresses the driving factors leading to the evolution of broadband networks from existing networks. No single factor is driving broadband but rather a combination of technology, standards, industries/business, and applications. All these factors are converging to create a new paradigm called *broadband networks* or *broadband communications network* or simply *broadband*. Figure 2.1 illustrates this convergence. In this chapter, the different potential applications are explained along with some potential migration of various network toward broadband.

2.2 Drivers for Broadband

This section addresses the various driving factors behind broadband and discusses its trends.

2.2.1 Technology

Several of the technologies behind the evolution of broadband are semiconductor, fiber-optic, and computers, and each is described in the following subsections.

2.2.1.1 Semiconductor Technology The cost of semiconductors is dropping every year, yet its complexity is simultaneously increasing (Fig. 2.2). For example, when IBM invented the PC, it had a 64K memory, two floppy drives running on Intel's 8080 microprocessor, and a monochrome monitor. If you tell your kids about this machine today, they will laugh and say "Do you mean that such a primitive computer existed?" Don't worry! Some day your children's computers will be obsolete because of the ever-

Figure 2.1
Drivers for BISDN.

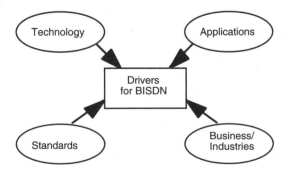

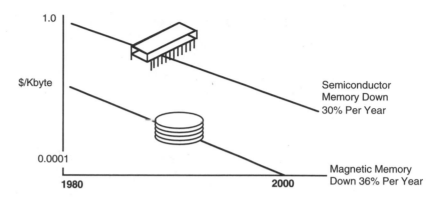

▬ ▬ ▬ ▬

Figure 2.2
Cost of semiconductors vs. complexity.

Source: Adaptive Corp.

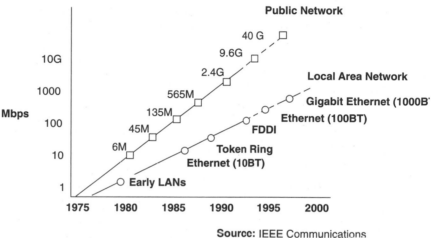

Figure 2.3
Fiber-optics technology.

Query: Figs 2-2, 2-3, 2-4 originally had boxes around certain elements. Can they be left out? They seem to be inconsistent.

Source: IEEE Communications

Key

M Mega - 10^6
G Giga - 10^9
T Tera - 10^{12}

changing technology. The cost of the early, primitive IBM PC was $2000 to $3000, while today, most complex IBM compatibles sell for less than $2000.

2.2.1.2 Fiber Optics The evolution of fiber-optics technology is shown in Fig. 2.3. The amount of data carried on a single strand of fiber has increased drastically, while, at the same time, the cost per bit carried on fiber optics has decreased so much. Today, fiber optics carry about 40 Gbps of traffic over a single strand of fiber, and terabits are expected to be on the market by the year 2000. These high-speed fiber systems are typically used in public backbone networks.

Recently, fiber optics has begun to penetrate LANs with ATM technology. In the past, fiber cost much more when compared with coaxial cable, which limited its penetration into LANs. Today, the cost of fiber optics is comparable to that of coaxial, thus enabling the use of fiber optics in the LAN environment.

2.2.1.3 Computing Technology Another factor driving broadband is the cost of computing equipment. The price of computers has dropped so much that it has become a commodity item available in every electronics retail outlet. The rule of thumb in this scenario is that the price drops are about three times in a year and the capacity doubles every 2 years. Today, about 45 percent of U.S. homes have a personal computer and more than 40 percent have access to the Internet. Figure 2.4 shows the comparative cost decrease in computing equipment. Cost is calculated based on the cost of processing information.

2.2.2 Applications

So far, we have seen the technological progress that has enabled the evolution toward broadband. In this section, we address the applications of broadband in detail by explaining their characteristics. Most of the protocols addressed in this book use these applications as their drivers. By understanding the characteristics of these applications, we can better

Figure 2.4
Computing technology cost.

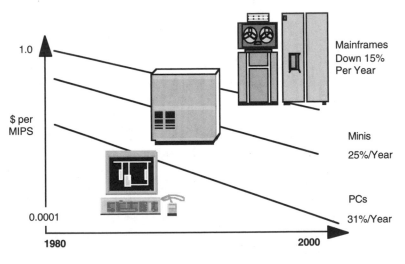

Source: Yankee Group

understand the use of the protocols. The applications discussed in this section are the following:

- LAN interconnect
- Computer-aided design (CAD)/computer-aided engineering (CAE)/computer-aided manufacturing (CAM)
- Visualization
- Imaging
- Supercomputing and channel extension
- Multimedia
- Internet access

2.2.2.1 LAN Interconnect LAN interconnect evolved in the late 1980s to connect computers within a building or campus. Initially, a LAN's backbone capacity was 4 Mbps, then 10 Mbps, 16 Mbps, 100 Mbps, and recently 1000 Mbps. Each one of these LANs is based on the IEEE 801.x protocol (x varies from 1 to 6). The number of LANs has also increased drastically from 30,000 in 1986 to 1.5 million in 1995, and the number is growing at double digit. The reason behind this expansion is the exponentially increasing number of PCs connected to LANs. Figure 2.5 shows how a network can interconnect two LANs.

Table 2.1 describes some applications that run on LAN and their characteristics in terms of bandwidth utilization rate. These applications are not the only ones that run on a LAN; they are just the potential applications that can impact LAN traffic because of their data rate or because they are more frequently used.

2.2.2.2 CAD/CAE/CAM Figure 2.6 shows a typical CAD environment. Typical traffic sources are engineering, computing, manufacturing, and design. It is essential to compare local traffic with remote traffic to characterize CAD traffic. Today, CAD traffic is primarily local and involves file transfers between workstations and the mainframe, all located at the same site.

Remote traffic is primarily offline transfer of files (offline possibly because of the limitations imposed by the network). The key characteristic of today's interactive CAD/CAM/CAE environment is that peak transmission rates are determined by the transfer protocol (X.25, frame relay, etc.) rather than by the workstation or PC. CAD workstations are becoming more powerful, and the cost for supporting higher millions of instructions per second (MIPS) or simply higher processing power, is

Figure 2.5
Typical LAN interconnect network.

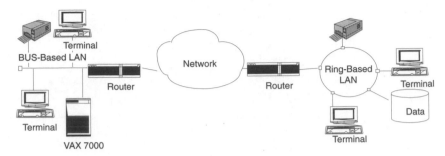

Figure 2.6
Typical CAD environment.

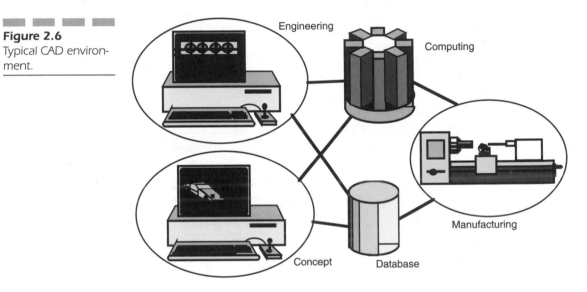

TABLE 2.1	**LAN Application**	**Typical Data Rate, in bits/s**
LAN Applications and their Data Rates	E-mail	9.6 to 56K
	File transfer	56K to 1.5M
	X-windows system	56K to 1.5M
	Remote database access	1.5M to 10M
	Imaging	1.5M to 45M
	Multimedia	3M to 45M

declining. With the fast migration toward distributed processing, more traffic is also imposed on the network. Speeds of 56 kbps to 1.5 Mbps are sufficient to meet today's stand-alone requirements. However, these speeds are not sufficient to meet the interactive response times required for most CAD/CAM/CAE applications.

2.2.2.3 Visualization Visualization is one of the upcoming applications where graphics workstations and vector processors are used to process large amounts of data and display them graphically, such that the human eye can process the important properties of information. Operating on the premise that "seeing is believing," visualization differs from CAD technology in the following two ways:

■ No known accurate physical model exists in visualization.

■ The graphics display is an abstraction of the object.

A good example of visualization is the modeling of molecular structures. Because molecules are invisible to humans, the models are simply a useful but abstract way of visualizing what we know about molecular structure. An effective visualization application depends on the reality of the presentation, i.e., high resolution must be displayed on a large viewing area. The abstraction is then structured to allow trends or patterns in a data set to be perceived.

Let's look at an example where the basic requirements for such a display are as follows:

■ Display using 1280×1024 pixels

■ Pixel of 24 bits of data

■ Pictures with alterations occurring 18 times per second or once every 55 ms

With these specifications, the required data rate is approximately 23 Mbps, which is obviously a very high bandwidth application that requires high-speed access. As a result, the economics of designing architecture for visualization are not very favorable. The visualization system also requires a supercomputer for processing, which makes the system even more expensive. Even with all these restrictions, about 100,000 visualization-capable systems are available. By the year 2000, about 1 million systems will exist.

Because the data rate requirement for visualization is 23 Mbps, a high-speed communication backbone is also needed to enable users residing at remote sites to access a supercomputer simultaneously shared by other users. Currently, visualization is a LAN-based solution or application, but, with the availability of cost-effective high-speed links, the application will go into MAN, WAN, and GAN.

2.2.2.4   Imaging   *Imaging* is defined as the process that digitizes and stores or retrieves documents, drawings, photographs, and other information in bit-mapped format. Systems that digitize, compress, and store this information are called *imaging systems.* The imaging application typically comes under three categories:

Item capture applications: Items such as checks, drafts, credit card slips, etc., are characterized by the need to process a large number of items quickly. These items are stored and only retrieved when the need arises. The applications are classified as capture- and store-intensive. American Express, for example, uses imaging to capture all credit card receipts.

Records management applications: Claim forms, loan documents, etc., are characterized by a low volume, small storage needs, but high frequency and the need for nationwide retrieval. These applications are classified as retrieval- and distribution-intensive. For example, in the insurance industry, a claim could be processed electronically by imaging the claims documents, thus enabling quick transfer for proper authorization. In the banking industry, loan applications could be processed quickly if they were processed electronically.

Medical and scientific applications: x-rays, scans, seismic data, satellite photos, etc., are characterized by a unique, near one-to-one capture-to-access ratio with little need for storage. These applications are classified as resolution- and distribution-intensive. They are usually stored in a tape backup system that can be retrieved in the future if the need arises. For example, a patient's x-rays could be imaged and electronically transferred from the x-ray lab to the doctor's office.

To better understand why imaging is a broadband application, let's look at the size of the imaging files. Say you are scanning a page at 300 dots per inch (dpi), using approximately 700K bytes of memory. If compressed, the page is between 80 and 250K bytes (depending on page content and compression ratio), which is about 0.25 to 2M bits (each byte is 8 bits). Using a 16-level gray scale, the size of the file is four times larger and with true color it would be 24 times larger. In other words, a true-color image can involve a file of 40MB (compressed). This application is currently LAN-based, but once it appears in MANs and WANs, it will become one of the predominant applications from user perspective because it uses most of the available bandwidth.

2.2.2.5 Supercomputing and Channel Extension Figure 2.7 shows a typical supercomputer/channel extension environment. The supercomputer is at a remote site, connected via a channel extender. The channel extender enables the supercomputer I/O bus to be extended, generally over a metropolitan area or campus, to support locations that have significant performance limitations or simply do not have a supercomputer.

Let's first address supercomputing in general. Many industries routinely use computers with enormous processing power. These high-powered computers are used for two types of applications:

Data reduction: In today's businesses, a vast array of data, from market facts to actual statistics, are increasingly encountered. Supercomputers manipulate and reduce such data to a usable format. This application is categorized as input-intensive.

Modeling and simulation: Models of business, scientific, or engineering processes are exercised repeatedly with varying parameters. Supercomputers accomplish thousands of exercises in reasonable amounts

Figure 2.7
Example of super-
computing/
channel extension
environment.

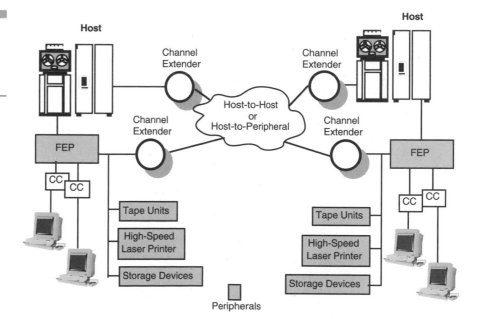

of elapsed time. These applications are typically output-intensive. In business models, supercomputers simulate a business environment. In a scientific environment, data collected from the Hubble telescope, for example, undergoes numerous processes before being interpreted. In engineering, many designs must be attempted using different parameters. For example, in designing a new car the supercomputer could experiment with different shapes and sizes to meet design requirements set by the user.

Now that we have addressed supercomputing, let's look at channel extension. Channel extension enables data transfer between mainframes/peripherals in one of the following ways:

■ By being directly attached to the I/O channel

■ By bypassing the front-end processor (FEP)

■ By serializing the information for transport on a communication link

Figure 2.7 shows a typical supercomputing channel extender environment. The channel extender is connected to the supercomputer and peripherals, enabling the peripheral to access the mainframe and bypass the FEP.

In the 1970s and 1980s, a small number of market segments used channel extenders at low speeds in a host-to-host communications environment. Since 1989, however, the characteristics of this application have tremendously changed. Current characteristics are summarized as follows:

■ Specialized systems

■ Increasing need for higher bandwidth

■ Media dependence

■ Large market

In recent years, the broad acceptance of T1 digital technology has been the most significant factor in the success of channel-extender applications. Host-to-host and host-to-peripheral applications, which are T1-capable, have been extremely successful. In addition, the installation of fiber by service providers in the public network has reduced the cost of high-bandwidth pipes.

2.2.2.6 Multimedia Multimedia is a combination of multiple forms of media in the communication of information between the user and the machine. A multimedia application is one that uses different forms of communication as one application. For example, information can be displayed on a computer using voice, text, and video simultaneously. Whether these applications are implemented as a stand-alone or shared system, they are usually bit-intensive, real-time, and very demanding on the networks. In this type of application, the source can be a location remote from the workstation, e.g., training a customer on setting up a new product. The customer can read relevant material, see a full-motion video demo of the product, and listen to warnings about possible hazards and so on—and all of these can be accessed from a remote location within the vendor's premises.

To support audio (voice) and video, a workstation must have vast amounts of data storage and processing capability. In the case of video, 10 min of uncompressed full-motion video consumes 22 GB of memory. Obviously, even a broadband network cannot handle this amount of data. One of the driving forces of multimedia is the compression technology and multimedia standard. Some of the compression standards available are joint photographic experts group (JPEG) and motion picture experts group (MPEG). Today, a compression ratio of 10:1 is available and is expected to reach 50:1. Compression converts a regular stream of data, called *continuous bit rate* (CBR), to variable bit rate (VBR) traffic. The problem with VBR is that an uneven bit stream results because of the compression. The compression algorithm is usually performed on a frame-by-frame basis. The content of the first frame is transmitted first, and then the change from the preceding frame is transmitted next. This variation in frame size results in the uneven data flow. In this book, we address the technology capable of handling this type of traffic.

2.2.2.7 Internet Access Internet access evolution is being driven primarily by strong demands for increasing bandwidth to support a growing variety of user services. Prior to 1994, traffic sent over the Internet was largely text-based information with file transfer and e-mail being among the most popular services. The users were from universities and research institutions around the world. The surge in growth of the Internet during 1995 was, in part, due to the commercialization of the Internet for business use and the increasing graphical nature of the content. A significant aspect of this shift is that graphical images generally consist of a large number of bits, and transfer of large graphical image files quickly with satisfactory performance meant that higher-speed access technologies were needed than those used to deliver relatively small text files. Each of these capabilities have been pushing the need for increasingly higher-speed access. Internet access itself is not an application but it is an enabler to a variety of applications, including some narrowband services. Based on a recent BRG[1] survey, the following were identified as the potential applications that will drive internet access demand. They are:

Information access/research: Research and education; database access; ability to access data from the federal government; access to business information; access to data; access to state/federal government data/information; database access, data warehousing; database searching; educational research; financial information; information access, e-mail; information and financial needs; information for teacher preparation; information gathering; legal research; power brokering, weather information; research in astrophysics; searching for regulatory/legal/technical updates and changes.

E-mail and messaging: E-mail; information access; FTP; WWW; document sharing; product information; Netscape, e-mail, FTP, telnet; messaging, data delivery, extended WAN services.

Web browsing: Custom-designed applications; e-mail, FTP, telnet; browse client sites; competition information; IS (information systems) staff Web access.

Collaboration: Decision-making applications; document management, videoconferencing; internet connection server, TCP/IP; project management, information sharing; proposal preparation; scientific collaboration; USEnet news for collaboration; workgroup collaboration.

Customer support: Customer access; customer access to financial products; customer interface, electronic transmission sales; customer requests for information; customer service; customer service for product inquiries, order status, technical specifications and troubleshooting.

Marketing: Competition, need to access new types of customers; marketing campaign, product and service awareness; marketing presentations; marketing to customers; providing information via home page; web site to attract television viewers.

Communication: Communication with customers; communication worldwide; customer contact, information delivery; customer site (remote) connectivity; web browser-based and text-based remote applications.

Internal/intranet information: Access to student information (class schedules, open classes); human resources; internal communication;

---

[1] Market research firm specializing in information technology.

plan/participant 401K information; publishing technical information on company intranet; student records; web pages for various departments and research groups.

Technical support: IS support for national applications; support tools; technical information—oil and gas; technical support; technical support for computers and machines; web access for technical support.

Electronic commerce: Electronic commerce; customer interface, electronic transmission sales.

Figure 2.8 is an example of the data rates needed to support various user services and the access rates that have become available over time. (The chart represents average user rate, but not peak burst rates on shared media.) It shows curves for three segments of the user population: the median, the upper 20th percentile, and the upper 2nd percentile of early adopters. Users are eager for audio and video services, and so is the challenge for access systems to meet that demand.

2.2.3   Business/Industry

With today's global economy, powerhouse companies averaging 3 percent growth in existing markets are looking for new markets to penetrate. Many new entrants are vying for partnerships that provide new services. Thus, new industries are forming. A recent example is the British Telecom's purchase of MCI and Sprint's alliance with Deuche Telecom and France Telecom. In the United States, the passage of the Telecom Act in 1996 has brought major changes in the industry. This act basically opened the door for convergence of voice, data, and video and thus the

Figure 2.8
Internet access rate
growth.

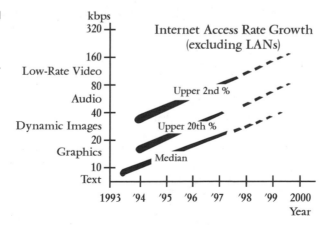

need for integrated broadband communications which enables service providers to provide cost-effective solutions to business customers.

Thus the Telecom Act of 1996 in the United States has forced traditional telecommunications providers to adopt a market-driven approach where reducing cost and increasing revenues become the name of the game to survive. The deregulation does not end with the United States. The year 1998 marks deregulation in Europe followed by other countries around the world.

2.2.4   Standards

Standards are very important in the success of a technology becoming commercial and ubiquitous. Many standards organizations around the world are working on the standardization of telecommunications networks and protocols so that any vendor can develop a product to be used in the worldwide network. A list of the standards organizations is given in Table 2.2. This list can only give you an idea on the number of organizations involved in the standards-making process. Chapter 22 describes some of the major international organizations, their relationships, and standardization processes.

2.3   Residential and Business Broadband Service Categories

The evolution toward a broadband network will allow broadband services to be provided to end users in addition to current services. The goal of the broadband network is thus to offer services to everyone, from business customers to residential customers using the same infrastructure resources. Providing services both to business and residential customers over the same network poses numerous problems, however, because of the different needs of each customer.

Three major categories of services exist: data, voice, and video. Figure 2.9 shows that both residential and business customers use voice, but data services are used only by business customers and video services only by residential users. This categorization does not mean that business users do not use video services or residential users do not use data services; it only represents the majority. For example, residential video services are

TABLE 2.2	Acronym	Standards Organization
Global Standards Organizations	AFNOR	Association Francaise de Normalisation
	ANSI	American National Standards Institute
	AOW	Asian-Oceanic Workshop
	ATM forum	Special-interest group focusing on ATM standardization
	ARC	Administrative Radio Conference
	BCS	British Computer Society
	BSI	British Standards Institute
	CCIR	International Radio Consultative Committee
	CCITT	International Telegraph and Telephone Consultative Committee
	CEN/Cenelect	Comite Europeane de Normalisation Electronique
	CEPT	European Conference of Postal and Telecommunication Administrations
	COS	Corporation for Open System International
	COSINE	Cooperation for Open System Interconnection Networking in Europe
	DIN	Deutsches Institut für Normung
	DOD-ADA	U.S. Department of Defense—ADA Joint Program Office
	ECMA	European Computer Manufacturers Association
	ECSA	Exchange Carriers Standards Association
	EDIFACT	Western European Electronic Data Interchange for Administration, Commerce, and Transportation
	EMUG	MAP/TOP User Group
	ETSI	European Telecommunications Standards Institute
	EWOS	European Open Systems Workshop
	GOST	USSR State Committee for Standards
	IAB/EITF	Internet Activities Board/Internet Engineering Task Force
	IEC	International Electrotechnical Commission
	IEEE	Institute of Electrical and Electronics Engineers
	ISA	Integrated Systems Architectures
	ISO	International Organization for Standardization

TABLE 2.2

(Continued)

Acronym	Standards Organization
ITRC	Information Technology Requirements Council
ITU-T	International Telecommunications Union—Telecommunications
JISC	Japan Industrial Standards Association
JSA	Japan Standards Association
JTC1	Joint Technical Committee 1—Information Technology
NIST	National Institute for Standards and Technology
NNI	Nederlands Normalisatie—Institut
OSF	Open Software Foundation
POSI	Pacific OSI Group
SAA	Standards Association of Australia
SCC	Standards Council of Canada
SIGMA	Unix Open Applications Group—Japan
SIS	Standardiseringskommissionen I Sverige
SMPTE	Society of Motion Picture and Television Engineers
SNV	Swiss Association for Standardization
SPAG	European Standards Promotion and Applications Group
T1	Standards Committee T1—Telecommunications
TTA	Telecommunications Technology Association of Korea
TTC	Telecommunications Technology Council
UAOS	Users Association for Open Systems
UI	Unix International
URSI	Union Radioscientifique Internationale
VESA	Video Equipment Standards Association
X/OPEN	Unix Open Applications Group

provided via CATV network. This service is the most dominant one used by the residential users, unlike data.

In the broadband world, all services are adapted to a single protocol, thus making the distinction impossible from a network point of view. For a service provider or an end user, however, the distinction is required to assign priority, quality-of-service, and allocation of bandwidth. To make these assignments, the service providers and end users must understand the characteristics and usage pattern of each service. For example, most business customers' traffic is voice-based and its peak usage is during working hours (8 a.m. to 5 p.m.), whereas the residential customer's peak time is during evenings and weekends.

Although future broadband promises to deliver all the previously mentioned services on a single unified network, in reality, it is a lot more difficult to achieve such objectives. The reason is that today's networks are designed to provide only cost-effective specific services. Therefore, it is cumbersome for a new network such as broadband to provide an overall cost-effective service compared to the existing specialized networks. So, to achieve this goal of providing all services in a single network, an evolution process must occur. New capabilities that have the best chance for success must be implemented in the broadband network, then allow other services to slowly migrate onto the broadband network on a justification basis. As mentioned in Chap. 1, there are basically three types of networks, i.e., voice-based telephone networks, data-based internet networks, and

Figure 2.9
Typical business and
residential services.

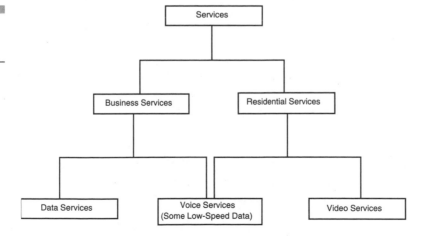

Figure 2.10
Approach to broad-
band-capable
network.

Requirements	Telephone world (telephone network)	Data world (Internet)	Radio/TV world (CATV/Wireless)
Intelligence			
Two-way communication			
Switching or Addressing			
Billing, Security			
Real-time capability			
Broadband capability			

video-based CATV/wireless networks. These networks show serious deficiencies, as shown in Fig. 2.10. The figure illustrates the deficiencies for each
network, such as the telephone network that lacks broadband capability;
the data network (Internet) that lacks the necessary billing, security, and
capacity; and the video network that lacks switching, addressing, reverse
channel capability for two-way communication, and the intelligence to
provide value-added services. For example, the present Internet resembles
more of an eastern bazaar than a modern supermarket, and the WWW
does not only stand for World Wide Web, but also, for World Wide Waiting.

To address some of the deficiencies mentioned Fig. 2.10, we propose a
possible evolution path to a broadband network for each of the networks
described in Chap. 1 using the technologies discussed in this book. The
evolution toward broadband can be defined in the following manner:

1. Start providing limited new services on an existing platform (network).
For example, CATV with its existing network cannot provide two-way
communication, billing, security, or real-time information. So, as a first
step, CATV providers are providing pay-per-view, where the customer
dials the number, and the CATV provider unscrambles the channel for
that specific decoder assigned to that particular home. From an infrastructure point not much needs to be done to perform this function.

Then, to improve the quality and reliability of the services, coaxial cable can be replaced by fiber optic cable.

2. Replace or enhance the platform, maintain backward compatibility with existing services and revenue streams while expanding the new service growth potential. For example, analog fibers can first be used in the network and then CATV providers can migrate to digital fiber in the distribution plant. At this point, CATV provider can upgrade their network with two-way capability and add features such as billing, security, and switching capability. This type of CATV network is typically called HFC (hybrid fiber, coaxial), which is discussed in Chap. 13. One of the reasons that CATV providers do not migrate to end-to-end digital systems currently is because television sets are still analog. Even if the network converts the signal to digital, the signal must be converted back to analog for ultimate viewing.

3. By adding features like switching and billing, CATV providers can start to interact with other networking services and systems to fill service gaps temporarily or permanently as best fits the needs of the business and leverage capability from other service providers.

Now that we have defined a generic evolution strategy, let's look at the evolution of the different networks already mentioned. Figure 2.11 shows the evolution path of the different networks toward the broadband vision, i.e., using ATM as the switching platform and SONET/SDH as the transmission platform. It also illustrates how the different existing networks can lead to the target network broadband by taking different paths suitable for the evolution from their current installed base. The figure does not specify the time line for the deployment of the different technologies but rather how some of the different technologies discussed in the book enable the evolution toward a broadband network from an infrastructure point of view.

2.4   Summary

This chapter addresses the various factors leading to the evolution toward broadband. The four basic categories that are driving the evolution for broadband are technology, applications, standards around the world, and

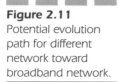

Figure 2.11
Potential evolution
path for different
network toward
broadband network.

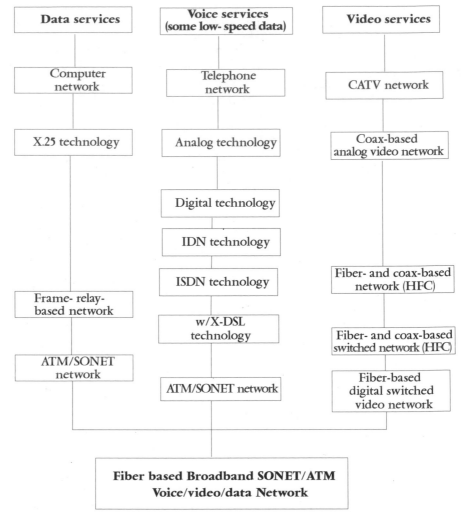

businesses/industries. Finally, we look at the evolution path taken by voice, data, and video networks to achieve the target network of broadband.

This evolution simply indicates how the different networks are converging to provide all the services, leveraging their existing service and customer base. The only technology that has been envisioned to be able to provide such a wide range of services is ATM-based broadband, with the help of SONET/SDH for transmission, ATM for switching, and IN to control these and other technologies.

PART 2

The Basics

In this part we provide an overview of the different broadband technologies that form the foundation for an end-to-end network. The different technologies covered are FDDI, DQDB, FR, SMDS, ATM, SONET, and broadband access technologies such as X- DSL, HFC, etc. Each one of these technologies is optimized for a certain application or a segment of the network. These technologies can perform the function of transmission or a switching or a combination of transmission and switching. Each one of these technologies is needed to work together in order to provide the service needed by the end user. This is where standardization plays an important role in defining the interworking of protocols. The detailed information on the standardization process at the international level is discussed in Part 7.

CHAPTER 3

FDDI and DQDB

3.1   Overview

This chapter explains the basic working standards and protocols of
FDDI and DQDB technologies. FDDI is included because, as per our definition, any service requiring more than 1.5 Mbps is considered broadband. Because FDDI is a LAN technology operating at 100 Mbps, it
therefore falls under our definition. In Chap. 15, we also see how ATM
technology competes against FDDI as the technology of choice in the
LAN environment. The evolution strategies for migrating from an
FDDI- to an ATM-based network architecture are also covered in that
chapter. Both FDDI and DQDB are quite similar. Both use fiber as the
transmission medium, and their targeted application is LAN interconnect, interworking with IEEE 802, capable of carrying both isochronous
(voice) and data traffic. Only FDDI-II, the second-generation FDDI, carries both voice and data. Differences do exist though: DQDB is intended
for the public network, whereas FDDI is intended for private LANs.
DQDB came into existence in the mid-1980s when the IEEE 802 committee recognized the need for an access technology to be used in the public MAN. In the 802.6 subcommittee, the different shared medium
topologies and access mechanism were discussed, resulting in the definition of DQDB. DQDB is based on a proposal that was initially called
queued packed synchronous exchange (QPSX) received from the University of Western Australia in 1988. IEEE 802.6 adopted the concept of
QPSX and renamed it DQDB. The IEEE 802.6 subcommittee was working on these standards at the same time that ITU-T was working on the
ATM standards. Thus, it was possible for each standards body to influence the standards of the other, allowing the DQDB standards to be
included in the CCITT standards wherever possible.

3.2   Fiber Distributed Data Interface (FDDI)

In this section, concepts, standards, and architecture of FDDI are discussed.

3.2.1   FDDI Concepts

Figure 3.1 illustrates the basic FDDI topology. FDDI is a token-passing LAN
technology that uses a timed-token protocol. This protocol guarantees that

Figure 3.1
FDDI ring configuration.

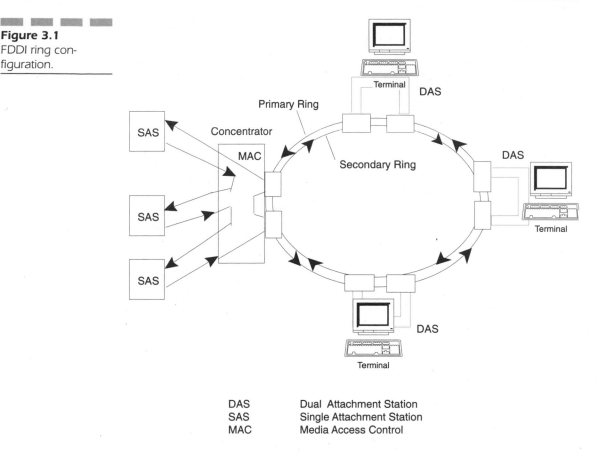

DAS	Dual Attachment Station
SAS	Single Attachment Station
MAC	Media Access Control

stations can gain access to the ring within a time period negotiated between stations each time a new station joins the ring.

An FDDI is constructed of nodes that connect together via links to form the ring. The nodes can be of two types: dual-attachment stations (DAS) or single-attachment stations (SAS). A special type of node, called a _concentrator,_ allows connection of stations into the ring and provides for greater fault tolerance than the basic ring architecture. One of the important features of FDDI is the use of dual-counter rotating rings. The dual rings are independent until a fault (such as a cable break) occurs, in which case the rings are joined together, or wrapped, to restore the ring to its operational state.

FDDI is based on the use of fiber-optic technology, which allows construction of rings up to a total fiber length of 200 km. Using multimode fiber, internode distances of 2 km are permitted, while single-mode fiber implementations enable internode distances that exceed 20 km. Recent enhancements in the FDDI standard have allowed the use of cheaper fiber optics for runs less than 500 m, and twisted-pair cable for runs of up to 100 m.

In addition to the dual-counter rotation rings, FDDI offers other features such as the following:

- Use of a token-passing MAC scheme based on the IEEE 802.5 token ring standard
- Compatibility with IEEE 802 LANs by using 802.2 logical link control (LLC)
- Ability to utilize multimode or single-mode optical fibers
- Operation at a data rate of 100 Mbps
- Ability to attach any number of stations (standards assume no more than 1000 physical attachments)
- Total fiber path of 200 km
- Ability to dynamically allocate bandwidth so that both synchronous and asynchronous data services can be provided simultaneously

3.2.2   FDDI Standards

Work on FDDI standards started in the early 1980s and still continues to enhance FDDI technology to meet ever-changing customer requirements. In this section, we address some of the basic standards of FDDI; for detailed technical information, refer to the individual ANSI (American National Standards Institute) or ISO document listed in Table 3.1.

The FDDI standards address the physical and data link layer requirements of the OSI reference model, as illustrated in Fig. 3.2. The FDDI (PMD, PHY, MAC, and SMT) standards, along with the IEEE 802.2 LLC standards, provide essential networking services to devices attached to an FDDI network. The PMD is the lowest sublayer of the OSI physical layer. It includes specifications for power levels characteristic of the optical transmitter and receiver, permissible bit-error rates, jittery requirements, acceptable media, etc. The PHY is the upper sublayer of the OSI physical layer. It deals with such issues as the encoding scheme, clock synchronization, and data framing. The lower sublayer of the OSI data link layer is the MAC. The MAC standard defines rules for medium access, addressing, frame formats, error checking, and token management. The station management standard specifies system management applications for

TABLE 3.1

ANSI/ISO FDDI
Standards

Standard Title	ANSI Standard No.	ISO Standard No.
Hybrid ring control (HRC)	X3.186	9314-5
Physical layer medium dependent (PMD)	X3.166	9314-3
Single-mode fiber physical layer medium dependent (SMF-PMD)	X3.184	9314-4
SONET physical layer mapping (SPM)	T1.105	
Station management (SMT)	—	—
Token ring physical layer protocol (PHY)	X3.148	9314-1
PHY-2	—	—
Token ring medium access control (MAC)	X3.139	9314-2
MAC-2	—	—

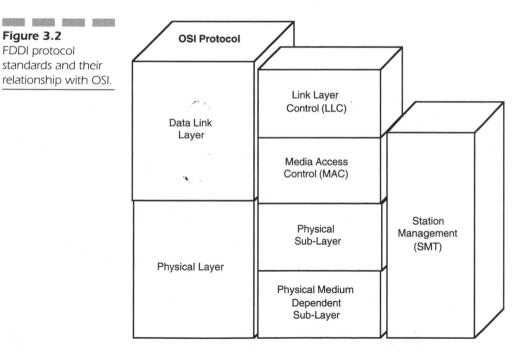

Figure 3.2
FDDI protocol
standards and their
relationship with OSI.

each of the FDDI protocol layers. In particular, it is concerned with the control required for correct operation of a station on an FDDI network. The details of these components and their functions are covered in the next section.

The FDDI standards comprise many separate documents. Before we go further, we need to understand the background of FDDI standards development. The initial idea of developing a new high-speed data interface for computers based on optical fiber dates back to October 1982. The ANSI X3T12 subcommittee was already addressing a similar high-speed data communications network using coaxial cable called the *local distributed data interface*. The subcommittee formed an ad hoc task group to examine the fiber-based concept in detail. It proposed that the working group formally start working on FDDI physical, data link, and network layer standards.

Initial proposals for the MAC and physical layers were put forth in 1983. The MAC layer corresponds to the lower half of the OSI data link layer. The task group decided to develop the FDDI MAC to operate below the IEEE 802.2 LLC standard, also under development at that time. The LLC corresponds to the upper half of the OSI data link layer, and all IEEE 802 MAC schemes are designed to operate under it. This choice by X3T12 made it possible for data link and network layer protocols to be FDDI-specific. The FDDI MAC protocol was formally adopted as an ANSI standard in 1987.

In 1984, the subcommittee recognized that fiber technology was changing rapidly, making the physical layer standard nearly impossible to complete in a timely fashion. The committee then decided to divide the physical layer into two protocol sublayers. The PHY corresponds to the upper half of the OSI physical layer and describes those physical layer issues independent of the network medium. Development of the PHY standard could continue in parallel with the MAC standard, and the PHY was later adopted by ANSI in 1988.

The second layer, the PMD sublayer, corresponds to the lower half of the OSI physical layer and deals with media-specific issues. The original PMD standard is written for multimode fiber (MMF) and was formally adopted in 1990. In 1987, meanwhile, the task group realized that the distance limitations of MMF were too confining, and it started to work on a single-mode fiber PMD (SMF-PMD).

Some FDDI users do not want to incur the expense of purchasing, installing, and managing their own optical fiber transmission facilities. Instead, they would prefer to use the high-speed transmission services available from public network providers. In 1989, recognizing that FDDI had applications using public network facilities, the task group created an interface between FDDI's PHY protocol and the emerging SONET standards. The standard defined an alternative to the PMD standards and allowed mapping of FDDI transmissions directly onto SONET-based networks. It was completed in 1992.

In 1984, the subcommittee also recognized the need for a separate standard describing station management issues. This standard had to conform to work already in progress by both the IEEE 802.1 committee and ISO on station and network management. With the development of integrated voice/data networks, and particularly ISDN, the subcommittee anticipated the requirement for a new type of network to carry this mixture of traffic. It started to develop plans for a second-generation FDDI capable of carrying voice, image, and video in addition to high-speed data. This second generation FDDI is commonly called FDDI-II. We do not address FDDI-II because of ongoing standards activity in this area.

3.2.3 FDDI Protocol Architecture

The previous section introduced the FDDI protocol model. Here, we look into the different components of FDDI and their functions (i.e., PMD, PHY, MAC, and SMT). As mentioned in Chap. 2, the lowest level of the OSI model is the physical layer. This level defines the transmission of bits on the physical medium. FDDI standards subdivide this OSI physical layer into two sublayers: PMD and PHY. These two sublayers separate the physical medium and transmission details into two distinct parts.

3.2.3.1 Physical Layer Medium Dependent. FDDI has standardized two PMDs. As highlighted in Fig. 3.3, PMD standards define how nodes (stations) physically attach to the FDDI ring and how stations are physically interconnected on the network by media type (optical fiber or copper).

The four types of PMD are the following:

■ *PMD.* Uses light-emitting diodes (LEDs) and multimode fiber. It was the first PMD developed by ANSI.

■ *SMF-PMD.* Uses laser diodes and single-mode fiber. It is used to interconnect stations separated by distances that exceed the 2-km limit imposed by the PMD.

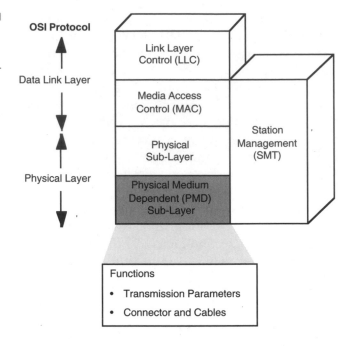

Figure 3.3
Physical medium
functions.

- *LCF-PMD.* Currently in development by ANSI, the low-cost fiber PMD also uses LEDs and multimode fiber. It spans 500 m between stations and is envisioned to be a low-cost alternative to PMD.

- *TP-PMD.* Also currently in development, the twisted-pair PMD will operate over copper media—shielded twisted-pair (STP) and some categories of unshielded twisted-pair (UTP). It is anticipated that the transmission distance between stations will be limited to 100 m.

Data is transmitted between stations by first converting the data bits into a series of signals, then transmitting these signals over the cable linking the two stations. The PMD standards deal with all areas associated with physically transmitting the data:

- Optical and electrical transmitters and receivers
- Fiber-optic or copper cable
- Media interface connector
- Optical bypass relay (optional in optical PMDs)

3.2.3.2 Physical Layer Protocol. The PHY standard, shown in Fig. 3.4, defines those portions of the physical layer that are media-independent.

Thus, new media such as twisted pair can be added without changing the PHY parameters.

The physical layer protocol provides the following functions:

- *Clock and data recovery:* Recovers the clock signal from the incoming data.

- *Encode/decode process:* Converts data from the MAC into a form for transmission over the FDDI ring.

- *Symbols:* Smallest signaling entities used for communication between stations. Symbols consist of five code bits.

- *Elasticity buffer:* Accounts for clock tolerances between stations.

- *Smoothing function:* Prevents frames from being lost because of shortened preambles.

- *Repeat filter:* Prevents the propagation of code violations and invalid line states.

3.2.3.3 Media Access Control. The second level of the OSI reference model is the data link layer. As shown in Fig. 3.5, the data link layer is divided into two sublayers: MAC and LLC.

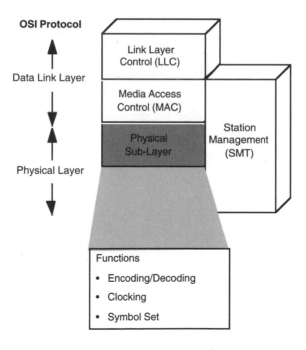

Figure 3.4
Physical sublayer functions.

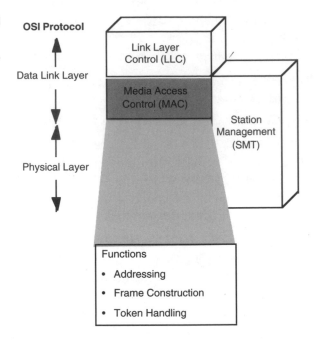

Figure 3.5
MAC functions.

The FDDI MAC standard defines the following functions:

- Fair and equal access to the ring through the use of the timed-token protocol
- Communication between attached devices using frames and tokens
- Construction of frames and tokens
- Transmitting, receiving, repeating, and stripping frames and tokens from the ring
- Various error-detection mechanisms
- Ring initialization
- Ring fault isolation

Although LLC is not part of the FDDI standard, FDDI requires LLC for proper ring operation and transmission of user data. Logical link control defines link-level services that allow the transmission of a frame of data between two stations. Figure 3.6 shows the relationship between LLC and FDDI. FDDI assumes implementation of the IEEE 802.2 LLC standard. Here, frames are used to transfer information between MAC layers in FDDI. FDDI defines three different types of frames:

- MAC frames that carry MAC control data
- SMT frames that carry FDDI-specific management information between stations
- LLC frames that carry LLC information

3.2.3.4 Station Management. The SMT standard provides the necessary services at the station level to monitor and control an FDDI station. SMT allows stations to work cooperatively within the ring and ensures proper station operation. FDDI stations can have multiple instances of PMD, PHY, and MAC entities, but only one SMT entity.

Station management contains three major components:

- Connection management (CMT)
- Ring management (RMT)
- SMT frame services

Figure 3.7 shows how these three SMT components are incorporated into the FDDI architecture.

3.2.3.4.1 Connection Management. CMT is the portion of station management that performs physical-layer insertion and removal of FDDI stations. Remember that FDDI stations can have multiple PHYs

Figure 3.6
Relationship between
LLC and FDDI.

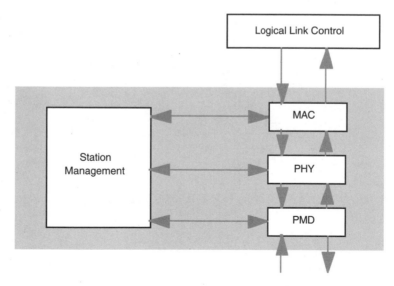

Figure 3.7
Relationship of SMT
components in FDDI.

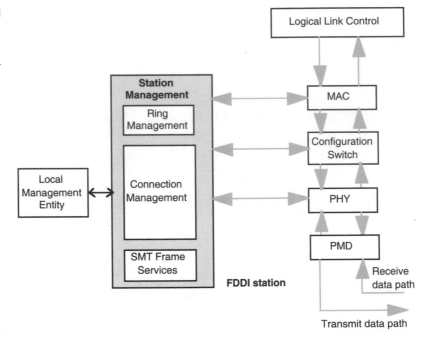

Figure 3.8
Connection manage-
ment portion of
station management.

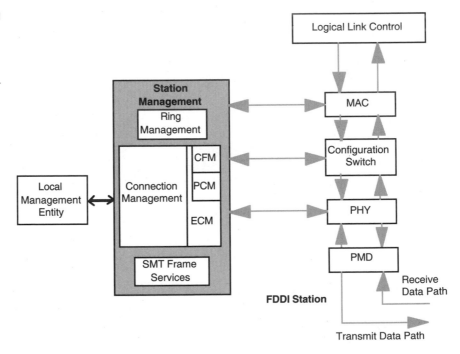

and MACs. Therefore, one of the functions of CMT is to manage the switch configuration (Fig. 3.8) that connects PHYs to MACs and other PHYs within a station. Connection management functions include:

- Connecting a PHY to its neighboring PHY
- Connecting PHYs and MACs via the configuration switch
- Using trace diagnostics to identify and isolate a faulty component

As shown in Fig. 3.8, CMT contains the following components:

- Physical connection management (PCM) provides for managing the physical connection between adjacent PHYs, including establishing the connection, testing the quality of the link before the connection is established (link confidence testing), and continuously monitoring error rates once the ring is operational (link error monitoring).
- Configuration management (CFM) provides for configuring PHY and MAC entities within a station.
- Coordination management (ECM) provides for controlling bypass relays, signaling to PCM that the medium is available and coordinating trace functions.

3.2.3.4.2 Ring Management. The RMT portion of SMT receives status information from MAC and CMT. Ring management then reports this status to SMT and higher-level processes. Services provided by RMT are the following:

- Stuck-beacon detection is a process by which a specialized frame called a beacon is used by MAC to announce to other stations that the ring is broken. A beacon indicates that a station cannot resolve a ring error condition detected in its receive path.
- Tracing process, which provides a recovery mechanism for beacon conditions on the FDDI ring.
- Determination of a MAC's availability for transmission.
- Detection of duplicate addresses, which prevent the proper operation of the ring even if the ring becomes operational.

3.2.3.4.3 SMT Frame Services. The SMT frame provides services on portions of SMT that control and observe stations on the FDDI network.

Different SMT frame classes and types implement these services. The frame class identifies the function that the frame performs, such as the neighborhood information frame (NIF), status information frame (SIF), parameter management frame (PMF), and status report frame (SRF). Frame type designates whether the frame is an announcement, request, or response to a request. These different classes of frames are described in the following subsections.

Neighborhood information frames: Stations determine their upstream and downstream neighbors by exchanging NIFs as part of the neighbor notification protocol. Stations also use the protocol to determine the existence of duplicate address conditions. Once upstream neighbor addresses are known to the stations, these addresses can be used to create a logical ring map showing the order in which each station appears in the token path.

Status information frames: Stations use SIFs to exchange more detailed information about their characteristics and configuration. SIFs also contain information about the status of each port in a station. The information in SIFs can be used to create a physical ring map that shows the position of each station, not only in the token path (logical ring), but in the topology as well. SIFs are divided into two types—SIF configuration frames and SIF operation frames. SIF configuration frames show the configuration details of a station, while SIF operation frames show operational detail such as error rates.

Parameter management frames: PMFs are used by the parameter management protocol to manage an FDDI station. Management is achieved by operations on the station's management information base (MIB) attributes. Operations are performed by exchanging frames between the manager and the station. If an attribute is initiated by a PMF Get Request frame from the management station, it is followed by a PMF Get Response frame from the target station. Changing an MIB attribute requires a Get Exchange (to check the current value), followed by a PMF set request/response exchange.

Status report frames: SRFs are used by the status report protocol to announce station status to management stations. SRF frames report conditions and events. Conditions are declared when a station enters certain states, such as Duplicate Address Detected. Events are instantaneous occurrences, such as the generation of a trace.

3.2.4 How FDDI Works

In FDDI, the standards define the functions that control ring operation and maintenance, whereas the technology attempts to provide survivability in case of failures. After receiving the token, an active station transmits a frame as a stream of symbols to the next active station on the ring. As each active station receives these symbols, it regenerates and repeats them to the next active device on the ring (its downstream neighbor). When the frame returns to the originating station, it is stripped by that station from the ring.

3.2.4.1 Dual Counterrotating Ring. The dual counterrotating ring is one of the basic concepts in the FDDI standards. It consists of two rings: a primary ring and a secondary ring. Both rings can carry data. As shown in Fig. 3.9, the data flows in opposite directions on the two rings. In most cases, particularly in high-bandwidth applications, it is best to use the primary ring for data transmission and the secondary ring as backup. This guideline is especially important when the FDDI ring undergoes its self-healing process during a fault condition. The configuration complexity and therefore the cost of FDDI increases if both rings are used for data transmission.

FDDI limits total fiber length to 200 km. Because the dual-ring topology effectively doubles the media length in the event of a fault condition, the actual length of each ring is limited to 100 km. The dual counterrotating ring is designed with the ability to restore ring operation if a device fails or a cable fault occurs. The ring is restored by wrapping the primary

Figure 3.9
Dual-ring topology.

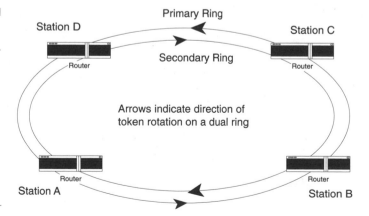

ring to the secondary ring, thus restoring the transmission path. This redundancy in the ring design provides a degree of fault tolerance not found in other network standards. In an FDDI ring, if a cable failure occurs, the stations on either side of the failure reconfigure by themselves. They wrap the primary ring to the secondary ring, effectively isolating the fault, restoring continuity to the ring, and thus allowing normal operation to continue. Figure 3.10 shows the fault-isolation technique.

When a wrap occurs, the dual-ring topology changes to a single-ring topology. When the fault is corrected, the topology reverts back to dual-ring. If multiple faults occur, the ring segments into many independent rings. Therefore, when more than one fault occurs in the dual ring, communication between all stations is not possible, but communication is possible within a portion of the ring.

We mentioned earlier that if an attached station fails, the devices on either side of the failed station reconfigure to isolate the station from the ring. Figure 3.11 shows this fault-isolation technique. In Fig. 3.11, station A is isolated from the ring. The ring remains operational by wrapping the primary and secondary rings at stations B and D. They remain wrapped until the fault is corrected, which is detected by transmission of a beacon frame, as shown in Fig. 3.12.

3.2.4.2   Ring Operation.   FDDI ring operation includes the following stages:

1. Connection establishment

2. Ring initialization

3. Steady-state operation

4. Ring maintenance

Figure 3.10
Dual-ring with fiber cut.

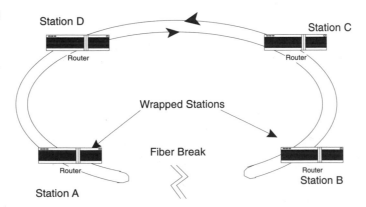

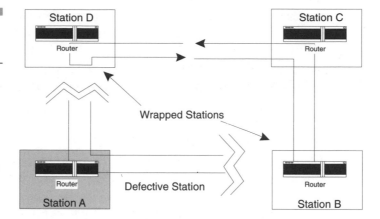

Figure 3.11
Defective station
isolation.

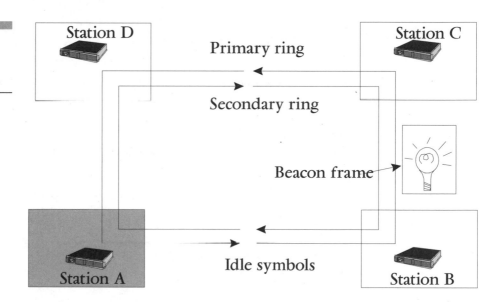

Figure 3.12
Detection of defec-
tive station using
beacon frame.

Each of these stages is monitored by timers that regulate the operations. Three timers are used by each FDDI station to perform the
function of regulating the ring operations:

Token-rotation timer: The TRT times the duration of operations in a station. This timer is critical to the successful operation of the FDDI
network. This timer controls ring scheduling during normal operation and fault recovery times when the ring is not operational. The
token-rotation timer is initialized to different values, depending
on the state of the ring. During steady-state operation, the token

rotation timer expires when the target token rotation time (TTRT) has been exceeded. Stations negotiate the value for TTRT via the claim process.

Token-holding timer: THT controls the length of time that a station can initiate asynchronous frames. A station holding the token can begin asynchronous transmission if THT has not expired. THT is initialized with the value corresponding to the difference between the arrival of the token and the TTRT.

Valid transmission timer: TVX times the period between valid transmissions on the ring. TVX detects excessive ring noise, token loss, and other faults. When the station receives a valid frame or token, the valid transmission timer resets. If TVX expires, the station starts a ring initialization sequence to restore the ring to proper operation. Now that we have seen timers used in the operation of FDDI, we can address the different operations.

3.2.4.2.1 Connection Establishment. To form the ring, stations must establish connections with their neighbors. The CMT portion of SMT controls this physical connection process. At power-up or on a connection restart, stations recognize their neighbors by transmitting and acknowledging defined line state sequence as illustrated in Fig. 3.13.

To establish a link, stations perform the following functions:

- Exchange information on port type and connection rules
- Negotiate the length of the link, which checks the quality of the links between stations
- Exchange results and status on the links and connections

Figure 3.13
Ring power-up.

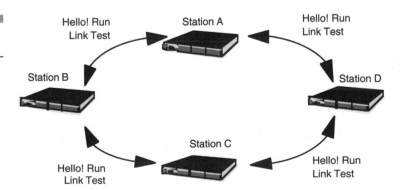

If the connection type is set up, the stations could complete the physical connection by transmitting another defined line-state sequence. This process is repeated for each link in the dual ring by each station. Eventually, all stations join the ring.

3.2.4.2.2 Ring Initialization. Once the connection is established, FDDI protocol requires the stations to bid for the right to initialize the ring (i.e., generate a token) by negotiating a TTRT, ensuring that stations receive guaranteed service time. The TTRT can be set based on:

- Number of attached stations
- Length of ring
- Time required by each station to transmit data over the ring
- Balance of low latency and adequate bandwidth

During ring initialization, stations negotiate the TTRT with other stations to determine which station can issue the token. This process of negotiation is called the claim process. The claim determines which station should initiate the ring. The claim process begins when the MAC entity in one or more stations enters the claim state. In this state, the MAC in each station continually transmits claim frames. A claim frame contains the station's address and bid for the TTRT. Stations in the ring compare the incoming claim frames with their own bid for target token rotation time. If the frame has a shorter time bid, the station repeats the claim frame and stops sending its own. If the frame has a longer time bid, the station removes the claim frame and continues sending frames with its own bid for TTRT.

When a station receives its own claim frame, that station wins the right to initialize the ring. If two or more stations make identical bids, the station with the longest and highest address wins the bidding. The winning station initializes the ring by issuing a token. This token passes around the ring without being captured by any station. Instead, as each station receives the token, it sets its own TTRT to match the TTRT of the winning station. On the second token rotation, stations can send synchronous traffic. On the token's third rotation, stations can transmit asynchronous data.

Figure 3.14 illustrates an example of the working of a claim process. The stations negotiate (or bid) for the right to initialize the ring. In this example, stations A and C are issuing shorter bids than stations B and D. Station C is issuing a shorter bid than station A.

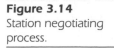

Figure 3.14
Station negotiating
process.

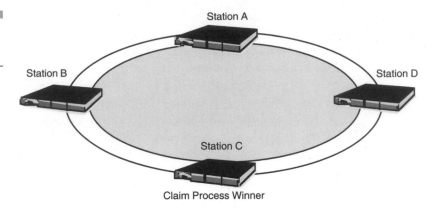

The process of negotiation is as follows:

1. All active stations start issuing claim frames.

2. Station D receives a shorter claim from station C, stops sending its own claim, and repeats station C's shorter claim to station A. Meanwhile

   ■ Station B receives a shorter claim from station A, stops sending its own claim, and repeats station A's shorter claim to station C.
   ■ Station C receives station A's claim frame but continues sending its own shorter claim frame.

3. Station A receives station C's shorter claim from station D, stops sending its own claim, and repeats station C's shorter claim to station B.

4. Station B receives station C's shorter claim from station A and repeats station C's shorter claim to station C.

5. Station C receives its own claim from station B. Station C sets the TTRT and issues a token to initialize the ring.

Thus, the negotiating process is achieved by supporting fair access to the ring.

3.2.4.2.3 Steady-State Operation.   Once the ring is initialized, FDDI goes into steady-state operation. When in the steady state, stations exchange frames using the timed-token protocol. The process is described in Fig. 3.15. The ring remains in the steady state until a new claim process is initiated, such as when a new station joins the ring. In the steady state, FDDI provides basically two types of services, namely asynchronous and synchronous services. Asynchronous services are designed for bandwidth-insensitive applications such as datagram traffic. Asynchronous frames are designed to be transmitted even when the station does not require the bandwidth, whereas synchronous frames are sent at any time, as long as the negotiated bandwidth is available. This service is useful for frames that must have guaranteed delivery within a time period of $2 \times$ TTRT. Such frames include compressed audio and video, among others.

The following is the process by which an FDDI station transmits a frame using time-token protocol.

When an FDDI station wants to transmit a frame it:

1. Waits until it detects the token

2. Captures the token

3. Stops the token repeat process (because no token is on the ring this action prevents other stations from transmitting data onto the ring)

4. Begins sending frames (frames can be sent until there is no more data to send, or the token holding rules require surrender of the token)

5. Releases the token onto the ring for use by another station

Once all active stations, except the sending station, on an FDDI network receive and repeat each frame, each station on the ring compares the destination address of each frame with its own and checks for frame errors. If addresses match, the receiving station copies the frame and sets status symbols (control indicators) to show that the station has recognized its address and copied the frame.

Repeating stations check for errors and retransmit the frames to the next station. If the station detects an error, it sets an error indicator. After the frame circles the ring, the station that sent the frame removes (strips) it from the ring. This stripping can cause partial frames, called *fragments*. These fragments are left on the ring. Each FDDI station must ensure that frame fragments do not degrade ring operation. The fragments are removed either by transmitting or operating a repeat filter at each station's PHY.

Figure 3.15
Frame transmission
process.

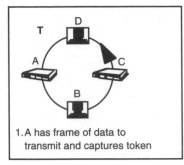

1. A has frame of data to transmit and captures token

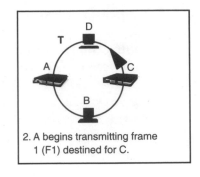

2. A begins transmitting frame 1 (F1) destined for C.

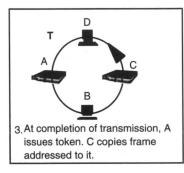

3. At completion of transmission, A issues token. C copies frame addressed to it.

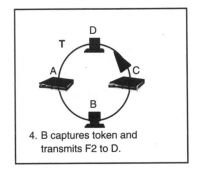

4. B captures token and transmits F2 to D.

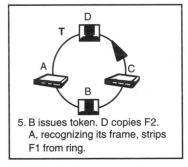

5. B issues token. D copies F2. A, recognizing its frame, strips F1 from ring.

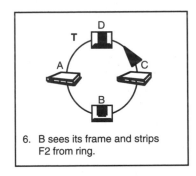

6. B sees its frame and strips F2 from ring.

Every time a device is attached to or removed from the ring, the ring reconfigures itself. During this process, stray frames can be introduced to the new topology. Sometimes, these stray frames have been generated by a device that is no longer part of the new topology. The frames can no longer be identified as belonging to any particular attached device. To remove these stray frames, a station sends a series of idle symbols to the ring. At the same time, MAC strips the ring of frames and tokens and this process is called scrubbing. Once this process is completed, the active stations enter the claim process. The time taken to scrub the ring guarantees that all frames on the ring have been created after the reconfiguration occurred, preventing old frames from continually circulating on the ring.

3.2.4.2.4 Ring Maintenance. The responsibility for monitoring the ring is distributed among all stations on the ring. Each station monitors the ring for conditions that require ring initialization, such as ring inactivity longer than the valid transmission time or a physical or logical break in the ring.

3.2.5 FDDI Network Topologies and Configurations

Like most other networks, FDDI networks can be described in terms of their physical and logical topologies. The physical topology refers to the physical arrangement of the stations and their physical interconnections. The logical topology refers to the path between MAC entities over which the information flows.

FDDI networks can be organized in many ways. A network configuration with only dual-attachment stations results in a logical and physical ring. FDDI allows for more versatility than this one configuration. For instance, when concentrators are added to the network, a branching tree topology develops.

FDDI can be implemented in three ways:

- A high-speed backbone connecting midspeed LANs, such as those found in IEEE 802.3 and IEEE 802.5 applications
- A high-speed workgroup LAN that connects workstations or servers
- A high-speed connection between host computers, or host computers-to-peripheral equipment, such as those found in a data center

The FDDI standards permit a number of topologies. The following four topologies are of particular importance:

- Standalone concentrator with attached stations
- Dual-ring

■ Tree of concentrators

■ Dual ring of trees

3.2.5.1 Standalone Concentrator Topology. The standalone concentrator topology consists of a single concentrator and its attached stations (Fig. 3.16). These stations can be either single-attachment station or dual-attachment station devices. For example, the concentrator can connect multiple high-performance devices in a workgroup. Figure 3.16 shows an independent workgroup topology that uses existing structured wiring, thus affording significant cost savings in prewired sites. The logical ring is formed by the stations and the concentrator, with the token path illustrated by the direction of the arrows.

3.2.5.2 Dual-Ring Topology. The dual-ring topology consists of dual-attachment stations connected directly to the dual ring. This topology is useful when there are a limited number of stations, as illustrated in Fig. 3.17. A dual ring of DAS devices, however, does not easily lend itself to additions, moves, or changes. Since each station is a part of the backbone wiring, the behavior of each user is critical to the operation of the ring. The simple act of a user disconnecting a dual attachment workstation causes a break in the ring.

In the event of a single failure, a dual ring self-heals by wrapping the primary and secondary rings. Multiple failures result in two or more segmented rings. Each ring is fully functional, but no access exists to the other rings. For this reason, dual rings should only be implemented when little risk exists of users disturbing the network connection.

3.2.5.3 Tree-of-Concentrators Topology. The tree of concentrators is the preferred choice when wiring together large groups of user devices. Concentrators are wired in a hierarchical star topology with one concentrator serving as the root of the tree. In this configuration, one FDDI concentrator is designated as the root (Fig. 3.18). Cables run from this concentrator to SASs, DASs, or other concentrators. This topology provides greater flexibility for adding and removing FDDI concentrators and stations, or changing their location without disrupting the FDDI LAN.

Additional concentrators can connect to the second tier of concentrators, as needed, to support new users. The tree configuration can connect all stations in a single building or a large number of stations on one floor of a building.

Figure 3.16
Standalone topology.

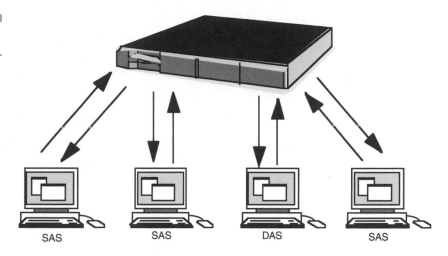

Figure 3.17
Dual-ring topology.

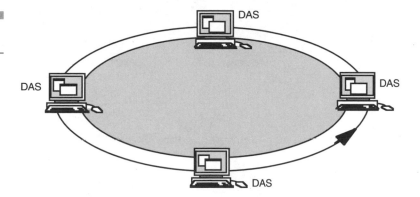

The tree topology is well-suited to structured cabling systems. Tree topologies also allow network managers to better control access of end-user systems to the network. Inoperative systems can be easily removed from the network by the concentrator. The network manager can also remotely access the concentrator to bypass the station.

3.2.5.4 Dual-Ring-of-Trees Topology.   The fourth topology described in the FDDI standards is the dual ring of trees. In this topology, concentrators cascade from other concentrators connected to a dual ring, as illustrated in Fig. 3.19, placing the dual ring where it is needed most—in the backbone.

Of all topologies defined, the dual ring of trees is the recommended topology for FDDI. It provides a high degree of fault tolerance and

Figure 3.18
Tree of concentrators.

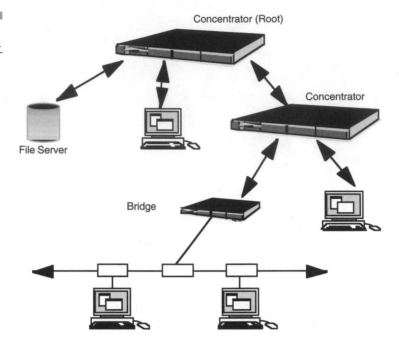

Figure 3.19
Dual ring of trees.

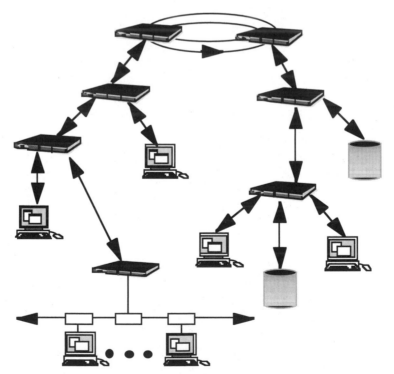

increases the availability of the backbone ring. The dual ring of trees is also the most flexible topology. The tree branches out by simply adding concentrators that connect to the ring through upper-level concentrators attached to the dual ring. Tree branches can be extended as long as the station number or ring distance limits are not exceeded. Stations attached to concentrators connected to the dual ring or configured in tree topologies can be removed from the FDDI LAN as needed. Concentrators can easily bypass inactive or defective stations without disrupting the overall network.

3.2.6 Applications of FDDI

FDDI was designed as a backbone network to connect smaller LANs within a building or college campus. Typically, networks connected to the FDDI are Ethernet and token ring at different speeds, such as 4, 10, and 16 Mbps. FDDI backbones typically run at 100 Mbps. FDDI's effective throughput is 30 Mbps, depending on the number of stations connected to it. Although FDDI-II was designed to carry isochronous (voice) traffic, in real-world applications it usually carries data only because voice on a typical campus environment is carried over PBX via the conventional public telephone network.

3.3 Distributed Queue Dual Bus

In the mid-1980s, IEEE 802 started working on MAN standards. In subcommittee 802.6, the different shared-media topologies and access mechanisms were discussed and compared, resulting in DQDB. The standards adopted by IEEE 802 were very much in line with ATM standards because the DQDB standardization process by IEEE and the ATM standardization process by ITU-T were almost parallel, with each process influencing the other.

3.3.1 DQDB Features

DQDB provides many features:

- Use of dual-bus architecture, where operation of each bus is independent of the other

- Compatibility with IEEE 802.X LAN standards
- Utilization of many types of media for transmission systems
- Looped dual-bus topology option for fault tolerance
- Operability of data at rates varying from 34 to 155 Mbps
- Operability independent of the number of users
- Simultaneous support of both circuit-switched and packet-switched services

3.3.2 DQDB Concept

A DQDB network is a dual-bus structure that consists of two unidirectional buses with opposite transmission directions. Such a bus is shared by multiple-access nodes, as depicted in Fig. 3.20. Each node is linked to a transmitter and receiver module through two unidirectional buses. Therefore, full duplex mode communication is possible between the nodes. The operations of the two buses are independent of one another with respect to data transmission; hence, a DQDB network has twice the capacity of a comparable system that employs only a single bus. The transmission of data in each bus is formatted into fixed-length units called *slots*. Nodes on the bus can write into the slot according to the rules of the access protocol. All slots originate at the head of the bus and terminate at the end of the bus, as shown in Fig 3.20. This concept is the most important one of DQDB. The other components of the DQDB architecture are the nodes. Each node on a subnet consists of an access unit (AU) and the physical attachment of the AU to the two buses, as shown in Fig. 3.21.

The access unit has two main responsibilities:

- It performs the node's DQDB layer functions, including access control and generation of information to place in the slots.
- It provides the physical attachment to each bus with a single read and write connection.

The AU writes on the bus using an OR-write process. It is called OR-write because writing on the bus is equivalent to the logical OR operation of the bit stream already on the bus and the bit stream that the node wants to transmit.[1] The read function occurs logically prior to the write function so that incoming data copied by a node is not affected by data written by the node. The read-and-write functions can be implemented using either active or passive techniques. An

Figure 3.20
DQDB dual-bus
structure.

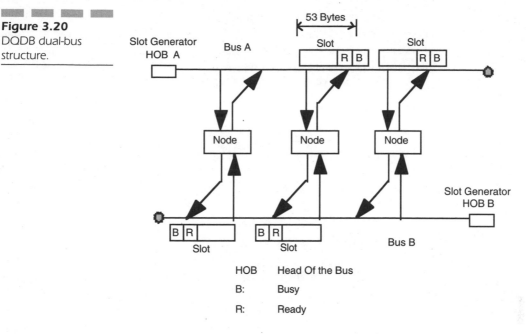

HOB   Head Of the Bus

B: Busy

R: Ready

Figure 3.21
DQDB node architec-
ture.

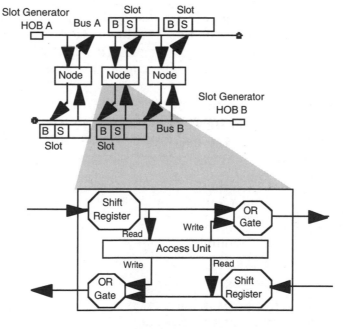

HOB   Head Of the Bus

B: Busy

R: Ready

active scheme would actually read data from the incoming bus, then regenerate it on the outgoing bus. A passive system would merely read the incoming data but never remove it from the bus. A passive technique limits the number of stations on the bus because each additional station becomes a source of signal loss.

A key feature of DQDB is that the operation of the bus is independent of the operation of the individual AUs. The node at the head of the bus has special functions that it must perform, called *head-of-bus* (HOB) functions. One of the functions is to generate the transmission slots mentioned earlier. The HOB must regularly create empty slots written into it by the other nodes on the bus.

3.3.3 DQDB Protocol

The IEEE 802.6 standard describes two protocol layers of the OSI protocol, i.e., the physical layer and data link (MAC) layer, as shown in Fig. 3.22. The physical layer of DQDB corresponds to the OSI physical layer and specifies how to use different underlying transmission media and speeds. The physical layer convergence protocol (PLCP) is part of the physical layer that adapts the capabilities of the transmission systems to provide the services expected by the DQDB layer. The PLCP is different for every transmission system option, but it is this part of the physical layer that allows the wide range of media and speed options supported by the network.

The 802.6 DQDB layer is equivalent to the MAC sublayer of the 802.3 to 802.5 LAN standards and corresponds to the lower sublayer of the OSI data link layer. It provides support for the following types of higher layer services, as shown in Fig. 3.23:

■ Connectionless (datagram) MAC service to the IEEE 802.2 logical link control sublayer, consistent with other IEEE 802 LAN and FDDI layers

■ Connection-oriented (virtual circuit) data service for the transfer of burst data, such as signaling or packet voice

■ Connection-oriented isochronous (circuit-switched) service

The MAC connection-oriented and isochronous convergence functions enhance the access control functions of the DQDB layer to meet the requirements of the higher-layer entity. These convergence functions are different for each type of higher-layer service and provide DQDB with enormous flexibility in terms of services that can be supported.

Figure 3.22
OSI relation with
DQDB.

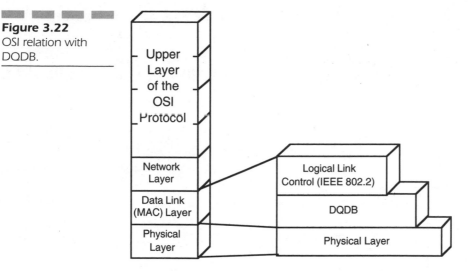

Figure 3.23
Functional structure
of DQDB.

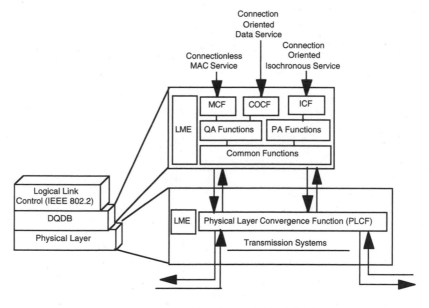

QA: Queued Arbitrated Access
MCF: MAC Convergence Function
COCF: Connection Oriented Convergence Function
ICF: Isochronous Convergence Function
LME: Layer Management Entity
PA: Pre-Arbitrated Access

The higher-layer services in DQDB are supported using two different access methods:

Queued-arbitrated access: The queued-arbitrated access method supports those services that are not time-sensitive, such as asynchronous or packet-switched data transfer. A distributed queued-access method allows users to request access to the medium as needed and is used in conjunction with the connectionless MAC service and the connection-oriented data service such as file transfer, database access, etc.

Pre-arbitrated access: The pre-arbitrated access method assigns specific octet positions within a transmission slot for use by different stations with time-sensitive applications, such as circuit-switched data transfer. This access method supports isochronous connection-oriented services such as voice and video.

3.3.4   How Does DQDB Work?

In a DQDB network, as shown in Fig. 3.24, the first node of each bus performs the HOB function, which entails continuously producing 53-byte empty slots or management information slots and releasing them into the bus. This node operates like a traffic cop, controlling and releasing the traffic onto the bus. A node with data to transmit does so by loading it onto the empty slots sent by the HOB with its own information using the distributed queuing method. Slots are divided into QA for nonisochronous traffic (data) and PA for isochronous traffic (voice or video).

DQDB is basically a bus structure, so a malfunctioning node can be easily disconnected from the bus so as not to affect the operation of the overall network. In the case of DQDB, if the first node in the bus acting as a traffic cop fails, this node is disconnected, and the rest of the nodes in the bus take the responsibility of traffic cop and generate slots and put them on the bus. If a node needs to put some information on the bus, depending on the information type, the node reads corresponding slots with the R bit from the bus. The node writes the traffic on the slots with the help of the access unit in the node. The node sets the bit in the slots to B (busy) and puts the slots in the bus. The destination node on the bus reads the slots and copies the information from the slots and resets the "busy" bit. This procedure enables the slots to be used by other nodes that need to present information. Thus, the information is transferred in a DQDB environment.

Figure 3.24
DQDB structure.

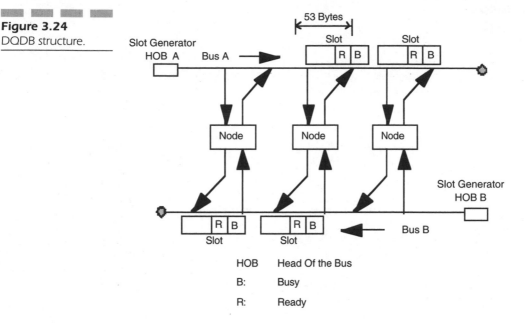

HOB　　Head Of the Bus

B:　　　Busy

R:　　　Ready

3.4　Summary

In this chapter, we explained the similarities and differences between two of the most popular access technologies, FDDI and DQDB. Both are based on fiber optics as the transmission medium. Their targeted application is LAN interconnect, they interwork with IEEE 802, and both are capable of carrying voice and data traffic. In the case of FDDI, only FDDI-II is capable of carrying both voice and data traffic. The main difference between FDDI and DQDB is that DQDB is designed for access to the public network, whereas FDDI is designed for private intercampus or intracampus applications. Numerous books are available that describe these technologies in detail. Several are mentioned in the reference section at the end of this book.

CHAPTER 4

Frame Relay

4.1 Overview

Frame relay is an emerging data communication concept sanctioned by ITU-T and ANSI. It is a fast packet technology developed to improve upon the X.25 packet technology. The development of fast packet was possible after the emergence of the various technologies mentioned earlier in Chap. 2. Frame relay gets its name from the frame designation of the OSI data link layer. It was essentially developed through two technologies:

- Widespread development of optical fiber-based transmission
- Intelligent customer premises equipment (CPE)

The frame-relay protocol supports data transmission over connection-oriented paths. The interface from the user to the frame-relay network is called *frame-relay interface* (FRI). FRI currently supports the following access speeds:

- 56 kbps
- $n \times 64$ kbps
- 1.544 Mbps (T1)
- 2.048 Mbps (E1 for Europe)

There are also some intermediate speeds, but the highest is T1 or E1.

FRI is an enhanced version of X.25 without error correction at the intermediate nodes. Error corrections in a frame-relay network occur in the intelligent CPE at either end of the connection, thus making frame relay much faster than X.25. Frame relay relies on the equipment to perform the functions previously done by the network. Advances in transmission technology and, of course, the terminal equipment has allowed this change to occur. These advances have made frame relay a standard in data communications from 56 kbps to T1- or E1-based applications and are slowly replacing the X.25-based packet-switched network. For speeds below 56 kbps, the X.25 packet-switched network is still ideal.

4.2 Frame-Relay Standards

The ITU-T has divided the functions and features of frame relay into three major standards, illustrated in Table 4.1.

TABLE 4.1

Frame-Relay
Standard
Documents
(ITUT/ANSI)

Standards Categories	ITU-T	ANSI Standards
Service description	I.233	T1.606
Core aspects	Q922	T1.618
Signaling	Q933	T1.617

4.2.1 Service Description Standard (ANSI T1.606, ITU-T I.233)

This standard outlines the overall frame-relay service description and specifications. In addition, recent documents examine connection management and ISDN multiplexing and rate adaptation. Connection management defines the speed the user is assigned to transmit data over the network as well as the burstiness of user data. Burstiness is random flow of information that varies in time in a unpredictable way. Connection management also describes how the network and end-user devices handle an overabundance of data traffic if every user transmits more than the committed data rate. The details of the service description are addressed in Chap. 5.

4.2.2 Core Aspects (ANSI T1.618, ITU-T Q.922)

This standard describes the core aspects of frame-relay specifications. The basics of frame relay, such as frame format, are discussed, along with the functions of different fields within the frame format, such as the DLCI (data link connection identifier) field. In addition, the congestion control mechanisms and methods of managing congestion are covered. The details of the core aspects are addressed in Chap. 5.

4.2.3 Signaling (ANSI T1.617, ITU-T Q.933)

This standard specifies a protocol for establishing and releasing switched frame-relay virtual connections and provides a means to inform users of permanent virtual circuits of failures and restorations. It sets out the procedure for the user-to-network signaling to support the frame-relay calls. The details of signaling are addressed in Chap. 5.

In addition to these standards, others such as data link control (ANSI: no standard planned, ITU-T Q.922) provide an optional end-to-end mechanism for ensuring the correct delivery of information across the network. This protocol is designed for implementation in end-user devices. It is not designed to be implemented in a frame relay network to carry user traffic because end-user devices usually rely on other protocols to ensure data accuracy.

4.3   Frame-Relay Field Format

This section provides an overview of basic frame information. The details are described in Chap. 5. Figure 4.1 shows the basic format of a frame-relay field. This format roughly conforms to the high-level data link control frame format, which is common to other protocols, such as IBM's Systems Network Architecture (SNA), X.25, and ISDN.

As shown in Fig. 4.1, the frame-relay format has five different fields, each of varying lengths. These fields are the flag field, frame-relay header, information field, frame check sequence field, and trailing flag field. Each of these fields is responsible for a specific function. Of these, the most important field is the frame-relay header field.

Figure 4.2 illustrates the field that forms the frame-relay header format. Flags delimit where the data frame starts and ends on each end of the frame-relay format.

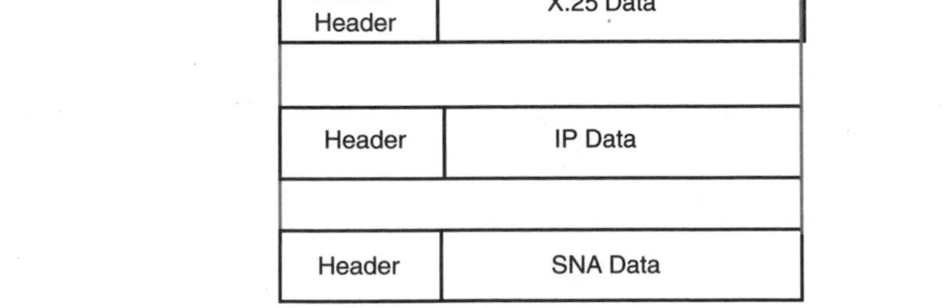

Figure 4.1
Frame-relay field format.

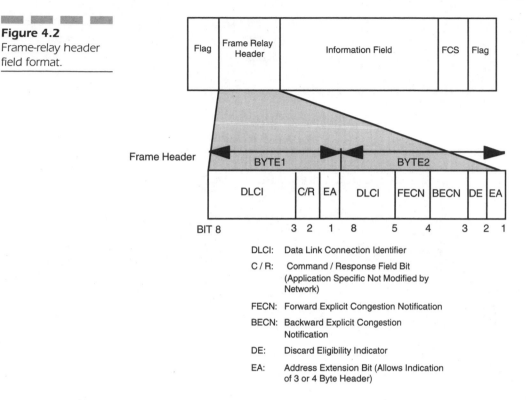

Figure 4.2
Frame-relay header
field format.

DLCI: Data Link Connection Identifier

C / R: Command / Response Field Bit
(Application Specific Not Modified by
Network)

FECN: Forward Explicit Congestion Notification

BECN: Backward Explicit Congestion
Notification

DE: Discard Eligibility Indicator

EA: Address Extension Bit (Allows Indication
of 3 or 4 Byte Header)

4.3.1 Data Link Connection Identifier (DLCI)

The central part of the frame-relay format is the data link connection
identifier. The DLCI distinguishes separate virtual circuits across each
access connection. Thus, specifying a DLCI rather than a destination
address transmits data coming into a frame-relay node. At the network
node, this connection specification is confirmed. If the specification
is in error, the frame is discarded. If not, the frame is relayed to its
destination. The details of this DLCI file and its usage are discussed in
Chap. 5.

4.3.2 Discard Eligibility

Discard eligibility (DE) is a one-bit field that can be set in low-priority
frames so they are discarded first in the event of frame loss. The DE bit is
set by the frame-relay network in any frame that exceeds a user's

subscribed rate. The network assumes that anything that exceeds the user's subscribed rate is low priority. The end-user equipment can also set the DE bit if it knows that certain frames are more important than others are.

4.3.3 Forward Explicit Congestion Notification

Forward explicit congestion notification (FECN) is similar to the congestion information field used in protocols such as Digital Equipment Corporation's Network (DECnet). In this network, the network sends a signal to the receiving or destination end point, advising it to slow down the receipt of information. At the end point, the destination device checks the FECN bits and if the field states that the user has exceeded the threshold, it alerts the sender accordingly.

4.3.4 Backward Explicit Congestion Notification

Backward explicit congestion notification (BECN) is usually used with an SNA-type network, where the network informs the source or transmitting end point and advises it to slow down the sending of information immediately. FECN and BECN perform congestion management in the frame-relay network. The implementation of FECN and BECN is called *explicit congestion management.* Some end-to-end protocols use FECN, while others use BECN. Both work well, but they are usually mutually exclusive options in end-user equipment.

4.3.5 Information Field

In Fig. 4.2, the information field is shown as a part of the frame-relay format that contains the actual information transmitted. The maximum allowed length of this information field can vary, depending on the design requirements of the network, from 262 to 8,000 octets or more.

4.3.6 Frame Check Sequence

Frame check sequence (FCS) performs error checking for the frame. Frame relay uses the error-checking technique known as cyclic redundancy check (CRC). The frame-relay CRC generates 2 bytes that are added at the end of the frame to detect bad data. The CRC algorithm uses an algebraic method to generate a unique bit pattern, which is recalculated at the far end. If the FCS at the source matches the FCS at the destination, the frame's integrity has (in most cases) been preserved.

When frame relay does discover a frame error, it merely drops the frame. As we have seen, frame relay does not request a retransmission of data if it finds errors in the transmission, but leaves this task up to the LAN station, X.25 switch, or other intelligent devices connected to the network.

4.4   Frame-Relay Architecture

Figure 4.3 shows the relationship between frame-relay architecture and the corresponding protocol stacks. For example, the router performs the function of the bottom three layers of the OSI protocol: network, data link, and physical. The protocol on the left in Fig. 4.3 shows the protocol stack for the originating terminal with all seven layers of the protocol stack.

The data is generated from this terminal and is then passed on to the originating router to which the terminal is connected. The router uses these three layers of the OSI protocol to route the data. From the router, the data goes to the frame-relay network, which uses the second layer of the OSI protocol and forwards the frames. At the terminating router,

Figure 4.3
Frame-relay protocol stack.

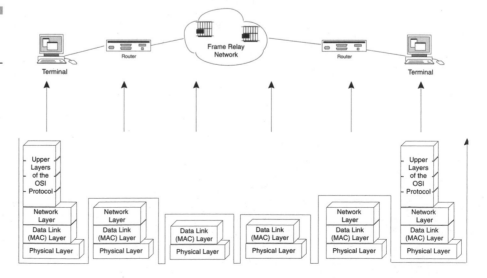

the data goes through the three layers and the terminating terminal for which the data was destined.

In the frame-relay network, the bottom two layers of the OSI protocol are used to forward the forms. The last, or physical, layer actively transports bits from one point to another. Next the data link layer performs the error check on the frames (or data) at each node in the network through which the data is routed. The FCS field in the frame-relay format performs this error checking. If this field reveals that the frame was corrupted during transmission across the communication channel, the node discards the frame. The field does not, however, send any acknowledgment stating that the frame has been discarded. It goes ahead and performs error checking with the next frame.

4.5 How Does Frame Relay Work?

Figure 4.4 shows a typical frame-relay network. Two routers are connected to the network via a standard FRI protocol. One router acts as an originator, and the other acts as a receiver. The data is originated and terminated at the end terminals.

Figure 4.5 shows the source side of the frame-relay network, where the originating router adds the header to the information payload with the upper-layer protocol. The header contains a 10-bit number, called *data link connection identifier*, which corresponds to a particular destination node. The router maps the actual destination address to the corresponding DLCI. This DLCI number is later used in the frame-relay network to route the frames. In the case of LAN interconnect, as in this example, the DLCI would correspond to a port to which the destination router is attached. With the appropriate DLCI in the address field, the router ships the frame to the frame-relay switch in the network. Figure 4.6 shows the second phase of the frame-relay service. The packet from the router is received at the first switch in the network with the DLCI number in the header.

Figure 4.4
Sample frame-relay network.

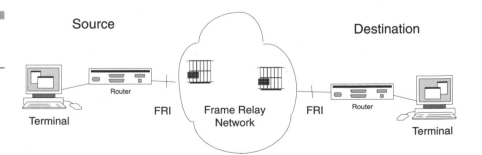

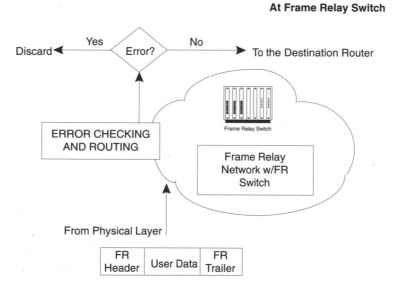

Figure 4.5
Sample frame-relay network, Phase I.

At Source

From Upper Layers

User Data

1

Address Routing Information

Router

Frame Relay Switch

Frame Relay Network w/FR Switch

Destination Router

| FR Header | User Data | FR Trailer |

To FR Switch

Figure 4.6
Sample frame-relay network, Phase II.

At Frame Relay Switch

Discard ◄ Yes — Error? — No ► To the Destination Router

ERROR CHECKING AND ROUTING

Frame Relay Switch

Frame Relay Network w/FR Switch

From Physical Layer

| FR Header | User Data | FR Trailer |

The data at the nodes follows three simple processes:

1. The frame-relay switch checks the integrity of the frame with the FCS field. If the frame has a flaw, the switch discards it.

2. The lookup table in the switch verifies the validity of the DLCI. If the DLCI is not defined in the table, the switch discards the frame.

3. If the DLCI is valid, the switch routes the frame to the appropriate port, in this case, to the destination router. This process is illustrated as a flow chart in Fig. 4.7.

The frame-relay switch works on the simple rule that if it finds an error in the frame, it discards that frame.

Once the frame reaches the router destination, the reverse function of the originating router is performed, i.e., the header field is stripped from the frame and the frame is forwarded based on the destination in the address field of the frame-relay header. This process is illustrated in Fig. 4.8. So far, we have seen how the data is transmitted in the frame-relay network, but we have not addressed what happened to the discarded frames and why they were discarded. We address those issues now.

A frame can be discarded due to one of the following reasons:

■ A bit error is found by the FCS field in the frame.

■ Network congestion occurs when the buffer at any node is full. When the node is full, the node begins to discard the frames so that the buffer can be made empty.

Figure 4.7
Flow chart for the frame-relay switch functions.

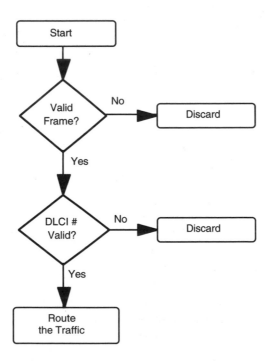

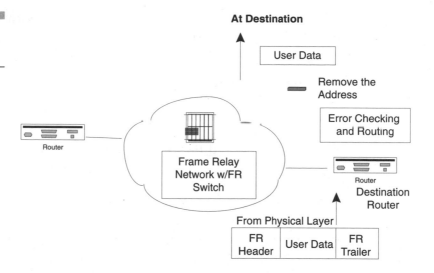

Figure 4.8
Sample frame-relay network, Phase III.

As mentioned earlier, the frame-relay network does not perform any error recovery. Error recovery is performed by the CPE at the other end of the connection.

4.6 Frame-Relay Services and Features

The frame-relay services are implemented using virtual circuits. The two types of virtual circuits are permanent virtual circuits based on ANSI T1.617 and ITU-T 933 and switched virtual circuits (currently not available).

A permanent virtual circuit (PVC) is a connection set by the service provider in a public network or by network operations in a private network. The PVC that is established on request can exist for weeks, months, or even years; use nailed-up circuits; or forgo call establishment, hence eliminating call setup delay.

In the case of a switched virtual circuit (SVC), the connection is set up like a regular telephone call with a call setup delay. The connection exists only for the duration of the call, as in an ordinary phone call. The standards for switched virtual circuit were completed in 1993. Currently, some vendors have added this service to their list of products. Vendors implemented SVC in 1996. Some of the service providers who have implemented SVC are BT (British Telecom), WorldCom, Sprint, AT&T, and MCI

Frame relay provides certain features along with the basic service, including:

- Interface signaling
- Committed information rate (CIR)
- Priority levels
- Multicast and global addressing

Each is discussed in the following subsections.

4.6.1 Interface Signaling

Interface signaling is the signaling across the FRI between the user and the network. It is accomplished by sending a frame with a DLCI field of 1023, called a *consolidated link layer management* (CLLM) message. Figure 4.9 illustrates this feature.

Interface signaling was included in the standard as an option. Service providers now are implementing it as a way of differentiating their service from that of their competitors. Signaling:

- Notifies the CPE that there is congestion in the network
- Communicates the status of the PVC
- Keeps the user informed of the access rate

Figure 4.9
Use of CLLM in signaling congestion.

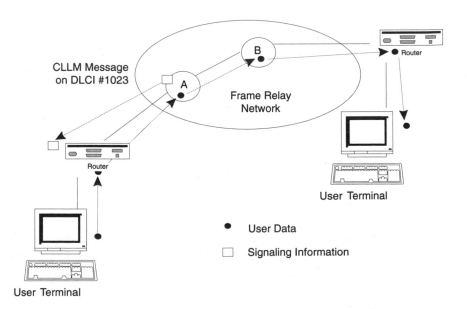

Signaling is accomplished by using certain bits called *explicit conges-tion notification* (ECN) bits in the header and by designating certain DLCI for specific purposes. The function of these bits is to inform the network that congestion has occurred. The two types of ECNs are FECN and BECN, which were discussed previously. As you recall, their function is to inform the forward and backward switches in the path about congestion. This concept is depicted in Fig. 4.10.

Another type of FRI signaling keeps the user informed of the sta-tus of the virtual connections, for example, sending "keep alive" mes-sages to keep the user informed that the connection is up and alive. This feature is useful when the users have not used the connection for a long period of time. It also informs the user about the congestion status of the nodes.

4.6.2 Committed Information Rate

A parameter called *committed information rate* allows the user to stipulate his average or normal traffic during a busy period. The network then measures the information flow on a dynamic basis. As long as the CIR is not exceeded, relay traffic (frames) is unaltered. If the user exceeds the CIR, the DE bit is set on those frames to signal the frame-relay switch to discard these frames first if congestion occurs. The CIR feature is explained further in Chap. 5.

4.6.3 Priority Levels

Frame-relay networks can assign priority levels to users so that lower-pri-ority traffic can be discarded first during congestion. Priority level is assigned by setting the DE bit. For example, the transaction traffic that is delay-sensitive would be given higher priority, and bulk file transfers would typically be given lower priority.

4.6.4 Multicasting and Global Addressing

Multicasting allows the broadcast of communications by assigning a certain DLCI to indicate multiple destinations. DLCI is not originat-ing port-specific with global addressing. In other words, a certain DLCI can route to a given terminal, no matter which port it is sent from.

Figure 4.10
Use of explicit con-
gestion notification.

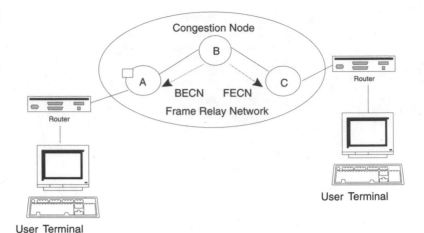

4.7 Frame-Relay Applications

We discussed some of the applications of broadband communications in
Chap. 2. Most of its applications are applicable to the technologies
(including frame relay) addressed in this book. As we know, the driving
application of frame relay is LAN interconnect, although other applications can also benefit from frame relay:

- IS applications
- Client-server computing
- CAD/CAM applications
- Graphics applications
- Other applications that generate bursty (variable bit rate) traffic

Let's look at an example of the economics of frame-relay service for
the LAN interconnection application and compare it to traditional leased
line service. Figure 4.11 shows a typical LAN interconnect solution. There
are five locations with routers at each site; these can be connected via a
network to provide LAN interconnect service across the United States.
Each router is connected to many LANs within a region, such as different buildings across a city. Let's assume that the network traffic is inter-
mittent but has high peak rates. Users thus have point-to-point-leased
lines of different capacities across the nation, depending on the traffic
pattern.

Based on this network (see Fig. 4.11), for the traditional leased lines the costs are as follows:

TABLE 4.2

Network Components	Number of Units	Cost/Unit, $	Total Cost (No. of Units × Cost/Unit), $
No. of routers (CSU/DSU)	5	15,000	75
No. of ports			
No. of 56K ports	8	400	3,200
No. of 256K ports	2	750	1,500
No. of 1.5M ports	4	1,500	6,000
		Total	85,700

The other cost components are the link lease from the interexchange carrier and the local exchange carrier. They are not separated as two different components because the IEC often provides direct access to the customer.

The traditional lease cost consists of two cost components, namely the one-time capital cost for the customer equipment and the monthly recurring cost. Table 4.2 shows the total capital cost of equiment at the customer site. Table 4.3 shows the recurring lease cost that customers pay on a monthly basis to the service provider. The cost drivers in lease cost are the number of links, the speed of the links, and the distance between the two points.

TABLE 4.3

No. of Links	Total Mileage for All Links	Lease Cost/ Month, $	Mileage Cost, $	Lease Cost/ Month, $
Four 56K links	7,500	75	0.25	1,950
One 256K link	2,000	150	0.50	1,150
Two 71 links	1,300	300	1.50	2,250
			Total	5,350

Based on the example, the lease cost for the proposed network is about $85,000.

Figure 4.11
LAN interconnect via
leased lines.

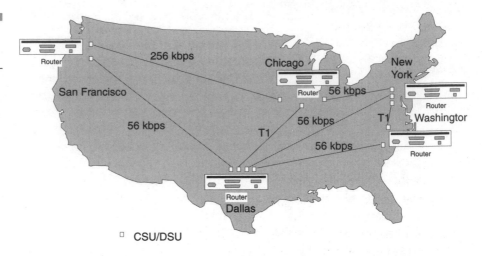

Now that we have seen the traditional method of calculating the cost for LAN interconnect, let's compare this cost with the cost when frame relay is used. Figure 4.12 shows the same network with a frame-relay backbone.

Based on this network, we have the following:

TABLE 4.4

Network Components	No. of Units	Cost/Unit, $	Total Cost (No. of Units × Cost/Unit), $
Number of routers (CSU/DSU)	5	15,000	75,000
No. of ports			
No. of 56K ports	2	400	800
No. of 256K ports	1	750	750
No. of 1.5M ports	2	1,500	3,000
		Total	79,550

The frame-relay network consists of similiar cost components. The cost drivers for frame relay are slightly different from the traditional lease cost. In frame relay the cost drivers are the number of ports, the speed of ports, the least cost of the port speed, and the access charge to connect to the network.

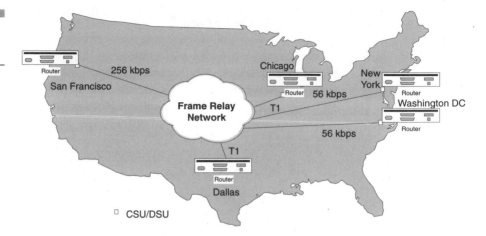

Figure 4.12
LAN interconnect via
frame-relay network.

Based on the example, the lease cost for the proposed network using frame relay is about $2,200 per month. The capital equipment cost is about $80,000, with a capacity to grow because of the number of ports consumed.

TABLE 4.5

Number of Ports	Lease Cost/Port/ Month (on the Network), $	Access Cost/Month, $	Total Lease Cost/Month, $	Annual Cost
Two 56Kports	75	75	300	3,600
One 256K ports	150	150	300	3,600
Two 71K ports	500	300	1,600	19,200
		Total	2,200	26,400

The other cost components are the frame-relay one-time installation costs for the different speeds of access to the network and the usage cost (usually in the number of packets or frames transmitted). Based on the current example, the savings obtained by using frame relay is approximately 60 percent when considering the usage cost savings may drop to 40 or 50 percent, which is still better than the traditional lease.

This example clearly demonstrates the cost savings obtained by migrating to frame relay. Of course, frame relay might not be a good solution for other applications. The only way to find out is to perform the calculation based on the usage pattern of that particular traffic.

4.8 Summary

As the name implies, frame relay relays the frames one behind the other in a predetermined path. Frame relay is a switched service positioned to improve communications performance through reduced delays, more efficient bandwidth utilization, and decreased equipment cost. Advantages of frame relay include the following:

- Port and link sharing
- Bandwidth on demand
- High throughput and low number of delays
- Ease of network expansion
- Ease of transition from existing X.25 network
- Simplified network administration
- Technology based on global standards
- Cost advantages

One of the obvious limitations of frame relay is the maximum access rate of T1 (1.544 Mbps) in the United States and E1 (2.048 Mbps) in Europe. The user cannot request more than T1 of bandwidth on a single connection. LAN interconnect is the driving application for the frame relay, but one must realize that frame relay is a connection-oriented service whereas LAN interconnect is an inherently connectionless application with traffic patterns of varying burstiness. But in recent years some service providers are providing T3-based frame-relay service.

CHAPTER 5

Advanced Frame Relay

5.1   Overview

In Chap. 4 we introduced the frame-relay standards, which are based on service description, core aspects, and access signaling. This chapter looks at these in detail. It also addresses the new standards for a network-to-network interface (NNI) between frame-relay nodes.

5.2   Service Description

This section addresses the frame-relay service description specification published in the ANSI T1.606 and ITU-T I.233 documents. We focus on service attributes such as information transfer, access, and other attributes of a frame-relay session. In addition, we look into the performance parameters used to measure frame relay. Examples of performance parameters are throughput, delay, and committed information rate.

5.2.1   Service Attributes

In frame relay, the service attributes are categorized into information transfer attributes, access attributes, and general attributes. Each is discussed in the following subsections.

5.2.1.1   Information Transfer Attributes.   Information transfer attributes are related to type of transfer mode and information transfer rate, i.e., the speed, in bits per second; type of communication establishment, such as switched virtual circuit or permanent virtual circuit; and method of transfer. It also includes information such as how traffic is sent across the network, such as point-to-point, point-to-multipoint, or broadcast. Table 5.1 summarizes the different information transfer attributes.

5.2.1.2   Access Attributes.   Both ANSI and ITU-T have defined the access attributes that determine the type of channels used and the type of protocols required at each layer for information and signaling (control access). Table 5.2 summarizes the access attributes.

5.2.1.3   General Attributes.   ITU-T and ANSI differ in their definition of general attributes. Currently, ITU-T has a list of provisional sup-

TABLE 5.1

Information Transfer Attributes

Attribute	Method of Transfer
Information transfer mode	Frame (packet in T1.606)
Information transfer rate	Less than or equal to maximum user channel bit rate (maximum access line capacity)
Transfer capability	Unlimited
Structure	Service data unit (SDU) integrity
Communication establishment	SVC, PVC
Configuration	Point-to-point, point-to-multipoint

TABLE 5.2

Access Attributes

Attribute	Method of Transfer
Access channel	D, B, and H channels
Signaling access protocol layer 1	I.430 or I.431 (ITU-T)
Signaling access protocol layer 2	Q.921 (ITU-T)
Signaling access protocol layer 3	Q.930 series (ITU-T)
Information access protocol layer 2 (core function)	Core function of Q.922
Information access protocol layer 2 (data link control)	User specified

plementary services, whereas ANSI has supplementary services defined for further study. Neither ITU-T nor ANSI have listed much information to date. Table 5.3 summarizes those ANSI and ITU-T general attributes that have been defined.

5.2.2   Performance Parameters

ANSI T1.606 has several definitions of frame-relay performance parameters, such as throughput and committed information rate (CIR). These parameters are used by the network operator when establishing service contracts with customers. In addition to these parameters, several others are described.

5.2.2.1   Throughput.   *Throughput* for frame relay is defined as the number of protocol data units (PDUs) successfully transferred in one direction per unit of time over a virtual connection. Q.933 defines

TABLE 5.3

Other Attributes

Attribute	Status
Supplementary services	For further study—ANSI provisional services—ITU-T
Quality of service	For further study
Interworking possibilities	ITU-T I.500 services ANSI T1.606
Operational and commercial	For further study

the interface in bits per second. A virtual connection can include any number of intermediate nodes between two end users. Figure 5.1 shows a virtual connection via two frame-relay nodes. A PDU includes all bits between the flags of the frame-relay frame. It includes the bits between the address field and the frame check sequence field, i.e., the information field (see Fig. 4.1). The term "successful transfer" means that the FCS check has acknowledged that the transfer has been completed successfully.

5.2.2.2 End-to-End Delay. *End-to-end* is the delay measured between two end points or end users. Typically, it includes the multiple transit delay, which is the delay measured between a pair of boundaries. ITU-T in its X.13 standard defines boundary as follows: "A boundary separates a network section for the adjacent circuit section, or it separates an access circuit section from the adjacent DTE (end user)."

Transit delay could define a boundary between international networks, national networks, or local-access and long-distance networks. Figure 5.2 shows the definition of transit delay, and Fig. 5.3 shows the definition of end-to-end delay.

Figure 5.2 shows the transit delay where it starts at time $T1$ when the first bit of the PDU crosses the boundary at the originating point. It ends at time $T2$, when the last bit of the PDU crosses the second boundary. Thus, the transit delay time is the time difference between $T2$ and $T1$, i.e.,

$$\text{Transit delay} = T2 - T1 = T_d$$

When this delay is added across multiple boundaries, it is called end-to-end delay, which is illustrated in Fig. 5.3.

5.2.2.3 Committed information rate. CIR describes the information transfer rate needed by the network to support a user during normal operation. In other words, the CIR is the throughput that the user asks

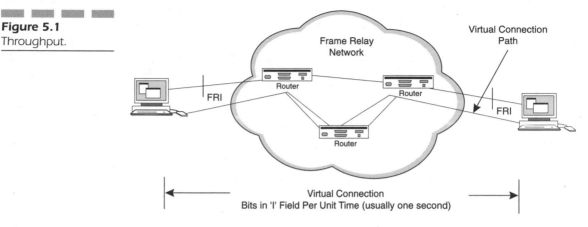

Figure 5.1
Throughput.

FRI   Frame Relay Interface

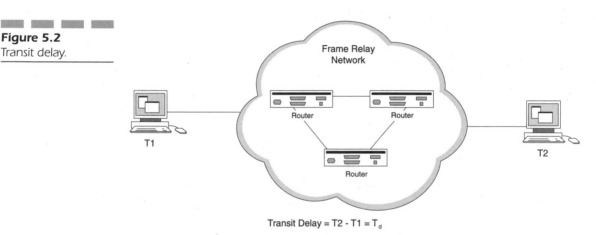

Figure 5.2
Transit delay.

Transit Delay = T2 - T1 = T_d

T1 - Time When First Bit Crosses the Originating Point
T2 - Time When Last Bit Crosses the Destination Point

for and the network guarantees for a particular SVC or PVC connection. For SVC, the CIR is negotiated during call setup. Figure 5.4 shows the CIR definition. Other measurement parameters work in conjunction with CIR, including measurement interval T_c, committed amount of data B_c, and excess amount of data B_e. Figure 5.5 shows these parameters.

The measurement interval, T_c, is defined as the time interval during which the user can send a committed amount of data, B_c, and an excess amount of data, B_e. B_c is defined as the data rate committed to by the user and guaranteed to be delivered error-free by network operators. B_e

Figure 5.3
End-to-end delay.

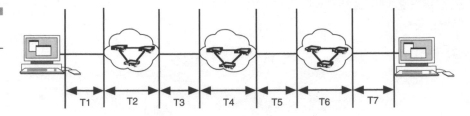

$$\text{End-to-End Delay} = \sum_{n=1}^{m} T_n$$

T_n = Transit Delay Between Two Points
m = Number of Transit Delays

Figure 5.4
CIR definition.

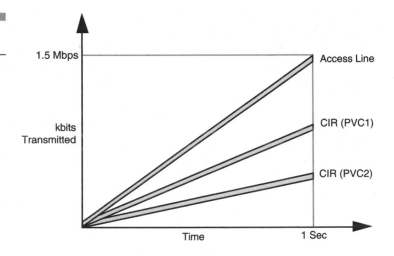

Figure 5.5
CIR parameters.

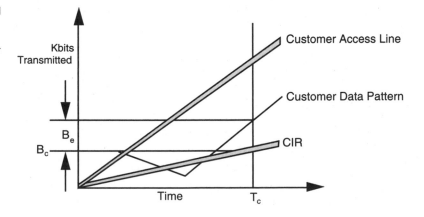

is defined as the amount of data that exceeded the committed amount of data, B_c, during the measurement interval.

The relationship between these parameters is as follows:

If

$$CIR > 0, \quad B_c > 0, \text{ and } B_e = 0$$

then

$$T_c = B_c/CIR$$

If

$$CIR = 0, B_c = 0, \text{ and } B_e > 0$$

then

$$T_c = B_c$$

Access rate (maximum access speed of $T1$)

The other parameter used for measurement is residual error rate (RER),

$$R = \frac{1 - \text{total correct SDUs delivered}}{\text{Total offered SDUs}}$$

An incorrect frame is one in which one or more bits are in error, such as:

- *Delivered error frame:* A frame delivered when the values of one or more of the bits in the frame are discovered to be in error.

- *Delivered out-of-sequence frame:* The arrival of a frame that is not in sequence relative to previously delivered frames.

- *Lost frame:* Frame is declared to be lost when the frame is not delivered correctly within a specified time.

- *Misdelivered frame:* A frame delivered to the wrong destination. In this situation, the DLCI interpretation can be in error, the routing table can be out of date, etc.

- *Switched virtual call establishment delay:* The time taken to set up a call across the network.

- *Clearing delay:* The time taken to clear a call across the network.

- *Premature disconnect:* The loss of the virtual circuit connection.
- *Switched virtual call clearing failure:* A failure to tear down the switched virtual call.

These are some of the parameters used to provide frame-relay service.

5.3 Core Aspects

This section examines the core aspects of frame-relay, as published in ANSI T.618 and ITU-T Q.922/Annex A. We introduced the core aspects in Chap. 4. In this section, the DLCI field in the frame-relay format and congestion control management are explained thoroughly.

5.3.1 Frame-Relay Format

In Chap. 4, we introduced the DLCI field and its usage. The DLCI field in the frame-relay frame can vary in size from 2 to 4 bytes, allowing the use of more DLCI numbers, and thus enabling more virtual circuit connections. Figure 5.6 illustrates the three formats.

In Fig. 5.6, the extended address (EA) bits are set to 0 to indicate that the header contains additional bytes. If the header and the EA are set to 1, it indicates the end of the header. The D/C field (1 bit) is called DLCI or DL-core control indication. This bit is set to 0 if the last DLCI byte contains DLCI bits. If the bit is set to 1, it contains DL-core information. The fields' forward explicit congestion notification, backward explicit congestion notification, and discard eligibility were explained in Chap. 4.

5.3.1.1 DLCI Values. We learned in Chap. 4 that the DLCI field identifies a logical connection multiplexed across a physical channel. The DLCIs with the same value always identify the same logical channel across a particular physical circuit. The DLCI values are explained in the ITU-T and ANSI core aspects document. The values and ranges depend on whether frame relay is being transmitted across the D or B channel. DLCI values vary depending on the use of 2, 3, or 4 bytes. The values are listed in Table 5.4.

Figure 5.6
DLCI frame formats.

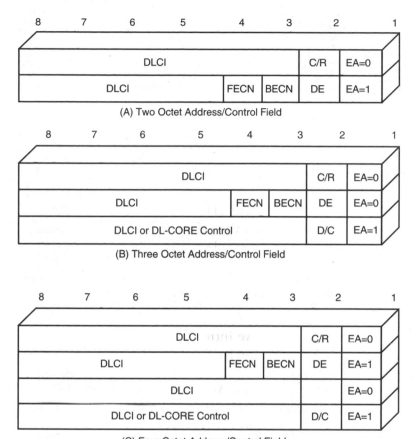

8	7	6	5	4	3	2	1
DLCI						C/R	EA=0
DLCI			FECN	BECN	DE	EA=1	

(A) Two Octet Address/Control Field

8	7	6	5	4	3	2	1
DLCI						C/R	EA=0
DLCI			FECN	BECN	DE	EA=0	
DLCI or DL-CORE Control						D/C	EA=1

(B) Three Octet Address/Control Field

8	7	6	5	4	3	2	1
DLCI						C/R	EA=0
DLCI			FECN	BECN	DE	EA=1	
DLCI							EA=0
DLCI or DL-CORE Control						D/C	EA=1

(C) Four Octet Address/Control Field

5.3.2 Congestion Control Management

As in any network, a frame-relay network must deal with congestion; it must have some form of congestion control management. The objective of such management is to meet the user's quality-of-service (QOS) request for each connection. To meet this requirement, an enhancement was added to frame relay. ITU-T and ANSI have developed the consolidated link layer management message to provide additional function to the frame-relay service, which was described in Chap. 4. In the frame-relay network, certain procedures must be accomplished prior to transferring information. This process is similar to a telephone call. In frame-relay, to initiate a data transfer, the user must signal the network (by sending certain connection control messages) that it would like to transfer data.

TABLE 5.4

DLCI Values Using Different DLCI Formats

DLCI Value	Function
Two-Octet Address Format	
0	In-channel signaling
1–15	Reserved
16–991	Assigned using frame-relay connection procedures
992–1001	Layer 2 management of frame-relay service
1002–1008	Reserved
1023	In-channel layer management
Three-Octet Address Format with D/C=0	
0	In-channel signaling
1–1023	Reserved
1024–63,487	Assigned using frame-relay connection procedures
63,488–64,511	Layer 2 management of frame-relay service
64,512–65,534	Reserved
65,535	In-channel layer management
Four-Octet Address Format with D/C=0	
0	In-channel signaling
1–131,071	Reserved
131,072–8,126,463	Assigned using frame-relay connection procedures
8,126,464–8,257,535	Layer 2 management of frame-relay service
8,257,536–8,388,606	Reserved
8,388,607	In-channel layer management

5.4   Access Signaling

This section examines the frame-relay specification published in ANSI T1.617 and ITU-T Q933 for setting up a switched virtual connection or call. Current frame-relay services are PVC-based. A rather extensive modification to Q933 is under way. The frame-relay forum has proposed a set of specifications for SVC. This proposal is different from the X.933/T1.617 specification in that it is simpler and appropriate for both

UNI (user network interface) and NNI. We discuss in this section the high-level description of SVC proposed by the Frame-Relay Forum (FRF). FRF is an interest group formed by service providers, users, and equipment manufacturers with respect to frame relay.

5.4.1 Frame-Relay Connection Process

The messages used for connection control can be grouped into three categories: call establishment, call clearing, and miscellaneous. Figure 5.7 illustrates the different messages in a network.

Setup: This message is sent by the frame-relay originator to the frame-relay network to establish a call. The setup message contains a

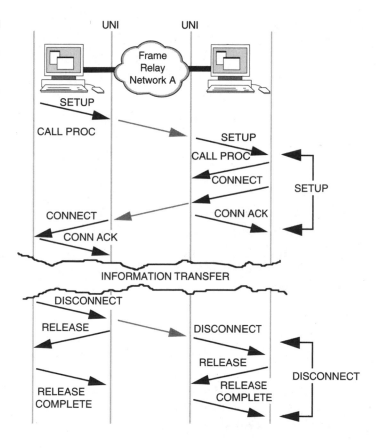

Figure 5.7
Connection establishment and release process.

number of fields that describe the type of message, the type of capabilities established along with the call, the appropriate DLCIs, the recommended end-to-end transit delay, and other parameters such as calling party address.

Connect: If the setup message is accepted by the called user, this user responds with a connect message sent to the local node and relayed via the network to the caller. It contains parameters such as transit delay, DLCI, etc.

Connect Acknowledge: This message is sent by the network to the called frame-relay user to notify the user that information transfer can occur. The destination user is informed with an ALERTIN message.

Call Proceeding: This message is sent by the called user to the network and relayed to the calling user to indicate that a call-establishment procedure has begun.

Progress: This message is sent by the network or the user to provide status of the call. The previous messages are for call establishment.

After this message, the data transfer begins. On completion of the call, the following messages are used for call disconnect.

Disconnect: This message requests the network to clear the frame-relay call.

Release: This message is sent by the user or the network indicating that the connection occurred, and if a DLCI has been used, it is released for further use.

Release Complete: This message clears the call and connection, freeing the channel for reuse.

In addition to these messages, others such as status and status inquiry are sent across the network to obtain information about the network (status information).

5.5   Network-to-Network Interface

The NNI was developed by the Frame-Relay Forum, and is currently published as a draft in the ANSI T1S1.2 working group. We examine some of the NNI functions and operations. The ANSI specification is important because it enables equipment from different vendors to inter-operate.

Initially, work on frame-relay was focused on user-network interface. Only recently has NNI been addressed. NNI defines the procedures for different networks to interconnect with each other to support the frame-relay operations.

Figure 5.8 shows the NNI in a typical frame-relay network. Some of the principal operations of NNI are

- Notification of adding a PVC
- Detection of deleting a PVC
- Providing notification of UNI or NNI failure
- Notification of PVC segment availability or unavailability
- Verification of links between frame-relay nodes
- Verification of frame-relay nodes

These operations occur through the exchange of status (S) and status inquire (SE) messages, which contain information about the status of the PVCs.

In Sec. 5.4, we described the SVC at UNI. The proposal also includes a specification for SVC capability at the NNI. Figure 5.9 shows the operations for a connection setup and connection release.

Figure 5.8
Typical FR network
with NNI interface.

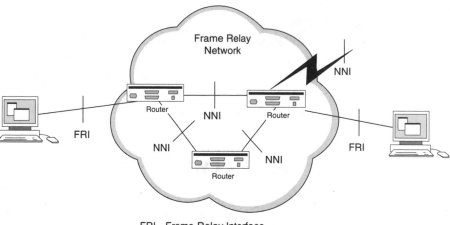

FRI   Frame-Relay Interface
NNI   Network Network Interface

Figure 5.9
Connection setup
and release in a
multiframe-relay
network.

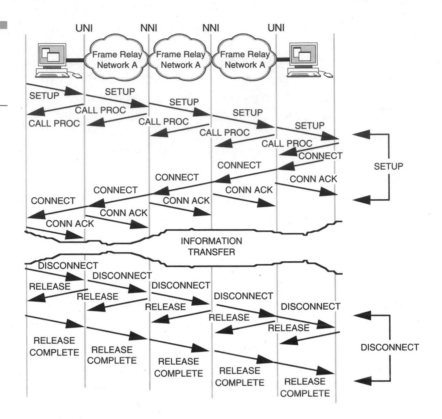

5.6 Summary

The advanced features of service, description, core aspects, and signaling in frame relay have been described. In addition, NNI was discussed in general. Currently, frame relay has all the important specifications required to provide SVC-based services, enabling frame relay to become even more popular for lower-speed traffic requirements (< 1.544 Mbps). In the next chapter, we see another technology—switched multimegabit data service—which is being designed as the first comprehensive technology and service for broadband.

CHAPTER 6

Switched Multimegabit Data Service

6.1 SMDS Overview

Switched multimegabit data service (SMDS) is similar to frame relay in many aspects. For example, each has

- An emerging data communication technique based on fast packet-switching technology
- A type of protocol for transferring data traffic
- A technology driven by LAN-interconnect traffic

SMDS is the first protocol designed for broadband communications to provide connectionless service. It is fixed cell-based and designed to be a broadband public network service and provide fully switched "any-to-any" connections.

SMDS was the creation of Bellcore, which adopted the connectionless data networking capability found in the IEEE 802.6 specification for its clients—the RBOCs. SMDS is designed for local, intra-LATA, and WAN services. The connectionless nature of SMDS is the most important distinction when compared to other technologies. Bellcore designed SMDS as a public broadband service to be provided by the RBOCs. Bellcore devised a set of specifications that spelled out the subscriber network interface specification, commonly known as a user network interface, or in the case of frame relay, frame-relay interface. Bellcore then defined the interswitching system interface (ISSI), which is the interface between switches within a network. Next came the intercarrier interface (ICI), which defines the interface between switches of two networks, such as local exchange and interexchange carriers. Finally came the operations systems (OSS) interface, which is used for billing and network administration.

In this chapter we tour SMDS, its working principles, and protocols.

6.2 SMDS Standards

Bellcore developed SMDS standards using its knowledge and expertise in telecommunications. Thus, it was able to cover every aspect of the network, such as the subscriber network interface, interswitching system interface, and intercarrier interface, allowing a local exchange network to be connected using a standard interface to any other network, such as an interexchange carrier's network (or long-distance network). In addition to these interfaces, Bellcore defined services and features not available in any new technology. Such comprehensive services would take a long time to be developed using a standards board. Bellcore developed many SMDS features that meet the needs of end users and the network operators. In fact, the international broadband committee is using Bellcore's document as the starting point in defining global BISDN standards. Table 6.1 lists the documents for which Bellcore provided detailed definitions on every aspect of the SMDS service definition and implementation.

6.3   SMDS Architecture

The reference network architecture of SMDS with various interfaces as defined by Bellcore in its standard document is shown in Fig. 6.1. Each interface has relevant Bellcore technical reference (TR) documents, which describe in detail the generic requirements that support SMDS.

The Bellcore specification defines how the data is to be converted to cells to pass through the subscriber network interface (SNI) via an SMDS

TABLE 6.1

List of SMDS-Related Documents

Document	Title
TR-TSV-000772	"Generic System Requirements in Support of SMDS" (May 1991)
TR-TSV-000773	"Local Access System Generic Requirements, Objectives, and Interface in Support of Switched Multimegabit Data Service" (June 1991)
TR-TSV-000774	"SMDS Operations Technology Network Element Generic Requirements" (March 1992, Issue 3)
TR-TSV-000775	"Usage Measurement Generic Requirement in Support of Billing for Switched Multimegabit Data Service" (June 1991)
TR-TSV-001059	ISSI generic requirements (December 1990)
TR-TSV-001060	"Switched Multimegabit Data Services Generic Requirements for Exchange Access and Intercompany Serving Arrangements (SMDS)" (December 1991)
TA-TSV-001061	"Operations Technology Network Element Generic Requirements in Support of Interswitch and Exchange Access SMDS" (May 1991)
TR-TSV-001062	"Generic Requirements for Phase 1 SMDS Customer Network Management Service (February 1992, Issue 2)
TR-TSV-001063	"Operations Technology Generic Criteria in Support of Exchange Access SMDS and Intercompany Serving Arrangements," Rev. 1 (March 1992)

Figure 6.1
SMDS reference
architecture.

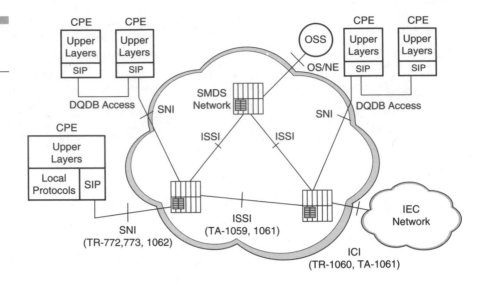

Figure 6.1
SMDS reference
architecture.

DQDB	Distributed Queue Dual Bus
SIP	SMDS Interface Protocol
SNI	Subscriber Network Interface
SS	Switching System
ISSI	Interswitching System Interface
OS/NE	Operations System/Network Element
DCN	Data Communications Network
OSS	Operations Systems
ICI	Intercarrier Interface
IEC	Interexchange Carrier

interface protocol (SIP), which indicates the end of the public network and the beginning of the customer premises. The SIP contains three protocol layers that give the frame structure: addressing, error control, and transport of the data at the SNI. These specifications provide a definition of the basic requirements for SMDS service. One can compare SIP to the X.25 interface protocol in a packet-switched network today because the SIP defines the network services and how they are accessed by the user, similar to the X.25 specification.

The other interfaces defined in SMDS are ISSI and ICI. The ISSI interface defines the interface between switching systems, such as between two SMDS switching systems. The interface can be between two SMDS switches or between an SMDS switch and an ATM/SONET-based BISDN switch. The ICI is an interface or boundary between the networks of two carriers providing SMDS service or one network providing SMDS service and another providing ATM-based broadband service. In the United States, the networks typically involved are an LEC and an IEC, as shown in Fig. 6.1.

6.4   The SMDS Protocol

The SMDS protocol is based on the three SIP layers. These three layers do not correspond to the layers of the OSI model, but the basic functionality of the bottom three OSI layers is used. For the customer to connect to the SMDS network, the customer interface must follow these three layers.

6.4.1   Layer 3 of SMDS Interface Protocol

Figure 6.2 shows the three-layer SIP protocol stack. The SIP provides the equivalent of the MAC and physical layers as described in the IEEE 802 standards. SIP minimizes the processing overhead performed at the SNI by the CPE. Minimal processing is particularly important because one of the goals of SMDS is to allow for simple CPE. Higher layers are not

Figure 6.2
SMDS protocol layers.

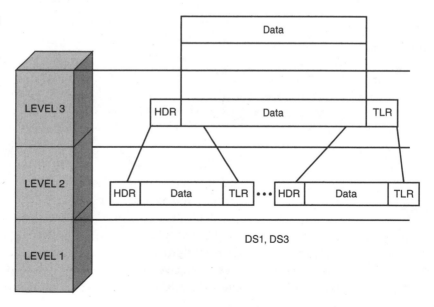

defined; instead, the protocol used in the existing bridges, routers, and gateways can be used here.

Level 3 of the SIP accepts data from the higher-layer protocols. The variable-sized SMDS SDU (SMDS data unit) has a maximum size of 9188 octets, big enough to accommodate IEEE 802.5 (4-Mbps version) and FDDI frames. Larger frames require an internetworking protocol to fragment the frame. Figure 6.3 shows the level 3 protocol data unit. Because SMDS used the IEEE 802.6 standards, the structure is similar in many ways to the DQDB protocol structure addressed in Chap. 7.

Figure 6.3
Layer 3 PDU frame format. (Bellcore TR-TSY-772, issue 1).

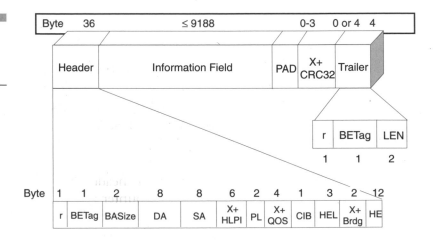

r	Reserved
BETag	Beginning-End Tag
BASize	Buffer Allocation Size
DA	Destination Address
SA	Source Address
X+	Unchanged by the Network
HLPI	Higher Layer Protocol Identifier
PL	PAD Length
QOS	Quality of Service
CIB	CRC32 Indication Bit
HEL	Header Extension Length
Brdg	Bridging
LEN	Length
HE	Header Extension

The SMDS PDU consists of the following main fields:

- Header field
- Information field
- Packet assembler and disassembler (PAD) field
- Cyclic redundancy check field
- Trailer field

In Fig. 6.3, the field X+ denotes those fields added to provide alignment with the cells produced in layer 2 of the SIP. These fields are not processed by the network. Each field is described in the following subsections.

6.4.1.1 Header Field. The header field is 36 bytes in length. The header is where the critical information related to the sender and destination resides. The fields that constitute the header field are as follows:

Reserved (r) field. A 1-byte field reserved by the standard and set to 0s. Its use is not currently defined.

Beginning-End Tag (BEtag) Field. A 1-byte sequence number that appears in both the header and trailer and ranges from 0 to 255. The number is used to associate the header and trailer of the level 3 entity at the receiving interface. A counter is maintained by the level 3 entity that is incremented after transmission of a frame so that the values 0 through 255 are cycled through as frames are sent.

Buffer Allocation Size (BASize) Field. This field is 2 bytes and indicates the size of the frame. It lies between the destination address and CRC32 fields. It is used to allow the receiving node to determine how many level 2 cells it can expect to receive.

Destination Address (DA) Field. This field is the 8-byte address used in SMDS to allow for individual or group addressing. The first 4 bits of the DA field are set to 1100 for individual addresses and 1110 for group addresses. The remaining 60 bits are used for the destination address, which is the address verified by the SMDS network before forwarding the cell through the network. The SMDS numbering plan has the same structure as the numbering scheme of the ITU-T E.164 ISDN numbers (telephone numbers).

Source Address (SA) Field. This field corresponds to the individual sender's address. It is the field verified by the SMDS network with its database of subscribers. If a match exists, the network allows the source to transmit via the SMDS network. In other words, this field checks whether the sender has subscribed to the SMDS services.

Higher-Layer Protocol Identifier (HLPI) field. A 6-bit field that is not processed by the network; it is included to provide alignment of the SIP level 3 protocol with the cells of the SIP level 2 protocol.

PAD Length (PL) Field. A 2-bit field that indicates the number of bytes in the PAD field and ensures that the level 3 entity is aligned on 32-bit boundaries. This 32-bit alignment is important for efficient implementation of this protocol on reduced instruction set computing (RISC) processors.

Quality of Service (QOS) Field. This 4-bit field is currently ignored by SMDS.

CRC-32 Indication Bit (CIB) Field. This bit indicates the presence of the CRC-32 field. If the bit is set to 1, CRC is present.

Header Extension Length (HEL) Field. A 3-bit field indicating the number of 32-bit words that populate the header extension (HE). At present, this field is set to 3 (binary 011) to indicate the fixed extension of 12 bytes.

Bridging Field. This 2-byte field provides 32-bit alignment.

6.4.1.2 Information Field. The next field of the layer 3 protocol is the information field, where the actual payload or data is carried. This field carries data from the higher layers. The payload can be up to a maximum of 9188 bytes.

6.4.1.3 Packet Assembler and Disassembler. The PAD field ensures that the information field is aligned on 32-bit boundaries. This field varies from 0 to 3 bytes in length.

6.4.1.4 Cyclic Redundancy Check CRC-32. If present, this field provides 32-bit error detection for the fields, covering the fields from the destination address up to and including CRC-32. This field does error detection in the following way: on the transmitting side, a calculation is performed on the bits of the PDU to be transmitted. The result, called an *error-detecting code,* is inserted as an additional field in the packet or frame. A calculation is performed on the same CRC-32 field on the received bits, and the calculated result is compared to the value stored in the incoming frame. If a discrepancy exists, the receiver assumes that an error has occurred and discards the PDU. Thus, CRC-32 performs error detection on the receiving side.

6.4.1.5 Trailer Field. This field is at the end of the frame-relay frame and consists of 4 bytes. The trailer field consists of three fields: reserved field, BEtag field, and length field (LEN). The first two fields are the same as in the header.

The BASize field value is placed in the LEN as an additional check to ensure the correct assembly of the SIP level 2 cells. These fields provide for the delivery of information and allow a number of checks to be conducted to ensure correct delivery. Errors that cause frames to be discarded include the following:

■ The header and the trailer BEtag fields do not match

■ The BASize field in the header and length field in the trailer do not match

■ The destination and source address formats are incorrect

The SMDS standards do not define how the CPE should react when delivery does not occur. This function is assumed to be part of the higher layers and is beyond the scope of these standards.

6.4.2 Layer 2 of SMDS Interface Protocol

The SIP level 2 protocol provides access control to the MAN. The level 2 SIP format is shown in Fig. 6.4.

Level 2 of SMDS is compatible with level 2 of IEEE 802.6; thus, equipment conforming to IEEE 802.6 (DQDB) protocol can work in an SMDS network. The level 3 frame is segmented into 44-byte data units for transmission in the level 2 cells. As with fragmented DQDB PDUs, the first cell is beginning-of-message (BOM) segment type, intermediate cells are continuation-of-message (COM) segment type, and the final cell is end-of-message (EOM) segment type, providing the receiving station with sufficient information to reassemble the frame.

6.4.3 Layer 1 of SMDS Interface Protocol

The SMDS access path is described in SIP level 1. This specification provides for the transmission of level 2 cells across the SNI. The operation is divided into the physical layer convergence protocol and transmission system sublayers. The transmission system sublayers define the digital carrier systems that can be used for the SNI. Currently, the specifications

Figure 6.4

SMDS layer 2 frame format (Bellcore TR-TSY-772, issue 3).

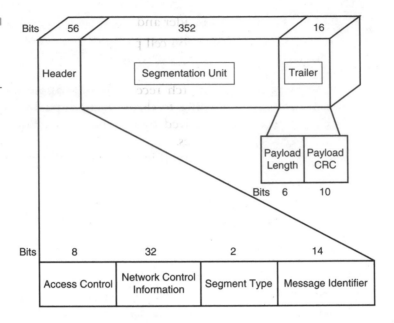

support DS-1 and DS-3. The PLCP defines how the level 2 cells are mapped onto the transmission systems. Thus to maintain compatibility with IEEE 802.6 systems, the PLCP is extracted directly from the IEEE standards.

6.5 How Does SMDS Work?

The basic network of SMDS is shown in Fig. 6.5. In the network, there is an originating and destination router, where the traffic is originated and terminated, respectively. The routers are connected via a high-speed serial interface (HSSI) running at 34 Mbps to an SMDS CSU/DSU, which in turn is connected to the public SMDS network at 45 Mbps, or at DS3 speed using the SIP specification. It is not necessary to have an HSSI interface; it can be bypassed and connected directly to the network.

The router generates the datagram traffic of variable frame length. On receiving the frame the CSU/DSU segments the frame into 48 bytes and adds the 5-byte header, to make cells totaling 53 bytes. The cells are generated at a speed of 45 Mbps. Figure 6.6 shows the SMDS cells at the SMDS switch. Once the SMDS cells reach the SMDS switch, the switch performs the following functions:

- Buffers the 5-byte header and the 48-byte payload
- Performs CRC check on cell payload
- Reads the segment type as BOM, COM, or EOM

Once the SMDS switch receives one of these messages, it processes each datagram according to the segment type. In our case, assume that the first datagram received by the switch is a BOM, with valid source and destination addresses.

Once the segment type is identified as BOM by the SMDS switch, the switch performs the following operations:

- Records the message identified (MID) in a new temporary location called call *record entry*
- Records the sequence number of this MID
- Performs source address validation

Figure 6.5
Example SMDS network.

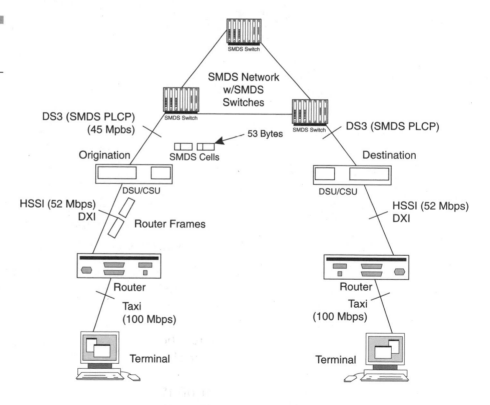

HSSI: High Speed Serial Interface
PLCP: Physical Layer Convergence Protocol

Figure 6.6
Cells at SMDS switch.

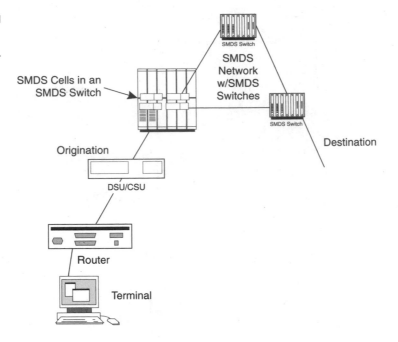

SMDS Cells in an
SMDS Switch

SMDS Switch

SMDS
Network
w/SMDS
Switches

SMDS Switch

Destination

Origination

DSU/CSU

Router

Terminal

- Performs destination address screening

- Associates destination address with MID in the call record

- If no routing table entry exists with this address, performs the shortest-path first-routing calculation and stores the routing information in the routing table, which is located in cache memory for quick retrieval

- Enters the routing information for the MID into call record

- Increments to the next expected sequence number

- Routes the cell to destination ISSI or ICI

On processing the datagram with a BOM segment type, the switch starts receiving the cells. The other cells following the first arrive with COM as their segment type from the level 2 PDU of the router. On receiving the new segment type, the switch performs the following functions:

- Looks up the temporary call record by the message ID for this particular SNI

- Verifies the sequence number

- Increments to the next expected sequence number

- Routes PDU based on the routing information in the call record

Upon processing the cell (or cells) with a COM segment type, the last cell arrives at the switch with an EOM segment type, indicating that this is the last of the series of cells and the end of the message. Once the EOM is received by the SMDS switch, the following functions are performed by the switch:

- Looks up the temporary call record by the message ID for this particular SNI
- Verifies the sequence number
- Routes PDU based on the routing information in the call record
- Clears the temporary call record
- Completes billing data collection at the ingress (destination) switch

If the cells must traverse more than one SMDS switch, the previously mentioned functions are performed at each switch until the destination address is matched by the SMDS switch. This process is called a *connectionless service*. In other words, there is no predefined connection between the source and the destination. Once the switch identifies the destination address and knows that it terminates at its location, it then forwards the cells to the SMDS CSU/DSU (channel service unit/data service unit), which is usually located at the customer premises (Fig. 6.7).

After receiving the cells, the CSU/DSU translates the cells into frames, maps the header address to the router address, and forwards it to the router. Thus, the SMDS switch routes each of the cells to the destination router. This router then sends the frames to the appropriate terminal, which is usually a part of the router address. One of the special features of SMDS is that customers can manage the network like their own private networks.

6.6   SMDS Features and Services

SMDS provides a number of features and services beyond the simple transmission of data through the network. In fact, SMDS differs from other protocols in the number of features provided to its users. For example, the security feature allows network security to screen the frames to verify if they can be legally transmitted to the destination or received from the source. This security feature allows a subscriber to build a virtual private network within a public network. Corporations can use the screening facilities to limit access to their resources. This

Figure 6.7
Cells at SMDS
destination.

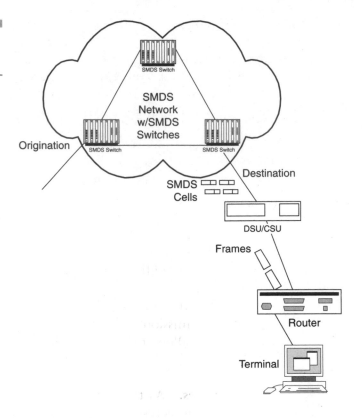

feature could provide a single point of entry for external systems, in order to control the information flow into and out of the corporation. This feature is also used by a number of companies to connect to the public backbone network. SMDS offers a variety of services both to the end user and the network operators. These services can be segmented into end-user features and network operator features.

6.6.1 End-User Features

SMDS, as a service, provides numerous features to the user:

- Address validation
- Group addressing
- Address screening
- Access classes
- Congestion control

Each is described in the following subsections.

6.6.1.1   Address Validation.   The network ensures the validity of the source address using address validation. The network verifies the source address at the SNI interface. If the address is invalid, the network prevents the user from accessing the SMDS network services.

6.6.1.2   Group Addressing.   A group address is used as a destination, allowing multicasting of the information to all members of the group. Group addressing is performed by the SMDS network. This feature in SMDS is similar to the point-to-multipoint capability provided by other technologies, such as ATM.

6.6.1.3   Address Screening.   Address screening is performed at the source on the destination address. The SMDS switch verifies the source address and allows delivery from a predefined list of senders only. If verification performed at the source on the destination addresses is valid, the switch allows transmission to a predefined list of destinations only. Address screening thus allows the implementation of logical private networks on the public network.

6.6.1.4   Access Classes.   As the name implies, this feature provides customers with different access, based on traffic requirements or characteristics. Although the capacity of the physical medium can be used entirely by the CPE for bursts of traffic, the access class defines a limit to the average rate of data transfer allowed over a longer period. Five types of access classes have been identified for DS3: 4, 10, 16, 25, and 34 Mbps. For each access class, the maximum DS3 speed can be used for the first 9188 bytes transferred in a burst. For subsequent bytes, the network operator can drop the data in excess of the subscriber's committed rate.

Access classes are useful for service provisioning. The operator can dimension a network based on the subscribed bandwidth rather than on the throughput of the access media. Access classes also provide flexibility in charging. More precisely, users can subscribe based on the power of their CPEs (i.e., the maximum bandwidth their CPE can use) rather than on the bandwidth of the access medium. In a regulated environment, access classes are mandatory for the RBOCs to be allowed to charge less than full DS3 access rates to subscribers who need only a fraction of the 45-Mbps bandwidth.

6.6.1.5 Congestion Control. Access classes are used in performing congestion control. SMDS relies on the access classes, which correspond to the rate of traffic and the burstiness subscribed to by the user. In case of congestion, the user is neither notified explicitly nor expected to reduce the traffic. The traffic measurement specified in SMDS simply allows the acquisition of information on traffic patterns.

6.6.2 Network Operators Features

Bellcore developed SMDS operations, administration, and maintenance (OAM) and billing features for network operators.

6.6.2.1 OAM. Many features are defined for OAM. The objective is to standardize the interface with service providers' OSS, which can provide a unified view, independent of vendors and switch equipment. The main functions covered are memory management, maintenance, traffic management, network data collection, customer network management, and other status and usage information.

6.6.2.2 Billing. One of the most important features that any service requires is a good billing mechanism. SMDS is a very good example of such a service. The billing system developed for SMDS consists of the description of usage measurement, performance, and operations-related information. Under performance objectives, the billing system addresses several areas. Examples are the maximum transit delay for a packet, probability of loss, error, missed delivery of packets, and service availability status. In fact, this billing concept is used as an example by the ISO for its work on BISDN standards.

6.7 Summary

SMDS is a high-speed protocol designed by Bellcore and backed by its clients, the RBOCs. From a standards perspective, the strength of SMDS is that it is defined by a coherent organization. The objective was to design a broadband protocol to provide public broadband data services. SMDS is a good candidate for customers who require high throughput or low latency delay for data transfer between disparate locations. Currently, customers can access the SMDS network via existing DS1 and DS3 facilities using the IEEE 802.6 DQDB protocol used for layer 2. In the future, DS1 and DS3 will be replaced by SONET STS3c. But because of lack of support from a major carrier SMDS is no longer a viable candidate for future broadband services. This is indicated by the service offering by service providers. Currently, MCI is a provider of SMDS service, although even MCI has identified that SMDS is not the long-term solution for broadband services and is in the process of migrating to ATM-based services.

CHAPTER 7

ATM

7.1   ATM Overview

Here ATM does not stand for automatic teller machine. In the telecommunications world, it stands for asynchronous transfer mode, whereby information packets are transferred asynchronously. This mode is another fast-packet switching mode. The first research on ATM and its related techniques was published in 1983 by two research centers, CNET and AT&T Bell Labs. In 1984, the research center of Alcatel Bell in Antwerp started to develop the ATM concept.

ATM has the same basic characteristics of packet switching, but also the delay characteristics of circuit-switching technology. This combination of characteristics is obtained by reducing the network functionality to a minimum. Initially, different names were proposed, and the standards organization settled on the famous acronym *ATM*. ITU selected ATM technology as the switching technology for BISDN, the foundation for all broadband communications. ATM is regarded as the technology of the twenty-first century, and its impact is expected to be similar to PCM, which is used widely around the world in digital telecommunications today.

The word "asynchronous" is used because ATM allows asynchronous operation between the sender clock and receiver clock. Inserting cells (filler cells) can easily solve the difference between both clocks and removing empty or unassigned cells (packets that do not contain any information) is very easy. We look into this in detail when we study ATM in the BISDN protocol. One of the special features that ATM provides is that it guarantees successful transport of any service [CBR, VBR, or ABR (available bit rate)] regardless of the characteristics of the originating service in terms of bit rate, quality requirements, or the bursty nature of traffic. ATM is applicable in all network environments, which is why most of this book is dedicated to the implementation of ATM. A network with such a service-independent transfer technique cannot suffer from disadvantages when compared to other transfer modes in terms of service dependence, inefficiency in the use of available resources, etc.

Before we leave this section, here is an analogy to help better understand ATM. We have all seen railway trains and railway lines (tracks). Have you ever wondered why all carriages are the same size, regardless of the type of cargo or passenger they carry? Why can't the railway department build differently sized coaches—one size for passengers, one for cargo? The reason is that it is easier to build only one size. The railroad then has the flexibility to add or drop coaches at intermediate junctions so that coaches can be put onto different tracks to reach different destinations. The same is true with ATM cells. By having a uniform ATM cell size, routing, adding, dropping, and multiplexing of ATM cells can be done faster without worrying about the information carried within the ATM cells.

7.2   The ATM Principle

This section addresses the basic principle behind ATM: *divide and conquer.* Sometimes, the best way to manage large chunks of information is to split the information into the smallest possible units, thus making the units easy to handle. For example, most of us have traveled with children in our lifetime. Sometimes the children pack all their stuff in one bundle and expect you to pack it into your suitcase, but you don't have space in your suitcase to keep the whole bundle as one. So what do you do? You unpack the sack and distribute the contents to different parts of the suitcase, wherever space is available. Keeping in mind the strength of segmentation, let's come back to the principle behind ATM. ATM does not care what the information is or its form. It simply cuts the information into equal-sized packets or cells and attaches a header so the packet can be routed to its destination. The headers in ATM have very little functionality, so the network can process them without delay. Figure 7.1 shows how traffic of different speeds, i.e., 64 kbps, 2 Mbps,

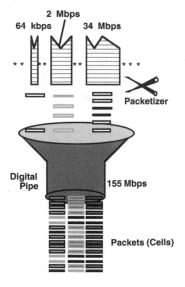

Figure 7.1
ATM principle.

and 34 Mbps, is chopped into equal-sized packets or cells by a "chopper" or "cell slicer." The different cells are put into a huge transmission pipe that mixes all the cells from different sources in such a way that the transmission pipe is optimized. The optimization is done via a technique called *statistical multiplexing.*

In an ATM network, several sources are combined or multiplexed on a single link. In a conventional time division multiplexing (TDM) network, the effective bandwidth is simply the sum of the individual sources' bandwidth. If two sources of bandwidth are x bps and y bps, their effective bandwidth is $(x + y)$ bps. The effective bandwidth in an ATM network, however, is z bps, where $z < (x + y)$ because all the information in bits is packed into ATM cells. The ATM switch then multiplexes the cells that carry valid information and discards cells with zero or invalid information. Thus, effective bandwidth is reduced. This bandwidth can also carry other users' traffic. Figure 7.2 shows a comparison of conventional TDM with statistical multiplexing. From Fig. 7.2 you can see that band-

Figure 7.2
Comparison of TDM and statistical multiplexing.

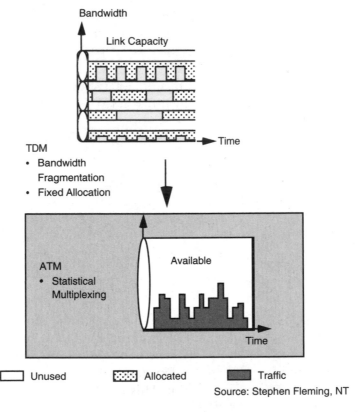

width is wasted in TDM due to the fixed allocation of the bandwidth. In the ATM environment no bandwidth is wasted because of statistical multiplexing. To achieve statistical multiplexing, all traffic, including voice, must be packetized, thus creating VBR traffic.

The ATM switch does not differentiate between the type of traffic carried within a cell. All it knows is that it has an input port, where cells come in, and a destination port, where cells go. A decision must also be made on the size of the cells or packets. Many issues come into play when making this decision. The most important among them are

- *Transmission efficiency:* The larger the packet, the longer the delay; the smaller the packets, the higher the ratio of overhead to information. In the case of ATM the overhead is about 10 percent of the payload, which is very high.

- *Delay:* The packet encounters various types of delays, such as basic packet transitive delay, queuing delay at each switching node, jitter, packetization, and depacketization.

- *Implementation complexity*

Unlike traditional circuit-switched or packet-switched networks, ATM deals with both network characteristics, thus making it complex to deploy. In an ATM network, the services are independent of technology, and ATM being new adds to the complexity. Many other contradicting factors, in addition to the ones mentioned, influence the choice of cell sizes. After long debate and argument by the ITU-T committee, the final decision was to choose between 32 and 64 bytes. This choice was based mainly on delay characteristics, transmission efficiency, and implementation complexity. Europe was more in favor of 32 bytes (because of echo cancelers for voice), but the U.S. and Japan were in favor of 64 bytes for transmission efficiency. Thus, in June 1989 in Geneva, ITU-T in its SGVIII meeting reached a compromise of 48 bytes. It then added 5 bytes more for header information. Thus, the peculiar 53-byte packet size came into existence for ATM.

7.3   ATM Standards

ATM standards are defined so that they are applicable to any environment around the world. The initial ATM-based broadband standards were defined by ITU. Later, the communication industry realized the time frame for ITU to develop standards and formed a special interest group called the ATM Forum. This group consisted of various players in the communications industry. This group defined specifications at a much faster rate. Even though this was not a standards group, their specifications have become the de facto standard in the ATM environment. Table 7.1 is a listing of all the specifications completed and approved as of May 1997 by the ATM Forum since its inception in 1991.

Technical Working Group	Approved Specifications	Approved Date
B-ICI	B-ICI 1.0	September 1993
	B-ICI 1.1	
	B-ICI 2.0 (delta spec to B-ICI 1.1)	December 1995
	B-ICI 2.0 (integrated specification)	December 1995
	B-ICI 2.0 Addendum or 2.1	November 1996
Data exchange interface	Data Exchange Interface version 1.0	August 1993
ILMI (integrated layer management interface)	ILMI 4.0	September 1996
LAN emulation	LAN Emulation over ATM 1.0	January 1995
	LAN Emulation Client Management Specification	September 1995
	LANE 1.0 Addendum	December 1995
	LANE Servers Management Spec v1.0	March 1996
Network management	Customer Network Management (CNM) for ATM Public Network Service	October 1994
	M4 Interface Requirements and Logical MIB	October 1994
	CMIP Specification for the M4 Interface	September 1995
	M4 Public Network view	March 1996
	M4 "NE View"	January 1997
	Circuit Emulation Service Interworking Requirements, Logical and CMIP MIB	January 1997
	M4 Network View CMIP MIB Spec v1.0	January 1997
	M4 Network View Requirements and Logical MIB Addendum	January 1997
Physical layer	Issued as part of UNI 3.1: 44.736 DS3 Mbps Physical Layer	

TABLE 7.1 ATM Standards

Technical Working Group	Approved Specifications	Approved Date
	100 Mbps Multimode Fiber Interface Physical Layer	
	155.52 Mbps SONET STS-3c Physical Layer	
	155.52 Mbps Physical Layer	
	ATM Physical Medium Dependent Interface Specification for 155 Mb/s over Twisted Pair Cable	
	DS1 Physical Layer Specification	September 1994
	Utopia	September 1994
	Midrange Physical Layer Specification for Category 3 UTP	March 1994
	6,312 Kbps UNI Specification	September 1994
	E3 UNI	June 1995
	Utopia Level 2	August 1995
	Physical Interface Specification for 25.6 Mb/s over Twisted Pair	June 1995
	A Cell-based Transmission Convergence Sublayer for Clear Channel Interfaces	November 1995
	622.08 Mbps Physical Layer	January 1996
	155.52 Mbps Physical Layer Specification for Category 3 UTP (See also UNI 3.1, af-uni-0010.002)	January 1996
	120-Ω Addendum to ATM PMD Interface Spec for 155 Mbps over TP	
	DS3 Physical Layer Interface Spec	January 1996
	155 Mbps over MMF Short Wavelength Lasers, Addendum to UNI 3.1	March 1996
	WIRE (PMD to TC layers)	July 1996
	E-1 Physical Layer Interface Specification	July 1996
	Interim Interswitch Signaling Protocol	September 1996
P-NNI	P-NNI V1.0	December 1994
	PNNI 1.0 Addendum (soft PVC MIB)	March 1996
	PNNI ABR Addendum	September 1996
	Frame UNI	January 1997

TABLE 7.1 *(Continued)*

Technical Working Group	Approved Specifications	Approved Date
Service aspects and applications	Circuit Emulation	September 1995
	Native ATM Services: Semantic Description	September 1995
	Audio/Visual Multimedia Services: Video on Demand v1.0	February 1996
	Audio/Visual Multimedia Services: Video on Demand v1.1	January 1996
	ATM Names Service	March 1997
	(See UNI 3.1, af-uni-0010.002)	November 1996
	UNI Signaling 4.0	July 1996
	Signaling ABR Addendum	January 1997
Testing	Introduction to ATM Forum Test Specifications	
	PICS Proforma for the DS3 Physical Layer Interface	December 1994
	PICS Proforma for the SONET STS-3c Physical Layer Interface	September 1994
	PICS Proforma for the 100-Mbps Multimode Fiber Physical Layer Interface	September 1994
	PICS Proforma for the ATM Layer (UNI 3.0)	September 1994
	Conformance Abstract Test Suite for the ATM Layer for Intermediate Systems (UNI 3.0)	April 1995
	Interoperability Test Suite for the ATM Layer (UNI 3.0)	September 1995
	Interoperability Test Suites for Physical Layer: DS-3, STS-3c, 100 Mbps MMF (TAXI)	April 1995
	PICS Proforma for the DS1 Physical Layer	April 1995
	Conformance Abstract Test Suite for the ATM Layer (End Systems) UNI 3.0	April 1995
	PICS for AAL5 (ITU spec)	January 1996
	PICS Proforma for the 51.84 Mbps Midrange PHY Layer Interface	January 1996
	Conformance Abstract Test Suite for the ATM Layer of Intermediate Systems (UNI 3.1)	January 1996
	PICS for the 25.6 Mbps over Twisted Pair Cable (UTP-3) Physical Layer	January 1996

TABLE 7.1 *(Continued)*

Technical Working Group	Approved Specifications	Approved Date
	PICS for ATM Layer (UNI 3.1)	March 1996
	Conformance Abstract Test Suite for the UNI 3.1 ATM Layer of End Systems	July 1996
	Conformance Abstract Test Suite for the SSCOP Sublayer (UNI 3.1)	June 1996
	PICS for the 155 Mbps over Twisted Pair Cable (UTP-5/STP-5) Physical Layer	September 1996
	(See UNI 3.1, af-uni-0010.002)	November 1996
Traffic management	Traffic Management 4.0 with ABR Addendum	April 1996
	Circuit Emulation Service 2.0	January 1997
Voice and telephony over ATM	ATM User-Network Interface Specification V2.0	January 1997
User-network interface (UNI)	ATM User-Network Interface Specification V3.0	June 1992
	ATM User-Network Interface Specification V3.1	September 1993
	ILMI MIB for UNI 3.0	1994
	ILMI MIB for UNI 3.1	

TABLE 7.1   *(Continued)*

7.4   ATM Protocol

As mentioned earlier, the 53-byte ATM cells carry an information payload of 48 bytes and a 5-byte header through the network, as shown in Fig. 7.3. Table 7.2 compares the packet-switching technologies such as X.25, frame relay, and ATM in terms of functionality. The existing packet-switched network (X.25) performs all of the three functions mentioned, such as packet retransmission, frame delimitation, and error checking.

One of the advantages of ATM is the reduced functionality of the ATM network, which is caused by using a smaller ATM header. As can be inferred, the reason for the reduced header is to simplify the switching and processing functionality in the network.

Figure 7.4 shows the protocol stack for ATM. The upper layer in the protocol performs additional functions that work closely with the ATM

Figure 7.3
ATM cell format.

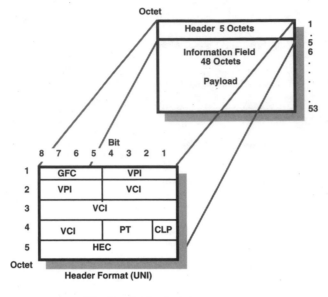

GFC: Generic Flow Control
VPI: Virtual Path Identifier
VCI: Virtual Channel Identifier
PT: Payload Type
CLP: Cell Loss Priority
HEC: Header Error Control

TABLE 7.2

Comparison of
Technology

Functionality	X.25 Packet Switching	Frame Relay	ATM Switching
Packet retransmission	X	—	—
Frame delimitation	X	X	—
Error correction	X	X	—

layer. ATM basically forms layer 2 of the BISDN protocol, which is explained further in Part 3, later in the book.

The higher layers convert the information into chunks of 48-byte cells that can be processed by ATM. The higher layer performs the functions required by various services. The ATM layer adds the 5 bytes of header to each cell as shown in Fig. 7.3. The header attached at the ATM layer carries sufficient information to route the cells in the ATM network. The ATM cell header consists of six different fields with varying sizes (in bits) based on their functions:

■ Generic flow control (GFC)

- Virtual channel identifier (VCI)

- Virtual path identifier (VPI)

- Payload type (PT)

- Cell loss priority (CLP)

- Header error control (HEC)

Each field performs certain functions, and the details of each field will be addressed later. The most important of these fields are the VPI and VCI, which are used for routing information in the ATM network. Before we explain routing in the ATM network, let's compare the VPI and VCI to something used in today's telecommunications world:

- VCI-based switching is similar to TDM in circuit switching

- VPI-based switching is similar to digital cross-connect (or slow switching)

Within the ATM cell header, there are two different formats: the user-to-network interface format, which is the header format for the cells between the user and the network as shown in Fig. 7.5, and the network-to-node interface format, which is the header format for the cells in between the switching nodes, as shown in Fig. 7.6.

7.4.1 Generic Flow Control

The GFC is envisioned as providing contention resolution and simple flow control for shared medium-access arrangements at the CPE. Thus, the GFC field is present at the cells between the user and the network.

Figure 7.4
ATM protocol stack.

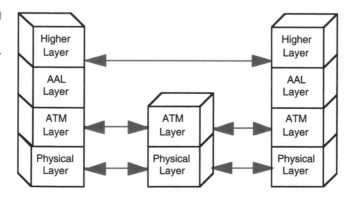

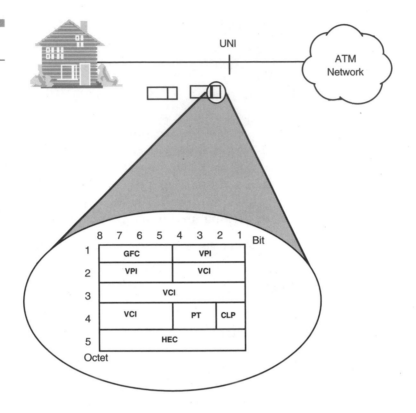

Figure 7.5
ATM cell at UNI.

7.4.2   Virtual Channel Identifier

The VCI is used to establish connections using translation tables at switching nodes that map an incoming VCI to an outgoing VCI. Circuits established using VCI connections are referred to as *virtual circuits,* and VCI end-to-end connections are called *virtual connections.* In this sense, the bandwidth is not utilized unless user information is actually transmitted. The VCI field in the header of the ATM has 16 bits. VCI is discussed further in Part 2 as part of the BISDN reference model.

7.4.3   Virtual Path Identifier

The VPI is used like VCI to establish a virtual path connection for one or more logically equivalent VCIs in terms of route and service characteristics. The VPI allows simplified network routing functionality and management. The VPI field has 8 or 12 bits, depending on the location of the ATM cell, and is used in setting up the end-to-end virtual path connection of multiple virtual path segments. A virtual path contains multiple virtual channels.

7.4.4   Payload Type

The PT, a 3-bit field, is used to differentiate the cells traversing the same virtual circuit. Cells can contain operation, administration, and maintenance information or user information.

7.4.5   Cell Loss Priority

The CLP is used to explicitly indicate cells of lower priority, by setting this 1-bit field to 1. The lower-priority cells might be discarded by the network, depending on network conditions. This bit is the *only* priority provided by the ATM network. All other priorities are at a higher layer of BISDN protocol.

Figure 7.6
ATM cell at NNI.

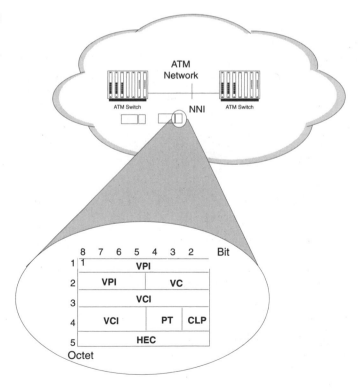

7.4.6 Header Error Control

The HEC performs a CRC calculation on the first 4 bytes of the header field for error detection and correction. The HEC sequence is utilized to reduce cell loss and misrouting because of cell header errors. The function of the HEC is described later. HEC performs error control only on the header of the ATM cell, and no error control is performed on actual payload.

7.5   How Does ATM Work?

So far, we have seen ATM as a technology and a set of principles. Now we will see how this technology can be applied as a service. A user can get ATM service in two ways—by setting up either a PVC or a SVC. Complete standards are available for both PVCs and SVCs. In this section, we address both types of methods. Table 7.3 shows the relationship of these two methods to today's environment.

In today's private line environment, the user calls the service provider requesting a private line from point *A* to point *B*. The service provider, based on circuit path and availability, "nails up" a circuit based on the capacity requested by the user. It usually takes from 10 days to 2 months to get the circuit nailed up. Usually, the contract between the user and the service provider is for several years. The user is committed to paying for the circuit even if it is not used for the duration of the contract.

7.5.1 PVC

Figure 7.7 shows the ATM PVC in an ATM network. In setting up a PVC, the following procedures, which are similar to requesting a private line service, are performed:

TABLE 7.3

Comparison of ATM Service to Today's Environment

ATM Service	Today's Environment
Permanent virtual circuit	Private line service
Switched virtual circuit	Switching concept similar to telephone network for voice from a user perspective

Figure 7.7
ATM PVC in an ATM
network.

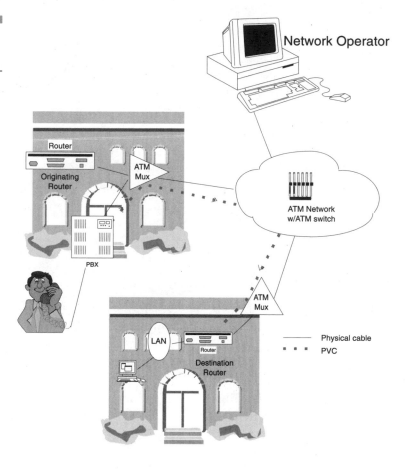

User calls the service provider with a request for PVC.

User provides the destination address, average bandwidth requirement or committed information rate, and duration of the PVC circuit.

Operator enters the information on the control terminal to set up the circuit path. This step is done almost in real time, as the user is on the telephone requesting a connection.

Circuit is established as requested.

User pays a monthly fee for a circuit and pays only for usage of that circuit. If that circuit is not used, the user pays only the monthly circuit fee. This contract is just like a basic monthly telephone bill, where the customer pays a fixed amount regardless of the telephone service usage.

PVC has the following advantages:

■ Negligible provisioning time (almost real time)

■ Almost real-time availability of the circuits

■ Bandwidth on demand

■ No call-establishment procedures

■ Nailed-up connection, which means a circuit always exists between points. The service provider is simply connecting the circuit via a remote terminal with the click of a button.

■ Easy extension of the circuit or disconnection of the circuit if not used. If the user needs more time for the circuit, it can be extended by a simple request to the service provider.

7.5.2 SVC

As mentioned earlier, SVC operation is similar to making a direct-dialed telephone call. When the call is set up, the only capacity or bandwidth assigned is exactly 64 kbps. And once the call is set up, the circuit is assigned to the user and dedicated for that use, whether the user actually transmits information or not. Of course, the user pays for the duration of the call regardless of usage, since others cannot use it because the circuit is dedicated to the user as long as the circuit is up.[1] Thus, one can see how the resource is wasted.

After recollecting the basics of a direct-dialed telephone call, let's see how the same call works in an ATM environment. The following procedures exist in either environment:

■ Call setup procedure

■ Call establishment procedure

■ Data transfer procedure

■ Disconnect procedure

■ Billing procedure

These procedures occur at different stages of a call. Figures 7.8 and 7.9 show a portion of the call process. The message flow for call establish-

[1]Many techniques such as TADI, TASI, and other DSP methods have been developed to use the bandwidth more efficiently.

ment and disconnect is shown in Fig. 7.10. The major differences between a telephone call in a regular network and one in an ATM network are in the call setup and call establishment parameters. We examine these differences next.

Figure 7.8 shows a call setup from a telephone over an ATM network. In an ATM network, one can set up a connection for video and data in the same way as for voice. For a voice connection, the call originator dials the destination number. The call is routed via the local PBX to the ATM hub, which adapts the signaling information to ATM cells. The ATM hub verifies the bandwidth requested, using the ATM payload information. The ATM hub can also identify the default bandwidth, depending on the CPE terminal connected to it. In this case, it is 64 kbps.

Default values are used because it is expected that existing, nonintelligent CPE will be used in the ATM environment for a long period of time, and this equipment cannot request variable bandwidth. The ATM hub thus sets the default values if it receives no specific bandwidth requests for connection. If the user attempts to set up a video

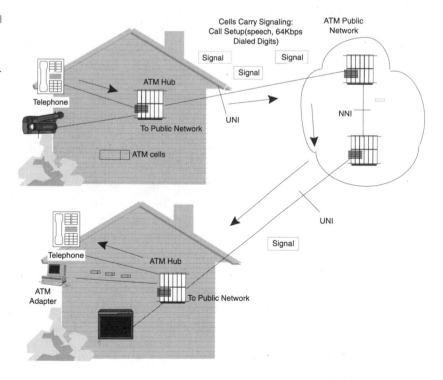

Figure 7.8
ATM call setup:
sample voice call.

Figure 7.9
ATM call establishment: sample voice call.

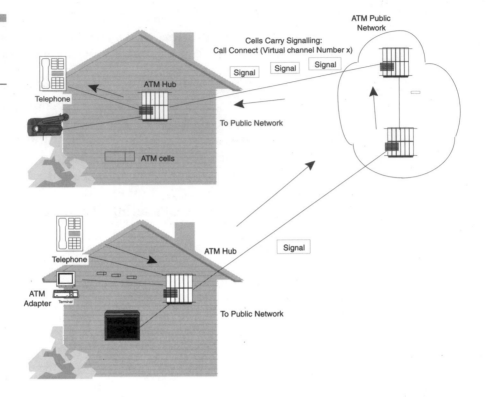

connection, the user must specify the bandwidth required, and the ATM hub fills in that information. In the case of a telephone call, the ATM hub fills in 64 kbps because it knows the CPE's capability. The ATM converts the information into cells using the signaling information, and these cells are carried into the network to the destination telephone for the circuit to be set up.

Once the cells reach their destination, the ATM hub at the destination address sends cells back with information for the virtual channel on which the originator needs to be connected to establish the connection. This connection is accomplished by sending the ATM cells to the originator with the VPI information carried on the payload of the cell, as illustrated in Fig. 7.9. Once the cells are received at the originating end, the ATM hub connects the call by assigning the cells to the appropriate VCI value. The network now knows where to route the cells so they can reach their destination.

Once the connection is set up, the information is carried in the ATM cells with the VCI number identified. This VCI, along with the VPI value in the ATM cell header, is used in routing the cells across the ATM network. In the network, each VPI and VCI value on the incoming cell is mapped to an outgoing VPI and VCI. These outgoing VPI and VCI values need not be the same as the ones defined by the end user during call setup; they have only local significance. Therefore, when the cells traverse the network, they can be mapped onto different VCI and VPI values in any ATM switch. All the network needs to know is that when leaving the network it must map the VPI and VCI values to the ones negotiated at call setup. (The details of how this mapping occurs within an ATM switch is covered in Part 4.)

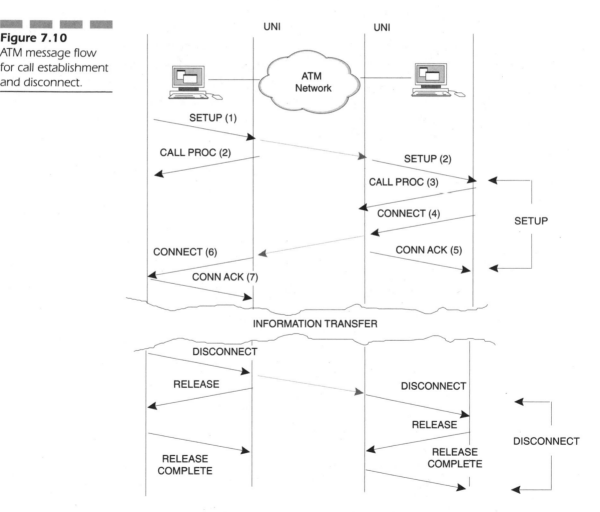

Figure 7.10
ATM message flow for call establishment and disconnect.

One of the users hangs up the telephone on completion of the call, so the call is disconnected and the destination switch stores the billing information. The billing in ATM can be done in various ways, such as by the number of cells transmitted, PVCs bandwidth used, etc. The billing system for SVC in the ATM environment is still in the early stages of definition.

7.6   ATM Application Environment

ATM technology has an upper hand when compared to other technologies, such as SMDS, frame relay, FDDI, etc., because ATM technology cuts across all spectrums of networks: LAN, WAN, GAN, and public networks. ATM is a technology for both switching and transmission. It can function as a switch, as a multiplexer, and as a cross-connect.

ATM can be used in many different ways in a LAN environment. The most obvious way is by having an ATM LAN hub, where terminals with ATM adapters are connected directly to the hub, as shown in Fig. 7.11. This configuration is a typical business environment where the ATM hub is the interface to the outside world.

The hub environment is called a pure ATM environment. This scenario is far from reality because in today's environment, with different existing LAN technologies, a migration strategy to ATM will be needed which requires very little investment to connect existing LANs to ATM. Thus, our ATM hub is in a slightly different environment from a regular ATM switching system. The differences and similarities between two application environments, i.e., the ATM hub switch and traditional ATM switch of ATM technology, are given below:

- Both switch ATM cells along their backplane
- Both look similar in functionality
- Both directly connect to the workstations, support a high-speed backplane, and provide access to public WAN
- An ATM hub supports Ethernet, Token ring, FDDI, TAXI, and ATM adaptation interface, whereas a conventional ATM switch does not
- An ATM hub has a maximum speed of OC3 interfaces, including a variety of legacy LAN interface speeds, whereas an ATM switch

■■■■ ■■■ ■■■ ■■
Figure 7.11
ATM hub environ-
ment with ATM inter-
faces only.

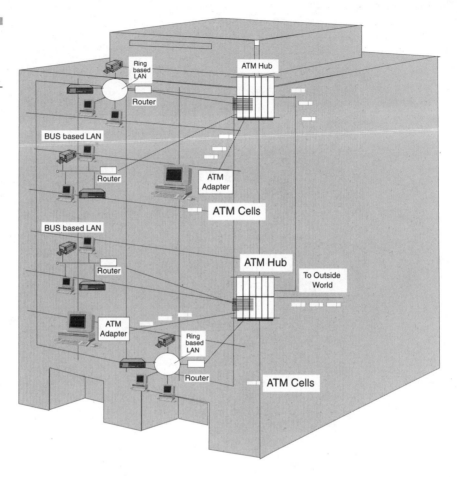

supports ATM interfaces operating at speeds from DS3, OC3,
OC12, or higher as it is needed

■ An ATM hub focuses on performing the adaptation function for
the ATM switch, whereas an ATM switch focuses more on
switching, routing, and call management features

Thus, an ATM hub in a LAN environment can be used as a backbone
switching mechanism, as shown in Fig. 7.12.

Now that we have seen ATM in a LAN, let's address ATM in a WAN or
GAN. Both environments can exist in private and public networks but
are found mostly in public ones. ATM has the following characteristics
in both environments:

Figure 7.12
ATM hub
environment.

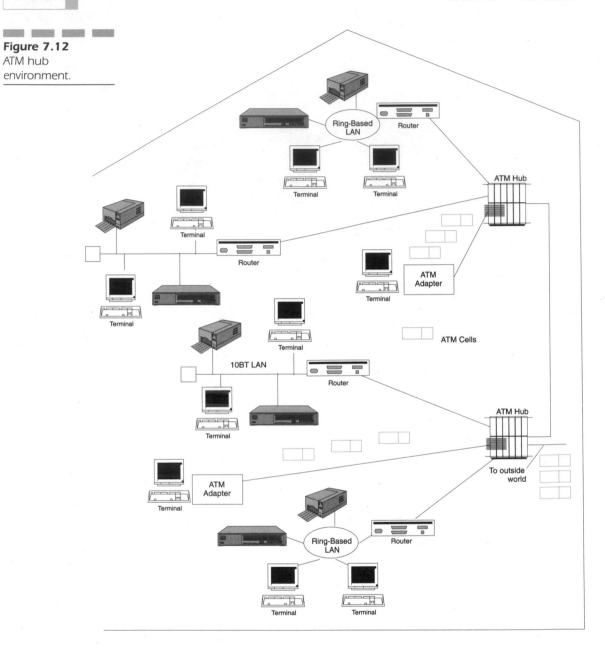

- Initially, ATM will support some subset of BISDN services.
- Its interface speeds of up to 150 Mbps (OC3) UNI are already defined, DS3 or ATM forum's 45-Mbps public UNI are used initially, and OC3 UNI and OC3 NNI will be used later as the need arises.

- It will support frame-relay and SMDS access
- It will support SVCs across multivendor ATM switch (standards are available since 1996)

Initial applications are likely to be:

- PVC for VPN (virtual private network) to connect multiple ATM LANs for LAN interconnect applications (data applications)
- SVCs for dialup service (mostly high-speed data)
- Backbone interconnection for FR and SMDS and transport for TDM services

Figure 7.13
Typical ATM network in WAN/GAN environment.

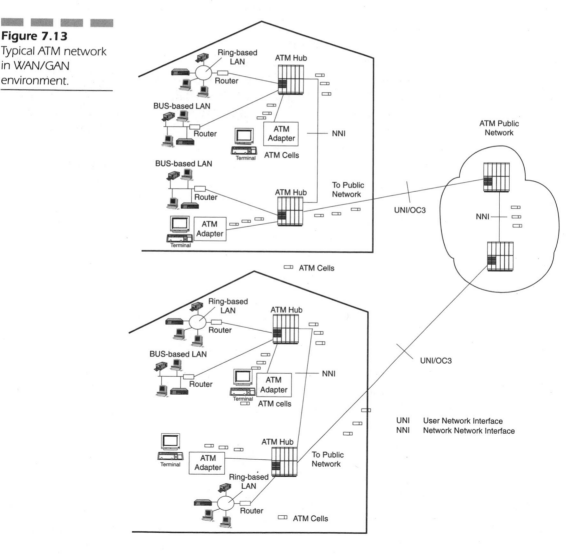

Figure 7.13 shows a typical ATM network in WAN/GAN environment. In this section, we refer to an ATM environment where we deploy the standard ATM switch. Here it uses two fields, called VPI and VCI, in the ATM header to do switching of ATM cells to reach their destination. If the same ATM switch uses only VPI to switch and route the cells, it is called ATM cross-connect. ATM cross-connect will be used as a traffic concentrator where an ATM switch cannot be justified.

ATM cross-connects can be used in place of existing digital cross-connects. Their multiplexing feature enables them to be used as an ATM multiplexer (mux) and cross-connect (XC) simultaneously in public networks. The details of an ATM switch (or cross-connect) are discussed in Part 4. A typical ATM network configuration uses ATM XC at the access interface where multiplexing and adaptation of traffic from different sources are performed; switching, however, is done in the backbone network.

The initial ATM PVC services became available from large IEC carriers since 1993. Even though carriers are planning to provide a wide range of services, their initial plans are for VPN-based LAN interconnect services. The other services will be provided based on customer demand. Much work still needs to be done related to ATM, especially in the area of VBR for real time. Current products on ATM are all hardware. Once the hardware is finalized or mature, more work must be done on intelligent software, where management functions for the ATM switches and network are performed. Here we will discuss some typical ATM environments where ATM will play a significant role. As mentioned earlier, ATM is designed to carry data, voice, and video. Lets look at how ATM can provide these services.

7.6.1   ATM LAN Emulation

One of the first applications targeted for ATM was the traditional data traffic in the LAN environment. The details are discussed in later chapters of this book. The most important application, however, is the interaction with the legacy LAN. Currently, ATM-based Ethernet switches and ATM workgroup switches are being deployed by end users at various corporate sites. The most widely used set of standards in the local ATM environments is the ATM LAN emulation (LANE) standard defined by the ATM Forum. ATM LAN emulation (Fig. 7.14) is used to make the ATM SVC network appear to be a collection of virtual Ethernet/IEEE 802.3 and token-ring/IEEE 802.5 LANs. The replication of most of the characteristics of existing LANs means that LAN emulation enables exist-ing LAN applications to run over ATM transparently, and this charac-teristic leads to its wide deployment. In ATM LAN emulation, most unicast LAN traffic moves directly between clients over direct ATM SVCs, while multicast traffic is handled via a server functionality. Bridg-ing is used to interconnect real LANs and emulated LANs running on ATM, while routing is used to interconnect ATM-emulated LANs and other WAN or LAN media for purposes of routing scalability, protocol mapping, or security firewalls.

The ATM Forum LANE implementation agreement specifies two types of LANE network components connected to an ATM network:

1. LANE clients that function as end systems such as
- Computers with ATM interfaces that operate as file servers
- End-user workstations or personal computers
- Ethernet or token-ring switches that support ATM networking
- Routers, bridges, and ATM ENS with membership in an emulated ATM LAN

2. LANE servers that support ATM LANE service for configuration management, multicast support, and address resolution.

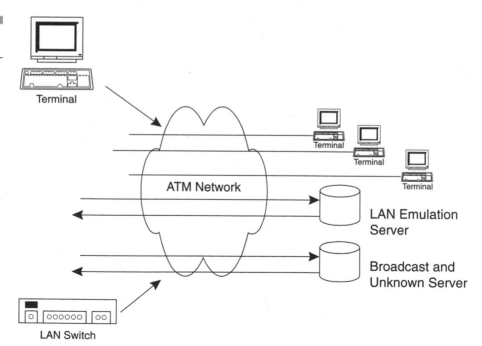

Figure 7.14
ATM LAN emulation.

The LAN-emulation service may be implemented using the same devices as the clients, or involve other ATM network devices. The communications interface, LAN-emulation user-network interface (LUNI), uses the IEEE 802.3/5 LANs interface format for transferring information. The component of the LAN-emulation service that deals with initialization (i.e., emulates plugging the terminal into a LAN hub) is the LAN-emulation configuration server (LECS). It directs a client to connect to a particular LAN-emulation server (LES). LES is the component of the LAN-emulation service that does the address registration and resolution. LES is responsible for mapping IEEE 48-bit MAC addresses and token-ring route descriptors to ATM addresses. One very important MAC address for clients is the MAC-layer "broadcast" address that is used to send traffic to all locations on a LAN. In LAN emulation, this function is performed by the broadcast and unknown server (BUS). ATM LANE is a comprehensive set of capabilities which has been widely deployed in ATM networks.

ATM LANE is an element of the multiple protocol over ATM (MPOA) architecture that is being defined by the ATM Forum. This work is addressing encapsulation of multiple protocols over ATM, automatic address resolution, and the routing issues associated with minimizing multiple router hops in ATM networks.

7.6.2 Voice Over ATM

The next important application targeted for ATM is the real-time voice over ATM. Since real-time voice services have been traditionally supported in the WAN via circuit-based techniques (e.g., via T1 multiplexer or circuit switching), it is natural to map these circuits to ATM CBR PVCs using circuit emulation and ATM adaptation layer 1 (AAL1). However, there is a significant disadvantage in using circuit emulation in that the bandwidth has to be dedicated for this type of traffic (whether there is useful information being transmitted or not), providing a disincentive for corporate users to implement circuit emulation as a long-term strategy. For example, a T1 1.544-Mbps circuit requires 1.74 Mbps of ATM bandwidth when transmitted in circuit-emulation mode. This disadvantage does not downplay its importance as a transitional strategy to address the installed base on a TDM network to an ATM network.

As technology has evolved, the inherent burstiness of voice and many real-time applications can be exploited [along with sophisticated compression schemes such as ADPCM (adaptive differential pulse code modulation), LD-CELP (low delay-code excited linear prediction), etc.] to significantly decrease the cost of transmission through the use of VBR-RT (variable bit rate-real time) connections over ATM. VBR (variable bit rate) techniques for voice exploit the bursty nature of voice communication, as there are periods of silence, which can result in increased efficiency. These periods of silence (in decreasing levels of importance) arise when:

- No call is up on a particular trunk, i.e., the trunk is idle during off-peak hours (trunks are typically engineered for a certain call-blocking probability, and at night, all the trunks could be idle)
- The call is up, but only one person is talking at a given time
- The call is up, and no one is talking

The addition of more bandwidth-effective voice coding (e.g., standard voice is coded using 64 kbps PCM) is economically attractive particularly over long-haul circuits and T1 ATM interfaces. Various compression schemes have been standardized in the industry (e.g., G.720 series of standards). Making these coding schemes dynamic provides the network operator with the opportunity to free up bandwidth when the network becomes congested. For example, when congestion begins, increased levels of voice compression could be dynamically invoked, thus freeing up bandwidth and potentially alleviating the congestion while diminishing the quality of the voice during these periods.

A further enhancement to the support of voice over ATM is to support voice switching over SVCs. This entails interpreting PBX signaling and routing voice calls to the appropriate destination PBX as shown in Fig. 7.15. From a traffic management perspective, the advantage is that connection admission controls can be applied to new voice calls; when the network is congested, these calls could be rerouted over the public networks and therefore not cause additional levels of congestion.

The ATM Forum has recently started to address VBR-RT voice. The development of this standard will drive the acceptance of ATM in the network as an end-to-end solution.

7.6.3 Video Over ATM

The next application of ATM is transporting video over ATM. Today, circuit-based videoconferencing streams (including motion JPEG running at rates around 10 Mbps or greater) are handled by standard circuit emulation using AAL-1. The ATM Forum has specified the use of VBR-RT VCs using AAL-5 for MPEG2 on ATM for video-on-demand

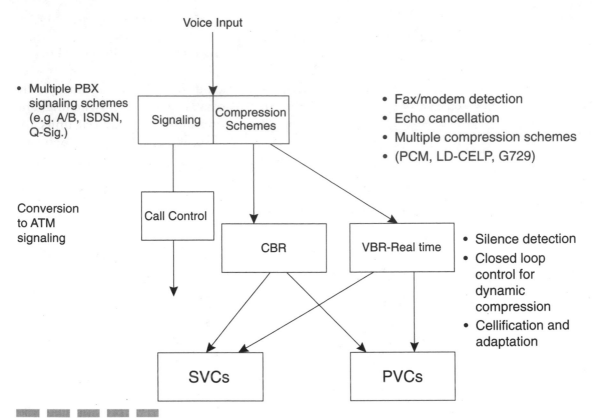

Figure 7.15
Voice processing over ATM.

applications as this approach makes better use of networking resources. Figure 7.16 shows the process of mapping MPEG2 signals on to an ATM environment.

7.6.4   ATM Advantages

ATM marks the beginning of a new era of end-to-end integration. It promises manageable and secure bandwidth on demand and is the proposed telecommunications standard for broadband ISDN. Two-way data, voice, and video can be transmitted on a common circuit using low-cost networking and low-cost technology. Any kind of information can be transferred and switched in real time or nonreal time at fixed or variable speed, depending on the characteristics of the steady or bursty data sources. In addition, there are many future benefits to ATM networking, the most important of which is that it will save the user money. ATM will provide direct bandwidth savings by securing the needed bandwidth from an application.

With ATM as the international standard for cell relay, it combines the efficiency of packet switching and the reliability of circuit switching. This is done by dividing all of the information into very small cell units and transferring and switching these units at superhigh speed. Most networks are either circuit-oriented, for transmitting delay-sensitive (isochronous) information such as video or voice, or packet-oriented, for high-speed data delivery. Circuit switching guarantees end-to-end delivery and response times but can waste expensive bandwidth. Packet switching makes the most out of its use of bandwidth but has variable packet delivery times, therefore making it unsuitable for isochronous transmission.

Statistical multiplexing is another advantage of ATM. If a good number of connections are quite bursty, then all of them could be

Figure 7.16
Video processing over
ATM environment.

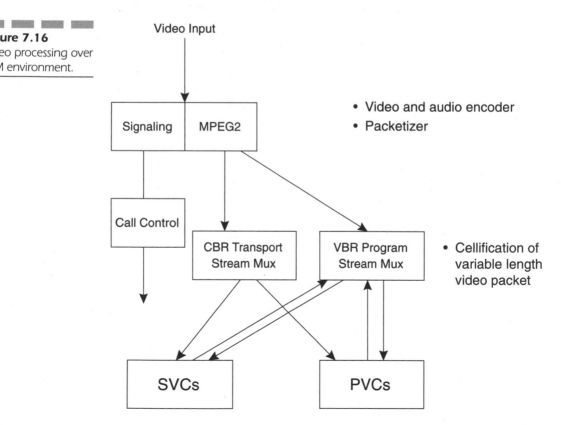

assigned to the same link since statistically they might not all burst at the same time. Yet, if some of them do burst simultaneously, the burst will be cushioned by the available elasticity until it is put in the next free buckets.

Therefore, ATM networks rely heavily on user-supplied information at connection setup time in order to provide the desired connection for transmission. They can secure a fixed bandwidth for an isochronous (repeating in time such as voice samples) connection carrying a continuous bit stream and a plesiochronous (variable frequency such as compressed video) connection for a variable bit stream, as well as rely on statistical sharing with no specific bandwidth for bursty sources. In ATM networks, the transmitter and receiver performance are also independent of one another. The transmitter side is constrained by flow control of the simultaneous connection streams with respect to bandwidth and other user requirements. The receiver side is constrained by asynchronous reception of cells at a variable rate and whether or not the adaptation layer is used. If the AAL layer is used, the reassembly of these cells into a higher layer PDU would also be done in the hardware of the receiver side. In trying to determine which protocol layer of the OSI stack[2] best fits ATM, it seems that it does not fit nicely into the defined abstract layered model, which can be attributed to the fact that within the ATM network itself, end-to-end connection, flow control, and routing are all done at the ATM cell level. However, ATM is ideal for switching fixed length packets in hardware over long distances in the Gigabit per second range. Thus, it should lie somewhere around the data link layer as in the OSI model. There are only a few higher layer functions present in ATM such as connectionless services. Another higher-layer service necessary for guaranteed delivery would be a TCP-type transport layer protocol. At the ATM layer, there is no end-to-end reliable delivery service and there are no retransmissions or acknowledgments of received data. If an error is detected, the cell is simply discarded. This allows very high transmission rates with little degradation, a positive result of recent optical fiber technology.

Through ATM technology, BISDN will be able to offer a variety of communication speeds and constant or variable bit rates for a variety of media. It will allow the terminal user to request a certain kind of service quality for communication without making any fixed assumptions. With the right kind of communications quality for every application, bit error

---

[2]Described in Chap. 1.

requirements will differ for low-speed and high-speed applications. However, many problems still need to be addressed before the introduction of actual BISDN systems, as ATM technology and its many advantages become the perfect mode of transmitting the mixture of voice, data, and video information.

7.7 Summary

ATM is a technology that can handle all types of traffic (voice, video, and data) multiplexed on the same network. In an ATM network, bandwidth can be reassigned in real time to different traffic, based on demand. ATM is the only technology common to all environments from LAN to GAN. The main reason for ATM's popularity is that it has been selected as the switching technology for future BISDN services and can handle future unknown services. ATM combines both circuit- and packet-switching modes and is thus able to handle traffic with different characteristics on the same network.

ATM, as a switching technology, is different from ATM-based services. ATM technology converts information into cells and then routes it to the appropriate destination. ATM as a service is an end-to-end service using ATM technology to provide higher-layer services. This ATM technology is transparent to the service and the user. In sum, the advantages ATM offers are:

■ Flexibility, since ATM can be easily evolved for future services

■ Efficiency in the use of its available resources

■ Capable of being one simple universal network

■ Reduction in operation, administrative, and maintenance costs

■ Reduction in transport costs (by statistical multiplexing)

■ Provision of dynamic bandwidth allocation

■ Statistical multiplexing of all types of traffic (voice, video, and data)

■ Flexible channel bandwidth allocation

■ Reduction in the number of overlay networks (data network, voice network, and video network)

■ Protection of existing investment for users by connecting existing system to ATM networks

■ Support of multimedia applications

■ High-speed access to the network (begins at DS1, or 1.544 Mbps)

CHAPTER 8

SONET/SDH

8.1 Overview

So far, we have discussed technologies for switching systems. This chapter describes the standard transmission technology to be used for the next generation of broadband communications, based on the BISDN protocol. Fiber optics has been selected as the medium of transmission. In a uniform optical transmission interface, standards bodies around the world have been developing a set of specifications that enable any vendors' transmission systems to be interconnected. As a result, synchronous optical network (SONET) and synchronous digital hierarchy (SDH) standards came into existence. The SONET specification was designed for the United States and Canada, while the SDH specification was designed for the European Community and other countries. Since little difference exists between SONET and SDH, this chapter uses SONET as an example and describes transmission systems with a reference to SDH whenever applicable.

8.1.1 SONET

SONET was first conceived by R. J. Bohm and Y. C. Ching of Bellcore. It was proposed as an optical communications interface standard to the ANSI T1 committee at the end of 1984. The objective was to produce a common standard for fiber-optic transmission systems that would provide for the operating companies a common, simple, economical, and flexible transmission network to operate. Just 5 years later, a stable base set of standards had emerged for SONET. SONET has been chosen as the transmission technology for the next-generation protocol, the BISDN, in the United States because it is capable of providing the infrastructure for the next generation of communication into the twenty-first century.

8.1.2 Synchronous Digital Hierarchy

In July 1986, the Consultative Committee on International Telegraph and Telephone (CCITT), with SG (Study Group) XVIII playing the central role, began the process of standardizing SDH. Like SONET, SDH is an optical transmission standard that operates by appropriately managing the payloads and transporting them through a synchronous transmission network. Before the advent of SDH, the most common digital hierarchy used was plesiochronous digital hierarchy (PDH), which is still widely used in Europe as E1, E2, and E3, and in North America as DS1, DS2, DS3, and DS4 (these are asynchronous transmission hierarchies). These PDH signals are multiplexed into an STM-n (synchronous transfer mode) signal. Compared to PDH, SDH appears to be extremely simple in operation. For example, mapping PDH tributaries into STM-n signals via synchronous multiplexing is not a trivial matter.

The term synchronous in SDH comes from the fact that multiplexing plesiochronous tributaries into STM-n adopts a synchronous multiplexing structure. Advantages of using synchronous multiplexing structure are

- Simplified multiplexing/demultiplexing technique
- Direct access to low-rate tributaries without demultiplexing/multiplexing all the intermediate signals
- Enhanced operations and OAM capabilities
- Easy transition to higher bit rates of the future in step with the evolution of transmission technology

Hence, one can conclude that the synchronous multiplexing structure is the very essence of SDH.

8.1.3 Advantages of SONET/SDH

Although slight differences exist between SONET and SDH, the advantages provided by both are similar because the same motivation is behind them—to develop a standard for a fiber-based synchronous network. In this section, we address the advantages that SONET/SDH provide:

- SONET and SDH standards are both based on the principle of direct synchronous multiplexing, which is the key to cost-effective and flexible telecommunications networking around the world. In essence, individual tributary signals can be multiplexed directly into a higher rate of SONET/SDH signals without intermediate stages of multiplexing. SONET/SDH network elements can then be interconnected directly with the obvious cost and equipment savings over the existing network.
- SONET and SDH both provide the advanced network management and maintenance capabilities required in a flexible network to

manage and maintain that flexibility effectively. Nearly 5 percent of the SONET/SDH bandwidth is allocated to support advanced network management and maintenance procedure and practices.

■ SONET and SDH signals can both transport all the tributary signals defined for the networks in existence today. Thus, SONET/SDH can be deployed as an overlay network to an existing network, and where appropriate, provide enhanced network flexibility by transporting existing signal types. In addition, SONET/SDH has the flexibility to readily accommodate new types of customer service signals that network operators will want to support in the future.

■ SONET and SDH can both be used in all three traditional telecommunications application areas: long-haul networks (backbone networks), local networks (access networks), and loop carriers. They can also be used in a CATV network to carry video traffic.

8.2   Standards

The following subsections address the different stages of SONET and SDH standards.

8.2.1   SONET Standards

In 1988, work by the standards committees resulted in the publication of a national standard for SONET. The SONET standards allow vendors to build equipment to transport information point-to-point, but they do not spell out the nature of the messages or commands that conduct performance monitoring or control, or allow equipment from different vendors to function together. SONET standards have been introduced in three phases, and each phase presents additional levels of control and operations, administration, maintenance, and provisioning (OAMP).

8.2.1.1   Phase I.   Phase I, which was approved by ANSI in 1988, defines transmission rates and characteristics, formats, and optical interfaces. This phase primarily defines the hardware specifications for point-to-point data transport. Phase I supports the initial requirement of an optical carrier-n (OCn) midspan to meet at payload level only. It also defines the standard data communications channels (DCC) with basic functions, as well as the basics of framing and interfaces.

8.2.1.2 Phase II. Phase II was built upon the midspan meet defined in Phase I for multiple vendor connectivity and management. Phase II defines:

- OAMP procedures
- Synchronization
- SONET-to-BISDN interconnectivity
- Pointer adjustments for wander and jitter
- Central office electrical interfaces
- Imbedded operation channels
- Common management information service elements (CMISE)
- Point-to-point, add/drop multiplexer capabilities

In addition, Phase II defines an intra-office optical interface (IAO), which allows equipment to be interconnected at the central office.

8.2.1.3 Phase III. Phase III is built upon Phase II by providing all of the OAMP required for a midspan meet. Additional network management, performance monitoring, and control functions are added, as are DCC standard message sets and addressing schemes for identifying and interconnecting SONET network elements, thus allowing the passing of DCC information between various vendor implementations of SONET. Phase III also provides for ring and nested protection switching using an automatic protection switching (APS) mechanism.

SONET standards set 51.84 Mbps as the base signal for the new multiplexing hierarchy called the *synchronous transport signal level 1* (STS-1). Its mirror signal for transmission over fiber-optic lines is optical carrier level 1 (OC1), which is a direct conversion from electrical to optical signaling.[1] Upper-level signals are multiples of OC1. Thus, OC3 carries three times more capacity than OC1, or 155.52 Mbps. Table 8.1 shows the SONET multiplexing hierarchy and line rates.

---

[1]There is a slight difference in speed between STS-1 and OC1.

TABLE 8.1

SONET Multi-plexing Hierarchy

Optical No.	Electrical No.	Speed	Multiple of DS3	Multiple of DS1	Multiple of DS0
OC1	STS-1	51.84 Mbps	1	28	672
OC3	STS-3	155.52 Mbps	3	84	2,016
OC12	STS-12	622.08 Mbps	12	336	8,064
OC24	STS-24	1.244 Gbps	24	672	16,128
OC48	STS-48	2.488 Gbps	48	1,344	32,256
OC192	STS-192	9.6 Gbps	192	5,376	129,024
OC768	—	40 Gbps	768	21,504	516,096

8.2.2 SDH Standards

ITU-T recommendations G.707, G.708, and G.709 were the result of efforts to create a worldwide standard for SDH. The recommendations were based on ANSI's North American standard for SONET. After much discussion and compromise, American and European parties arrived at a unified standard that accounted for both the European hierarchy, with its 2.048-Mbps (E1) basic bit rate, and the North American hierarchy, with its 1.544-Mbps (T1 or DS1) bit rate. The new SDH standard has a common bit rate of 155.52 Mbps.

In addition to these three recommendations, the ITU-T specified a number of supplemental recommendations for SDH. Table 8.2 shows the full range of recommendations related to SDH.

8.3   SONET/SDH Protocol

The current asynchronous broadband network has grown on an ad hoc basis, where problems in construction, operation, or maintenance must be resolved individually, resulting in an excessively complex network structure. Consequently, these networks are difficult to operate, maintain, and expand. The SONET standards groups have sought to resolve this problem by defining a hierarchical layered structure. Also, in an effort to manage information better in SONET, information is accessed at the byte level instead of the bit level, as in asynchronous systems. Each layer can handle intralayer communications independently and is responsible for a portion of the overall link management. Although analogous to the layering of the OSI communications model in some respects, SONET layering as described in this section is concerned with the frame itself, which applies only to the OSI data link layer. The exception to SONET/SDH is the communication overhead bytes, used for operations and maintenance, which transmit information generated by lower layers to higher OSI layers as required.

TABLE 8.2

ITU-T SDH Recommendations

Standard	Type of Recommendation
G.702	Digital hierarchy bit rates
G.703	Physical/electrical characteristics of hierarchical digital interfaces
G.707	Synchronous digital hierarchy bit rates
G.708	Network node interface for the synchronous digital hierarchy
G.709	Synchronous multiplexing structure
G.773	Protocol suites for Q interfaces for management of transmission systems
G.781	Structure of recommendations on multiplexing equipment for the synchronous digital hierarchy
G.782	Types and general characteristics of synchronous digital hierarchy multiplexing equipment
G.783	Characteristics of synchronous digital hierarchy multiplexing equipment
G.784	Synchronous digital hierarchy management
G.955	Digital line systems based on the 1.544-Mbps hierarchy on optical fiber cables
G.956	Digital line systems based on the 2.048-Mbps hierarchy on optical fiber cables
G.957	Optical interfaces for equipment and systems relating to the synchronous digital hierarchy
G.958	Digital line systems based on the synchronous digital hierarchy for use on optical fiber cables
G.652	Characteristics of a single-mode optical fiber cable
G.653	Characteristics of a dispersion-shifted single-mode optical fiber cable
G.654	Characteristics of a 1,500-nm wavelength loss minimized single-mode optical fiber cable
M.30	Telecommunications management network

Figure 8.1 shows the different layers in SONET and how they interact. The SONET layers have a hierarchical relationship—each layer starts with the path layer and requires the services of all lower-level layers to perform its own functions.

From a bottom-up approach, each layer builds on the services provided by the lower layers. The four layers are

- Photonic layer
- Section layer
- Line layer
- Path layer

8.3.1 Photonic Layer

This layer provides optical transmission at a very high bit rate. Issues dealt with at this layer include optical pulse shape, receiver and transmitter power levels, and operating wavelength. Electrooptical equipment communicates at this level. The main function of the photonic layer is to convert the electrical signal to optical signals and map the electrical STS-n frame into an optical OC3-n frame. The reason for this mapping is that the higher layers perform their functions in an electrical domain, whereas the physical transmission system is in an optical domain.

Figure 8.1
SONET protocols
stack.

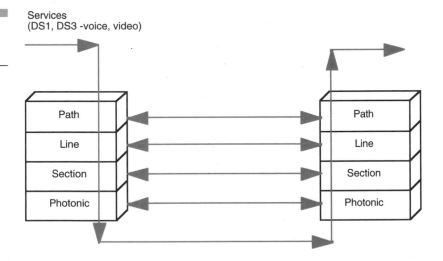

8.3.2 Section Layer

The section layer deals with the transport of STS-n frames across the physical medium. Functions include framing, scrambling, section-error monitoring and communicating, and addition of the section-level overhead. A section of the transmission facility includes termination points, between either a terminal network element or a repeater or two repeaters.

8.3.3 Line Layer

The line layer deals with the reliable transport of the path layer payload and its overhead across the physical medium. The line layer provides synchronization and multiplexing for the path layer. A line is the transmission medium required to transport information between two consecutive network elements (e.g., an OC-n/OC-m multiplexer), one of which originates the line signal and the other of which terminates it. The network elements are also called *terminating equipment* because the signals terminate in them.

8.3.4 Path Layer

The path layer deals with the transport of services (e.g., DS1 or DS3) between path terminating equipment. The main function of the path layer is to map the services of the path overhead (POH) into an STS SPE, which is the format required by the line layer. The path overhead uses pointers to identify the beginning of DS1 or DS3 signals.

8.4 Basic SONET Frame

Figure 8.2 shows the basic SONET frame format, with a bit rate of 50.688 Mbps. The concept of the synchronous transport system goes beyond the basic needs of a point-to-point transmission system to include the requirements for telecommunications networking. SONET can therefore be used in all three of the traditional network applications (voice, video, and data) where the growth in bandwidth and the provisioning of new customer services are expected to happen in the near future.

Figure 8.2
STS-1 SONET frame.

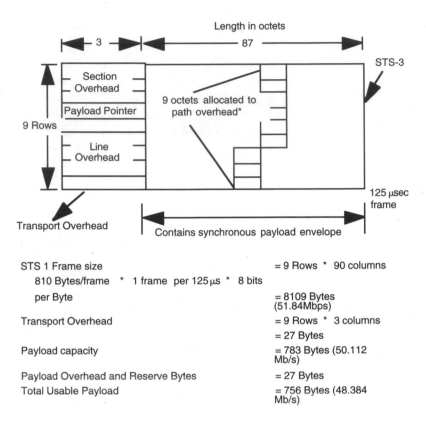

STS 1 Frame size	= 9 Rows * 90 columns
810 Bytes/frame * 1 frame per 125 μs * 8 bits per Byte	= 8109 Bytes (51.84Mbps)
Transport Overhead	= 9 Rows * 3 columns
	= 27 Bytes
Payload capacity	= 783 Bytes (50.112 Mb/s)
Payload Overhead and Reserve Bytes	= 27 Bytes
Total Usable Payload	= 756 Bytes (48.384 Mb/s)

This basic signal is STS-1. Before we describe the different components of the SONET frame, we need to understand the frame size in bytes. The lowest SONET frame is STS-1. This frame consists of 9 rows and 90 columns, where each row and column is 1 byte, thus making the total frame 810 bytes. The time taken to transmit this frame is 125 μs with 8 bits/byte. This frame has the capacity of 51.84 Mbps, and is divided into different components to perform certain functions. The components are:

- Transport overhead (TOH)
- Section overhead (SOH)
- Line overhead (LOH)
- Path overhead (POH)
- STS synchronous payload envelope (SPE)

Each is discussed in the following subsections.

8.4.1 Transport Overhead

In Fig. 8.2, the first three columns of the STS are TOH, which are reserved for transport information. The TOH has been assigned 27 bytes, of which 9 bytes are reserved for the section overhead and 18 bytes are reserved for the line overhead.

8.4.2 Section Overhead

The section overhead contains the information required for the section elements only (i.e., repeaters). This section overhead information is processed at each section terminating point, which is usually between any two pieces of SONET transmission equipment. Section overhead provides the following functions:

■ Detection of STS-1 frame alignment

■ Section performance monitoring and fault isolation

■ Data communications channel for OAMP

■ Channel for voice communications for maintenance personnel

8.4.3 Line Overhead

Line overhead contains the information required between the line termination equipment, such as an add-drop terminal. It provides the following functions:

■ STS payload pointer

■ Line performance monitoring and signal failure detection

■ Automatic protection switch signaling channel (bidirectional)

■ Data communications channel for alarm gathering, remote provisioning, and other OAMP

■ Channel for voice communication for maintenance personnel

8.4.4 Path Overhead

The path overhead is assigned to and transported with the payload until the payload is demultiplexed. The POH is carried with the payload envelope and supports the transport of the payload from the point it enters the SONET network to the point it leaves. There is a corresponding POH for every payload. The POH performs the following functions necessary to transport the payload between path-terminating equipment:

■ Monitors end-to-end transport of the payload and its performance when transferring the network

■ Identifies that a correct connection was made

■ Identifies payload type

■ Provides a user channel for carrying the service provider's information

8.4.5   STS Synchronous Payload Envelope (SPE)

Envelope payload is the bandwidth within the STS frame, and it is aligned to the STS frame that carries the STS SPE. This bandwidth can be combined with several STS-1s to carry a higher bandwidth payload. The STS SPE consists of 87 columns by 9 rows of bytes (the remaining bytes of TOH), which is the capacity reserved for the payload and path overhead, as shown in Fig. 8.2. Column 1 contains the STS path overhead (9 bytes), the remaining 774 bytes are available for the payload to carry the actual information. The STS SPE can begin anywhere in the STS envelope capacity (it can start in one frame and end in the next), as illustrated later in this chapter.

8.5   SONET Overhead Capabilities

As mentioned earlier, the SONET overhead consists of three components: section, line, and path. Before we address each one of the overheads, we need to understand the relationship of these overheads to the network elements. Figure 8.3 shows the originating and terminating element for the section, line, and path overheads.

For network management and maintenance purposes, the SONET network can be described in terms of three different network spans:

■ The path span allows network performance to be maintained from a service end-to-end perspective.

■ The line span allows network performance to be maintained between transport nodes (or between two active terminals).

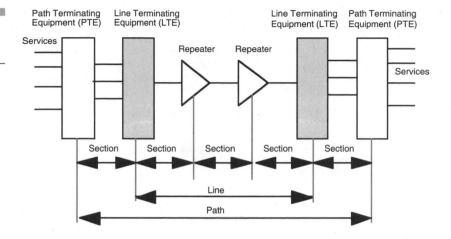

Figure 8.3
SONET network spans.

- The section span allows network performance to be maintained between the SONET network elements. Section spans can be regenerators or repeaters between any SONET network elements.[2]

Let's look into the functions provided by each of the SONET overheads and the details of bytes within each.

8.5.1 Path Overhead

Figure 8.4 shows the POH within a SONET frame. The functions provided by the path overhead are

- End-to-end transport of services
- Sequencing of cells
- Path-terminating element status
- Continuity
- Error detection
- User-defined functions

The POH of the SONET frame consists of 9 bytes of the STS. It is carried in the STS SPE and comprises the following bytes:

---

[2]Repeaters and regenerators are actually different. A repeater amplifies the incoming signal and transmits it, in which case even the noise is amplified. A regenerator increases the original signal and transmits it. In this case the noise is suppressed.

Byte	Use
J1	The J1 byte is used to repetitively transmit 64-byte information. It consists of a fixed-length string, so that continued connection to the source of the path signal can be verified at any receiving terminal along the path.
B3	The B3 byte provides BIP-8 (bit interleaved parity) path error for monitoring. The path BIP-8 is calculated over all bits of the previous SPE, and the computed value is placed in the B3 byte before scrambling.
C2	The C2 byte indicates the construction of the STS SPE by means of a label value assigned from a list of 256 possible values (8 bits).
G1	The G1 byte is used to convey back to the originating STS PTE the path termination status and performance. This feature allows the status and performance of a two-way path to be monitored at either end or at any point along the path.
F2	This byte is allocated for the user's purpose between the path terminations.
H4	This byte provides a multiframe phase indication for virtual tributary (VT) payloads.
Z3 to Z5	These three bytes are reserved for future use.

Figure 8.4
Path overhead (POH)
in STS-1 frame.

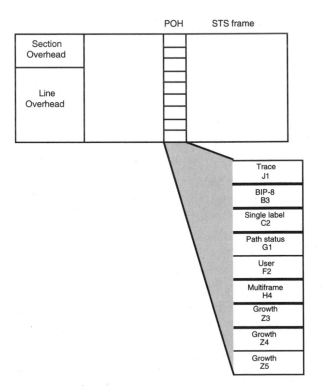

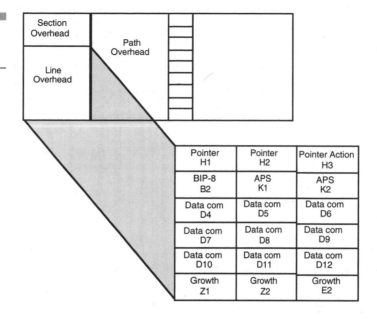

Figure 8.5
Line overhead of
STS-1.

8.5.2 Line Overhead

Figure 8.5 shows the LOH bytes in an STS-1 frame. The functions provided by the line overhead are:

- Communication between the line-terminating equipment (LTE)
- Synchronization between LTEs
- Payload location or identification within the payload
- Multiplexing
- Error detection
- Automatic protection switching

The 18 bytes of the STS-1 line overhead are comprised as follows:

Byte	Use
H1 to H3	These three bytes facilitate the operation of the STS-1 payload pointer and are provided for all STS-1s in an STS-n.
B2	This byte provides BIP-8 line error monitoring. The line BIP-8 is calculated over all bits of the line overhead and payload envelope capacity of the previous STS-1 frame before scrambling, and the computed value is placed in the B2 byte. This byte is provided for STS-1 in an STS-n signal.

Byte	Use
K1 to K2	These two bytes provide APS signaling between line-terminating equipment and are defined only for STS-1 number 1 in an STS-n signal.
D4 to D12	These nine bytes provide a data communications channel at 576 kbps for administration, monitoring, maintenance, alarms, and other communications messages needs between line termination equipment. These bytes are defined only for STS11 of an STS-n signal.
Z1 to Z2	These two bytes are reserved for functions not yet defined.
E2	This byte provides an express order-wire channel for voice communications between line terminating equipment and is only defined for STS-1 of an STS-n signal.

8.5.3   Section Overhead

The last of the three overheads in the transport portion of the SONET header is the section overhead. Figure 8.6 shows the bytes of the section overhead. The functions provided by the section overhead are

■ Frame alignment pattern
■ STS-1 identification

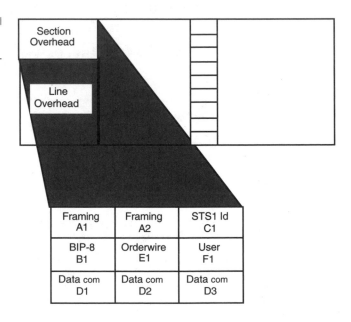

Figure 8.6
Section overhead.

- Parity check
- Data communication channel
- Voice communications (order-wire)
- User channel

The nine bytes of the STS-1 section overhead are made up as follows:

Byte	Use
A1 to A2	These two bytes provide a frame-alignment pattern (11110110 00101000). These bytes are provided in all STS-1s within an STS-n. These two bytes identify the beginning of the SONET STS-1 frame.
C1	This byte is set to a binary number corresponding to its order of appearance on the byte interleaved STS-n frame and can be used in the framing and de-interleaving process to determine the position of other signals. This byte is provided in all STS-1s within an STS-n, with the first STS-1 being given the number 1 (0000 0001).
B1	This byte provides section error monitoring by means of a bit-interleaved parity (BIP-8) code using even parity. In an STS-n, the section BIP-8 is calculated over all bytes of the previous STS-n frame after scrambling, and the computed value is placed in the B1 of the STS-1 number before scrambling.
E1	This byte provides a local order-wire channel for voice communications between the regenerators and network elements.
F1	This byte is allocated for the user's purpose and is terminated at all section-level equipment.
D1 to D3	These three bytes provide a data communications channel for administration, monitoring, alarm, maintenance, and other communications messages needs at 192 kbps between section termination equipment.

8.6 How Does SONET/SDH Work?

To explain the operation and functions of SONET/SDH, we can take SONET as an example. By now we know that SONET works on the principle of synchronization. So first let's look into a basic synchronous signal structure, as shown in Fig. 8.7. A synchronous signal comprises a set of bytes (8 bits each) organized into a frame structure. Within this frame structure, the identity of each byte is known and preserved with respect to a framing or marked byte. In Fig. 8.7, a single frame in the serial signal stream is shown in a two-dimensional format. It consists of

Figure 8.7
Synchronous signal
structure.

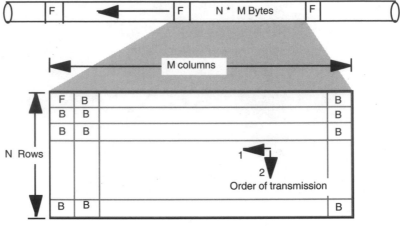

N rows and M columns of boxes, each representing 1 byte (8 bits) of the synchronous signal. A framing byte, or F-byte, appears on the top left corner of the box to provide the frame reference byte location. This signal is transmitted in a sequence starting from the top left-hand corner byte (the F-byte), followed by those in the second byte in row 1 and so on, until the bits in the Mth byte, i.e., the last byte in row 1, are transmitted. Then, the bits in the first byte of row 2 are transmitted, followed by the bits in the second byte of row 2, and so on, until the Mth byte of the Nth row is transmitted. This whole sequence is repeated for the next STS frame.

Figure 8.8 shows the next stage of the synchronous signal structure, called the *synchronous transport frame*. A synchronous transport frame comprises two distinct and readily accessible parts within the frame:

- Synchronous payload envelope
- Transport overhead

SPE is where the actual information is carried by the signal. In SPE, individual tributary signals, such as DS1 and DS3, for instance, are mapped onto the payload. These signals are assembled and disassembled only once, even though they might be transferred from one transport system to another many times on their route through the network to its destination.

A portion of the signal capacity is reserved for transporting what is called *signal overhead*. We explained the function of the overhead in Sec. 8.4.

The overhead, in general, provides information such as alarms, maintenance, bit error monitoring, etc., which is carried across the network to support and maintain the transportation of the SPE between the nodes in a synchronous network.

Within each STS-1 frame, there is a pointer to the payload envelope, known as the STS-1 payload pointer. This pointer provides a method for flexible and dynamic alignment of the STS SPE within the STS envelope capacity. The alignment is independent of the actual contents of the envelope. This dynamic alignment means that the pointer can accommodate differences in the phases and frame rate of the STS SPE and the transport overhead (i.e., when network elements are running at slightly different clock rates). This difference occurs when the frame is transported from one network to another and when each derives its master clock from different sources. Synchronization and timing are covered in Part 4.

Figure 8.9 shows the link between the transport overhead and the SPE. To facilitate efficient multiplexing and cross-connection of signals in the synchronous network, the SPE is allowed to float within the payload capacity provided by the STS-1 frames. Thus, the STS-1 SPE can begin anywhere in the STS-1 payload capacity and is unlikely to be wholly contained in one frame. Usually, the STS-1 SPE begins in one frame and ends in the next. When an SPE is assembled into the transport frame, additional bytes, referred to as payload pointers, are made available in the transport overhead. These bytes contain a pointer value that indicates the location of the first byte (J1 is part of the POH byte) of the STS-1 SPE. The SPE is allowed to float freely within the space made available for it in the transport frame, so that timing phase adjustments can be made

Figure 8.8
Synchronous transport frame structure.

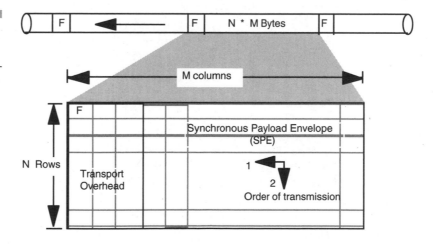

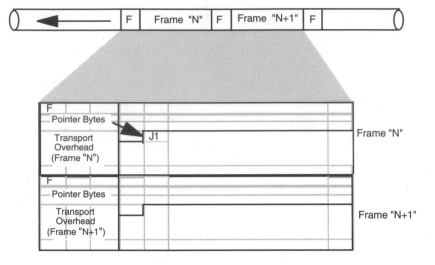

as required between the SPE and transport frame. The payload pointer maintains the accessibility of the SPE by identifying the location of the first byte of the SPE.

We have discussed the pointer in the link between the transport overhead and SPE. Now let's address the functions of payload pointers. Basically, payload pointers allow asynchronous operation in a synchronous network. Because SONET works only on a synchronous network, mapping asynchronous network traffic can be achieved using pointers. Ideally, this means that all synchronous network nodes should derive their timing signals from a single master network clock. Current synchronous network timing scenarios, however, do allow for the existence of more than one master network clock.

For example, networks owned by different network operators or service providers must have their own independent master timing references. These clocks operate independently and, therefore, at slightly different rates. Also, situations exist in which a network node loses its timing reference and operates on a standby clock, which might not be as stable as the master clock. Therefore, synchronous transport must be able to operate effectively between network nodes operating asynchronously within certain limits. To accommodate clock offsets, the SPE can be moved (justified) positively or negatively 1 byte at a time with respect to the transport frame. Moving the SPE is achieved by simply recalculating or updating the payload at each SONET network node. In addition to clock offsets, updating the payload pointer also accommodates any other timing phase adjustments required between the input SONET signals and the timing reference of the SONET node.

Of course, payload processing does introduce new signal impairment known as payload adjustment jitters. This jitter impairment appears on a received tributary signal after recovery from an SPE that has been subjected to payload pointer changes. Excessive jitter on a tributary signal influences the operation of the network equipment that is processing the tributary signal immediately downstream. Therefore, care should be taken in the design of the timing distribution of the synchronous network to minimize the number of payload pointer adjustments and level of tributary jitter that could be accumulated through synchronous transport.

8.6.1   Synchronous Multiplexing of STS

So far, we have seen how an STS-1 frame is transported carrying a payload. Now we study an example. Figure 8.10 shows how synchronous multiplexing is done. *Synchronous multiplexing* of STS is defined in SONET as a procedure for multiplexing the individual bytes of a signal such that each signal is visible within the multiplexed signal, i.e., it eliminates complete demultiplexing of an STS-n to access one STS-1. An STS-n signal is formed by byte interleaving of n STS-1 signals. For example, an STS-12 comprises 12 STS-1s, each separately visible (meaning each can be accessed). The individual STS-1s could be carrying different payloads, each with a different destination. Figure 8.10 shows an example of three STS-1 signals multiplexed onto an STS-3 signal. Here, the three STS-1s are

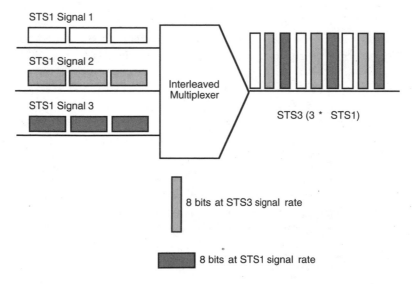

Figure 8.10
Example of synchronous multiplexing.

multiplexed to form an STS-3 signal by making the output of the equipment operate at a rate three times the input rate. For example, at the input each STS-1 takes 125 ms to transmit, whereas on the output, the STS-3 frame takes only 125 ms to transmit. Thus, three STS-1 signals can be multiplexed onto one STS-3 frame.

Multiplexing of SONET signals provides benefits such as transporting narrowband and broadband signals together in the most economical way. This feature reduces the number of network elements required and allows the transport elements to be dynamically provisioned.

8.6.1.1 Payload Mapping So far, we have addressed some of the basics of the SONET frame and its multiplexing. Now let's look into mapping information into the payload. As mentioned earlier, SPE is the location in the SONET frame where the actual information is stored and carried in the network. The process of carrying the information consists of the SPE assembly and disassembly processes.

8.6.1.2 SPE Assembly Process Figure 8.11 shows the assembly process of the STS payload. In this example, the process of mapping a tributary signal such as DS3 into a synchronous payload envelope is explained. Once assembled, this payload is transported across a synchronous network. This process is part of the fundamental principle defined in the SONET standards. The process of assembling the tributary signal into an SPE is referred to as *payload mapping*. To provide uniformity across all SONET transport capabilities, the payload capacity provided for each individual tributary signal is always slightly greater than that of the required tributary signal. Thus, the essence of the mapping process is to synchronize the tributary signal with the payload capacity provided for transport by adding extra stuffing bits to the signal stream as part of the process as shown in Fig. 8.11.

For example, in Fig. 8.11, a DS3 tributary signal at a nominal rate of 44.74 Mbps needs to be desynchronized with a payload capacity of 48.54 Mbps provided by the STS-1 SPE. The addition of path overhead completes the assembly of the STS-1 SPE and increases the bit rate of the composite signal to 50.11 Mbps.

8.6.1.3 SPE Disassembly Process Figure 8.12 shows the disassembly process of the STS payload. At the disassembling point, the tributary signal that has been transported over the network must be recovered from the SPE that provided the transportation facility for the original signal. The process of disassembling the original tributary signal from the SPE is referred to as *payload demapping*. The SPE consists of path overhead, which was added during the payload mapping process, and the tributary signal to carry the payload. Thus, the essence of the demapping process is to desynchronize the tributary signal from the composite SPE signal and reproduce this tributary signal to its original form as precisely as possible.

So, in our example, an STS-1 SPE carrying a mapped DS3 payload arrives at the disassembly location with a signal rate of 50.11 Mbps. Stripping the path overhead and stuffing bits from the SPE results in a discontinuous signal, representing the transported DS3 signal with an average signal rate of 44.74 Mbps. These timing discontinuities are reduced by means of a desynchronizing phase-locked loop (PPL) to produce a continuous DS3 signal at the same average signal rate.

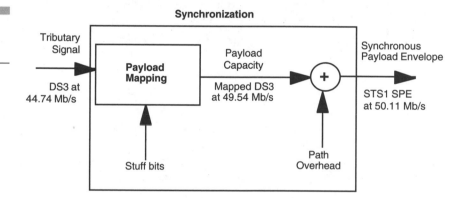

Figure 8.11
SPE assembly
process.

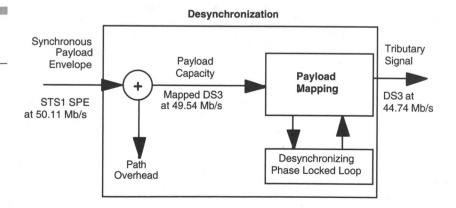

Figure 8.12
SPE disassembly
process.

8.6.2   Virtual Tributary

In a SONET environment, mapping DS3 onto an STS-1 payload is relatively straightforward because of the compatibility between the speed of the two signals. In a real-world environment, however, very few users have a DS3 amount of traffic. Usually, this amount of traffic is available only in the backbone. So SONET standards-making bodies defined mapping of T1 or DS1 onto the SONET STS-1 payload in the form of virtual tributaries, enabling access to each of the VTs without the need to demultiplex the whole payload to get one VT. We know a DS3 can accommodate 28 DSIs. Thus, to access each one of the VTs (DSI) within an STS payload, different types and modes of VT are present. The STS SPE can be divided into VTs for transporting and switching payloads smaller than the STS-1 rate (e.g., DS1, DS2, and PCM30). Four types of VTs are defined, which are shown in Table 8.3.

Let's go through an example of a VT mapping onto an STS-1 SPE. For simplicity, we take VT1.5 (DS1), which is popular among VTs because it maps the DS1 signal. Figure 8.13 shows how VT1.5 is packaged onto an STS-1 payload.

In an SPE payload, 28 VT1.5s can be packaged for transportation. The 3-column by 9-row structure of the VT1.5 fits neatly into the same 9-row structure of the STS-1 SPE. Thus, 28 VT1.5s can be packaged into the 86 columns of the STS-1 SPE payload capacity, still leaving two spare columns in the STS-1 SPE payload capacity. These spare columns are filled with fixed-stuff bytes that allow the STS-1 SPE signal structure to be maintained in case of nonsymmetric timing. These VTs can operate in two modes: floating and locked.

8.6.2.1   Floating Mode   This mode has been designed to minimize the network delay and provide efficient cross-connection of transport signals at the VT level within the synchronous network. This goal is

TABLE 8.3

Different Types of VT

VT Size (Type)	Capacity, Mbps	Payload Name	Rate, Mbps
	Optical Levels		Payload Example
VT1.5	1.728	DS-1	1.544
VT2	2.304	E-1	2.048
VT3	3.456	DS-1C	3.152
VT6	6.912	DS-2	6.312

Figure 8.13
VT1.5 packaged in
STS-1 payload.

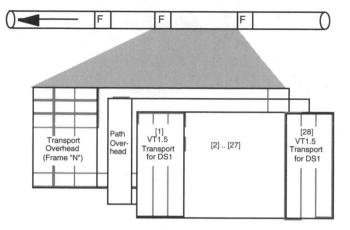

achieved by allowing VT SPE to float with respect to the STS-1 SPE to avoid the use of unwanted slip buffers at each VT cross-connect between different transport systems without unwanted network delay. This mode allows a DS1 to be transported effectively across a SONET network. The problem in this mode is to identify the beginning of the VT because the source of VT is not fixed.

8.6.2.2 Locked Mode. Locked mode has been designed to minimize the interface complexity and support bulk transport of DS1 signals for digital switching applications. This goal is achieved by locking individual VT SPEs in fixed positions with respect to the STS-1 SPE. Each VT1.5 SPE is not provided with its own payload pointer. It is not possible with this mode to route a selected VT1.5 through a SONET network without unwanted network delay and extra cost caused by having to provide slip buffers to accommodate the timing synchronization issues. This mode does have the advantage, though, of mapping VTs in a predefined location within the payload. The disadvantage is the delay and inefficient use of the SPE payload.

8.6.2.3 SONET Synchronization. In a synchronous system such as SONET, all clocks are locked onto a reference frequency. Every clock can be traced back to a highly stable reference clock source. The STS-1 rate remains at a nominal 51.84 Mbps. A synchronous system allows simpler multiplexing and direct payload visibility, as compared to an asynchronous environment, where the bit stuffing does not allow direct payload visibility. Because of the use of payload pointers, the STS-1s and their contents (the individual bytes) are easily accessed at higher STS-n rates.

TABLE 8.4

Comparison of
SONET and SDH
Frames

Speed	SONET	SDH	Optical equivalent
50 Mbps	STS-1	—	OC1
150 Mbps	STS-3	STM-1	OC3
622 Mbps	STS-12	STM-4	OC12
2.4 Gbps	STS-48	STM-16	OC48
9.6 Gbps	STS-192	STM-64	OC192
40 Gbps	—	—	OC768

SONET can thus transport between smaller networks with different clocks using a pointer-adjustment facility or when part of the network loses its timing reference because of fault conditions.

8.7 Summary

In this chapter, we addressed one of the most important fiber-optics transmission technologies for broadband communication, SONET. The reason for its importance is that SONET has been selected as the transmission technology for fiber-based transmission systems for BISDN. We also addressed SDH, which is the European counterpart of the SONET as defined by ITU-T for the European Community and others who adopt the E1-based standard. Although some differences exist in the basic frame format, SONET and SDH are the same beyond the STS-3 signal level, as shown in Table 8.4.

To generalize the terminology, one could use STM-n for SDH and STS3-n for SONET. Standards have been developed in such a way that both are compatible from the second level (i.e., STS-3 or STM-1) and their lower tributaries can be mapped interchangeably between the two formats from there onwards. We also discussed the overheads, the working of SONET payload mapping, and tributary mapping onto the SONET payload.

Broadband Access Technologies

9.1   Overview

The rapidly changing and expanding communications market will bring about many opportunities for service providers, especially in the access areas. Many initiatives related to new broadband access technologies and architectures are currently under way, and it is certain that in the future some will be deployed for the mass market. These new broadband access technologies will change the way that service providers like cable companies, telephone companies (local and long distance), and others do business. No one is exactly sure of the path these service providers will take, yet many providers are pursuing new technologies and architectures with the hope of expanding their service offerings. Some have chosen a specific direction with respect to technology, while others are hedging their bets by testing several new technologies while they wait to determine what their optimal path will be.

This chapter addresses an important component of the network, the access to the customer, which is currently the bottleneck in providing a wide range of broadband services (including narrowband services) in a cost-effective way. Thus, broadband access technologies that are capable of providing broadband and narrowband services for the various service providers are examined in this chapter. This chapter does not cover the potential fiber-based access technologies such as PON (passive optical network). Although this was quite popular in the early 1990s when the fiber-to-the-home architecture discussion dominated studies in the telecommunications industry, in recent years, it has become clear that any technology leveraging an existing embedded base will gain over a technology involving building a new infrastructure such as a fiber network to the mass market.

Many access technologies are currently being considered to provide integrated broadband voice, data, and video services. The service provider must select an appropriate access technology that fits the existing network and plan a service strategy for both the short and long term. The background on some of the potential architecture and access technologies, along with potential strategies that service providers can pursue with respect to these technologies, follows.

9.2   Broadband Access Technologies

The broadband access technologies discussed here are x-digital subscriber loop (x-DSL) which include technologies such as

- ADSL (asymmetrical digital subscriber loop)
- HDSL (high-speed digital subscriber loop)
- RADSL (rate-adaptive digital subscriber loop)
- SDSL (symmetrical digital subscriber loop)
- VDSL (very high-speed digital subscriber loop)
- IDSL (ISDN digital subscriber loop))

In addition, we will discuss some of the CATV technologies and supporting modulation techniques used in x-DSL technologies such as carrierless amplitude phase (CAP) and discrete multitone (DMT).

9.2.1 Modulation Techniques

All of the x-DSL technologies mentioned here are adaptable to one of the modulation techniques such as DMT or CAP. There is another modulation technique called 2B1Q used in HDSL and IDSL, but it is not discussed in this book. There are other techniques used, such as QAM, which is a variation of CAP techniques. So, before we discuss the most popular x-DSL, we will address some of the modulation schemes used.

9.2.1.1   Basics of CAP   CAP is a two-dimensional multilevel multiphase encoding modulation scheme. As the name implies, it uses both multilevel amplitude modulation (i.e., multiple voltage levels per pulse) and phase modulation. This results in values that are produced by a combination of two amplitude values, each separated by a 90° phase shift. Figure 9.1 shows how CAP is an extension of the 2D binary line.

Presently, CAP transceivers can use multiple constellations that create $2n$ values, yielding many bits per hertz. However, in reaction to different line conditions, CAP algorithms can expand and contract these constellations (i.e., to 512-CAP, 64-CAP, 4-CAP, etc.). This ability to change constellation size is one of the two ways that CAP systems provide rate adaptation. The other method is to simply reduce the total amount of frequency spectrum used. These two simple methods give CAP its inherent rate adaptive quality.

Unlike other multicarrier-based systems, such as DMT, CAP systems do not subdivide the bandwidth available above the 4-kHz range into fixed intervals (bins) of bandwidth. Instead, CAP algorithms can evenly distribute energy across the entire range of frequencies in a channel. Hence, CAP systems have a rate adaptation granularity of as little as 1 bit/s, i.e., CAP can expand or contract the entire frequency spectrum used in increments of 1 Hz. However, this

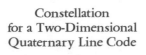

Figure 9.1.
Constellations for a
two-dimensional
binary line code and
64-CAP.

Constellation
for a Two-Dimensional
Quaternary Line Code

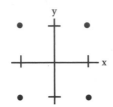

Constellation
for 64-Cap
(a Two-Dimensional
Multilevel Line Code)

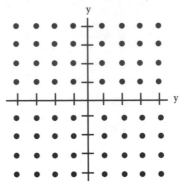

extreme degree of rate adaptation granularity is not particularly useful for practical purposes and, therefore, is not usually employed. In CAP systems (see Fig. 9.2), only two channels are required above the 4-kHz frequency used for POTS: one upstream channel (for transmission from the service subscriber to the network) and one downstream channel (for transmission from the network to the service subscriber). These channels are separated by a technique called *frequency division multiplexing* (FDM).

The CAP system incorporates forward error correction (FEC) scheme in the downstream direction to ensure reliable transmission in the presence of bursty error events resulting from impulse noise.

9.2.1.2 Basics of DMT DMT is a multilevel encoding scheme, which achieves its high bit rate by encoding groups of bits in discrete subchannels, commonly referred to as bins. These bins are created through the use of a fast fourier transform (FFT) at the receiver and inverse fast fourier transform (IFFT) at the transmitter. DMT's algorithms aim for a maximum of 15 bits/Hz inside each bin.

At a very basic level, DMT X-DSL systems can be thought of as employing 256 "minimodems," 4 kHz each, that run simultaneously in a single chipset. Figure 9.3 shows how DMT utilizes the frequency spectrum above 4 kHz. Many DMT vendors have deviated from the T1.413 specification and are deploying nonstandard, nonuniform products. Alcatel, as an example, uses 3-kHz subchannels.

For a T1.413-compliant DMT system, whatever efficiency has been gained by increasing the efficiency in an individual 4-kHz bin is reduced as the processor must coordinate the assignment of bits to up to 256 bins.

In a DMT system, bits are assigned to bins on the basis of each bin's signal-to-noise ratio, and the bins that have the highest ratio take the most bits. If noise increases above a certain level on a given bin, bits from that bin are moved to bins with lower noise (i.e., a higher signal-to-noise ratio). In T1.413, DMT's 256 bins are grouped into larger channels, four unidirectional downstream and three bidirectional downstream and upstream. Most DMT systems use echo cancellation techniques to separate these channels (although there is at least one DMT implementation that uses FDM). Hence, DMT is initially designed for asymmetrical applications, i.e., ADSL. But, there are products in recent days that are capable of providing symmetrical bandwidths using DMT.

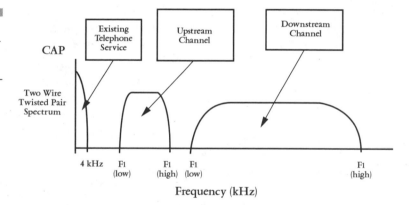

Figure 9.2.
Upstream and downstream channels in CAP systems.

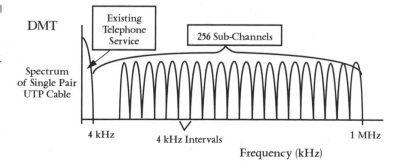

Figure 9.3
DMT's frequency spectrum distribution.

9.2.2 x-DSL Technology

x-DSL technology enables telephone operating companies with existing twisted-pair loops to offer single/multiple video channel or high-speed data (symmetrical and asymmetrical bandwidth) along with telephone service. Since x-DSL uses existing twisted-pair loops currently deployed around the world, it is easy to rapidly implement new services, such as high-speed data access and multimedia services. For instance in the United States, there are currently 170 million telephone lines using twisted-pair loops. Of these, about 70 percent of the loops are within 18,000 ft and therefore are potential x-DSL candidates. This shows the potential opportunity for this technology worldwide. Table 9.1 shows the distribution of the loop plant. x-DSL comes in many flavors. First-generation x-DSL was HDSL that provided a two-way 1.5-Mbps wideband channel designed to deliver T1-based services to subscribers up to 12,000 ft over two pairs of twisted copper pair. Later generations of DSL were ADSL, SDSL, HDSL, VDSL, etc., which were capable of transmitting variable bandwidth both downstream and upstream containing video or data traffic. It has been demonstrated[1] that ADSL can provide 1.5-Mbps bandwidth for up to 18,000 ft. In the demonstration just cited, ADSL carried 1.5 Mbps of information from the network to the customer location and a 16-kbps control/data channel from the customer to the network. This was in addition to a full-duplex baseband channel used for POTS service. In recent years with the development of VDSL technology, the bandwidth has been increased to 25 Mbps if the loop length is 3000 ft and 52 Mbps if the loop length is 1000 ft. Table 9.1 shows the potential opportunity in the United States for x-DSL type technology. With more than 600 million twisted pairs deployed around the world, the potential opportunity for this technology is enormous.

All of the x-DSL technologies mentioned here are designed for point-to-point application. Thus, they are well suited for switched architecture such as the one used by telephone operating companies. A variety of x-DSL rates and technologies have been standardized, or are in the process of standardization, by ANSI and the ADSL Forum. As Fig. 9.4 shows, the higher rates are more complex because of the design of the chip set. The x-DSL is compared with traditional narrowband technologies such as ISDN, IDSL, and analog modems.

---

[1]Demonstration by US West in Denver, Colorado. Published in Telephony, January 1996.

TABLE 9.1

LEC Loop Plant
Distribution

		1983 Survey	1998
Residential		63% of loop is ≤12 kft	?
		53% of loop is ≤10 kft	?
		15% of loop is ≤3 kft	?
		5% of loop is ≤1 kft	?
Business		75% of loop is ≤12 kft	?
		60% of loop is ≤10 kft	?
		33% of loop is ≤3 kft	?
		10% of loop is ≤1 kft	?

Source: SR-TSV-002275 BOC Notes on the LEC network, 1990.

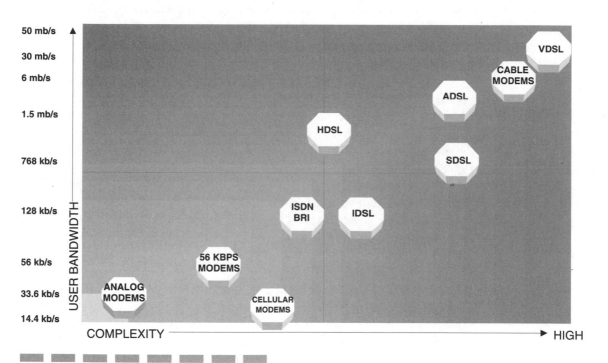

Figure 9.4
Bandwidth versus complexity of technology.

9.2.2.1   ADSL   ADSL delivers asymmetric transmission rates typically up to 10 Mbps downstream and 16 to 604 kbps upstream as shown in Fig. 9.5. However, like all copper transmission systems, the faster they run, the shorter range they will have. Hence, most operators are currently using no more than 4 Mbps downstream (usually 1.5 to 2 Mbps) with no more than 400 kbps (usually 64 to 250 kbps) upstream for Internet and remote LAN access. When ADSL is operated at these lower speeds, it typically has a range around 4.8 km (18 kft). ADSL is specifically designed to operate on the line at the same time as POTS (by operating at frequencies above the voice band). ADSL has been widely tested in real time around the world and the initial service offerings (mainly by small ISPs) began to appear in late 1996. It is expected that a few telephone companies will start to deploy ADSL for tariffed services in 1998 with larger-scale deployments appearing in 1999.

The architectures used by the early service providers are typically based on connecting DSL line cards into Ethernet-based switches, hubs, or routers at the central office to consolidate a number of line cards into a router port. This architecture has the benefit of being available using today's off-the-shelf components. However, it is based on a data communications solution as opposed to a telecom solution. As a consequence, most large telephone companies have only chosen to use this architecture for marketing, technology, or performance trials. Some of the companies such as Bell Atlantic, Ameritech, and Microsoft have used it as their trial architecture. There are concerns about the scalability, manageability, security, and future ability to evolve to support multiple service offerings over this Ethernet/router architecture.

ANSI and the ADSL Forum have endorsed DMT (discrete multitone) technology. However, CAP technology has the most market share so far, with 30 times as many ADSL lines using CAP. DMT and CAP modems are incompatible, but the issue is not nearly as great as with voice-band data modems.

9.2.2.2   HDSL   HDSL technology is a symmetric base-band transmission system using 2B1Q line coding. It requires two copper pairs for T1 bit rates or two or three copper pairs for E1 bit rates (see Fig. 9.6). HDSL technology using two or three pairs is mature now and has been commercially deployed over the past 3 years to carry T1/E1 services by many telephone companies in Europe and the United States. The typical range of such systems is around 2.5 to 3.5 km (9 to 12 kft). A new single-pair HDSL system (S-HDSL or HDSL-2), which delivers T1 or E1 over one pair, is currently

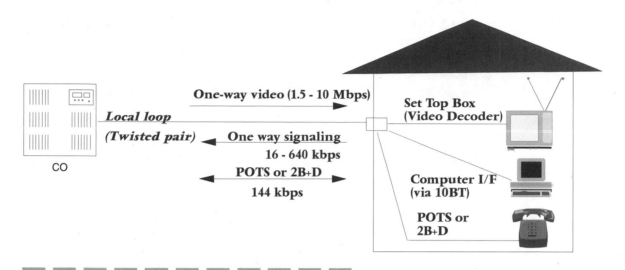

Figure 9.5
ADSL architecture in a typical telephone network environment.

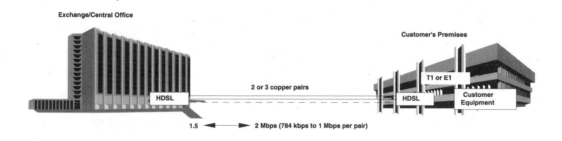

Figure 9.6
HDSL architecture.

available from several vendors and the ANSI and ETSI standards bodies. At present, there are some spectral compatibility and range concerns with the S-HDSL technology which are being validated. Overall, the technology has made a huge impact on the competitive access providers.

The current HDSL transceivers that use a two- or three-pair system but only one copper pair enables bit rates of around 784 kbps to be delivered over one pair. This could then be used for transporting fractional primary rate services or multiple 64-kbps private circuits or basic rate ISDN lines. This lower-rate one-pair operation of mature HDSL equipment is easily confused with the full T1/E1 S-HDSL currently under development.

9.2.2.3 RADSL As the name implies, RADSL modems adjust the data rate to match the quality of the twisted-pair connection. Emerging software should make this an automated process with little human intervention.

RADSL represents a significant advancement over other DSL implementations because its transmission speed is rate-adaptive, based on the length and signal quality of an existing telephone line. RADSL products will have the option of selecting the highest practical operating speed automatically or as specified by the telecom service provider. This variable-rate feature ensures high-quality service to all customers, even those residing farther from the telephone company's nearest equipment location.

Its variable rate capability offers significant savings for equipment manufacturers who can sell one DSL product to support a range of data rates, with both symmetric and asymmetric transmission modes.

9.2.2.4 SDSL SDSL refers to single-line DSL or symmetric DSL. SDSL is similar to HDSL, but requires only one pair of wires. SDSL is simply a single-line version of HDSL, transmitting T1 or E1 signals over a single twisted pair and (in most cases) operating over plain old telephone service (POTS), so a single line can support POTS and T1/E1 simultaneously. However, SDSL has one important advantage compared with HDSL in that it suits the market for individual subscriber premises, which are often equipped with only a single telephone line. The potential for SDSL will be for any application needing symmetric access (such as servers and power remote LAN users); therefore, it complements ADSL, which is discussed earlier in this section. It should be noted, though, that SDSL has distance limitations in that it will not reach much beyond 10,000 ft, a distance over which ADSL achieves rates above 6 Mbps.

SDSL offers a range of transmission rates from 144 kbps up to 2 Mbps which optimizes network service application needs. SDSL operates over a range of transmission rates. Matching transmission rates with application needs allows DSL equipment suppliers to optimize product costs. It also allows telephone companies to optimize the availability of network services and make them more cost-effective.

9.2.2.5 VDSL VDSL is clearly becoming the telephone companies' favorite twisted-pair technology. Many are predicting that VDSL will be their next generation broadband access technology. This technology is well suited with access architecture such as fiber to the node (FTTN), fiber to the building (FTTB), fiber to the curb (FTTC), etc.

In simple terms, VDSL transmits high-speed data over short reaches of twisted-pair copper telephone lines, with a range of speeds depending upon the actual line length. The maximum downstream rate under consideration is 52 Mbps over lines up to 1000 ft in length. Downstream speeds as low as 1.5 Mbps over lengths beyond 12,000 ft are also possible. Upstream rates in early models will be asymmetric, just like ADSL, at speeds from 1.6 to 2.3 Mbps. In VDSL, both data channels will be separated in frequency from bands used for POTS and ISDN, enabling service providers to overlay VDSL on existing services. At present the two high-speed channels will also be separated in frequency. As the need arises for higher-speed upstream channels or symmetric rates, VDSL systems may need to use echo cancellation.

9.2.2.5.1 VDSL Capabilities While VDSL has not achieved the same degree of maturity as ADSL, it has advanced far enough to discuss realizable goals and standardize with data rate and range. Downstream rates derive from submultiples of the SONET and SDH canonical speed of 155.52 Mbps, i.e., 51.84, 25.92, and 12.96 Mbps. Each rate has a corresponding target range, as shown in Table 9.2.

Early versions of VDSL will certainly incorporate the slower asymmetric rate. Higher upstream and symmetric configurations may only be possible for very short lines.

Like ADSL, VDSL must transmit compressed video, a real-time signal unsuited to error retransmission schemes used in data communications. To achieve error rates compatible with compressed video, VDSL will have to incorporate FEC with sufficient interleaving to correct all errors created by impulsive noise events of some specified duration. Interleaving introduces delay on the order of 40 times the maximum length of the correctable impulse.

9.2.2.5.2 Line Code Candidates for VDSL VDSL uses the standard DSL line codes such as CAP and DMT. There are other line codes proposed to address issues related to very high speeds. So far, four types of line codes have been proposed for VDSL, i.e., CAP, DMT, DWMT, and SLC.

TABLE 9.2

VDSL Bandwidth
Versus Range

Bandwidth, in Mbps	Range, in ft (m)
12.96—13.8	4500 (1500)
25.92—27.6	3000 (1000)
51.84—55.2	1000 (300)

CAP: Carrierless AM/PM is a version of suppressed carrier QAM. For passive NT configurations, CAP would use QPSK upstream and a type of TDMA (time division multiple access) for multiplexing (although CAP does not preclude an FDM approach to upstream multiplexing).

DMT: Discrete multitone is a multicarrier system using discrete fourier transforms to create and demodulate individual carriers. For passive NT configurations, DMT would use FDM for upstream multiplexing (although DMT does not preclude a TDMA multiplexing strategy).

DWMT: Discrete wavelet multitone is a multicarrier system using wavelet transforms to create and demodulate individual carriers. DWMT uses FDM for upstream multiplexing but also allows TDMA.

SLC: Simple line code is a version of four-level baseband signaling that filters the baseband and restores it at the receiver. For passive NT configurations, SLC would most likely use TDMA for upstream multiplexing, although FDM is possible.

9.2.3   CATV Technology

The technology used in CATV is typically designed for the transport of video signals. Currently, three basic technologies comprise the CATV system:

- AM (amplitude modulation)
- FM (frequency modulation)
- Digital

Table 9.3 compares the bandwidth, cable length, distortion, video signal-to-noise ratio (SNR), and audio dynamic range of the three systems. Since the current CATV system with its coaxial analog technology cannot provide any of the additional channels or bandwidth required to provide residential broadband service, CATV providers will have to adopt a new technology. Although the CATV network providers are familiar with the AM and FM modulation schemes, they are not familiar with digital technology. A general tendency within CATV network designers is to continue to maintain or improve AM and FM technology for their network upgrades. The CATV network equipment providers like this mindset because it prevents major equipment providers from entering their marketplace. Some CATV companies are against deploying digital technology in the CATV network because the current televisions are all analog,

TABLE 9.3

CATV Technologies

AM System	FM System	Digital System
Cable length: 30 km	Cable length: 40 km	Cable length: 40 km
Bandwidth/fiber: 40 chs	Bandwidth/fiber: 16 chs	Bandwidth/fiber: 8–12 chs
(420 MHz)	(700 MHz)	600 MHz–1.2 GHz)
Intermodulation and reflection distortions	Intermodulation noise	No intermodulation noise, but noise from AD to DA conversion
Channel spacing design	Channel spacing design	Channel spacing design not required
Regeneration on amplifier generates distortion	Regeneration on amplifier generates distortion	Regeneration without distortion
Video SNR: 55 dB	Video SNR: 65 dB	Video SNR: 57–67 dB
Audio dynamic range:	Audio dynamic range: 65 dB	Audio dynamic range: 65–85 db

and additional equipment would have to be deployed for a digital-to-analog conversion, which would be expensive.

In the digital system, a CATV network will not require the expensive telemetering and monitoring systems typically used in telecommunications transmission systems. Thus, digital CATV networks can be built at much lower cost. Advantages of using digital technology in the CATV system are in its performance, which is far superior to the AM/FM system and ease of migration from a coaxial- to a fiber-based system, quality of service (QOS), and long-term cost effectiveness. Digital technology also makes it easy to provide additional services and channels. By compressing the digital signal, more services can be provided because the bandwidth per channel is decreased, depending on the type of compression used. One major disadvantage of using digital technology, as mentioned earlier, is that it must be converted back to analog technology because input to the television sets has to be analog. Thus, the additional equipment that converts analog to digital signals and vice versa, called A/D and D/A converters, is required at some point in the network.

Fiber-optics technology in CATV networks is also important. No network will benefit more from fiber-optic technology than the CATV network. Its inherent characteristics eliminate most of the bottlenecks existing in today's network, such as increasing the channel capacity and reducing the number of amplifiers in the network. We mentioned earlier that, in coaxial cable systems, there are repeaters every 1000 to 2000 ft to regenerate the signal, causing the deployment of numerous amplifiers in the network at additional capital, maintenance, and operations costs. By deploying fiber, a typical CATV network can reduce the number of amplifiers to four or six, and still get substantial gain in bandwidth and cost. Fiber can be used to carry both analog and digital signals, so fiber does not need to be replaced if the technology evolves. Only the fiber terminals at the end of the physical fiber cable will have to be replaced. Fiber terminals are located every 40 km or greater if single-mode fibers are used. The CATV network that is based on fiber and coaxial is called a hybrid-fiber coax (HFC) network.

9.3   Summary

As we consider the need to support the growing demand for broadband access, we can see that the access technologies mentioned here offer the carrier community and service providers an unsought but beneficial opportunity. Faced with the challenge of deploying solutions that meet the growing needs of an expanding market, service providers are quickly coming to the conclusion that each one of the technologies have their niche markets. Thus, it has become critical that they understand their business and market needs in order to provide cost-effective service to the customer.

New services such as internet access, telecommuting, and LAN access are driving services providers to pursue different technologies to meet customer needs. Figure 9.7 shows a high-level mapping of various technologies to the services.

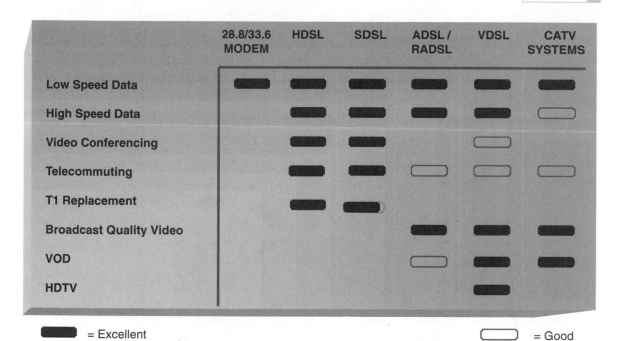

Figure 9.7
Service to technology mapping.

PART 3

Broadband Architecture

In this part, the BISDN protocol reference model is described as defined by ITU-T. Here, each layer of the BISDN is covered in detail. In addition to defining each of the BISDN protocol layers, the service delivery and service management aspects are covered: service control, service provisioning, and traffic management. Part 3 gives the reader a background on broadband protocol, which is the basis of the broadband communications network architecture described later in this book.

10

BISDN
Lower Layers

10.1   Overview

In telecommunications, broadband services are referred to as *BISDN,* for *broadband integrated services digital network.* It is an extension of ISDN as the name implies, at least in terms of naming terminology. The intent of the name was to state that BISDN is an extension of ISDN in terms of capabilities, i.e., it not only has the narrowband capability of ISDN but also broadband capability. Thus, since the introduction of BISDN, ISDN has been renamed N-ISDN, or narrowband-ISDN. N-ISDN, according to ITU-T, is defined as any service requiring a bandwidth of less than 64 kbps or up to a regular voice channel. Anything above 64 kbps and below 1.544 Mbps is defined as wideband. As mentioned earlier, any service inquiry with a speed greater than 1.544 Mbps is defined as broadband. Thus, any communications based on this speed are called *broadband communications.*

BISDN is an extension of ISDN only in terms of the name. Everything else is different, including its protocol, architecture, transmission and switching technology, and platforms. If someone is an expert in ISDN, he or she is not necessarily knowledgeable about BISDN.

BISDN is not a totally new concept. Many of the ideas are extracted and enhanced from ISDN and other telecommunications and data communication protocols. The reason for such extraction is that the fundamental objective of BISDN is to achieve complete integration of services, ranging from low-bit-rate bursty signals to high-bit-rate continuous real-time signals. Services include voice-band services, such as telemetry, low-speed data, telephone, and facsimile and broadband services, such as high-quality video conferencing, high-definition television (HDTV) video transmission, and high-speed data transmission.

Thus, to meet its objective, BISDN must adapt the characteristics of each of the different services and integrate them into a common transmission and switching platform. For instance, the packet-switching concept is used for data transmission and the circuit-switching concept is used for voice transmission. In BISDN, both concepts are used so that both types of traffic can be handled. Of course, some technical difficulties exist in achieving such an objective. But, in this case, the benefits outnumber the difficulties.

Why do we need a protocol that is completely different from those already in existence? The reason is the increasing demand for various types of broadband services. Although some broadband services are available in a disintegrated form, those services currently available in private networks are expensive because of the inefficient utilization of such network resources. The BISDN protocol is the right solution for such inefficiencies. From the user's perspective, BISDN will offer a single interface that provides for all the required communication needs—voice, data, video—and will carry both signal and user information. The interface between the user and the network will be identical for all users of BISDN. This network provides a high level of transparency to the user, which means that the user will not be concerned with the mechanics of how the service is provided, but only with the services received from the network. Figure 10.1 shows the basic concept of BISDN from the user's perspective.

Now that we have looked at BISDN from a user's perspective, let's see how a network operator or service provider views it. A typical network operator might be a telephone company or other large company. The following are some of a network operator's objectives for any network:

- Maximum efficiency or utilization of the network, considering grade of service to maintain performance levels demanded by the users of the network

- Single-operation interface for all network elements and terminals attached to the network

- Ability of network operators to rapidly identify, isolate, and thus minimize the impact of faults occurring in the network

- Ability to manage the traffic transiting through the network in terms of automatic rerouting in case of congestion

Figure 10.1
BISDN user network interface.

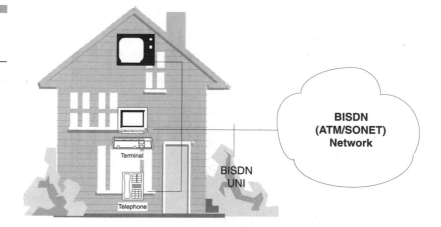

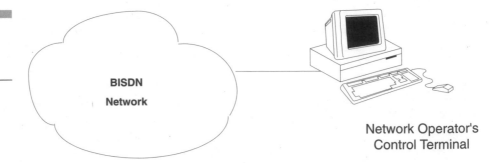

Although these are the objectives of any network operator, they are not that easy to achieve. One consideration to keep in mind is the ability of equipment to "talk" to other equipment in the same language or protocol, which is far from the reality of today's world. Figure 10.2 shows a view of the network from the operator's perspective.

To come anywhere close to the previously mentioned objectives, it becomes necessary to perform a lot of protocol conversions that degrade the system's efficiency. BISDN is the first technology or network that addresses these problems and achieves most of the network operators' objectives, at least in the long term. BISDN can achieve these goals because of its capability of carrying different types of traffic under a single network and still maintaining the application characteristics independent of another application's traffic. Currently, no complete list of applications or services is defined that could be provided by BISDN, but ITU-T has listed some of its potential current and future applications, which are mentioned in Chap. 12.

Of course, Rome cannot be built in a day. Different phases will be necessary before a complete BISDN network can be achieved. Several of the transitions for different environments where BISDN/ATM is applicable are addressed in Part 5 of this book.

In this chapter, we address the lower layers of the BISDN protocol for the proposed target network.

10.2   Broadband Protocol Reference Model

BISDN protocol architecture is a vertical layered architecture which covers the transport, switching, signaling and control, user protocols, and applications or services. The architecture model covers the complete set, including management. For an individual function such as switching or transmission, a subset of the protocol model applies, along with its respective upper-layer functions, such as the management functions. The protocol architecture divides the functions of each layer so that appropriate functions are used to support a given application.

The BISDN reference protocol model, or simply BISDN PRM, consists of three planes as shown in Fig. 10.3. The three planes are

- Management plane
- User plane
- Control or signaling plane

Each is discussed in the following subsections.

10.2.1 Management Plane

Two types of functions exist in this plane: layer management functions and plane management functions. All the management functions that relate to the whole system (end-to-end) are located in the plane management. Its task is to provide coordination between all the different planes. No layered structure is used within this plane.

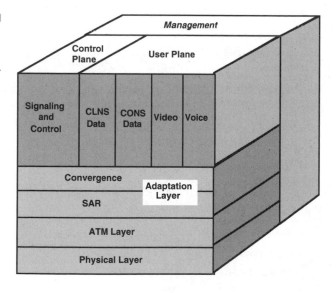

Figure 10.3
BISDN protocol reference model.

The layer management functions are in a layered structure. This structure performs the management functions relating to the resources and parameters residing in its protocol entities, such as signaling. For each layer, the layer management handles the specific O&M information flow, described in Chap. 11.

10.2.2   User Plane

The function of the user plane is to transfer the user information from point *A* to point *B* in the network. All associated mechanisms, such as flow control, congestion control, or error recovery are included. A layered approach is used with the user plane to identify the different functional components involved in providing services to the user.

10.2.3   Control or Signaling Plane

A layered structure is also used for the control or signaling plane. This plane is responsible for call control and connection control functions related to setting up a connection and tearing down a connection of the call. These are all the signaling functions necessary to set up, supervise, and release a call or connection. The functions of the physical and ATM layers are the same for the control and user planes. The difference in function occurs at the ATM adaptation layer, or AAL, and in the higher layers. The control plane is discussed in detail in Chap. 11.

10.2.4   ATM Cell Types

Before we go into the detail of each layer, we need to understand the cell terminology, used in both the physical and the ATM layer. According to ITU-T, "A cell is a block of fixed length. It is identified by a label at the ATM layer of the BISDN PRM."

Many different types of cells exist in BISDN protocol layers:

- Idle cell
- Valid cell
- Invalid cell
- Assigned cell
- Unassigned cell

Figure 10.4 shows the relationship between the different cells with respect to BISDN physical and ATM protocol layers.

Idle Cell (Physical Layer). These cells are used by the physical layer to adapt the ATM cell rate to the transmission rate using a predefined header. The cells are added at the physical layer at the originating end and removed at the physical layer at the terminating end. These cells are not seen by the ATM layer. Thus, they are switched.

Valid Cell (Physical Layer). A cell with no header errors that is not modified by the HEC verification process is called a valid cell. This cell is present only at the physical layer and has no significance to the ATM layer.

Invalid Cell (Physical Layer). An invalid cell is one whose header has errors, has not been modified by the cell HEC verification process, and is discarded by the physical layer. These cells are relevant to the physical layer only.

Assigned Cell. These cells carry valid information for a service in the upper layers with a valid header. They originate from the ATM layer with appropriate header values for routing. At the destination side, these cells are passed on to the ATM layer on completion of error checking by HEC. Assigned cells are the last cells to be discarded in case of congestion or any other problem on the network.

Unassigned Cell. A cell that contains no valid information or preassigned header is called an unassigned cell. These cells, again, originate from the ATM layer or above. They carry predefined header values and payloads. These cells are most often used for OAM, signaling, etc., where certain values are reassigned for identification by the switch for special purposes. We address some of these functions again in their respective layers. In the later sections of this chapter, we address each of the layers in some detail.

Figure 10.4
Cell types.

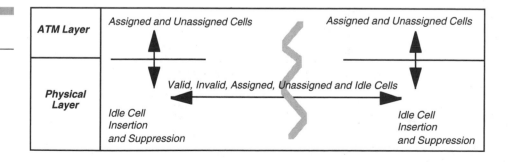

10.3   Broadband Functional Architecture

The functional reference architecture identifies the network function performed by each layer in the broadband protocol.

A good functional architecture should be designed in a way that provides mobility of function between different physical elements. Figure 10.5 shows the functions of BISDN layers in the BISDN protocol. It gives an overview of the functions of the different layers of the protocol. In this section, we address only the high-level functions of each layer. The details of each layer are given later.

Figure 10.5
Function of BISDN layers.

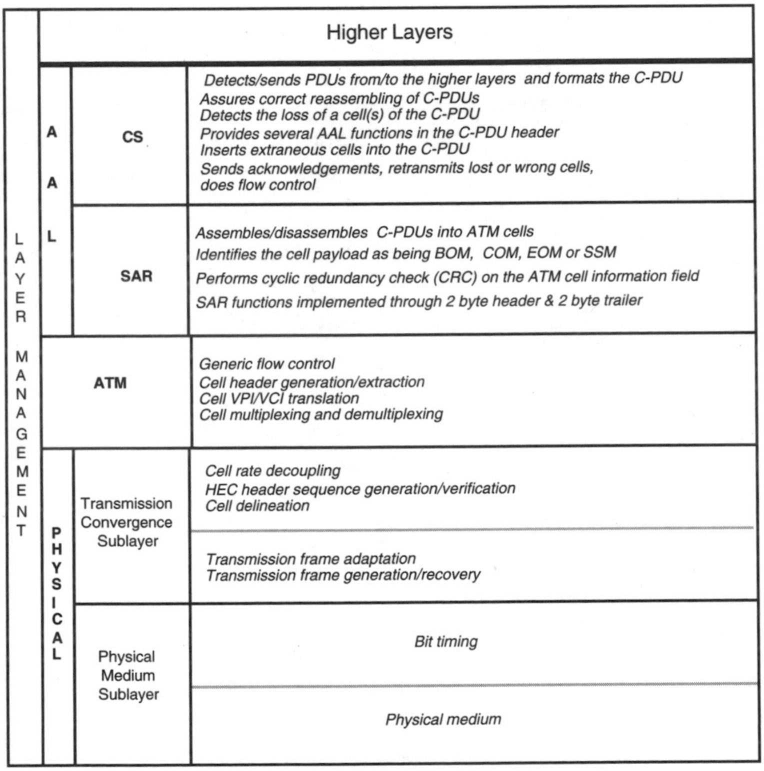

L A Y E R M A N A G E M E N T	A A L		**Higher Layers**
		CS	*Detects/sends PDUs from/to the higher layers and formats the C-PDU* *Assures correct reassembling of C-PDUs* *Detects the loss of a cell(s) of the C-PDU* *Provides several AAL functions in the C-PDU header* *Inserts extraneous cells into the C-PDU* *Sends acknowledgements, retransmits lost or wrong cells, does flow control*
		SAR	*Assembles/disassembles C-PDUs into ATM cells* *Identifies the cell payload as being BOM, COM, EOM or SSM* *Performs cyclic redundancy check (CRC) on the ATM cell information field* *SAR functions implemented through 2 byte header & 2 byte trailer*
	ATM		*Generic flow control* *Cell header generation/extraction* *Cell VPI/VCI translation* *Cell multiplexing and demultiplexing*
	P H Y S I C A L	Transmission Convergence Sublayer	*Cell rate decoupling* *HEC header sequence generation/verification* *Cell delineation*
			Transmission frame adaptation *Transmission frame generation/recovery*
		Physical Medium Sublayer	*Bit timing*
			Physical medium

AAL	ATM Adaptation Layer
ATM	Asynchronous Transfer Mode
CS	Convergence Sublayer
HEC	Header Error Control
SAR	Segmentation and Reassembly
VPI	Virtual Path Identifier
VCI	Virtual Channel Identifier

Figure 10.6
Physical layer
functions.

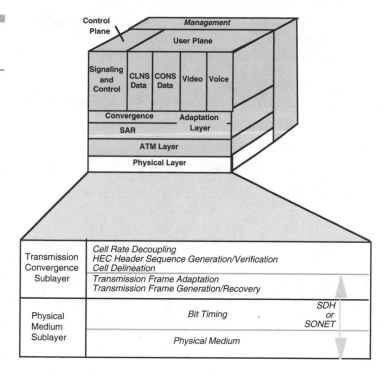

10.3.1 Physical-layer Functions

Figure 10.6 shows the physical-layer functions in the BISDN protocol. The physical-layer function again is divided into two sublayers:

- Physical medium (PM) sublayer
- Transmission convergence (TC) sublayer

10.3.1.1 Physical Medium Sublayer. The physical medium sublayer is the lowest layer of the BISDN protocol, and it includes functions that are only physical-medium-dependent. The physical medium provides bit transmission capability, including bit alignment. The physical medium itself provides line coding and, if necessary, electrical-to-optical conversion. The physical medium itself can be of any material such as optical fiber, coaxial, or even air. ITU-T, however, defined BISDN using optical fiber as the physical medium. In addition to the functions already mentioned, the physical medium provides bit timing where generation and reception of waveform is performed.

10.3.1.2   Transmission Convergence Sublayer.   The TC sublayer is the second layer of the physical layer. Figure 10.6 shows the TC sublayer functions, and they are listed here:

- Cell rate decoupling
- HEC header sequence generation/verification
- Cell delineation
- Transmission frame adaptation
- Transmission frame generation/recovery

Each is described in the following subsections.

10.3.1.2.1   Cell Rate Decoupling.   Idle cells are inserted during transmission and removed during reception. This mechanism is called cell rate decoupling. The purpose of this mechanism is for the ATM cell rate to adapt to the payload capacity of the transmission system. Other cells are passed untouched. As mentioned earlier, idle cells have no significance at the ATM layer.

10.3.1.2.2   HEC Header Sequence Generation/Verification.   The HEC sequence is inserted in the 1-byte HEC field in the header of the ATM cell during transmission. At the receiving side, the HEC value is recalculated and compared with the received value. If there are single-bit errors, error correction is performed; otherwise, the cell is discarded. The details of HEC are covered in Sec. 10.4.

10.3.1.2.3   Cell Delineation.   Cell delineation enables the receiver to recover cell boundaries. This mechanism is described in ITU-T recommendation I-432. To protect the cell delineation mechanism from malicious attack, the information field of a cell is scrambled before transmission and descrambled on the receiving side.

All of the previous functions are common to all possible transmission frames. The next two functions are transmission-frame-specific.

10.3.1.2.4   Transmission Frame Adaptation.   This adaptation is responsible for all actions necessary to adapt the cell flow according to the payload structure of the transmission system used in the sending direction. In the opposite direction, the reverse is done. The frame can be a cell equivalent, such as SONET envelope or DSS PLCP frame. The details of a SONET envelope were described in Chap. 8.

10.3.1.2.5 Transmission Frame Generation/Recovery. The lowest of all functions is the generation and recovery of the transmission frame. Its basic function is to generate the required frames so that ATM cells can be mapped. The frame size depends on the transmission speed on the transmitting side. On the receiving side, transmission frame recovery is performed by identifying the frame so that ATM cells can be identified and recovered from the payload envelope.

10.3.2 ATM Layer Functions

The next layer of the BISDN protocol is the ATM layer. Figure 10.7 shows the ATM layer and its functions in the BISDN protocol.

This layer has characteristics independent of the physical medium. Simply stated, the function of this layer is switching. The functions provided by this layer can be categorized as follows:

■ Generic flow control

■ Cell header generation/extraction

Figure 10.7
ATM layer functions
of BISDN.

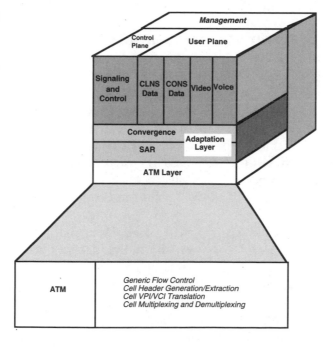

- Cell virtual path identifier/virtual channel identifier translation
- Cell multiplexing and demultiplexing

Each is described in the following subsections.

10.3.2.1 Generic Flow Control. As mentioned earlier, the GFC function is defined only at the BISDN user network interface (UNI) to provide access flow control. It supports control of ATM traffic flow from customer networks or premises. GFC can be used to alleviate short-term overload conditions. The specific information is carried in assigned or unassigned cells.

10.3.2.2 Cell Header Generation/Extraction. Cell header generation/extraction is done at the terminating points of the information or payload in the ATM layer. The cell header is added, except for the HEC, in the transmit direction, after receiving the ATM payload from the adaptation layer (48 bytes). The VPI and VCI values that are part of the header are obtained from the service access point (SAP) identifier. In the receive direction, the cell header is extracted, and the payload is forwarded to the AAL layer. Only the cell information field is passed to the higher layer (AAL layer). Here, the VPI and VCI values are translated into an SAP identifier.

10.3.2.3 Cell VPI/VCI Translation. Cell VPI/VCI translation is the basis of ATM switching. It is performed at the ATM switching nodes or cross-connect nodes where the VPI and VCI values are translated. In a virtual path (VP) switch, the incoming VPI values within a cell are translated into a new outgoing VPI value. Here, the VCI values within the VPIs are preserved, not changed. In a VC switch, the values of the VPI as well as the VCI are translated. The VP switch is called an ATM cross-connect, and the VC switch is called an ATM switch. It is not necessary that the VPI and VCI values be translated just because the traffic passes through a switch. The values of VPI and VCI end-to-end could be preserved if necessary.

10.3.2.4 Cell Multiplexing and Demultiplexing. In the transmitting direction, cells from the individual VPs and VCs are multiplexed into one resulting cell stream. This function is called cell multiplexing and is accomplished by changing the VCI or VA value accordingly. The composite stream is normally a noncontiguous cell flow. At the receiving side, the cells are demultiplexed into individual cells, and they flow into appropriate VP or VC to their destination.

10.3.3   ATM Adaptation Layer Function

Figure 10.8 shows the AAL layer in the BISDN protocol. The basic function of AAL is the enhanced adaptation of the services provided by the ATM layer until the requirement of the higher layer's services are met. In this layer, the higher layer PDUs are mapped onto the information field of the ATM cell, which is 48 bytes long. The ATM layer adds a header with appropriate VPI and VCI values to this cell.

To perform its functions, AAL is divided into two sublayers: the convergence sublayer (CS) and the segmentation and reassembly sublayer (SAR).

10.3.3.1   Convergence Sublayer.   The functions of this layer are service-dependent and provide the AAL service at the AAL-SAP. Figure 10.9 shows the CS-PDU structure of the convergence sublayer. Details of the CS sublayer are discussed later in this chapter.

The following are the five classes of AAL services:

- AAL 1 or Type 1 constant bit rate or circuit emulation
- AAL 2 or Type 2 variable bit rate video and audio
- AAL 3 or Type 3 connection-oriented data transfer

Figure 10.8
AAL layer in BISDN.

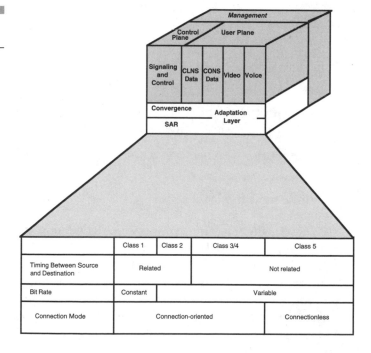

	Class 1	Class 2	Class 3/4	Class 5
Timing Between Source and Destination	Related		Not related	
Bit Rate	Constant		Variable	
Connection Mode	Connection-oriented			Connectionless

Figure 10.9
CS-PDU structure.

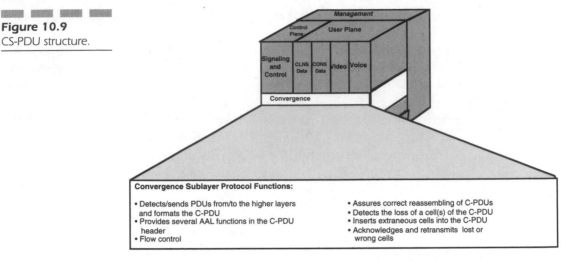

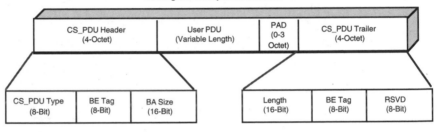

- AAL 4 or Type 4 connectionless data transfer
- AAL 5 or Type 5 high-speed data transfer

To obtain the different classes and services, each of these are classified based on three basic parameters:

- Time relationship between source and destination
- Bit rate
- Connection mode

10.3.3.1.1 *Time Relationship Between Source and Destination.* Some services have a time relationship between source and destination, and in others, no such time relationship exists. For instance, voice traffic requires a time relationship between source and destination. If a timing problem occurs, the information will not arrive in the same manner as transmitted. For example, say the information transmitted is "Good Morning." If there is no timing synchronization, the information can arrive as "Morning Good." For data traffic, the information could arrive out of sync with no harm done because no real-time delivery is required. The traffic is reassembled using the sequence number in each 3-PDU and can be delivered in the correct order to the end user. But the integrity of the PDU must be maintained.

10.3.3.1.2 Bit Rate.   Some services, such as conventional voice traffic, have a continuous bit rate and others, such as data traffic, have a variable bit rate. Of course, if the voice is packetized, it becomes a VBR type of traffic. Video traffic can be either CBR or VBR. In an ATM environment, it is preferred that video be VBR. With statistical multiplexing, real bandwidth savings can be achieved via sharing.

10.3.3.1.3 Connection Mode.   There are two types of connection modes: connection-oriented and connectionless. In services that are connection-oriented, a connection must be established before any information is transferred. Two examples are frame-relay and circuit emulation traffic. The connectionless modes require no prior connection to transfer information. In this service, each packet has the source and destination address so that it can be individually routed in the network. An example of such a service is SMDS. Thus, a service typically inherits each one of these characteristics and transfers them across the network.

10.3.3.2 Segmentation and Reassembly Sublayer.   The SAR at the transmitting side segments the incoming higher-layer PDUs into a suitable size so they can fit into the information field of the ATM cell (48 bytes). At the receiving side, the information from different cells is reassembled and passed on to the higher layer as PDUs in the original form. Simply stated, the segmentation process is like cutting a long string into 48-byte pieces for easy handling; reassembly is piecing the string back together. For example, the PDU size for frame relay is different from that of SMDS. Figure 10.10 shows the generic SAR-PDU and the functions of SAR.

10.4   Physical Layer of BISDN Protocol

Figure 10.11 shows a more detailed physical layer in the BISDN protocol than in Fig. 10.10.

Figure 10.10
SAR-PDU structure
and functions.

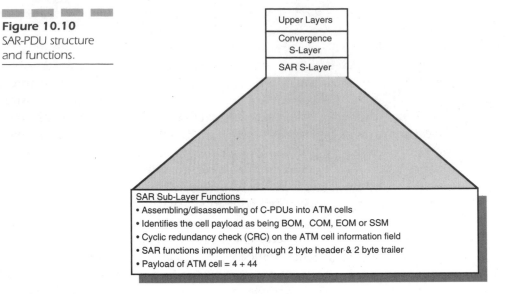

Figure 10.11
Physical layer of
broadband protocol.

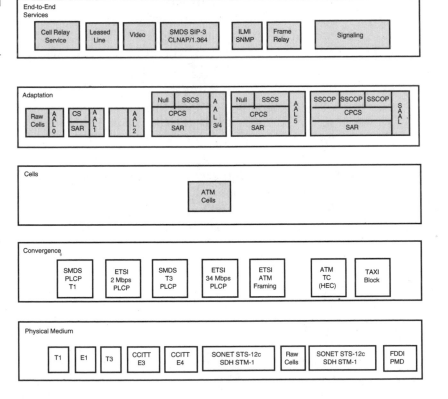

As mentioned earlier, the physical layer is subdivided into two layers: the physical medium sublayer and the transmission convergence sublayer. ITU-T has defined the physical medium as fiber optics. To accommodate existing physical media for smooth transitions, however, coaxial cables are included. Currently, ITU-T has defined the physical medium interface based on the SONET/SDA for fiber and PDH for coaxial. Using these physical media, ITU-T has defined the interface between customer (user) and the network, known as UNI. Recently, the ATM Forum provided the details of the UNI specification which, in some cases, is in addition to ITU-T specifications. Table 10.1 shows the UNI specifications addressed by ITU-T and ATM Forums.

The ATM Forum, a special interest group formed by manufacturers from computer and telecommunications industries, has been defined as an additional interface to accommodate and expedite the deployment of ATM in existing interfaces. Some of the potential physical medium interfaces shown in Fig. 10.11 are T1 (1.544 Mbps), E1 (2 Mbps), T3 (45 Mbps), E3 (34 Mbps), E4 (140 Mbps), SONET STS-3c/SDH STM-1 (155 Mbps), mapping of a raw ATM cell on any medium beginning (155 Mbps), SONET STS 12c/SDH STM-4 (622 Mbps), and FDDI PMD (100 Mbps).

Each of these physical medium types has a corresponding transmission convergence layer protocol to act as a translator for different physical media and speeds to the ATM layer. The ATM layer can only process ATM cells with a 48-bytes payload and 5-bytes header. The following transmission convergences have been defined to process the different specifications from the physical medium. The different protocols are

- SMDS PLCP T1
- ETSI PLCP E1
- SMDS PLCP T3
- ETSI PLCP E4

TABLE 10.1

Comparison of UNI Specifications Between ATM Forum and ITU-T

	ITU-T 1990	ATM Forum 1992
45 Mbps DS3	—*	x
STS1	—*	—†
155 Mbps or STS 3c	x	x
622 Mbps or STS 12c	x	—†

*Not an international standard.
†This rate was not chosen by the ATM Forum.

■ ETSI ATM framing

■ ATM TC (HEC)

■ TAXI block

Figure 10.12 shows the mapping of the PM protocol to the TC sublayer protocol. Of the different media protocols, ITU-T has defined three basic physical-layer interfaces for BISDN so far:

■ ATM cell-based interface

■ SDH/SONET-based interface

■ Digital interface

10.4.1 ATM Cell-Based Interface

In this interface, a continuous stream of ATM cells is transported without any regular framing. In this cell stream, special cells conveying OAM information concerning the physical layer itself are transmitted. These cells are identified by special header values. These special OAM cells are not delivered to the ATM layer; they have significance only at the physical layer. Table 10.2 shows the values that identify these cells.

These are preassigned values of the cell header (excluding the HEC octet). They perform functions such as monitoring, detecting, and trans-

Figure 10.12
Mapping of physical medium to transmission convergence in physical layer.

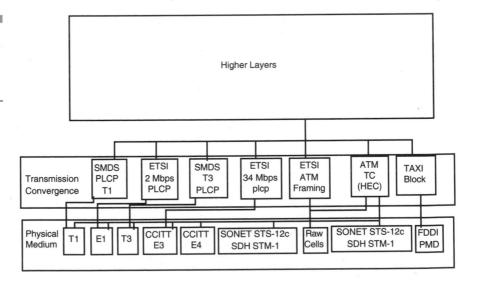

TABLE 10.2

Preassigned ATM Cell Values

	Octet 1	Octet 2	Octet 3	Octet 4
Reuse by physical layer	PPPP0000	0	0	0000PPP1
Unassigned cells	AAAA0000	0	0	0000AAA0
Physical layer OAM	0	0	0	00001001
Idle cells	0	0	0	00000001

Note: A—bit available for use by ATM layer. P—bit available for use by physical layer.

Figure 10.13
ATM cell stream.

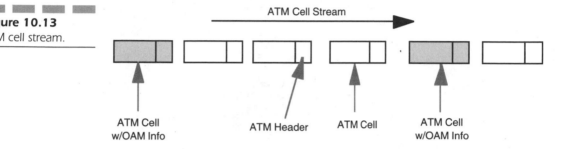

ATM Cell Stream

ATM Cell w/OAM Info   ATM Header   ATM Cell   ATM Cell w/OAM Info

mission errors reporting by calculating an error code over the block of cells between two subsequent physical layer OAM ATM cells. This error code is transmitted in the information field of the physical-layer OAM cells. Figure 10.13 shows the ATM cell stream with OAM cells. However, no external frame exists to carry the ATM cells.

10.4.2   Physical Layer for SONET/SDH Interface

Here, the ATM cells are carried in a SONET/SDH STS-3c frame as shown in Fig. 10.14. The cells are mapped into an STS-3 payload with a POH pointer indicating the beginning of the ATM cells. ATM cell bytes are aligned within a payload but can cross the STS-3 frame. The H4 pointer of the POH is the pointer that points to the beginning of a cell in the payload. At the receiving end, the pointer used to identify the beginning of the cell boundary can be optionally used to help the cell delineation based on the HEC mechanism. The OAM implementation is in accordance with SONET/SDH implementation. The OAM allows frame alignment, error monitoring and reporting, etc.

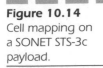

Figure 10.14
Cell mapping on
a SONET STS-3c
payload.

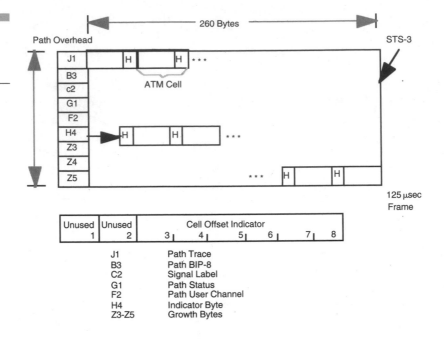

10.4.3 Digital Interface

This interface was proposed to accommodate the existing asynchronous digital transmission signal as part of the broadband interface to enable easy evolution to BISDN. Existing digital standards, such as DS1, DS3, E1, and E3, are used in this interface. The cells are directly mapped onto the digital signal using a function called the PLCP. Mapping is defined for asynchronous rates with frame on HEC (not PLCP) format. Figure 10.15 depicts the DS3 PLCP frame format.

  We mentioned earlier that five functions are performed by the transmission convergence sublayer. Here, we look into two important functions: header error control and cell delineation and scrambling.

10.4.4 Header Error Control

As the name indicates, the basic function of HEC is to reduce the number of errors that occur in the header. The HEC algorithm is implemented in such a way that this objective is achieved in two stages. Stage 1 detects errors. If the detected error is a single-bit error, the algorithm performs error correction. If a multiple-bit error is detected, the algorithm discards the cell. Figure 10.16 shows the basic operation of the HEC algorithm.

In normal (detection) mode, if the receiving side detects a single-bit error, it enters the correction mode. The error is corrected, and the state at the receiver switches back to detection mode. In the detection mode state, all cells detected with multiple-bit errors are discarded. Headers without errors are examined and forwarded to a higher layer. On the transmission

Figure 10.15
DS3 PLCP.

<1>	<1>	<1>	<1>	<53 Bytes>
A1	A2	P11	Z6	L2_PDU
A1	A2	P10	Z5	L2_PDU
A1	A2	P9	Z4	L2_PDU
A1	A2	P8	Z3	L2_PDU
A1	A2	P7	Z2	L2_PDU
A1	A2	P6	Z1	L2_PDU
A1	A2	P5	F1	L2_PDU
A1	A2	P4	B1	L2_PDU
A1	A2	P3	G1	L2_PDU
A1	A2	P2	M2	L2_PDU
A1	A2	P1	M1	L2_PDU
A1	A2	P0	C1	L2_PDU	Trailer: 13-14 Nibbles

A1, A2	Framing Bytes
P11-P0	Path Overhead Integrity
Z1-Z6	Growth Bytes
F1	PLCP Path User Channel
B1	BIP-8
G1	PLCP Path Status
M1,M2	SIP Level Counter
C1	Cycle/Stuff Counter
PLCP	Physical Layer Convergence Procedure

125 µs

Figure 10.16
HEC algorithm
operation.

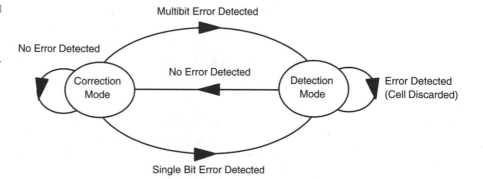

side, the HEC value is calculated using the polynomial generated by header bits (fields other than the HEC field), which are multiplied by 8 and divided by $x^8 + x^2 + x + 1$. The remainder of this calculation is transmitted as the 8-bit HEC field and verified at the receiving end to check the validity of the ATM cells. Figure 10.17 depicts the HEC flowchart.

10.4.5   Cell Delineation and Scrambling

Cell delineation is the process that allows cell boundaries to be identified. Identification is based on the correlation between the header bits to be protected and the relevant control bits. Figure 10.18 shows a state diagram of HEC- based cell delineation.

The cell delineation algorithm works as shown in Fig 10.18. When in hunt state, a bit-by-bit check of the assumed header field is performed. If a correct header is found, the algorithm goes to presync state and the HEC correlation check is performed cell by cell. If δ consecutive correct HECs are found, the algorithm goes to sync state. If not, the system goes to hunt state. The system leaves sync state only if α consecutive incorrect HECs are identified. The default values recommended by ITU-T for α and δ are 7 and 6, respectively.

With $\alpha = 7$, at 155 Mbps, the ATM HEC will be correct for more than a year with bit-error probability of about 10^4. With $\delta = 6$, the same system with the same bit-error probability will need about 10 cells, or 28 μs, to reenter sync after the loss of cell synchronization.

This cell delineation method could fail if the HEC correlation were imitated in the information field of ATM cells. In such cases, the information field contents are scrambled, using a self-synchronizing scrambler with the polynomial $X^{43} + 1$. The scrambler is on only in the presync and sync states and is disabled in the hunt state.

10.5   ATM Layer of the BISDN Protocol

The second layer of BISDN protocol is the ATM layer, as shown in Fig. 10.19. Five basic functions are performed in this layer. Table 10.3 summarizes the different functions and their corresponding parameters, which were explained in an earlier section.

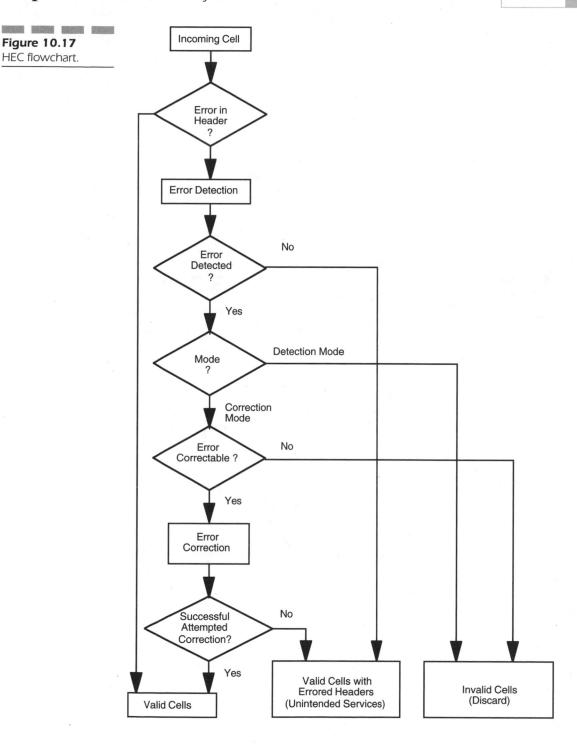

Figure 10.17
HEC flowchart.

Figure 10.18
Cell delineation state diagram.

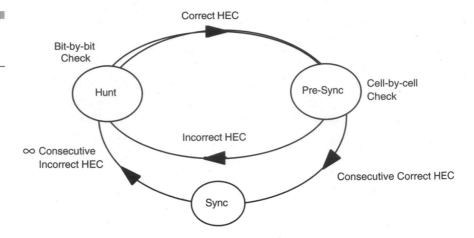

Figure 10.19
ATM layer of BISDN.

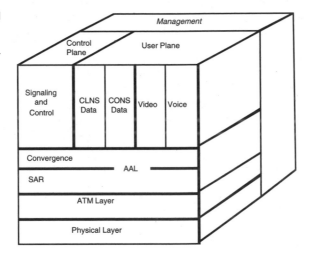

TABLE 10.3

Functions Supported at the UNI (U-Plane)

Functions	Parameters
Multiplexing among different ATM connections	VPI/VCI
Cell rate decoupling (unassigned cells)	Preassigned header field values
Cell discrimination based on predefined header field values	Preassigned header field values
Payload type discrimination	PT field
Loss priority indication and selective cell discarding	CLP field, network congestion state

The ATM layer provides certain services along with its functions. It provides for the transparent transfer of fixed-size ATM layer service data units (ATM-SDUs) between communicating upper-layer entities (e.g., AAL entities). This transfer occurs on a preestablished virtual ATM connection according to a traffic contract. A negotiated traffic contract consists of a QOS class, a vector of traffic parameters, a conformance definition, etc. Each ATM end point is expected to generate traffic that conforms to these parameters. We mentioned that transfer occurs on a preestablished virtual ATM connection; two levels of virtual connections exist through which transfer occurs.

Two levels of virtual connections can be supported at the ATM UNI:

■ A point-to-point or point-to-multipoint virtual channel connection (VCC), which consists of a single connection established between two ATM VCC end points.

■ A point-to-point or point-to-multipoint virtual path connection (VPC), which consists of a bundle of VCCs carried transparently between two ATM VPC end points.

Table 10.4 shows predefined header field values that are defined at UNI by the ATM Forum in their UNI specification working document. These values are used to discriminate the ATM cells based on the ATM header values so that processing can be done accordingly.

Within the ATM header exists the payload type indicator (PTI) field, which has certain predefined values. Table 10.5 shows the predefined cells based on PTI.

The ATM layer routes the cells based on the values of different fields in the header and PTI values. The basic function of the ATM layer from the protocol perspective, however, is in the transmitting direction. The ATM layer utilizes the information received from the higher layers and the management plane to generate the header with certain values and then appends the header to the user information field, which is received from the AAL layer. These cells subsequently are sent down to the physical layer for transmission. In the receiving direction, the cells received from the physical layer are disassembled to extract the header information and process it, while the payload is sent to the AAL layer. To take the cell from the higher layer at one end and deliver it to the higher layer at the other end, the ATM layer performs an ATM connection. An ATM connection is a transparent connection provided by the ATM layer to the higher layer. It is connected end-to-end through a concatenation of connection elements.

Use	Value[1,2,3,4]			
---	Octet 1	Octet 2	Octet 3	Octet 4
Unassigned cell indication	00000000	00000000	00000000	0000xxx0
Metasignaling (default)[5,7]	00000000	00000000	00000000	00010a0c
Metasignaling[6,7]	0000yyyy	yyyy0000	00000000	00010a0c
General broadcast signaling (default)[5]	00000000	00000000	00000000	00100aac
General broadcast signaling[6]	0000yyyy	yyyy0000	00000000	00100aac
Point-to-point signaling (default)[5]	00000000	00000000	00000000	01010aac
Invalid pattern	xxxx0000	00000000	00000000	0000xxx1
Point-to-point signaling[6]	0000yyyy	yyyy0000	0000000	001010aac
Segment OAMF4 flow cell[7]	0000aaaa	aaaa0000	00000000	00110a0a
End-to-end OAMF4 flow cell[7]	0000aaaa	aaaa0000	00000000	01000a0a

TABLE 10.4

Predefined Header Field Values

[1]"a" indicates that the bit is available for use by the appropriate ATM layer function.
[2]"x" indicates "don't care" bits.
[3]"y" indicates any VPI value other than 00000000.
[4]Indicates that the originating signaling entity sets the CLP bit to 0. The network may change the value of the CLP bit.
[5]Reserved for user signaling with the local exchange.
[6]Reserved for signaling with other signaling entities (e.g., other users or remote networks).
[7]The transmitting ATM entity sets bit 2 of octet 4 to 0. The receiving ATM entity ignores bit 2 of octet 4.
Source: ATM Forum, UNI Specification version 3.0.

10.5.1 ATM Layer Connections

Before we explain the ATM connection, we need to understand the basics of VPI and VCI. Figure 10.20 shows the relationship between a VPI and VCI. A physical path can be coaxial-based DS3 (44.76 Mbps) or fiber-based SONET OC3 (155 Mbps and above). Within this physical path a certain number of virtual paths could exist. The number of virtual paths depends on the number of bits allocated as the VP value in the cell header. Using the VPI value in the ATM cell header, each virtual path is identified. Usually, 12 bits are allocated for the VPI value at the user interface. Having explained the relationship between the physical path and the virtual path, let's look into the relationship between the virtual path and the virtual channel. Within a virtual path there are many virtual channels. The number of virtual channels per virtual path depends on the number of bits allocated to the VCI value in the ATM cell header. Usually, 16 bits are allocated for the VCI value. In an ATM network, the ATM cells are routed using the VP and VCI values in the header of each cell.

In the real ATM world, two types of ATM connections exist: VCC and VPC. A VC connection is a logical connection between two end points for the transfer of ATM cells, whereas VPC is a logical combination of VCCs. Each VCC is assigned a VCI value, and each VPC is assigned a VPI value. Within a VPC, VC links different from one another exist, and each is differentiated through the use of VCI. On the other hand, VCs belonging to different VPs can possess the same VCI as one used in another VPC. A VC can be completely identified solely on the basis of its corresponding VCI and VPI values. Thus, in an ATM environment, switching of cells is performed based on the VPI and VCI values. The mechanism of switching in an ATM node is explained in Part 4.

TABLE 10.5

Predefined Cells Based on PT Identifier

PTI Coding (MSB First)	Interpretation
000	User data cell, congestion not experienced, SDU-type=0
001	User data cell, congestion not experienced, SDU-type=1
010	User data cell, congestion experienced, SDU-type=0
011	User data cell, congestion experienced, SDU-type=1
100	Segment OAM F5 flow-related cell
101	End-to-end OAM F5 flow-related cell
110	Reserved for future traffic control and resource management
111	Reserved for future functions

Figure 10.20
VPI and VCI concepts.

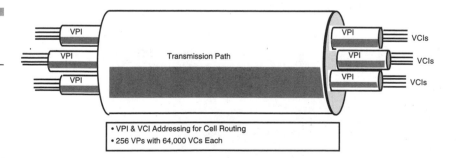

In an ATM network, if the VCI value is not modified but the VPI value is, that function is called a VP switch, ATM cross-connect, or ATM add-drop, and its equipment is called cross-connect equipment or a concentrator. If the function of the equipment is to alter both VPI and VCI values (incoming VPI/VCI values are mapped to outgoing VPI/VCI values), that equipment is called ATM switch or VC switch. Figure 10.21 shows the concept of VP and VC connections using VP and VC switches. The VP switch corresponds to the add-drop multiplexer and the VP/VC switch corresponds to a normal switching function.

VC or VP connections are defined based on the switching elements used. A VCC refers to a concatenation of VC lines for achieving connection between ATM service access points. In the VC link, the VCI is assigned, gets translated, or is removed. The VCC provided by the ATM switching element can be set up as a permanent or semipermanent connection. The integrity of the cell sequence is ensured within the same VCC. A VCC user is provided with a set of parameters, such as cell delay and cell loss rate, by the network. At the time of VCC setup, user traffic parameters are prescribed through negotiation between the user and the network, and the network monitors these parameters for the duration of the connection. At the user-network interface, four different methods can be used to establish the VCC:

1. The signaling procedure. In this connection, setup or release is achieved through a reservation. This method applies to permanent or semipermanent connections.

2. The metasignaling procedure. A signaling VC is established or removed through the use of metasignaling VC.

3. The user-network signaling procedure. A signaling VCC is used to establish or release a VCC for end-to-end communication.

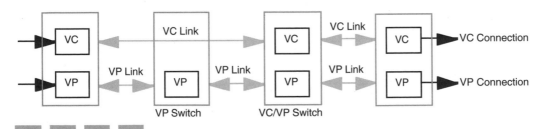

Figure 10.21
VC and VP connections.

Figure 10.22
Example of VCC.

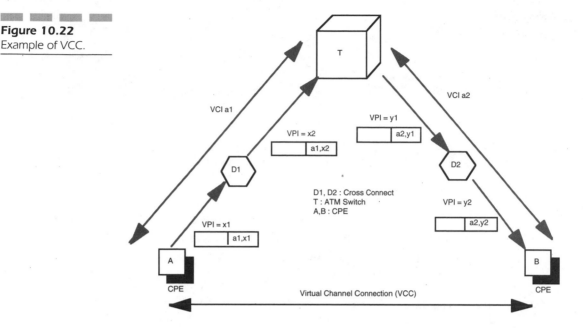

4. The user-to-user signaling procedure. A signaling VCC is used to establish or release a VCC internal to a VPC preestablished between two UNIs.

Once a VCC connection is established using any of these methods, ATM cells flow through the network. Each cell header is processed at the network element, such as the cross-connect and ATM switch, which translates the VPI and VCI values to reach their destination. Figure 10.22 shows a typical VCC connection and the location where the VPI and VCI values are translated. *A* and *B* are the CPE, D1 and D2 are the ATM cross-connects, where only the VPI values are translated, while the VCI values are preserved. *T* is the ATM switch that performs the translation of VPI and VCI values. Figure 10.22 clearly depicts the concept behind the VCC.

Figure 10.23 shows a blowup of *D*1 or *D*2 which is a VP switch, and Fig. 10.24 shows a blowup of the *T* which is a VC switching function. So far, we have addressed the VC connection and the network elements that participate in the completion of a VC connection. Another type of connection exists called a VP connection, or virtual path connection, or simply VPC.

This VPC refers to the concatenation of VP links for connecting the points at which a VPI is assigned, translated, or removed. A VPC was

Figure 10.23
VP switching.

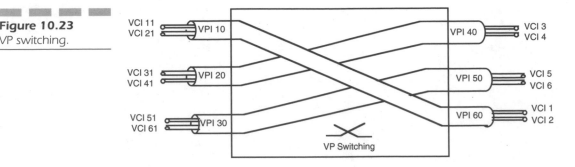

shown in Fig. 10.22. A VPC can be provided through switching equipment and can be permanent or semipermanent. Cell sequence is ensured for each VCC within the same VPC. A VPC between the VPC end points can be established or released in two possible ways:

1. Without a signaling procedure. The setup and release of a connection is achieved using a reservation.

2. By user or network control. VPIs are assigned in advance by the user or the network service provider.

These are the basic ways through which the ATM layer provides transparent transfer of cells between higher layers at either ends.

10.6 ATM Adaptation Layer of BISDN Protocol

Figure 10.25 shows the ATM adaptation layer of the BISDN protocol. As depicted in Fig. 10.25, four different classes of AAL exist, each with certain characteristics. Each class has different AAL functions, i.e., timing, bit-rate type, and connection mode. Each of these classes maps onto existing services so that they can be adapted to ATM-based broadband networks. In Sec. 10.2 we discussed the functions of AAL.

Certain changes in the AAL classes have occurred from the ones initially proposed by ITU-T. For example, a new AAL class has been included to address the need of high-speed data transfer. In this class, the overhead bytes for a packet are reduced compared to class 3/4. AAL 3 and 4 have also been merged together as a single class. A proposal has been put forth to eliminate class 2, which addresses packetized voice and video, but it has been postponed until other important issues are resolved.

Today's equipment manufacturers are thus developing equipment based on AAL classes 1, 3/4, and 5. In addition to these, a proposal exists for AAL 2 for mapping of MPEG 2 video signals into ATM. In this section, we address each of the AAL classes with regard to

- Characteristics
- Functions
- Services provided
- Protocol data unit structure
- Mapping of AAL1-PDU to ATM and physical layer

Figure 10.24
VC switching.

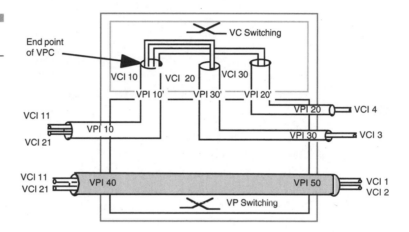

Figure 10.25
AAL layer classes.

	CBR Voice Class 1	VBR Video Class 2	CL (VBR) Data Class 3/4	CO (VBR) Data Class 5	
Service Specific Coordination Function (SSCF)	AAL1-SSP	AAL2-SSP	Null	SSCP Access Signaling | SSCP Network Signaling	Service Specific Convergence Sublayer
				SSCOP	Service Specific CO Sublayer
Convergence Part Sublayer (CS)	AAL1-CP	AAL2-CP	AAL 3/4-CS	Null	Common Part(CP) Convergence Sublayer
			AAL 3/4-SAR	AAL 5-CP	Segmentation and Reassembly (SAR) Sublayer

CBR	Constant Bit Rate
VBR	Variable Bit Rate
CL	Connectionless
CO	Connection Oriented
SSP	Service Specific Part
CP	Common Part
CS	Convergence Sublayer
SAR	Segmentation and Reassembly Sublayer

10.6.1   AAL 1 or Class 1

Services that have CBR use class 1, because it receives and delivers SDUs with constant bit rate from and to the layers above. Along with data, class 1 transfers certain characteristics of CBR, such as the timing information, between the source and destination. An indication of lost or errored information is sent to the higher layers if or when failures cannot be recovered. This section addresses the AAL 1 characteristics, services, SDU functions, and how the mapping is accomplished to the ATM and physical layer of the BISDN protocol.

Characteristics.   As mentioned previously, CBR type of services typically falls under class 1. The following are characteristics of this class:
- The traffic is called isochronous traffic, where blocks of data appear at known constant intervals, e.g., 193 bits every 125 μs for T1 or DS1.
- The traffic is very intolerant to any variation in delay.
- The traffic is intolerant of missequenced information.
- The traffic is very tolerant of compression.

Functions.   The functions provided by AAL for class 1 services are
- Segmentation and reassembly of user information
- Handling of cell delay variation
- Handling of lost and misinserted cells
- Source clock recovery
- Monitoring for bit errors and handling those errors
- Structure pointer generation and detection

Services provided.   This class of AAL provides constant bit-rate service that can be voice, video, or data. It takes incoming structured (bytes) or unstructured (bits) information and maps it into 48-byte payloads to be shipped to the lower layer.

Protocol data unit structure.   Figure 10.26 shows the format of the SAR-PDU for AAL class 1. Three fields exist, i.e., the SN (sequence number), SNP (sequence number protection), and SAR-PDU (segmentation and reassembly-protocol data unit). SN detects the loss or misinsertion of cells. SNP provides error detection, which is done by CRC process, and correction capabilities. The SAR-PDU carries the actual payload of the information to be transported.

Mapping of PDU to the ATM and physical layer.   Figure 10.27 shows a high-level view of how unstructured CBR DS1 traffic is mapped onto the ATM layer and then to the physical layer. In this example, the physical layer uses the SONET format for carrying the ATM cells.

Figure 10.26
AAL 1 SAR-PDU
structure.

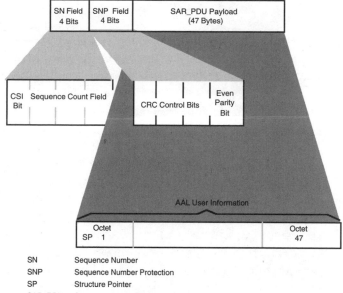

SN	Sequence Number
SNP	Sequence Number Protection
SP	Structure Pointer
SAR_PDU	Segmentation and Reassembly—Protocol Data Unit
CSI	Convergence Sublayer Indication
CRC	Cyclic Redundancy Check

Figure 10.27
Mapping of AAL1
PDU to physical layer.

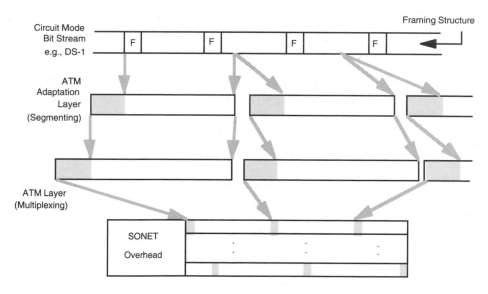

10.6.2   AAL 2 or Class 2

Class 2 addresses the same type of traffic—voice and video—but with different characteristics. Class 2 addresses variable bit-rate traffic, which is usually data. This type of traffic is not widely used, and the standards for this layer have not been well defined because converting voice traffic to variable bit-rate traffic has numerous problems. The obvious ones are sequencing the data and preserving the timing. These parameters are very critical for real-time voice traffic, but they are not critical to data. Converting voice to VBR needs additional processing by the upper layer. For example, the upper layer should sense silence during a voice conversation and suppress those data units and transmit only the ones with information. At the same time, the timing integrity between source and destination must be maintained. Thus, the standards body has decided to postpone working on this class of service because it will take a while to be used. There are other basic issues that also need to be defined.

Characteristics.   Characteristics of AAL class 2 service are the following:
- The traffic has burst characteristics from time to time.
- A time stamp for each packet is required so that it can be reassembled.
- The traffic is very intolerant of missequenced information.

Functions.   The following are the functions performed by AAL class 2 to enhance the services provided to the ATM layer:
- Segmentation and reassembly of user information
- Handling of cell delay variation
- Handling of lost and misinserted cells
- Recovery of source clock at the receiver
- Monitoring for bit error and handling of these errors
- Monitoring the user information field for bit errors and possible corrective actions

PDU structure.   Figure 10.28 shows the AAL 2 protocol structure. The structure consists of three fields: header, payload, and trailer. The information is carried in the payload. The SN in the PDU header detects lost or misinserted cells. The IT indicates the type of information being carried, such as BOM, COM, or EOM. In the PDU trailer, LI is used to indicate the number of CS-PDU bytes carried in the SAR-PDU payload field. The CRC protects the PDU against bit errors.

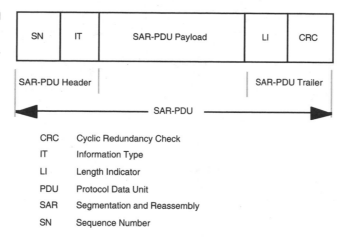

Figure 10.28
AAL 2 PDU structure.

CRC	Cyclic Redundancy Check
IT	Information Type
LI	Length Indicator
PDU	Protocol Data Unit
SAR	Segmentation and Reassembly
SN	Sequence Number

10.6.3   AAL 3/4 or Class 3/4

In this section we address AAL 3 and 4 as one service. The initial definition of BISDN was AAL 3 as connection-oriented and AAL 4 as connectionless. The new class is defined as a connectionless-based service, and
the services provided by AAL 3 are adopted by the new class called
AAL 5.

Characteristics.   The characteristics of class 3/4 are different from that of
the other classes. Most of them are an extrapolation of the characteristics of existing VBR traffic:

■ Burst of information with variable frame length
■ Delay that is not critical, as in case of class 1 or class 2 service such
as voice or video
■ Because delay is not critical, packets can be resequenced based on
the sequence number

Services provided.   Two models of services are defined for AAL 3/4 class:
message mode and streaming mode. Message mode is used for
framed data transfer, and streaming mode is suitable for the transfer
of low-speed data with low delay requirements.

PDU structure.   Figure 10.29 shows the AAL 3/4 PDU structure. This
PDU has three parts: SAR-PDU header, payload, and trailer. The header
consists of fields ST (segment type), SN (sequence number), and MID
(multiplexing identifier). The segment type consists of 2 bits and
indicates whether the packet is beginning, or continuing, the end of
the message with a 2-bit code. The next 4 bits are for the sequence

Figure 10.29
AAL 3/4 PDU
structure.

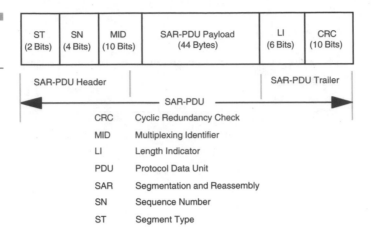

ST (2 Bits)	SN (4 Bits)	MID (10 Bits)	SAR-PDU Payload (44 Bytes)	LI (6 Bits)	CRC (10 Bits)

SAR-PDU Header | SAR-PDU Trailer

◄──────── SAR-PDU ────────►

CRC	Cyclic Redundancy Check
MID	Multiplexing Identifier
LI	Length Indicator
PDU	Protocol Data Unit
SAR	Segmentation and Reassembly
SN	Sequence Number
ST	Segment Type

number. The SN is incremented by one relative to the previous PDU belonging to the same source connection. The next 10 bits (MID field) are used to assist in the interleaving of ATM-SDUs from different CS-PDUs and reassembly of these CS-PDUs at the other end.

The second major field is the payload field, which consists of 44 bytes used for CS-PDU data. If this field is not fully filled, the remaining unused bits are coded as 0s. The third major segment is the trailer, and it consists of two fields: LI (length indicator) and CRC (cyclic redundancy check). The LI consists of 6 bits and contains the number of bytes from CS-PDU that are included in the PDU payload field. Its maximum value is 44. The CRC is a 10-bit field filled with the results obtained from a CRC calculation performed over the SAR-PDU header.

Mapping of PDU to the ATM and physical layers. Figure 10.30 shows the mapping of user data into the ATM and the physical layer of the BISDN protocol. It also shows how a user's data is segmented into 44 bytes of information in the AAL layer and mapped into the ATM layer of 48 bytes by the addition of 4 bytes, where 2 bytes are for the header and 2 bytes are for the trailer by the AAL layer.

10.6.4   AAL 5 or Class 5

Class 5 service was not part of the BISDN standards initially proposed. It was proposed by the computer and data processing vendors to the standards bodies in the United States in August 1991 for two major reasons:

- AAL 5 has a low overhead compared to AAL 3/4.
- A TCP/IP acknowledgment fits into a single cell with AAL 5, versus two cells in AAL 3/4.

This class is optimized for local usage. The AAL 5 class uses 48 bytes of information in the cell payload, which is achieved by removing the MID field and reassembling it based on VCI values only. The message type in this class is indicated based on the PT (payload type) field in the ATM cell header. They are as follows:

0X1: EOM

0X0: BOM or COM

Here, X is don't care, i.e., it can be 0 or 1.

The BOM is the first cell of a particular VPI/VCI value with a PT value 0X0, followed by cells with a PT value of 0X1. By using this technique, a tremendous performance improvement can be obtained. The receiving end simply has to queue the cells until it encounters the EOM message bit, which is the indication of the last cell. On receiving the last cell, the CRC and LI get checked and are passed on to the higher layers.

Figure 10.31 shows the PDU structure of AAL 5. The structure is similar to AAL 3/4 except that no MID field exists in the SAR-PDU structure. In the AAL 5 convergence layer, all cells except the last cell of the

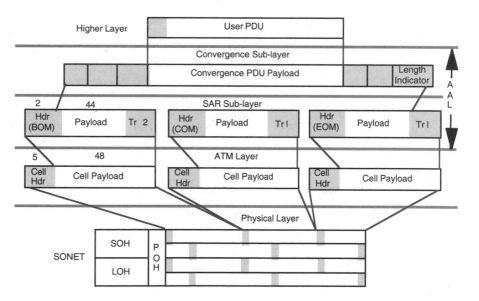

Figure 10.30
Mapping of user data in AAL 3/4.

Figure 10.31
AAL 5 PDU structure.

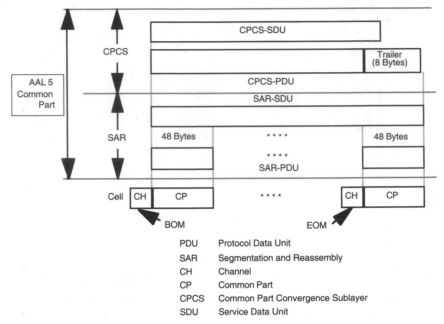

PDU	Protocol Data Unit
SAR	Segmentation and Reassembly
CH	Channel
CP	Common Part
CPCS	Common Part Convergence Sublayer
SDU	Service Data Unit

packet are completely filled with 48 bytes of data. The CS-SDU trailer has four fields: a 1-byte user-to-user indication (UU) field, a 1-byte common part indicator (CPI), a 2-byte field, and a 4-byte CRC field. The UU and CPI fields are currently unused and set to 0.

10.7   Summary

In this chapter, we addressed the lower layers of the BISDN protocol, i.e., the physical layer, ATM layer, and the ATM adaptation layer, along with their respective functions. Each layer of the BISDN has certain basic functions. The physical layer deals with transport of bits, the ATM layer deals with routing and switching of the ATM cells to the destination, and the AAL layer deals with the adaptation of different protocols, such as frame relay, SDMS, etc. The adaptation layer inherits the characteristics and function of the protocol, such as frame relay, SMDS, etc., so as to make it as transparent as possible to the user who has subscribed to that service. The AAL layer maps the information into the ATM payload so that the AAL layer at the destination can recover the information with the same characteristics with which it was transmitted.

CHAPTER 11

BISDN Higher Layers

11.1 Overview

In the previous chapter, we addressed the lower layers of the BISDN protocol reference model: the physical, ATM, and ATM adaptation layers. These lower layers provide the basic functions, such as transmission (transportation of cells), switching (routing of cells), and adaptation of the other protocol-based services, including frame relay, SMDS, etc.

In this chapter, we address the higher layers of the BISDN protocol. The higher layers are the management plane, user plane, and control or signaling plane. The functions of these layers are independent of the lower layers. These layers perform functions to provide the BISDN services and features to the end user. The BISDN protocol uses the existing higher layers, such as the SS7 network for signaling and IN for providing intelligence to the services, and, of course, adapting user protocols to the ATM-based BISDN protocol. This chapter discusses the functions and services provided to the user by these layers.

11.2 Management Plane

The management plane performs the management-related functions for the BISDN protocol. This plane is divided into two sublayers: plane management and layer management. Figure 11.1 shows the two management sublayers.

11.2.1 Plane Management

This layer performs the management functions related to the whole system. Its main task is to coordinate functions between all planes, including gathering the status of information on each plane and informing the other planes of that status.

11.2.2 Layer Management

The functions of this sublayer are categorized by how it affects each of the plane layers. Layer management performs the management functions relating to performance, operations, administration, resource management,

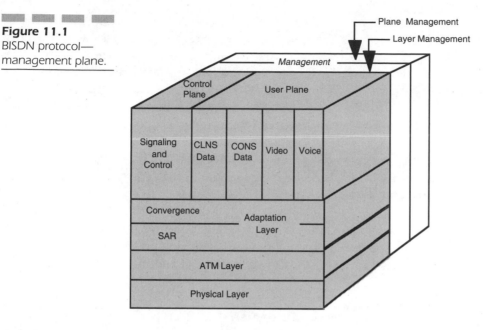

Figure 11.1
BISDN protocol—
management plane.

and parameters for each of the user plane layers. For each of the user plane layers, such as the physical layer, ATM layer, etc., layer management handles specific performance and operations, administration, and management functions. The initial view on OAM functions is provided in ITU-T recommendation I.610. In this recommendation, ITU-T defined the basic OAM principle, which is based on controlled maintenance. The OAM provides status, testing, and performance monitoring information for different protocols to prevent errors.

To obtain an optimal functionality with OAM, the following functions have been defined by ITU-T:

- Performance monitoring
- Defect and failure detection
- System protection
- Performance information
- Fault localization

Each function is described in the following subsections.

11.2.2.1 Performance Monitoring. In normal operation, performance monitoring continuously checks or periodically controls functions to guarantee that maintenance information is provided. The performance information obtained by the relevant performance monitoring mechanisms is transported via cells to the applicable OAM entities, which use this information for long-term system evaluation, short-term service quality control, or to initiate preventive actions, if necessary.

11.2.2.2 Defect and Failure Detection. By continuous or periodic checking of the functions, failures can be detected or made known. If a failure is detected, the necessary actions can be initiated to localize the failure, such as disconnecting the failed equipment from other equipment in the network.

11.2.2.3 System Protection. If a failure is detected, the failed entity is excluded from operation, thereby minimizing the effect of the failure on the whole system. This process protects the rest of the system from failure.

11.2.2.4 Performance Information. If an entity fails, other management entities are informed in a timely manner on the status of the entity. Status information is also exchanged with other entities. This status information about the failed entity is used by the system in the protection phase so that the system can exclude failing entities. The information is also used by neighboring entities to ensure that a failure message is spread over the entire network. These entities can then update their routing table so as to avoid the failed entity.

11.2.2.5 Fault Localization. Internal or external test devices determine the exact location of the failed entity. When the faults are identified exactly, the system enters into the protection phase, where the failing entities are excluded.

To identify the fault exactly, ITU-T has defined five physical hierarchical OAM levels, and an associated information flow exists in the layer management sublayer with each of these levels. These five levels are illustrated in Fig. 11.2. In Fig. 11.2 two levels are defined in the ATM layer: virtual channel level, identified by F5, and virtual path level, identified by F4. The other three levels are in the physical layer. The transmission path level is identified by F3, the digital section level by F2, and the regenerator section level by F1. These levels are not present in all parts of the network. In case of a fault condition, the relevant OAM functions are performed on a higher level. These levels are described in the following subsections.

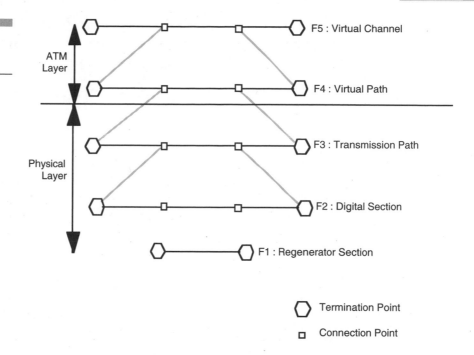

Figure 11.2
OAM hierarchical levels.

11.2.2.5.1 Virtual Channel (F5). Both end points perform virtual channel identifier termination functions for a broadband connection. Such a connection comprises several virtual paths. The OAM functions are performed on a VCI level and might provide input to any of the five OAM categories mentioned previously. For example, it is possible to conduct performance monitoring on a VCI level using the PTI bits on the ATM cell header. Performance monitoring occurs at the ATM layer in the BISDN protocol.

11.2.2.5.2 Virtual Path (F4). Both end points perform virtual path identifier termination functions for a broadband connection. Such a connection comprises several physical transmission paths. Again, one of the five OAM categories might be involved in the virtual path maintenance. This virtual path maintenance is performed at the ATM layer in BISDN protocol.

11.2.2.5.3 Transmission Path (F3). Both end points perform the assembly/disassembly of the ATM payload and the OAM-related functions of a transmission system. Because cells must be recognized at a transmission path to extract OAM cells, cell delineation and HEC functions are required at the termination point of each transmission path. A transmission path consists of several digital sections. Assembly/disassembly is performed at the physical layer of the BISDN protocol.

11.2.2.5.4   Digital Section (F2).   Both end points are section termination points. Every digital section comprises a maintenance entity, capable of transporting OAM information between adjacent digital sections. This function is performed at the physical layer of the BISDN protocol.

11.2.2.5.5   Regenerator Section (F1).   This is the smallest recognizable physical entity for OAM and is located between repeaters. The mechanism provides OAM functions, and the information flows associated with it depend on the respective OAM layer.

11.2.3   Physical-Layer Mechanisms

At the physical layer, the OAM information flow of F1, F2, and F3 depends on the type of transmission system. In plesiochronous transmission systems (G.702, G.703), the bit-error rate per section is monitored via CRC by counting the number of code violations. In SONET/SDH, special bytes in the SOH and POH transport error measurement codes such as BIP-8 (bit interleaved parity). In a cell-based transmission system, OAM is performed by special OAM cells called *PLOAM* (physical-layer OAM) cells. These cells are valid only on the physical layer and are not passed to the ATM layer. The OAM information is transferred in different ways based on the physical transmission systems defined.

11.2.4   ATM Layer Mechanisms

At the ATM layer, the OAM information flows of F4 and F5 have dedicated cells used to perform virtual channel and virtual path maintenance. These cells can also be used to transport OAM information. Here, the payload type indicator bits can be used to identify the OAM cells.

11.2.5   OAM of the Physical Layer

Let's look into some examples of OAM flow in the physical layer. To achieve end-to-end OAM information flow, different sections of the physical layer must be maintained separately. A possible physical configuration of the network is shown in Fig. 11.3.

We see that the F1 flow is terminated by LTs (line terminations) and a regenerator, whereas F2 is terminated solely by LTs. The F3 flow requires the recognition of ATM cell streams.

In each of the OAM information flows, different errors can be recognized and assigned to one of the three levels described. For example, in SONET/SDH-based transmission systems, the OAM information flow identified for each of the different levels is as follows.

For F1, F2:

▨ *Loss of frame.* In SONET/SDH, frame synchronization is lost.

▨ *Degraded error performance.* The quality of the received bit stream is not at an acceptable level, i.e., too many bits are in error, which could be caused by a bad transmission system, an out-of-sync clock, etc.

For F3:

▨ *Loss of cell delineation.* The cell delineation algorithm is no longer in the SYNC state (see Fig. 10.19), i.e., the algorithm cannot identify the beginning of the cells.

▨ *Uncorrectable header.* The header has more errors than can be corrected (i.e., multiple bit errors). This error is detected using the HEC mechanism.

Figure 11.3
Example of a physical configuration and OAM flows at the physical and ATM layers.

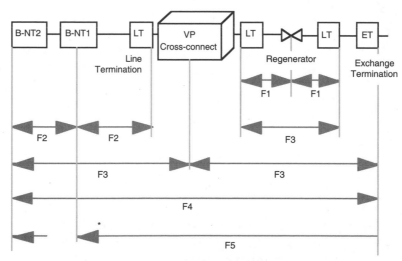

Note: * Termination of F5 at the B-NT1 is for further study

- *Degraded header error performance.* There are too many header bit errors. This information can be detected by the HEC mechanism.

- *Loss of H4 pointer.* The H4 pointer of the SONET/SDH is not identified, resulting in an unrecognizable SONET payload.

- *Degraded error performance.* The grade of service is no longer acceptable. This performance level is measured by inserting special OAM cells or by calculating a BIP-8 over the preceding cells, or by using a special pattern in the information fields of the unassigned cells.

- *Failure of insertion and suppression of idle cells.* If too many idle cells arrive, no useful information can be transported.

If a cell-based transmission system is used, the errors detected could be similar to ones in a SONET/SDH-based transmission system. The errors detected in a cell-based transmission system are as follows:
    For F1, F2:

- *Loss of PLOAM cell recognition.* This error occurs when the receiver does not recognize PLOAM cells. Thus, no performance monitoring can be done or provided.

    For F2:

- *Degraded error performance.* This error is the same as for a SONET/SDH-based transmission system.

    For F3:

- Loss of cell delineation
- Uncorrectable header
- Degraded header error performance
- Failure of insertion and suppression of idle cells

The description for all the F3 errors is the same as for the SONET/SDH-based transmission system.

11.2.6 OAM of the ATM Layer

An example of the physical termination points of the ATM layer OAM flows was shown in Fig. 11.3. In Fig. 11.3, an end-to-end virtual path and virtual channel is maintained with the F4 and F5 information flows.

Two possible failures are identified by ITU-T in the ATM layer. For F4:

■ *Path not available.* In this case, the virtual path cannot be established and requires a system protection action to prevent it from setting up a virtual path. This situation can occur if the required bandwidth is not available (end-to-end) or if the number of virtual path connections is exceeded.

For F4, F5:

■ *Degraded Performance.* The ATM cells arriving at the VCI/VPI processing nodes (switching nodes) do not meet performance requirements. This degraded performance can be caused by cell loss, cell insertion, too high a bit-error rate in the information field, etc.

ITU-T Recommendation I.610 is only the first document on the maintenance principles of an ATM network. Further work on this subject is continuing.

11.3 User Plane

The higher layers of the user plane contain all the service-specific protocols necessary for the completion of end-to-end communications. The higher-layer protocols should be independent of the protocols used at the underlying layers. The nonshaded portion of Fig. 11.4 shows the different services on top of the BISDN protocol layers. These services have a protocol independent of the protocol used by the BISDN layers. In fact, the higher-layer service-specific protocols can provide services regardless of the lower-layer protocol.

These services typically form end-to-end communications with the BISDN protocol in the network portion. Some of these protocols are addressed in Part 2 of this book (FDDI, DQDB, frame relay, ATM, and SMDS). These protocols have functions duplicated by the BISDN protocol layers. Thus, in many cases, some of the protocols' functions are unnecessary. In the long run, if protocols similar to the one used in BISDN, such as ATM, are used for end-to-end communications, the duplicated functions can be eliminated. This increased efficiency will, in turn, enhance the performance of the network.

Figure 11.4
BISDN user plane
higher layers.

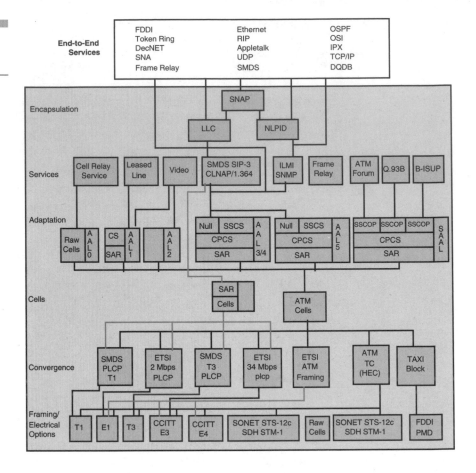

Figure 11.4
BISDN user plane
higher layers.

11.4   Control or Signaling Plane

The control plane of the higher layers provides signaling message transport and connection/call control capabilities. Signaling specifications (ATM UNI signaling protocol for SVC) are completely defined by ITU-T approved in their SG11 meeting in September 1994. Current commercial ATM implementation is based on permanent virtual circuit, which is an operator-assisted connection setup. For the customer to receive more flexible services, such as bandwidth on demand, SVCs are required, which calls for the implementation of the signaling protocols. There are two BISDN signaling specifications—Q2931 (formerly known as Q.93B) and B-ISUP (Q.2761). The standards bodies plan to implement the signaling requirements in two phases or releases. Phase 1 is short term and Phase 2 is to address the long-term requirements.

The ATM Forum in its June 1993 working document, "ATM User-Network Interface Specification Version 2.2," defined the Phase 1 requirement for signaling.

In this section, we address only Phase 1 of the signaling requirements definition and the features provided as part of Phase 1. As far as Phase 2 is concerned, nothing has yet been proposed. We can speculate on the type of signaling that might be defined for the long term, which is in addition to the Phase 1 signaling requirements.

Figure 11.5 shows the protocols required to support signaling in the BISDN protocol. Before we detail the signaling phases, we must understand the need for signaling to provide SVC service, which is simply an automatic call setup, and, at a high level, similar to the regular voice-based phone conversation.

We can now define the procedures for dynamically establishing, maintaining, and clearing ATM connections at the user-network interface. The procedures are defined in terms of messages, and the information elements are used to characterize the ATM connection and ensure interoperability. This implementation agreement is based on a subset of the broadband signaling protocol standards (formerly known as Q93B; now Q.2931). Additions to these Q.2931 specifications have been made wherever necessary to support capabilities identified by the ATM Forum for early deployment and interoperability of ATM equipment.

Figure 11.5
BISDN layers required for providing switched services.

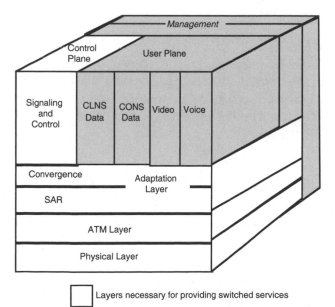

Layers necessary for providing switched services

The primary areas where the standard has been supplemented are to support point-to-multipoint connections, additional traffic descriptors, and private network addressing issues.

The procedures proposed by the ATM Forum in its signaling implementation agreement apply to the interface between the terminal or end-point equipment and a public network, referred to as public UNI, and terminal or end-point equipment connected to a private network, referred to as private UNI. Note that the term "Phase 1" or "Release 1" refers to the protocol as described in this section.

11.4.1   Reference Configuration

Before we go further, we need to understand the reference configuration. The protocol specified as part of the ATM Forum is valid for the private and public UNI as defined in Fig. 11.6. For this UNI, the protocol must be symmetrical, i.e., it must also apply to the interface in the configuration on both ends of the ATM network or even end-to-end. The purpose of a reference configuration for the UNI signaling specification is to list all the elements of an ATM network and the links between them to which this signaling specification applies.

Network elements in this context are

- End-point equipment
- Private ATM network
- Public ATM network

For the purposes of this section, let's assume a network, public or private, consists of one or more ATM switching platforms under the same administration. The possible reference configuration is illustrated in Fig. 11.6. The references to public UNI and private UNI refer to Phase 1 of signaling.

11.4.2   Phase 1 Signaling Capabilities

In this section, we mention the signaling capabilities defined in Phase 1 at a high level. The basic capabilities supported by the Phase 1 signaling release are:

- Switched connections
- Point-to-point and point-to-multipoint switched connections

Figure 11.6
Reference con-
figurations.

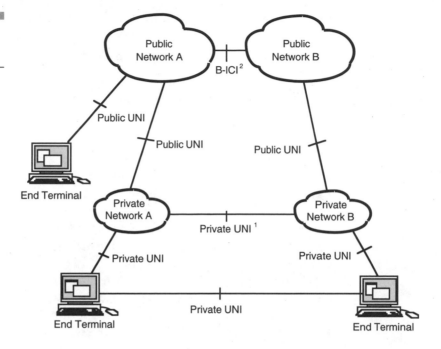

[1] Private ATM networks can be connected using the private UNI signaling. Features specific to private network interworking, however, are not a requirement for Phase 1 of the protocol. In releases after Phase 1, such internetworking features can be implemented in a private network-to-network interface (NNI) specification.

[2] The connection between public networks is outside the domain of the UNI specification. It is addressed by the B-ICI (Broadband Intercarrier Interface) specification of the ATM Forum.

- Connections with symmetric or asymmetric bandwidth requirements
- Single-connection (point-to-point or point-to-multipoint) calls
- Basic signaling functions via protocol messages, information elements, and procedures
- Class A (AAL 1), class C (AAL 3/4), and class D (AAL 5) ATM transport services
- Request and indication of signaling parameters
- VPI/VCI assignment
- A single, permanently defined out-of-band channel for all signaling messages
- Error recovery

- Public and private UNI addressing formats for unique identification of ATM end points
- A client registration mechanism for exchange of addressing information across a UNI
- Multicast service addresses
- End-to-end compatibility parameter identification

Each are described in the following subsections.

11.4.2.1 Switched Connection. The purpose of this specification is to support switched connections. The switched connections are established in real time using certain signaling procedures. These on-demand connections can remain active for a certain amount of time but are not automatically reestablished after a network failure. In contrast, permanent connections are those set up and torn down via provisioning by the service provider. These connections remain established for long periods of time and are automatically reestablished in the event of network failure. The reestablishment is usually done by the service provider. Phase 1 of the signaling deals only with switched connections.

11.4.2.2 Point-to-Point and Point-to-Multipoint Switched Connection. A point-to-point connection is a collection of associated ATM VC or VP links that connect two end points (see Fig. 10.25). The Phase 1 signaling supports point-to-point connections.

The point-to-multipoint connection is defined as a connection that is a collection of related ATM VC or VP links with associated end-point nodes. For ease of understanding, the following properties are assumed:

- One ATM link, called the *parent link,* serves as the parent in a simple tree topology. This parent node originates the call. When the parent node sends information, all the remaining nodes requesting a connection, called *child nodes,* receive copies of the information.
- In Phase 1, only zero-return bandwidth (i.e., from the child to the parent) is supported.
- In this connection type, the child nodes cannot communicate directly with each other. The only way two child nodes can communicate is by going through the parent's connections.
- A distributed implementation can be used to connect leaves to the tree. For example, each child node can act as a parent node

and make connection to other nodes, which then become the child nodes.

A typical point-to-multipoint connection setup is achieved by first establishing a point-to-point connection between the parent node and one child node. After this setup is complete, additional child nodes can be added to the connection by "add party" requests by the parent node. In addition, the Phase 1 signaling specified by the ATM Forum supports the ability of the parent node to have multiple add party requests pending at one time (i.e., the parent node does not have to wait for a response from one add party request before issuing the next). The add party response identifies the child that was added (or that failed to get added) so that responses can be paired with requests. Note that the parent node could choose to add child nodes serially, i.e., the parent could wait for each add party to be completed before issuing the next, even though the network allows child nodes to be added in parallel.

A child node can be added or dropped from a point-to-multipoint connection at any time after establishing the connection. A new child node can be added to an existing connection via the parent node issuing an add party request. A child node can be dropped from a connection as a result of a request sent by either the parent node or by the child node to be dropped (but not by another child).

This point-to-multipoint connection is different from a multipoint-to-multipoint connection, where every node can communicate with every other node in the call or group. Multipoint-to-multipoint connections are not supported in Phase 1 signaling. Multipoint-to-multipoint connections can be achieved using point-to-multipoint connections in the following ways:

- Each node in a group that wishes to communicate can establish a point-to-multipoint connection to all the other nodes in the group. For example, a group of N nodes requires N point-to-multipoint connections.

- Each node in the group that wishes to communicate can establish a point-to-point connection to a multicast server. The multicast server is the parent node in a point-to-multipoint connection to each node in the group. Any information sent by a node in the group to the multicast server is transmitted back from the multicast server through the point-to-multipoint connection to each of the nodes in the group. For a group of N nodes, this requires N point-to-point connections and one point-to-multipoint connection.

11.4.2.3 Connections with Symmetric or Asymmetric Bandwidth. Point-to-point, bidirectional connections usually have the same bandwidth in both directions, but the specifications allow bandwidth to be specified independent of the other direction. Forward and backward directions can have different bandwidths. The forward direction is from the calling party to the called party, while the backward direction is from the called party to the calling party.

For point-to-multipoint connections, the Phase 1 signaling specification supports only nonzero (identical) bandwidth in the forward direction from the parent node to each child node, and zero bandwidth in the reverse direction from each child node to the parent node.

11.4.2.4 Single Connection per Call. Here, one and only one connection per call is supported. The single connection can be either a point-to-point or point-to-multipoint connection.

11.4.2.5 Protocol that Supports Basic Signaling Functions. The signaling protocol that supports the basic signaling functions at the UNI interface are

- Call setup
- Call request
- Call answer
- Call clearing
- Reason for clearing
- Out-of-band signaling

Each is discussed in the following subsections.

11.4.2.5.1 Call Setup. This protocol supports the establishment of a connection or call between different parties. The call establishment includes call request and call answer.

11.4.2.5.2 Call Request. The function of the call request protocol is to allow an originating party to request the establishment of a call to a certain destination. In this request, the originating party might provide information related to the call. The request might contain information, such as destination number, bandwidth required, etc.

11.4.2.5.3 Call Answer. The function of the call answer protocol is to allow the destination party to respond to an incoming call request. In other words, it is an acknowledgment. The destination party can include information related to the call. (Rejection of the call request is considered part of the call-clearing function.)

11.4.2.5.4 Call Clearing. The function of the call-clearing protocol is to allow any party involved in a call to initiate its removal from an already-established call. If the call is between two parties only, the whole call is removed. This function also allows a destination party to reject its inclusion in a connection or call.

11.4.2.5.5 Reason for Clearing. The function of this protocol is to allow the clearing party to indicate the cause for initiating its removal from a connection or call.

11.4.2.5.6 Out-of-band Signaling. The function of this protocol is to specify that call-control information uses a channel different from the channels used for exchanging data information between the end parties for carrying control information (i.e., a specific VPI/VCI value is used for the call control signaling channel—SS7).

11.4.2.6 Class A, Class C, and Class D ATM Transport Services. These three classes relate to AAL 1, AAL 3/4, and AAL 5 basic services, respectively. Each is described in the subsections following.

11.4.2.6.1 Class A (AAL 1) ATM Transport Service. Class A service is a connection-oriented, constant-bit-rate ATM transport service. Class A service has certain characteristics, such as end-to-end timing requirements, that might require stringent cell loss, cell delay, and cell delay variation performance. The user chooses the desired bandwidth and the appropriate quality-of-service during the setup procedure to establish a class A connection (e.g., voice traffic).

11.4.2.6.2 Class C (AAL 3/4) ATM Transport Service. Class C service is a connection-oriented, variable-bit-rate ATM transport service. Class C service has no end-to-end timing requirements. The user chooses the desired bandwidth and QOS with appropriate information during the setup procedure to establish a class C connection (e.g., frame-relay type connection).

11.4.2.6.3 Class D (AAL 5) ATM Transport Service. Class D service is a connection-oriented ATM transport service where the AAL, traffic type (VBR or CBR), and timing requirements are user-defined (i.e., transparent to the network). Class D service is also known as AAL 5 service. The user chooses only the desired bandwidth and QOS with appropriate information during the setup procedure to establish a Class D connection (e.g., SMDS type traffic).

Thus, Phase 1 signaling specifications support class A, C, and D services. Class D service is not directly supported by signaling. It can be supported via a class D or class C connection to a connectionless server, however.

11.4.2.7 Request and Indication of Signaling Parameters. The Phase 1 signaling specification does not provide support for the negotiation of signaling parameters (e.g., QOS, cell-transfer rate, end-to-end compatibility parameter values). Instead, the sender chooses a value for each parameter to be sent during the connection setup request, and the receiver indicates whether or not the chosen values can be accommodated.

11.4.2.8 VPI/VCI Support. The Phase 1 signaling specification supports the virtual path connection identifier (VPCI) to identify the virtual path across the UNI, with the restriction that a one-to-one mapping exists between VPCI and VPI, and hence values beyond 8 bits are restricted.

The following list describes the Phase 1 signaling capabilities with respect to VPIs, VPCIs, and VCIs.

1. It provides for the identification of virtual paths (using VPCIs) and virtual connections within virtual paths (using VCIs).

2. It does not (in Phase 1) include negotiations of VPCIs or VCIs but does not preclude negotiation in future releases.

3. It does not (in Phase 1) include provisions to negotiate or modify allowed ranges for VPCIs or VCIs within virtual paths but does not preclude this in future releases. (Negotiation or provisioning of VPCI/VCI ranges is outside the scope of the signaling protocol for Phase 1.)

11.4.2.9 Support of a Single Signaling Virtual Channel. For single point-to-point signaling virtual channels, VCI of 5 and VPCI of 0 are used for all signaling in Phase 1. The association between signaling entities should be permanently established. Metasignaling is not supported in Phase 1. Broadcast signaling using a virtual channel is also not supported either.

11.4.2.10 Error Recovery. The error recovery capabilities of Phase 1 signaling are

■ *Detailed error-handling procedures.* One such signaling entity informs its peer when it has encountered a nonfatal error (i.e., insufficiently severe to force call clearing). Examples of nonfatal errors are message format errors, message content errors, and procedural errors (messages or message contents received in a state other than what is expected).

■ Procedures for recovery from signaling AAL reset and failure (and, by extension, from physical layer outages and glitches).

■ Mechanisms for signaling entities to exchange status information for calls and interfaces and to recover gracefully if a disagreement occurs. These procedures must operate in error conditions by requesting a signaling entity (i.e., status enquiry).

■ Capability to force calls, VCCs, and interfaces to be disconnected, either by manual intervention or due to severe error(s).

■ Cause and diagnostic information for fault resolution provided with call clearing, nonfatal errors, and recovery from errors affecting the whole interface.

■ Mechanisms to recover from loss of individual messages (e.g., timers and associated procedures).

11.4.2.11 Public and Private UNI ATM Addressing. Phase 1 signaling supports a number of ATM address formats to be used across the public and private UNIs to unambiguously identify the end points in an ATM connection.

11.4.2.12 Client Registration Mechanism. Phase 1 signaling supports a mechanism for the exchange of identifier and address information between an end system and a switch across a UNI. The basic capability allows a network administrator to manually configure ATM network address information into a switch port, without having to configure that information into any terminal later attached to that port. Instead, the terminal uses the client registration mechanism to exchange its identifier information for the ATM address information configured in the switch port. The client registration mechanism allows this exchange to take place, for example, whenever the terminal is initialized, reinitialized, or reset.

At the conclusion of the client registration exchange, the terminal has automatically acquired the ATM network address as configured by the network provider, without any requirement for the same address to have been manually provided to the terminal. The terminal can then use and transfer its network address as needed by higher-level protocols and applications. This function is similar to the client-server mechanism used in LAN equivalents, such as FDDI, where each station connected to the network can be identified with a unique address.

11.4.2.13 Multicast Service Addresses. The addressing format contains a field called an *end system identifier* (ESI) to satisfy the following requirements related to multicasting:

- The addressing schemes allow for multicast service addresses to be distinguishable. For example, when an IEEE 48-bit media access control address is used as an ESI value, a multicast address is distinguished by a 1 in the multicast bit of the address.

- An ATM end point can have multiple multicast service addresses (e.g., when multicast is supported on top of the network by a multicast server, the server can have a separate multicast service address for each multicast address it supports plus its own nonmulticast address).

- The significance of a multicast service address can be restricted to an administrative domain or it can be global.

- Multicast service addresses can be carried within the called party identifier in a point-to-point connection to a multicast service, and within the calling party identifier in a point-to-multipoint connection originated by a multicast service.

11.4.2.14 End-to-End Compatibility Parameter Identification. On a per-connection basis, the following end-to-end compatibility parameters can be specified:

- AAL type (e.g., type 1, 3/4, or 5)
- Method of protocol multiplexing (e.g., LLC versus VC)
- For VC-based multiplexing, the protocol that is encapsulated (e.g., any of the list of known routed protocols or bridged protocols)
- Protocols above the network layer

11.4.2.15 Example of ATM Signaling for Point-to-Point Connection. Now that we have addressed different capabilities of signaling in Phase 1, let's address some of the features of Phase 1 signaling and explain how some of these capabilities operate. Of all the capabilities, the most important are point-to-point and point-to-multipoint connections, and both types are addressed. Figure 11.7 shows a basic ATM network signaling for setting up point-to-point connections.

ATM signaling is based on the existing SS7 protocol used in today's narrowband ISDN. Because the signaling is based on an existing signaling protocol, no new messages are required or created. In this protocol, however, the B-ISUP (Q2761) (similar to ISUP for ISDN) messages are carried as cells in the signaling VC between the ATM switches. The same message is carried as frames between the STPs and non-ATM switches, as shown in Fig. 11.8.

The point-to-point signaling is carried on VC=5 and VP=0. The protocol used for access and network signaling is based on Q2931.

11.4.2.16 Example of ATM Signaling in Point-to-Multipoint Connections. The signaling for point-to-multipoint connections is based on setting up multiple point-to-point connections. In this type of connection, each virtual path has a separate signaling channel (VC=1). The signaling is used to establish, monitor/maintain, and tear down signaling VCs. This signaling channel is also used to carry the service profile information between the end points. Figures 11.9, 11.10, and 11.11 show

Figure 11.7
ATM signaling in point-to-point mode.

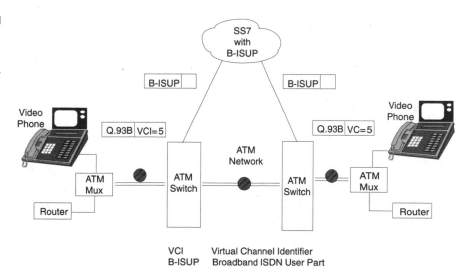

Figure 11.8
ATM signaling in SS7
network architecture.

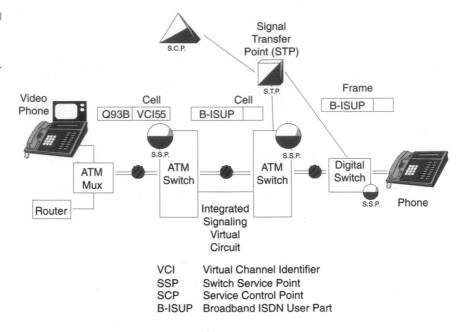

VCI   Virtual Channel Identifier
SSP   Switch Service Point
SCP   Service Control Point
B-ISUP   Broadband ISDN User Part

Figure 11.9
ATM signaling in
point-to-multipoint
(connection request).

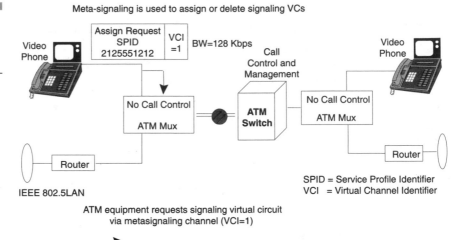

the different stages in setting up a point-to-multipoint connection: connection request, acknowledgment, and connection setup.

In Fig. 11.9 (connection request), the ATM CPE equipment requests the signaling VC using signaling channel VC=1 and VP=0. The information such as the bandwidth requirement and service profile identifier

(SPID) is carried within the cell to the ATM switch via the ATM mux, where the actual call control or connection setup occurs.

Once the cell with the information is received by the ATM switch, the switch performs call control and forwards the cell to the appropriate child node. Upon receiving the cell, the child node sends an acknowledgment with information on the channels to be used. This process is repeated for every child node in the parent's list, as explained earlier. Figure 11.10 shows an answer or acknowledgment with the cell carrying the appropriate VC higher-bandwidth value.

Once the CPE equipment receives the appropriate channel for the transmission of information, the setup acknowledgment is sent on the appropriate channel (VC number), which is followed by the actual information transfer as shown in Fig. 11.11.

Figure 11.10
ATM signaling in
point-to-multipoint
(acknowledgment).

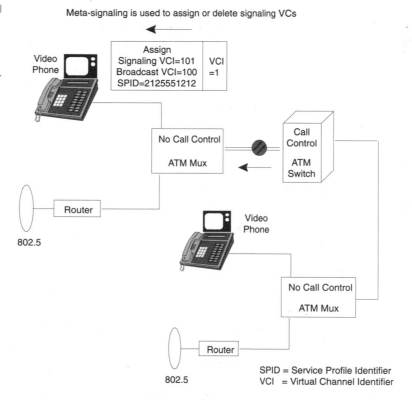

11.4.3 Phase 2 of ATM Signaling

As mentioned earlier, not much is defined by the standards bodies as to what features are to be incorporated in Phase 2. It is speculated that the signaling features in Phase 2 will be based on a multipoint-to-multipoint connection, multimedia type of call setup, compared to Phase 1 signaling, where even point-to-multipoint connections are achieved by setting up point-to-point connections. Figure 11.12 shows an example of a type of signaling that might be done in an ATM environment. In this example, the call control or connection occurs at the ATM mux level, and a connection request carries multiple connection requests on different channels of different bandwidths, such as low bandwidth for voice and high bandwidth for video traffic. Once this information is received by the network, it sets up the appropriate connection for information transfer, thus enabling a multimedia type call. Here, each of the calls is independent in terms of channel. Synchronization occurs between different channels in a multimedia call. The issues of synchronization for a multimedia call are still under investigation.

Figure 11.11
ATM signaling in point-to-multipoint (connection setup).

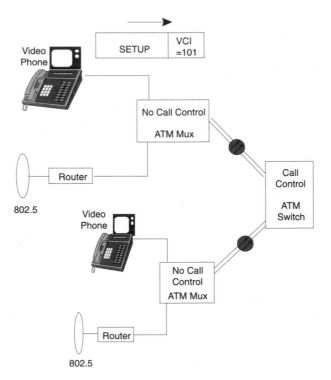

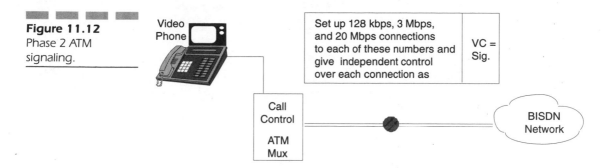

Figure 11.12
Phase 2 ATM signaling.

11.5 Summary

In this chapter, we addressed the higher layers, such as user plane, management plane, and control/signaling plane of the BISDN protocol, and their functions. In the management plane, there are two sublayers: plane management and layer management. The management plane's main functions are related to OAM and performance of the ATM network. In the control or signaling plane, we addressed the features or capabilities proposed for signaling implementation in Phase 1.

12

Other Aspects of BISDN

12.1   Overview

In this chapter, we address the BISDN service aspects (I.211), BISDN network aspects (I.311), and BISDN user-to-network interface aspects (I.413, I.432). The BISDN service aspects define the different types of services that ITU-T has proposed for both residential and business needs for various types of bit-rate traffic. In the network aspects, we address the network layering structure, signaling principles, and traffic control mechanisms. In the BISDN UNI, we address the customer network configuration and its different topologies, as recommended by ITU-T.

12.2   Broadband Service Aspects

The broadband service aspects are defined by ITU-T recommendation I.211. In this recommendation, ITU-T has defined the different classes of services, taking into consideration features such as:

■ Services that have the capability of increasing the flexibility of a connection

■ Services that have the capacity for flexible bandwidth allocation

In addition, video-coding aspects are considered where visual services come into play. In a broadband environment, the capacity available to the user increases dramatically, enabling support of a range of services. ITU-T has classified the services that could be provided by a broadband network into interactive services and distribution services, as illustrated in Fig. 12.1.

12.2.1   Interactive Services

Interactive services are those services in which a two-way exchange of actual information (other than control signaling information) occurs between two subscribers or between a subscriber and a service provider. These services include conversational services, messaging services, and retrieval services.

12.2.1.1   Conversational Services.   Conversational services provide bidirectional, real-time communication with end-to-end information

Figure 12.1
BISDN service classification. (ITU-T Recommendation I.211, Fig. 1, reprinted with permission.)

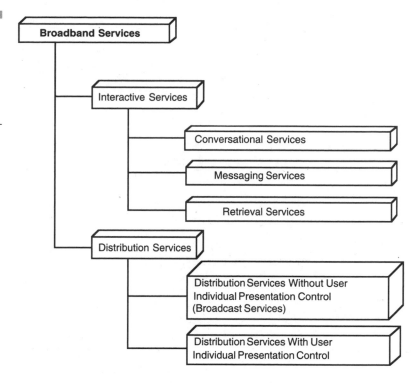

transfer between two users or between a user and a service provider. These services support the general transfer of information specific to a given user application, i.e., the information is generated by, and exchanged between, users; it is not public information.

This category encompasses a wide range of application types. Table 12.1 divides conversational services into four categories: moving pictures (video), sound, data, and document (text). Of these, one of the most important for broadband service is conversational video, such as video telephony service, which is based on video telephones, and desktop video, which uses a computer terminal and video camera.

Video services simply means that the service includes both voice and picture. Currently, two vendors offer video telephone products, and both operate on a regular phone line (64 kbps). In the future, with better compression algorithms, the quality of video can be improved. Higher bandwidth has already improved the quality drastically.

Another video service in this category is video-conferencing. The simplest form of this service is a point-to-point video-conference, which connects conference rooms in two locations. A point-to-point

Type of Information	Examples of Broadband Services	Applications	Some possible Attribute Values
Moving pictures (video) and sound	Broadband*,† video telephony	Communication for the transfer of voice (sound), moving pictures, and video-scanned still images and documents between two locations (person-to-person)† • Tele-education • Tele-shopping • Tele-advertising	• Demand/reserved/permanent • Point-to-point/multipoint • Bidirectional symmetric/bidirectional asymmetric • (Value for information transfer rate is under study)
	Broadband† video-conference	Multipoint communication for the transfer of voice (sound), moving pictures, and video-scanned still images and documents between two or more locations (person-to-group, group-to-group)† • Tele-education • Business conference • Tele-advertising	• Demand/reserved/permanent • Point-to-point/multipoint • Bidirectional symmetric/ bidirectional asymmetric
	Video surveillance†	• Building security • Traffic monitoring	• Demand/reserved/permanent • Point-to-point/multipoint • Bidirectional symmetric/ bidirectional asymmetric
	Video/audio information transmission service	•Television signal transfer • Video/audio dialogue • Contribution of information	• Demand/reserved/permanent • Point-to-point/multipoint • Bidirectional symmetric/ bidirectional asymmetric
Sound	Multiple-sound program signals	• Multilingual commentary channels • Multiple program transfers	• Demand/reserved/permanent • Point-to-point/multipoint • Bidirectional symmetric/ bidirectional asymmetric

Type	Service	Applications	Attributes
Data	High-speed unrestricted digital information transmission service	• High-speed data transfer • LAN interconnection • MAN interconnection • Computer-computer inter-connection • Transfer of video information • Transfer of video and other information types • Still image transfer • Multisite interactive CAD/CAM	• Demand/reserved/permanent • Point-to-point/multipoint • Bidirectional symmetric/bidirectional asymmetric • Connection-oriented connectionless
	High-volume file transfer service	• Data file transfer	• Demand • Point-to-point/multipoint • Bidirectional symmetric/bidirectional asymmetric
	High-speed teleaction	• Real-time control • Telemetry • Alarms	
Document	High-speed telefax	User-to-user transfer of text images drawings, etc.	• Demand/reserved/permanent • Point-to-point/multipoint • Bidirectional symmetric/bidirectional asymmetric
	High-resolution image communication service	• Professional images • Medical images • Remote games and game networks	
	Document communication service	• User-to-user transfer of mixed documents‡	• Demand • Point-to-point/multipoint • Bidirectional symmetric/bidirectional asymmetric

*This terminology indicates that a redefinition of existing terms has taken place. The new terms may or may not exist for a transition period.

†The realization of the different applications may require the definition of different quality classes.

‡"Mixed document" means that a document may contain text, graphic, still and moving picture information as well as audio annotation.

Source: ITU-T Recommendation I.211, Fig. 2. (Reprinted with permission.)

TABLE 12.1

Conversational Services

video-conference has additional features such as facsimile and document image transfer and special equipment such as electronic blackboards. Today's video-conference speed ranges from 128 kbps (T1) to 1.554 Mbps (E1). Another type of video-conferencing is the multipoint-to-multipoint service, which allows participants in multiple locations access to a video-conference connection without leaving their workplaces. This application can be accomplished using a video-conference server within the network. Such a system would support a small number (e.g., five) of simultaneous users. In this system, one participant (the one who speaks) would appear on all screens at the same time, and it would be managed by the video-conference server.

Another type of video service in this category is video surveillance. Video surveillance is not a distribution service because the information delivery is limited to a specific intended subscriber. This type of service is typically applicable to building security and traffic monitoring. In both cases, users might like to control the camera (change orientation, etc.). Attributes of these services can be on-demand, which can be point-to-point or point-to-multipoint.

The next type of service is audio. In audio (sound), multiple-sound program signals could be transmitted. This service has all the attributes of video services.

As shown in Table 12.1, the next service is data. Examples of data applications that could use this service are the following:

- File transfer in a distributed environment, where file servers are distributed across the network high-speed or large-capacity transmission of measured values or control information

- Computer-aided design and manufacturing (CAD/CAM)

- Connection of multiple LANs, MANs, and WANs distributed across a large region

Finally, there is the conversational transfer of documents. The document could be very high-resolution images, with voice annotation and/or a video component.

12.2.1.2 Messaging Services. Table 12.2 shows the messaging services. Messaging services offer end-user-to-end-user communication, usually between an individual user and a file server for electronic mail, video mail, etc. Video mail is an enhancement to e-mail. In video mail, all video, text, and voice can be sent simultaneously. Messaging services can also edit, process, and convert the information. In contrast to conversa-

Type of Information	Examples of Broadband Services	Applications	Some Possible Attribute Values

Moving pictures (video) and sound	Video mail service	Electronic mailbox service for the transfer of moving pictures and accompanying sound	• Demand
			• Point-to-point/multipoint
			• Bidirectional symmetric/
			  bidirectional asymmetric unidirectional
			  (for further study)

Document	Document mail service	Electronic mailbox service for mixed documents	• Demand
			• Point-to-point/multipoint
			• Bidirectional symmetric/
			  bidirectional asymmetric
			  unidirectional (for further
			  study)

TABLE 12.2

Messaging Services

tional services, messaging services are not in real time. Hence, messaging services place less demand on the network and do not require that both users be available at the same time. These messaging services are analogous to narrowband services such as X.400 and teletex. They have all the standard attributes of other services.

12.2.1.3 Retrieval Services Table 12.3 shows the retrieval services.

Broadband videotext is basically an enhancement of the existing videotext system. The user will be able to select a variety of sound, images, video, and text. Examples of broadband videotext services are:

■ Retrieval of encyclopedia information

■ Results of consumer goods comparisons

■ Electronic mail-order catalogs and travel brochures with the option of placing a direct order or making a direct booking

Another retrieval service is video retrieval. With this service, a user could order full-length films or videos from an online film/video library facility. Because the provider might need to satisfy many requests,

TABLE 12.3

Retrieval Services

Type of Information	Examples of Broadband Services	Applications	Some Possible Attribute Values[6]
Text, data, graphics, sound, still images, moving pictures	Broadband videotext	• Videotext including moving pictures • Remote education and training • Telesoftware • Teleshopping • Tele-advertising • News retrieval	• Demand • Point-to-point • Bidirectional asymmetric
	Video retrieval service	• Entertainment • Remote education and training	• Demand/reserved • Point-to-point/ multipoint • Bidirectional asymmetric
	High-resolution image retrieval service	• Entertainment purposes • Remote education and training • Professional image communications • Medical image communications	• Demand/ reserved • Point-point/ multipoint • Bidirectional asymmetric
	Document retrieval service	• Mixed documents retrieval from information centers, archives, etc.[1,2]	• Demand • Point-to-point/ multipoint[3] • Bidirectional asymmetric
	Data retrieval service	• Telesoftware	

1 Mixed document means that a document can contain text, graphics, still and moving picture information, and audio annotation.

2 Special high-layer functions are necessary if postprocessing after retrieval is required.

3 Further study is required to indicate whether the point-to-multipoint connection represents a main application in this case.

bandwidth considerations dictate that only a small number of different video transmissions can be supported at any time. A realistic service would offer perhaps 500 movies or videos for each 2-hour period. If each subscriber used a 50-Mbps video channel, it would require a manageable 25-Gbps transmission capacity from video suppliers to distribution points. With advances in video compression technology such as MPEG and JPEG coding, however, systems such as ADSL, which run from 1.5 Mbps, are available to provide video over existing copper-based networks.

12.2.2   Distribution Services

Distribution services are services in which the information transfer is primarily one way, such as from service provider to broadband subscriber. The information transfer can be via broadcast services, for which the user has no control over the presentation of the information, or cyclical services, which allow the user some measure of information presentation control.

12.2.2.1   Broadcast Distribution Services.   Services in this category are also referred to as services without user presentation control. These services provide a continuous flow of information distributed from a central source to all users connected to the network. Each user can access the flow of this information but cannot control the presentation. In particular, the user cannot control the starting time or order of the presentation of the broadcasted information. All users simply tap into the flow of information. A good example of this is the CATV network. Table 12.4 shows the different types of broadcast distribution.

In CATV networks, the signals are broadcast to every subscriber on the network. With broadband communications, these types of services can be integrated with telecommunications services. In addition, higher resolutions and better services can be achieved with the availability of higher bandwidth.

12.2.2.2   Cyclical Distribution Services.   Services in this class are very similar to broadcast services. With these services, the user can individually access the distributed information by controlling the starting point and order in which the information is presented.

Table 12.5 shows cyclical distribution services. The information is actually a one-way broadcast of a video signal. Currently, the information capacity is limited to the available bandwidth.

Examples of information presented by such a system are stock market reports, weather reports, news, leisure information, and recipes. This type of information is currently available through online services such as America On Line (AOL), Earth Link, etc.

A broadband environment can enhance this service. In the narrowband environment, a very small bandwidth is available. With broadband, a service could use a full digital broadband channel to transmit the information, using text, images, video, and audio. Broadband service can provide low-cost access to timely and frequently requested information,

Type of Information	Examples of Broadband Services	Applications	Some Possible Attribute Values
Data	High-speed unrestricted digital information distribution service	Distribution of unrestricted data	Permanent Broadcast Unidirectional
Text, graphics, still images	Document distribution services	Electronic newspaper Electronic publishing	Demand (selection)/permanent Broadcast/multipoint† Bidirectional asymmetric/unidirectional
Video and sound	Video information distribution services	Distribution of video/audio signals	Permanent Broadcast Unidirectional
Video	Existing quality TV distribution service (NTSC, PAL, SECAM)	TV program distribution	Demand (selection)/permanent Broadcast Bidirectional asymmetric/unidirectional
	Extended quality TV distribution service	TV program distribution	Demand (selection)/permanent Broadcast Bidirectional asymmetric/unidirectional
	Enhanced definition TV distribution service High quality TV		
	High-definition TV distribution service	TV program distribution	Demand (selection)/permanent Broadcast Bidirectional asymmetric/unidirectional
	Pay-TV (pay-per-view, pay-per-channel)	TV program distribution	Demand (selection)/permanent Broadcast/multipoint Bidirectional asymmetric/unidirectional

*ITU-T/I.211, Table 1, reprinted per permission.

†Further study is required to indicate whether the point-to-multipoint connection represents in this case a main application.

TABLE 12.4

Distribution Services Without User Presentation Control*

such as an electronic newspaper that uses public networks, or an in-house information system for trade fairs, hotels, or hospitals. A typical system like this can access up to 10,000 pages in 1 second. Table 12.6 shows the characteristics of broadband service in terms of bandwidth utilization.

12.3   Network Aspects

According to ITU-T Recommendation I.327, the information transfer capabilities of a broadband network include:

- Broadband capabilities
- 64 kbps-based ISDN capabilities
- User-to-network signaling
- User-to-user signaling

Figure 12.2 depicts the information transfer capabilities of broadband. In a broadband network, ATM provides the information transfer. As we know, the ATM data unit is a 53-byte cell, of which 5 bytes are the header. The header carries the information necessary to identify the cell so it can be routed to its appropriate destination.

TABLE 12.5

Distribution Services with User Presentation Control

Type of Information	Examples of Broadband Services	Applications	Some Possible Attribute Values
Text, graphics, sound, still images	Full-channel broadcast videography	Remote education and training Tele-advertising News retrieval Tele-software	Permanent Broadcast Unidirectional

'ITU-T/I.211, Table 1, reprinted per permission.

TABLE 12.6

Characteristics of Broadband Services

Service	Bit Rate (Mbps)	Burstiness'
Data transmission (connection-oriented)	1.5 to 155	1 to 50
Data transmission (connectionless)	1.5 to 155	1
Document transfer/retrieval	1.5 to 45	1 to 20
Videoconference/video-telephony	1.5	1 to 5
Broadband videotex/video retrieval	1.5 to 155	1 to 20
TV distribution	1.5 to 50	1
HDTV distribution	155	1

'Burstiness = peak bit rate/average bit rate.

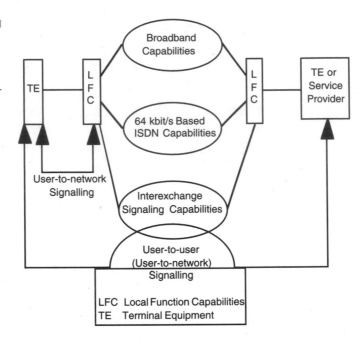

Figure 12.2
Information transfer and signaling capabilities.

ATM is a connection-oriented technique, and a typical connection within an ATM layer consists of more than one link, each of which is assigned an identifier. These identifiers remain unchanged for the duration of the connection. For signaling, the control information is carried on a different connection using a separate identifier (via an out-of-band signaling mechanism).

Although ATM is a connection-oriented technique, it offers a flexible transfer capability common to all services, including connectionless services such as SMDS. The broadband network aspects can be categorized into the following:

- Network layering
- Signaling principles
- Traffic control

Each is described in the subsections following.

12.3.1 Network Layering

The layered structure of a broadband network is addressed in ITU-T Recommendation I.311, which is depicted in Fig. 12.3. In Fig. 12.3, BISDN is divided into two categories: the higher layer functions and the ATM transport layer. Because the ATM transport network layer handles network aspects of BISDN, we address only ATM transport layer functions in this section.

The ATM transport network layer is split into two parts: the physical layer and the ATM layer. Both are hierarchically structured. The physical layer consists of the transmission path level, digital section level, and regenerator section level.

The transmission path extends between network elements that assemble and disassemble the ATM payload of a transmission system. The digital section extends between network elements that assemble and disassemble continuous bit or byte streams. The regenerator section is a portion of a digital section extending between two adjacent regenerators.

The ATM layer has two hierarchical levels: virtual channel level and virtual path level. The VC and VP are used for switching the ATM cells. Typical applications of VC/VP-based connections are between user-to-user, user-to-network, and network-to-network segments of the network. All cells with specific VP/VC connections are transported along the same route through the network. The cell sequence is preserved (first sent—first received) for all virtual connections, which is an advantage of ATM-based

Figure 12.3
BISDN layered
structure.

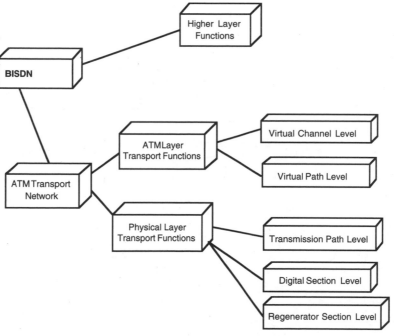

| ATM | Asynchronous Transfer Mode |
| BISDN | Broadband Integrated Services Digital Network |

switching, where the timing between the cells is maintained from source to destination. The relationship between the different layers of the broadband transport network are shown in Fig. 12.4.

12.3.2   Signaling Principles

A broadband network follows the principle of out-of-band signaling similar to the one in N-ISDN using the SS7 signaling network. In BISDN, however, the VC concept provides the means to separate logical signaling channels from user channels.

In Chap. 11, we described the signaling features to be implemented in Phase 1 of signaling as part of the control layer function. Here, we give an overview of the different capabilities of broadband signaling. It has been recommended that the existing signaling function according to ITU-T recommendation Q.2931 is to be included as part of broadband signaling. However, broadband signaling is based on the ATM transport network, which has been designed to address the increasing desire for advanced forms of communications, such as multimedia services.

In broadband networks, ATM network-specific signaling capabilities are

Figure 12.4
Hierarchical layer-to-layer relationship principles.

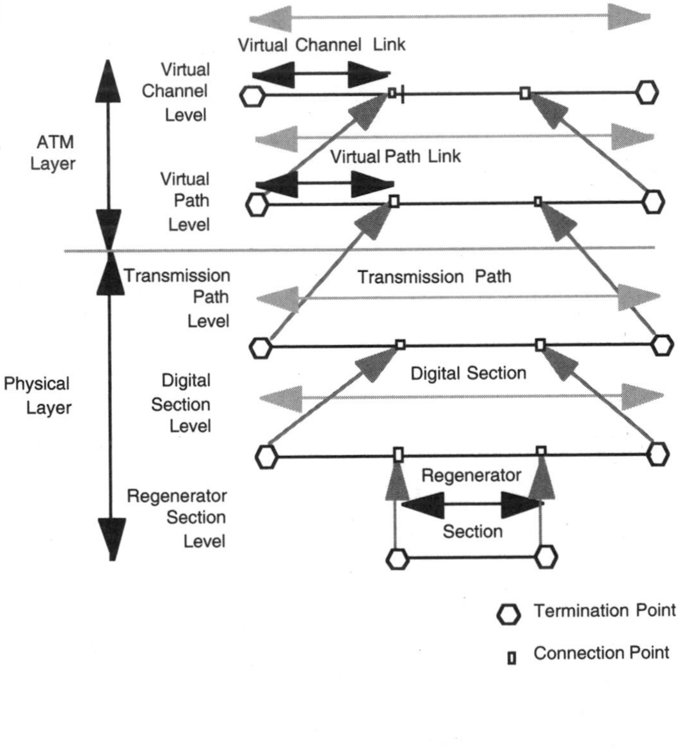

- Establish, maintain, and release ATM virtual circuit connection and virtual path connection for information transfer
- Negotiate the traffic characteristics using usage parameters for a connection

Other signaling requirements are not ATM-related. Examples are the support of multiple connection calls and multipoint calls.

As mentioned earlier, in a broadband network, signaling messages are conveyed by out-of-band signaling techniques in dedicated switched virtual channels. Table 12.7 shows the different types of SVCs, which are described as follows

Metasignaling channel: One channel exists per interface. This channel is bidirectional and permanent. It is an interface management channel used to establish, check, and release the point-to-point and selective SVCs.

General broadcast SVC: This channel is unidirectional, in the network-to-user direction. It sends signaling messages to all signaling end points.

Selective broadcast SVC: This channel is also unidirectional. It sends signaling messages to selected end points. The selective broadcast SVC can also be provided as a network option to address all terminals belonging to the same service profile category.

Point-to-point SVC: This channel is allocated to a signaling end point only while it is active. A signaling end point at the user side can be located in a terminal. In a multifunctional terminal, multiple signaling end points can occur, which are bidirectional. This channel is used to establish, control, and release VCC or VPCs to carry user data.

12.3.3   Traffic Control

To provide desired broadband network performance, ITU-T in Recommendation I.311 identified a set of traffic control capabilities:

TABLE 12.7

Different Types of SVCs

SVC Type	Directionality	No. of SVCs
Metasignaling channel	Bidirectional	One
General broadcast SVC	Unidirectional	One
Selective broadcast SVC	Unidirectional	Multiple
Point-to-point SVC	Bidirectional	One per signaling-end point

- Connection admission control (CAC)
- Usage parameter control (UPC)
- Priority control (PC)
- Congestion control (CC)

Figure 12.5 shows where the different traffic controls are applied in the reference broadband network. Each segment of the network contains some sort of traffic control mechanism. For instance, network A has the traffic control mechanisms of CAC, resource management (RM), and PC implemented in its network.

12.3.3.1 Connection Admission Control. CAC is defined as the set of actions taken by the network during the call setup phase (or during call renegotiations) to establish whether a VC/VP connection can be accepted.

A connection can only be accepted if sufficient network resources are available to establish the connection end-to-end at its required quality of service. The quality of service that already exists in the current network connections must not be influenced by the new connection. Thus, the resources can be requested in terms of bandwidth, average information rate, peak information rate, etc. Two classes of parameters are foreseen to support connection admission control: (1) a set of parameters to describe the source traffic characteristics and (2) a set of parameters to identify the required QOS class.

Source traffic can be characterized by its

- Average bit rate
- Peak bit rate
- Burstiness
- Peak duration

12.3.3.2 Usage Parameter Control. UPC is defined as the set of actions taken by the network to monitor and control user traffic in terms of traffic volume, cell loss, and cell routing validity. Its main purpose is to protect network resources from malicious and unintentional traffic misbehavior, which can affect the quality of service of other already established connections. UPC monitors and detects violations of negotiated parameters. Usage parameter control applies during the information trans-

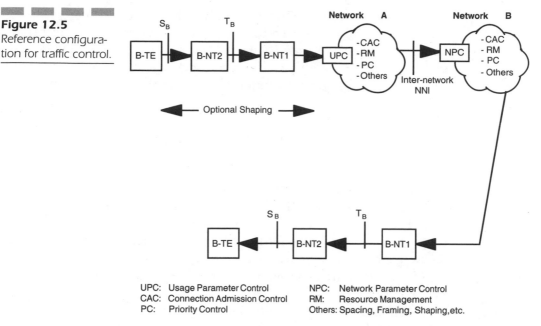

Figure 12.5
Reference configuration for traffic control.

UPC: Usage Parameter Control
CAC: Connection Admission Control
PC: Priority Control

NPC: Network Parameter Control
RM: Resource Management
Others: Spacing, Framing, Shaping, etc.

fer phase of a connection only. Connection monitoring encompasses all connections crossing the user-network interface, including signaling. Usage parameter monitoring includes the following functions:

- Checking the validity of VPI/VCI values.

- Monitoring the traffic volume entering the network from individually active VP and VC connections to ensure that parameters agreed upon are not violated.

- Monitoring the total volume of accepted traffic on the access link.

- Discarding those cells that violate the negotiated traffic parameters. In some cases, the "guilty" connection might be released. Another less rigorous option is to reroute the violating cells. These cells can be transferred as long as they do not cause serious harm to the network. Thus, the overall throughput of ATM cells might possibly be raised.

Let's illustrate the different UPCs used in a broadband network. Figure 12.6 shows different access network arrangements. The appropriate usage parameter control measures are applied to VCs or VPs at the access point where they are terminated within the network. In case A, a user is connected directly to a VC switch. Usage parameter control is performed within the VC switch on each VC before switching it. In case B, a user is connected to a VC switch via a concentrator. Usage parameter control is performed within the concentrator on each VC only. In case C, a user is connected to a VC switch via a VP switch. Here, usage parameter control is performed within the VP switch on each VP and within the VC switch on each VC. In case D, a user is connected to another user via a VP switch. Usage parameter control is performed within the VP switch on each VP connected to the user.

12.3.3.3 Priority Control.   Two levels of priority are available in the ATM cell header field called CLP (cell loss priority). These priority classes could be treated separately by connection admission control and usage parameter control. Different buffering mechanisms are used in different switching systems with the two priorities. The mechanisms are common buffer with pushout mechanism, partial buffer sharing, and buffer separation.

In common buffer with pushout, cells of both priorities share a common buffer. If the buffer is full and a higher priority cell arrives, a cell with lower priority (if any is available) is pushed out and lost. A complicated buffer management mechanism is necessary to guarantee the cell sequence integrity.

In partial buffer sharing, low-priority cells can only access the buffer if the total buffer size is less than a given threshold S_L (where S_L<total buffer capacity). High-priority cells can access the whole buffer. By adjusting the threshold, S_L, it is possible to adapt the system to various load situations.

In buffer separation, each of the priorities have different buffers. This mechanism is simple to implement, but cell sequence integrity can only be maintained if a single priority is assigned to each connection.

12.3.3.4 Congestion Control.   Congestion in broadband networks is defined as a status of network elements (e.g., switches, concentrators, transmission links) in which, due to traffic overload or control resource overload, the network cannot guarantee the negotiated quality of service to the already established connections and the new connection request. Congestion can be caused by unpredictable statistical fluctuations of traffic flows or fault conditions within the network. For example, a user or users can use more resources than they have requested at the time of connection setup negotiations.

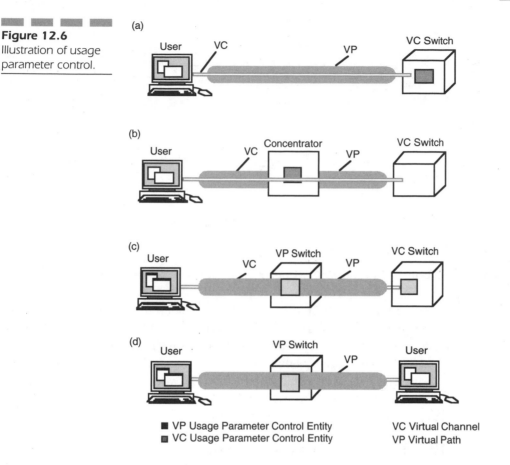

Figure 12.6
Illustration of usage parameter control.

12.4 User-Network Interface Aspects

One of the essential parts of the BISDN network is the customer network. It is sometimes referred to as the customer premises network (CPN) or subscriber premises network (SPN).

Figure 12.7 shows the reference configuration of BISDN UNI, which was extended from ISDN UNI as described in ITU-T Recommendation I.411. This ISDN configuration was general enough to be considered for BISDN UNI configuration. The BISDN UNI consists of the following:

- Functional groups
- ~B-NT1: Broadband-Network Terminal 1
- ~B-NT2: Broadband-Network Terminal 2

Figure 12.7
Reference configura-
tion of the BISDN UNI.

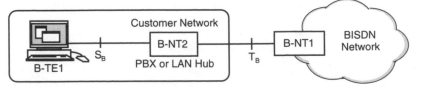

B-NT Network Termination for BISDN
B-TE Terminal Equipment for BISDN

• Functional Groups: B-NT1, B-NT2 and B-TE1
• Reference Points: T_B and S_B

■ ~B-TE1: Broadband Terminal Equipment 1

■ Reference points: T_B, S_B.

The B-NT1 performs line transmission termination and related OAM functions. The B-NT2 can be a PBX or LAN interface that performs multiplexing and switching of ATM cells. The reference point T_B is the interface between the CPN and the public network. A number of customer network categories exist, depending on the aspects of the customer network, such as environment, number of users, or topology. The major categories of broadband customer network are residential customer network or business customer network.

12.4.1   Residential Network

In this network, a small number of users use broadband services mainly for entertainment purposes. In this case, no internal switching capabilities are necessary within a customer network.

12.4.2   Business Network

This category can be divided into the subcategories of small, medium, and large businesses. The subcategory is based on the number of users in each environment. For example, in the case of small business, the number of users varies from 1 to 20; their requirements are similar to residential users, except that the end use is not for entertainment but business purposes.

Two requirements exist for this CPN: service requirement and structural requirement.

- Service requirements include the consequences of supporting these services. Each of the services has different requirements, such as bit rate, quality, grade of services, and delay variation. The customer network should be designed in such a way to handle a wide variety of services. For instance, to carry switched video services, the customer network should be able to handle high bandwidth, high-quality video signal, which requires certain levels of delay and grade of service (GOS).

- Structural requirements are the physical arrangements of the network elements. The structure should be flexible, modular, reliable, and provide maximum performance at low cost. Flexibility deals with the ability to cope with system changes in case of failure or other outages. There are four points: adaptability, expandability, mobility, and interworking. Modularity is the ability to have flexible structure and add additional equipment to the existing network configuration. Reliability is the ability to perform without any mishaps or errors in traffic under extreme environments, and it can also sometimes require redundancy (backup) of the customer network components. All these requirements enhance or maintain the performance at a reduced cost.

Figure 12.8 shows the physical configurations typically used in a customer network. The configurations can be one of the following:

- Star configuration
- Dual-bus medium (shared-medium) configuration
- Combination of star and shared-medium configuration

These configurations are typically used for LANs. To connect different LANs located in geographically dispersed areas, an interconnection is needed. Figure 12.9 shows a typical example of the interworking of LANs via a MAN and the interworking of multiple MANs with a broadband network. The interworking unit (IWU) was created for this purpose. The IWU can be attached directly to a B-NT1 at the reference point T_B or the LAN/MAN can be connected via an IWU through S_B or B-NT2 (if present) as shown in Fig. 12.9.

Figure 12.8
Physical configurations of customer premises network.

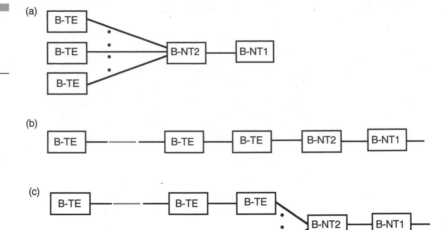

(a)

(b)

(c)

B-NT Network Termination for BISDN
B-TE Terminal Equipment for BISDN
Dashed Box Means the B-NT2 May or May Not Exist

Figure 12.9
Interworking LAN/MAN with BISDN.

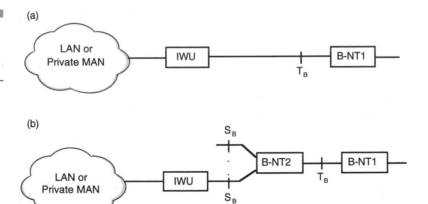

(a)

(b)

B-NT Network Termination for BISDN
B-TE Terminal Equipment for BISDN

LAN   Local Area Network
MAN Metropolitan Area Network

12.5 Summary

In this chapter, we addressed the different aspects of BISDN, such as service, network, and the user or customer-to-network interface. In service aspects, we addressed the different categories of service that ITU-T has defined in its recommendation: interactive and distribution services. The interactive services were subdivided into conversational services, messaging services, and retrieval services, while the distribution services were subdivided into distribution without user presentation control and distribution with user presentation control. The network aspects were divided into three subcategories: network layering, signaling principles, and traffic control. The final section covered aspects related to the user or customer-to-network interface, and that section discussed the requirements and topologies of customer networks.

CHAPTER 13

Broadband Access Architecture

13.1   Overview

This chapter addresses the broadband access network architecture, which is currently the bottleneck in providing a wide range of services in a cost-effective way. In this chapter we discuss various broadband-capable access architectures using some of the technologies mentioned in Chap. 9. Access is one of the areas where ATM will be the last environment to penetrate because of the difficulty in the financial justification for such an implementation. Although ATM will play a major role in the access environment at some future time, initial broadband access architecture and technology will have to support the current heterogeneous protocols and technologies, leveraging existing facilities. The adaptation to ATM will be performed at the first point of interface in the network, if needed.

There are many issues related to the deployment of these architectures by service providers, and it is important to understand these issues before making any decisions. An understanding of how the architectures and technologies work together is also necessary for a firm grasp of the concepts. Some architecture implementations may use all of the technologies discussed in Chap. 9, while other implementations may not use any of them. Naturally, the costs associated with implementing and using broadband architectures and technologies are a major factor to everyone interested in broadband networks or applications. Implementation costs vary widely, depending on such factors as technology, technology maturity, and reuse of existing network components. Service providers must plan carefully to ensure that implementation costs can be recovered by providing enhanced services and by achieving operational savings within an acceptable period of time. Finally, the differences among the various types of architectures need to be understood for an appreciation of how each is best utilized. Once the major differences between different types of architectures are understood, issues related to their deployment need to be evaluated before using the technologies as part of the architecture.

13.2   Broadband Access Architecture

We discussed some of the broadband technologies in Chap. 9. Here we will discuss the broadband architectures: IDLC (integrated digital loop carrier), hybrid fiber/coaxial (HFC), fiber to the curb (FTTC), fiber to the home (FTTH), multichannel multipoint distribution service (MMDS), local multipoint distribution service (LMDS), and direct broadcast satellite (DBS).

13.2.1 IDLC Architecture

Currently, IDLC (Integrated Digital Loop Carrier) architecture is the most widely deployed in public telephone networks around the world, and it is used as a means to bring digital technology closer to the subscribers. This architecture complements existing star-based telephone network architecture. In his architecture most of the access plant is copper-based and designed to transport primarily telephone services. IDLC equipment uses fiber/digital technology to support various services. The access rates are DS1, fractional DS1, 64 kbps, and BRI. The trunk transport rate is usually DS1, DS3, OC-3 or OC-12. Most deployed equipment in his architecture is SONET-compatible and based on Bellcore specifications (as contained in TR-303 or GR-303). IDLC provides a migration path from current analog to SONET-based broadband transport. IDLC is designed to support both basic and enhanced telephony services. The hardware architecture and software features vary from vendor to vendor. In general, the following system features are supported by most of them:

■ Remote software provisioning capability

■ Compact and rugged shelf design to sustain outside plant operation

■ OAMP features that are SONET-compatible

■ Flexible hardware architecture to accommodate future software upgrades

■ Digital service to the end users if needed.

This architecture can be complemented with X-DSL technologies discussed in Chap. 9 as the next phase of migration toward an end-to-end broadband network designed to handle the convergence of services. This system architecture is depicted in Fig. 13.1.

13.2.2 HFC Architecture

HFC architecture was once considered the easiest and most logical way to provide all the services to the end user by means of the existing CATV

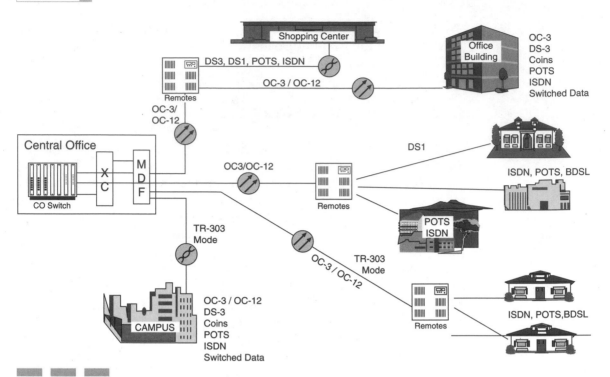

Figure 13.1
IDLC architecture.

infrastructure because of the high bandwidth coaxial drop to each customer. Theoretically, HFC is capable of supporting all existing and emerging narrowband and broadband services including telephony, TV broadcasting, video dial tone, video on demand, distance learning, etc. HFC can support both analog and digital services and offers a migration path to pure optical service and an all-digital network in the last mile.

Figure 13.2 shows the HFC architecture from the head end down to the interface node between the fiber and coaxial cable. Modulation techniques such as QPSK, QAM, or VSB are used between the head end and optical network interface (ONI), where the signal is mapped to a particular frequency and carried onto the network until it is converted back to the original format for the subscribers. Digital or analog information within the frequency is unconverted to a narrowband channel at high frequency for the transmission. Analog signals can be unconverted using any frequency modulator. Thus, QPSK, QAM, or VSB technology enables multiplexing several sources, each modulated with one or more frequency signals that can be combined optically in a CATV network.

In an HFC-based CATV system, the broadcast video and switched video signals are transported via fiber to the ONU (optical network unit) or ONI. The ONI connects the fiber backbone to the coaxial cable distribution plant. At the ONI, the signals are frequency-shifted to the appropriate channel and fed to an amplifier for transmission over coaxial cable. The conventional analog, video, data, and voice signals can be carried simultaneously in different frequencies. The final segment of coaxial cable requires two-way amplifiers for the bidirectional signals on the cable. The ONU performs additional functions like separation of upstream and downstream signals.

Some of the current issues with the HFC architecture in providing telephony service are grade of service, network powering requirement, and ingress noise generated by noncable subscribers. Also, the reverse channel currently uses the low-frequency range that is bandwidth-limited. For data services, the issue is still reverse bandwidth and ingress noise. Recently, alternative proposals for reverse bandwidth, such as using telephone lines, have been considered.

13.2.2.1 Capacity. Hybrid fiber/coaxial utilizes the 0 to 50 MHz band for upstream traffic and the 50 to 750 MHz band for downstream traffic. As shown in Fig. 13.3, the upstream usable bandwidth will continue to increase and move into different regions of the spectrum as enhancements to modulation techniques are realized. In most cases, the 0- to 50-MHz range bandwidth is used for upstream traffic.

HFC architectures may fall into one of three categories based on

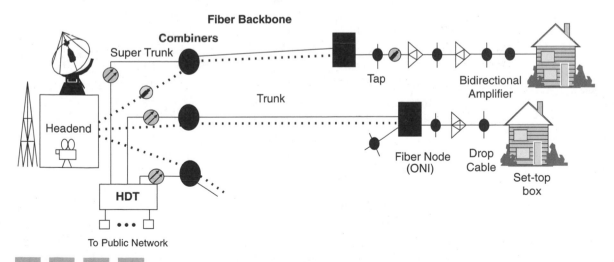

Figure 13.2
HFC access architecture.

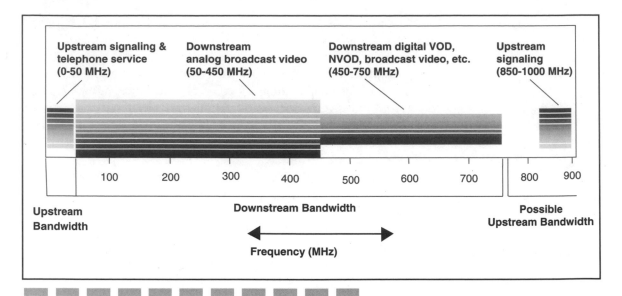

Figure 13.3

An example of possible spectrum allocation in an HFC network.

the signal type used: all analog hybrid fiber-coaxial, analog and digital hybrid fiber-coaxial, and all digital hybrid fiber-coaxial. In the first category, the downstream bandwidth is utilized to provide broadcast analog video channels, premium PPV (pay-per-view) channels, and/or subscription channels. The upstream bandwidth is not typically used in all analog HFC implementations. An analog and digital HFC architecture permits transmission of both analog and digital signals and makes use of the back channels to provide interactive television, video on demand, and administrative features. A set-top box with a decoder on top of the television is required at the subscriber's premise to decompress and convert digital signals to analog format. In an all-digital HFC network, the digital signals travel via fiber and coaxial to a box at the subscriber's premise. The back channel is used for control over content received through the forward channels and for administrative features.

The downstream bandwidth, which is between 50 and 750 MHz, translates to approximately one hundred 6-MHz analog video channels. In the case of digital signaling, each 6 MHz of the carrier channel can carry 27 to 38 Mbps of digital payload. A compressed digital video channel of VHS quality translates to 1.544 Mbps. A video channel of NTSC

(National Television System Committee) quality requires 7 Mbps. Assuming a 4-bit/Hz QAM encoding, a bandwidth of 1.75 MHz is required by one conventional NTSC program. Typically, in HFC, the lower end of the forward bandwidth, 50 to 450 MHz, is used for analog video. Elsewhere, the upper portion of the forward bandwidth, 450 to 750 MHz, is reserved for digital video. Some HFC implementations may use bandwidths above 850 MHz for upstream signaling (Fig. 2.7).

One proposal for an HFC network claims a capacity of 70 analog video channels and 240 compressed digital video channels for broadcast purposes and 80 compressed digital video channels for VOD services (quite a leap from 40 CATV channels). This network utilizes the bandwidth from 0 to 30 MHz for upstream traffic and 50 to 750 MHz band for downstream traffic (30–50 MHz is not used).

13.2.2.2 Services Supported. Hybrid fiber-coaxial networks offer a flexible suite of analog and digital services. Current analog television equipment is adequate for receiving basic analog video through HFC. A digital television or a digital-to-analog converter within a box and an analog television are required to receive digital video using HFC. It is also possible to send telephone signals through the HFC network via an interface between local central offices switches and the head end. HFC, however, does not provide good telephone connections due to the use of a shared reverse channel and the poor quality of cable plant, which can cause interference problems. In spite of these problems, the following services are possible over HFC networks:

- Analog video and sometimes voice
- Digital video (compressed or uncompressed) and data

  The types of applications available using HFC are

- Regular analog TV
- High-speed LAN-type (shared) data transport
- Telephone service
- Video on demand
- Home shopping
- Video games
- Pay-per-view channels
- Electronic news delivery

13.2.3 FTTH, FTTC, FTTB, and FTTN Architectures

These architectures are similar to the IDLC architecture, with the exception that fiber is being used as the transmission medium in the distribution plant. If fiber is used all the way to the home, it is called *fiber to the home* (FTTH). If fiber is used up to the curb of the home, it is called *fiber to the curb* (FTTC). If fiber is used to the basement of the office building or complex, then it is called *fiber to the building* (FTTB). If the fiber is deployed all the way to a node, which is equivalent to the pedestal at the curb, then it is called *fiber to the node* (FTTN). This fiber, combined with switching network elements like ATM switches that are capable of handling all services (voice, video, and data), will make FTTC, FTTH, FTTB, or FTTN into a network that can provide all services. Since all the different architectures are a variation of FTTC architecture, the remainder of this section will address FTTC architecture. FTTC is the most popular architecture deployed and is adopted as part of a FSAN (full-service access network) study.

In an FTTC architecture, digital signals travel from the service provider to the central office via backbone links. The signals from the CO are routed through to an ONU. At the ONU, the optical signal from the fiber is converted into an electrical signal and transported over copper or coaxial cables, or even wireless cables in some cases, to the customer.

For telephone operating companies providing services, twisted-pair wires from the curb are used to connect to the customers' premises. In the case of a CATV provider, coaxial cables may be used. FTTC is usually implemented as a switched network with multiple fibers for bidirectional signal flow. But it can be implemented with HFC architecture as well. Figure 13.4 illustrates an FTTC architecture in a typical telephone environment using a switched star architecture.

13.2.3.1 Capacity. FTTC networks allow for dedicated downstream information transport from an optical network unit to each subscriber at 51 Mbps and upstream traffic of 1.62 Mbps per subscriber. This 51-Mbps switched information stream is capable of concurrently carrying six or seven unique high-quality data programs to each subscriber. Along with this data traffic, FTTC can support other high-speed data services and telephone services to each subscriber.

As mentioned earlier, if fiber goes all the way to the home, the architecture is called FTTH. Considerable bandwidth can be achieved for each customer with this type of network architecture, but currently

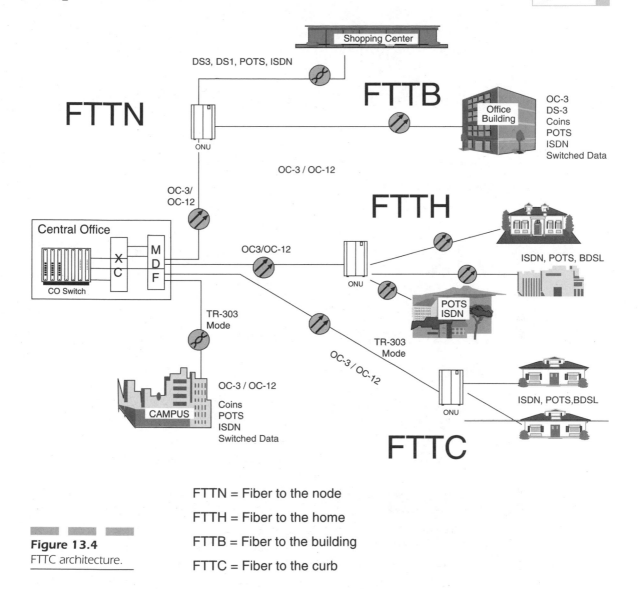

Figure 13.4
FTTC architecture.

FTTN = Fiber to the node

FTTH = Fiber to the home

FTTB = Fiber to the building

FTTC = Fiber to the curb

there is no business case to justify that amount of bandwidth to the end-user. However, it could be justified if the current twisted-pair architecture could provide the needed bandwidth in a cost-effective way for all the services needed by the customer. This is where some of the x-DSL technologies discussed in Chap. 9 become valuable. Thus FTTC combined with one of the x-DSL solutions will be able to provide the required bandwidth at the price point that could make business sense.

13.2.3.2 Services Supported. FTTC and FTTH are architectures optimized for the transport of end-to-end digital signals. As such, the transport of analog video channels, while possible, is not practical or cost-effective when compared to today's cable technology and its architecture. This fact limits FTTC/FTTH architectures to providing only digital services. Some of the services that can be provided in the digital form are

- Voice
- Digital video and data
- Telephone service (including video telephone services)
- High-speed LAN-type data transport
- Digital video (high definition)
- Video on demand, near video on demand, and interactive video on demand
- Highly interactive real-time video games

13.2.4 LMDS Architecture

Of all the different wireless technologies that exist, LMDS is mentioned because it is one of the few wireless technologies that addresses broadband multimedia on wireless media.

The FCC has allocated a 1-GHz frequency on a 28- to 32-GHz frequency band for a wide range of wireless broadband services. This wireless system is capable of providing all the advanced two-way multimedia services including telephony and high-speed data. This service enables service providers like IXCs (interchange carriers) who don't have the infrastructure to provide local access in a cost-effective way to both residential and business customers in the least amount of time.

The basic architecture of this system is illustrated in Fig. 13.5. In this architecture, the last mile, or the local loop, is a wireless interface. The antenna at the customer's location must be in line of sight (LOS) with the cell site. The cell site is connected to the network, which provides all the customer-required services.

13.2.5 MMDS Architecture

MMDS, or microwave multipoint distribution system, is a type of broadcast network similar to LMDS but it operates at a 2.4-GHz frequency. Also, the operating bandwidth range in this frequency is limited to provide a

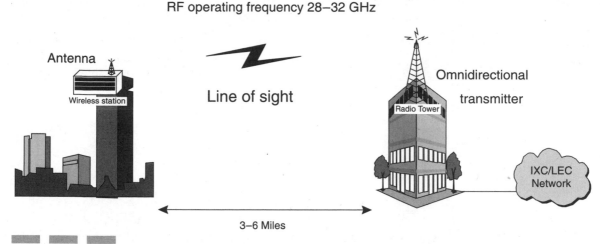

Figure 13.5
LMDS architecture.

variety of services. Currently, MMDS frequency is used by CATV providers to connect multiple head end locations to broadcast analog video signals. With the telecommunications deregulation, the use of this frequency is open to other services such as telephony and interactive services.

Unlike LMDS, MMDS is less susceptible to interference from external environmental factors such as rain, thunderstorms, etc. Thus, it is less stringent in terms of distance from the cell site. Typically MMDS covers a radius of 50 miles whereas LMDS has a radius of 3—6 mi.

13.2.5.1 Capacity. The 2.2- to 2.7-GHz band is used to transmit analog video signals from towers to receiving antennae located at the subscribers' premises. Up to 33 channels can be used for broadcast purposes through this system. Subscribers within a 25- to 30-mi radius of the transmitting tower can pick up these signals. If the video signals are digitized and compressed, 100 to 150 channels are possible.

A MMDS license owner is guaranteed four of the 11 MMDS channels allocated in the 2.2- to 2.7-GHz range by the Federal Communications Commission (FCC). The license owner must acquire any additional channels from institutions or other individuals who own the rest of the spectrum allocated to wireless cable. Table 13.1 provides details regarding the FCC's spectrum allocations in the United States.

If instructional television fixed service (ITFS) channels are acquired, the owner must ensure that at least 20 hours of educational programming

TABLE 13.1

MMDS Spectrum
Allocation in the
United States

Frequency Range, kHz	Number of Channels	Type of Service
2150—2162	2	MDS
2500—2596	16	ITFS
2596—2644	8	MMDS
2644—2686	4	ITFS
2644—2686	3	MMDS
2686—2689.875	31	MMDS

will be broadcast. If multiple ITFS channels belong to MMDS implementers, all the educational programming may be transmitted on a single
ITFS channel. The remaining channels may be utilized for entertainment
video. It is clear from the information in Table 13.1 that, if a single
provider owns the rights to the entire frequency range, the provider will
have the total capability to broadcast 33 analog channels.

13.2.5.2 Services Supported.   MMDS can be used to provide either
analog or digital video. Receiving analog video requires a relatively simple antenna on the rooftop and a box on top of the television consisting
of a down-converter and a descrambler. In the case of digital MMDS, the
converter is more intricate and expensive. With recent developments in
technology, equipment vendors have developed equipment that is capable of providing high-speed data and voice services in addition to traditional analog and digital video services.

13.2.6   DBS Architecture

The current DBS is the third-generation satellite-based video broadcast
service. Recently, this service has become very attractive with the advent
of digital technology and a smaller dish antenna at each customer's location. This, in turn, enables better quality video and audio. DBS provides
a type of service similar to that currently provided by conventional analog satellite systems. The attractiveness of DBS is that the signal is transmitted in a digital format, which is decoded by the converter box at each
customer's location. This box, in addition to converting signals from digital to analog, has built-in intelligence to provide many new advanced
services, such as interactive TV, information on demand, etc. The basic
DBS architecture is shown in Fig. 13.6.

13.2.6.1 Capacity. True direct broadcast satellites operate in the broadcast satellite services (BSS) portion of the Ku-band spectrum. This is equivalent to a spectrum range of 12.2 to 12.7 GHz (DirecTV and USSB broadcast operate at these frequencies). Subscribers of DBS may receive 150 to 200 channels with digital video using MPEG-2 compression technique. Some DBS service providers are also planning data broadcasts in the Ku band.

13.2.6.2 Services Supported. DBS systems provide digital video broadcast services to subscribers. Although they are capable of providing analog video, DBS systems usually utilize digital video using MPEG-2 compression for the most efficient bandwidth use. DirecTV and USSB provide a combined total of 170 digital channels: 70 channels of major cable services, 30 channels of subscription sports, 20 channels of special interest programming, and 50 PPV channels. Primestar offers 90 channels

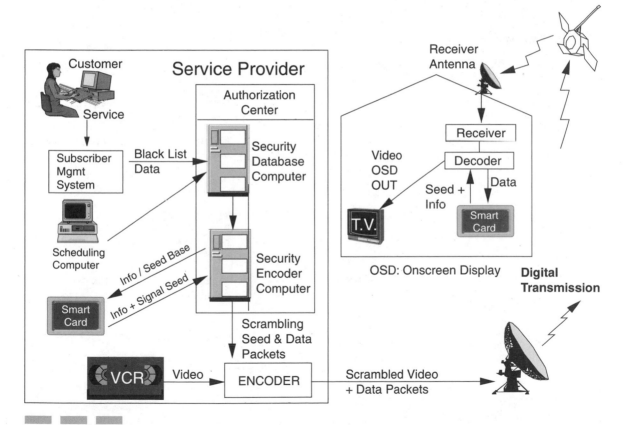

Figure 13.6
DBS architecture.

to subscribers. Recent developments in DBS systems can support one-way broadcast data and will use traditional telephone lines for control channel. Some of the services supported by DBS are: satellite broadcast video services, educational programming, pay-per-view movies, and, more recently, Internet via satellite.

13.3   Summary

Table 13.2 summarizes all the different access technologies described in this chapter and the type of transmission media used to transport the

TABLE 13.2   Summary of Broadband Access Network Architectures

			Architecture		
	IDLC	**HFC**	**FTTC/FTTH**	**LMDS/MMDS**	**DBS**
Transmission media	Twisted	Coaxial fiber	Fiber twisted	Broadband wireless fiber	Broadband satellite
Service providers	Telco	CATV	CAP, Utility, Telco	Cellco, CATV, new players	Satellite providers, new players
Customer	Residential/business	Residential	Business/residential	Residential/business	Residential/business
Bandwidth availability	Broadband	Broadband	Broadband	Broadband/wideband	Wideband
Technology	SONET, TDM	MPEG2, ATM, AM, FM	MPEG2, ATM, TDM, PON, WDM, x-DSL	TDMA, CDMA, FDM, TDMA, AM, FM, ATM MPEG-2	FDM, TDMA, AM, FM, ATM, MPEG-2
Advantages	Widely deployed (global)	High bandwidth, (mostly U.S.)	High bandwidth, good reach	Mobility, mass distribution High bandwidth	Global coverage, mass distribution
Disadvantages	Legacy OSS, last mile QOS	CATV reliability; limited two-way, upgrade cost scalability	Infrastructure cost, need to deploy	Expensive frequency, license required, reliability	Shared bandwidth, one-way (limited two-way)
High-speed Internet	Medium	Medium	High	Medium	Limited
Broadband (integrated voice/data/video)	Limited	Medium	High	High	Medium

signal to the customer. This is done because service providers will use one of the transmission media mentioned to provide access to the customer.

As we consider the need to support the growing demand for broadband access, we can see that the access architectures mentioned here offer service providers an amazing opportunity. Faced with the challenge of deploying solutions that meet the growing needs of an expanding market, service providers are quickly coming to the conclusion that each one of the architectures has its niche market. Thus, it has become very critical that they understand their business and market needs in order to provide cost-effective services to the customer.

New services, such as Internet access, telecommuting, and LAN access, are driving services providers to pursue appropriate architectures to meet the customer needs, depending on their current embedded base, strength, and experience.

Broadband Access, Switching, Transmission, and Intelligent Network

In this part, we look into the different components that constitute the end-to-end broadband network, i.e., broadband access, transmission, switching, and the intelligent network. We know by now that ATM is the switching technology for broadband networks, and SONET/SDH is the fiber-based transmission system standard used for future BISDN. But, we also know there is no one preferred method of access for broadband networks and no preferred method to control and provide value-added services over intelligent networks. Here are some of the broadband access architectures that are capable of carrying high bandwidth services with or without ATM and broadband intelligent networks options to control and provide timely service in the new broadband environment. Several options are discussed with respect to broadband IN architecture, where ATM is the transport for signaling information. In addition, we examine the building blocks of the ATM switching system, its working principles, and the different types of ATM switching fabrics currently in use along with the various ways SONET/SDH systems are deployed and used.

14

ATM-Based Broadband Switching

14.1   Overview

Since ATM is the switching technology for broadband networks, we focus on ATM switching concepts, including the basic architecture, requirements, principles, and building blocks. Numerous books and papers have been published which address issues of switch design to increase the speed, capacity, and overall performance of ATM switching systems. Appendix C lists numerous reference materials. This chapter gives an overview of ATM switching systems and the core components.

14.2   Switching Technology Background

Before we focus on ATM switching technology, we will look into where ATM fits in the spectrum of switching. Figure 14.1 shows the spectrum of switching technologies available, ranging from traditional circuit switching on one end to packet switching on the other.

One of the first uses of switching technologies used in telecommunications was telegrams sent via "packets" or "messages" from one relay station to another. This packet contained the source and destination address along with the contents of the message.

The next switching technology, which was introduced at the end of the last century, was circuit switching. It is used even today for plain old telephone service (POTS), the classical telephone service. In this application, a circuit must be established and dedicated for the duration of the call (i.e., the connection remains intact).

Next came the requirement to interconnect a computer and terminals. Circuit switching was not suitable because the need for data interconnection was more stringent than for voice (large bursts for a short duration and error-free transmission). Circuit switching was thus replaced by packet switching. In a packet-switched network, the data stream is broken into a sequence of packets, and each packet is appended with the source and destination address, just like the address in a postal letter. These packets are received, stored, processed, and retransmitted at each node until they reach the matching destination address on the packet. In this technique, many users can share network resources

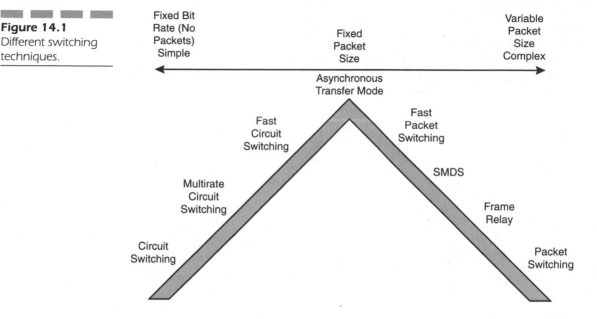

Figure 14.1
Different switching
techniques.

because no one can reserve the rights for a channel at any given time. The network can therefore use resources more efficiently. To help your understanding of packets, compare a packet to a postal envelope, as shown in Fig. 14.2.

The following information is in the header of a packet:

- Source address
- Destination address
- Size of the packet

There are two types of packet switching: datagram (connectionless) and virtual circuit (connection-oriented). Table 14.1 shows the difference between circuit switching, datagram packet switching, and virtual-circuit packet switching.

For future broadband networks that satisfy broadband types of applications, the existing switching techniques cannot be used efficiently. Therefore, we must devise a generic switching technique that is independent of the type of application in use and can adapt to future services needed. The following section is a thorough review of the broadband switching technology, i.e., an ATM that can meet these requirements and its applications in different environments.

Figure 14.2
Comparison between
postal envelope and
data packet.

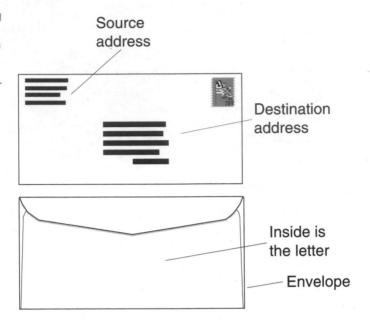

Generic Packet Structure

Header	User Information

14.3 ATM-Based Switching

Switching systems developed for conventional voice or data networks are not directly applicable to broadband systems. Hence, a more flexible switching technology, ATM, had to be developed and adopted for broadband-based networks. Two major requirements impact the definition of broadband ATM switching systems:

High-speed interfaces (50 Mbps to 2.4 Gbps) to the switch, with switching rates up to 80 Gbps in the backplane

Statistical capability of the ATM streams passing through the ATM switching systems

To meet these requirements, the ATM switches had to be completely different from conventional switches. A large number of alternatives exist for ATM switches based on different factors, and they are addressed in this chapter.

First, however, we need to understand the basic ATM switch. A generic ATM switch can be divided into two categories—hardware architecture and software architecture—which are, in turn, subdivided. Each is explained in the architecture sections that follow.

14.3.1   Hardware Architecture

The hardware architecture of an ATM switch is divided into two main components: the switch core, which performs the switching of cells, and

TABLE 14.1

Differences Between Switching Types

Circuit Switching	Datagram Packet Switching	Virtual-Circuit Packet Switching
Dedicated transmission path	No dedicated path	Dedicated path
Continuous transmission of data	Transmission of packets	Transmission of packets
Fast enough for interactive	Fast enough for interactive	Fast enough for interactive
Message not stored	Packets stored until delivered	Packets stored until delivered
Path is established for entire conversation	No path is established	No path is established
Call setup delay	Packet transmission delay	Call setup delay
Busy signal if the party is busy	Sender can be notified if the packet is not delivered	Sender is notified of the connection denial
Overload can block call	Overload increases packet delay due to queuing	Overload might block call setup, increases packet delay
User responsible for lost message	Network responsible for lost packets	Network responsible for packet sequences
Usually no speed or code conversion	Speed and code conversion	Speed and code conversion
Fixed bandwidth transmission	Dynamic use of bandwidth	Dynamic use of bandwidth
No overhead bits after call setup	Overhead bits in each packet	Overhead bits in each packet

the switch interface, which performs the external input and output functions in addition to adaptation functions from legacy technologies. Recent developments in standards, such as LANE. MPOA, etc., have accelerated the use of ATM products in the LAN environment. Figure 14.3 depicts the ATM switch and its physical interfaces. Each interface is connected to the switch core through two ATM core interfaces, one for input and the other for output.

14.3.1.1 Switch Interface. The switch interface is the connection between the access devices and the ATM switch core whenever needed. The bit rate and format of the ATM cells are adapted by the switch interface to fit the switch core. In addition, almost all functions that handle ATM cell labeling reside in the switch interface, including virtual path identifier/virtual channel identifier assignment, addition of routing information to cells, and discarding cells if needed. The switch interfaces can be designed for various bit rates. Currently, 1.5-Mbps, 50-Mbps, 155-Mbps, 622-Mbps, and 2.4-kbps interface speeds have been developed for different physical-layer protocols. The VP and VC switching are simultaneously supported by the switch interfaces, which results in valuable cell-routing flexibility.

To summarize, a switch interface performs optical-to-electrical signal conversion, cell synchronization, header translation, and insertion and extraction of routing information both at the input and output line card. Figure 14.4 shows the various functions performed by the input and output line cards.

14.3.1.2 Switch Core. The switch core is a space switch that supports both point-to-point and point-to-multipoint connections. It is equipped

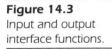

Figure 14.3
Input and output interface functions.

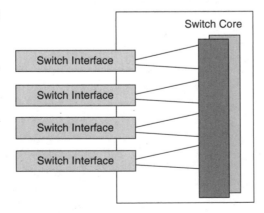

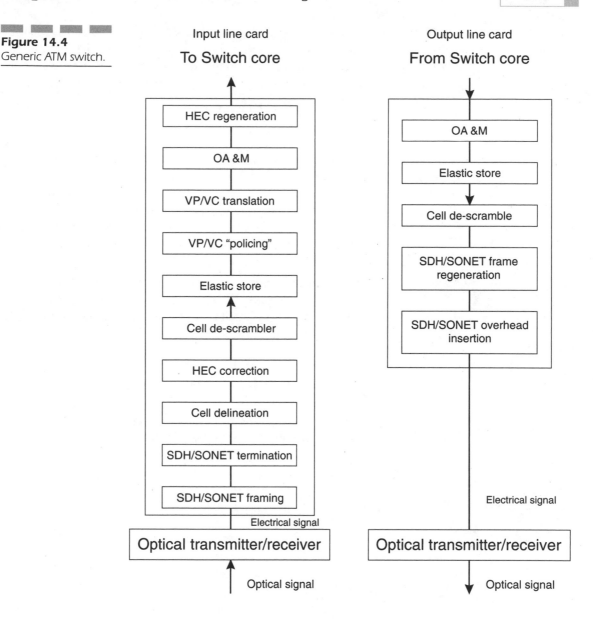

Figure 14.4
Generic ATM switch.

with large buffers at the output or input connections to cope with variations in the asynchronous cell flow. The decision to put buffers at the input or output, or both, is an aspect of ATM switch design and varies depending on vendor methodology. The switch core is comprised of three different functional units: concentrators, multiplexers, and switching matrix.

When combined, these three can be cost-effective to meet the various capacity requirements for a switching node. Using additional switch cores can increase switch capacity. Figure 14.5 shows a switch core containing all three type units.

Concentrators and multiplexers: Devices with a lower bit rate at the switch interface are connected to the switching matrix via a concentrator to better utilize the incoming link connected to the switch matrix. Thus, a concentrator aggregates the lower variable bit-rate traffic into a higher bit rate so that the switching matrix can perform the switch at a standard interface speed. Multiplexers are used when switching matrix interfaces are at a higher link speed than the switch interface. In this process, the cells from a number of interfaces are multiplexed into a single cell stream. The output cell stream is at the cell rate required by the switching matrix.

Switching matrix: The incoming cell streams are passed through the switching matrix. No switching occurs in the concentrators and multiplexers; the switch core always contains the switch matrix. Many types of switching matrices exist, some of which are discussed in Sec. 14.7.

14.3.2   Software Architecture

The ATM switch is controlled and supervised by software. The software architecture in an ATM switch is usually divided into three functional

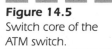

Figure 14.5
Switch core of the
ATM switch.

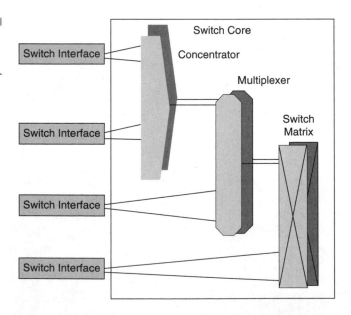

categories: traffic management, operation and maintenance, and system functions. Each of these categories is further divided into seven functional areas:

- Connection handling
- Configuration management
- Fault management
- Performance management
- Billing management
- Security management
- System functions

An essential requirement when designing software for the ATM switch has been the ability to partition the software into hardware-dependent and hardware-independent components. Software blocks have well-defined interfaces to other software blocks and entail as little interdependency as possible. This modular approach is a prerequisite for a simplified systematic upgrading of the switch when introducing new functionality.

Each of these seven functional areas controls the ATM switch. Each performs certain functions related to a call. For example, performance management provides statistics on the performance of the network on a VP- or VC-connection basis. In addition, statistics such as delay and throughput are available. Very little work has been done so far in software architecture of the ATM switch.

Usually, the ATM cells in the switch must be transported from an input to one or more outputs. The switching from input to output can be combined with concentration, expansion, multiplexing, and demultiplexing of the ATM traffic. From a functional point of view, an ATM switch is the same as a packet switch. The main difference between the ATM switch and the packet switch is the switching speed, processing of the packets or cells, and the packet size.

14.4 ATM Switching Principle

Having seen the basic architecture of the ATM switch, let's go through the principle behind it, which is shown in Fig. 14.6. Here, the incoming ATM cells are physically switched from an input, I_n, to an output, O_q, while the cell's header values are translated from an incoming value, β, to an outgoing value, δ. Each incoming and outgoing link has unique header

Figure 14.6
ATM switching
principle.

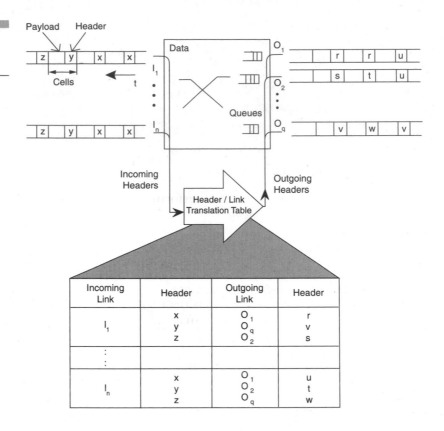

values, but identical headers can be found in different links (e.g., X on link I_q and I_n). The translation tables map the incoming header value to the outgoing header value. For example, the cells with a header value of x on incoming link I_1 are switched to output O_1, with their headers translated (switched) to value r. Similarly, all cells with header value x in link I_n are switched to output O_1 with header value u.

In this switching system, however, it is possible that two cells of inputs I_1 and I_n arrive simultaneously at the ATM switch and are destined for the same output (O_1). In such a case, the cell cannot be put on output at the same time, and the switch must buffer the cells that cannot be served. Buffering is typical of an ATM switch.

14.5   ATM Switching Requirements

As mentioned earlier, a broadband network must be capable of transporting all types of information, ranging from low-bit-rate basic voice to high-bit-rate high-definition video. Each of these services has different requirements in terms of bit rate, characteristics, temporal behavior (constant bit rate or variable bit rate), semantic transparency (cell loss, bit error rate), and time transparency (delay, delays jitter). The broadband ATM switches must meet these different service requirements.

To address these services, the following are classified as the basic requirements for an ATM switch:

- Ability to handle different information rates
- Capability to do broadcast and multicast
- Ability to have high performance in terms of bit error rate, delay, and throughput

14.5.1 Information Rates

Because the information rates of the different services are very diverse, a large number of information rates must be switched in broadband switches. These rates range from a few kilobits per second to values as high as 150 Mbps. Currently, ATM switches have a maximum bit rate of about 150 Mbps per port. Thus, the internal backplane switching capacity of an ATM switch can vary from 2 to 260 Gbps, depending on the number of ports in a switch.

14.5.2 Broadcast and Multicast

In typical voice and packet switches, only point-to-point connections are available because information must be switched from a logical input to a logical output. In broadband networks, however, additional requirements arise because of the new services. As mentioned in Chap. 12, some services are distributive in nature (requiring the broadcasting of information from one source to all destinations) and others are multicast (providing the information from one source to selective destinations). CATV distribution is an example of broadcast. Both multicast and broadcast facilities require trunk circuits to subscribers.

14.5.3 Performance

Typically, the performance of a switch is characterized by throughput, call blocking probability, bit error rate (BER), and switching delay. In an

ATM switching environment, however, two additional parameters are also important, i.e., cell loss or cell insertion probability and jitter on the delay.

In ATM switches, as in conventional switches, the performance characteristics are based on the technology and dimensioning of the system. We addressed the different technology drivers for broadband in Chap. 2.

In this section we address the three parameters: connection blocking probability, cell loss or cell insertion probability, and switching delay.

Although ATM switching is based on ATM cells, it is inherently connection-oriented. Thus, a connection must be established between an input and an output interface through the switching matrix, which does not mean that ATM switch implementation is internally connection-oriented.

Connection blocking probability: Connection blocking is determined as the probability that not enough resources are available between the input and output of the switch to guarantee the quality of all existing connections as well as the new connection. Thus, if enough resources (i.e., guaranteed bandwidth) are available on the switch for all the connections, no blocking occurs. The number of connections depends on the internal design of the switch because resources in the switch must be allocated internally for every new connection. The blocking probability of the switches is determined by the dimensioning of the switch, such as the number of internal connections and the load (or bandwidth utilized) on those connections.

Cell loss/cell insertion probability: In ATM switches, there could be instances when too many cells are destined for the same link. The consequence of this situation is that a particular link receives more cells than it can handle, forcing cells to be discarded or lost. The probability of losing cells should be kept within specified limits to ensure a high semantic transparency. Typical values for cell loss probability for ATM switches are in the range of 10^{-8} to 10^{-11}. In other words, as an approximation, only one cell per billion should be lost (10^{-9}).

Switching delay: Switching delay is the time taken to switch an ATM cell through the switch. Typical values mentioned for the delay in ATM switches range between 100 and 1000 μs, with a jitter of a few hundred microseconds. This delay is negligible compared to the switching delay of 20 μs that is found in a packet switch.

14.6   ATM Switch Building Blocks

An ATM switching network or fabric comprises basic building blocks called *switching elements*. Switching elements consist of queues and switching matrices. First, we focus on the building blocks, then we look at the different switching matrix types.

ATM switching elements are typically small. Currently, elements vary from two inputs and two outputs at 155 Mbps each to a maximum of 32 inputs and 32 outputs at 155 Mbps. The number of ports varies depending on the interface speed of the switch and also on the technology used and the level of integration achieved by the switch manufacturer. In this section, we discuss the queues of switching elements. Typically, the switching element acts as a statistical multiplexer, which resembles queuing. A cell is "queued" when two cells arrive at two inputs destined for the same output. Depending on the architecture of the switching element and on internal speed, the cell can be queued at the input, the output, or internally in the switching element (i.e., between two switching matrices). Depending on the queue location, a switching element is called an input-queued switching element, an output-queued switching element, or a central queued switching element. Each is described in the following sections.

14.6.1   Input-Queued Switching Element

Figure 14.7 shows the switching element with an input-queuing mechanism. In this approach, the contention problem is resolved at the input. Each input port consists of a dedicated buffer to store the incoming cells until the arbitration logic determines that the buffer (queue) can be served. On clearing the queue, the cell goes to the switching transfer medium, which transfers the ATM cells from the input to the output without any internal contention or blocking. The arbitration logic decides which input port is to be served. This logic can be the basic round-robin algorithm, or any complex selection algorithm that uses the information switch as quality of service to select the queue to be processed. The switching matrix in the switching element with input queues transfers the selected cells (the number of cells is less than N) from the N input ports to the N selected output ports during one cell time. In this phase, the queue size depends on the switch algorithm.

Figure 14.7
Switching element
with input queues.

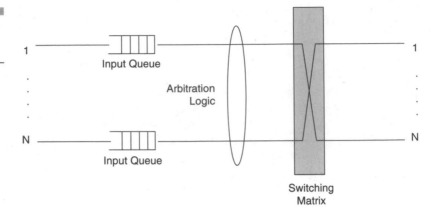

Typically, the queue size ranges from 320 to 640 cells. If the incoming cells exceed the queue length, the switch drops the lower-priority cells from the queue.

14.6.2   Output Queuing

Figure 14.8 shows a switching element with output queues. A collision can occur if several input cells are hunting for the same output. This problem is resolved by using queues at each output of the switching element. Each output consists of a dedicated buffer that stores multiple cells that might arrive during one cell time. To ensure that no cell is lost in the switching matrix, the matrix must transfer the cells at a rate of N times the speed of input ports before the cells arrive at the output queue. The system must then write N cells in the queue in one cell time. Here, no arbitration logic is required in the switching elements because all the cells can arrive at their respective output queues. The control of the output queues is based on a simple first-in—first-out (FIFO) logic, ensuring that the cells remain in the correct sequence.

14.6.3   Central Queuing

Figure 14.9 shows the switching element with central queuing and multiple switching matrices within the switching element. In central queuing, the queuing buffers are not dedicated to a single input or output port of the switching matrix but are shared between all inputs and outputs. In this case, each incoming cell is stored directly in the central queue. Every output selects the cell destined for it from the central queue using FIFO.

14.7   ATM Switching Matrix or Network

We mentioned one of the building blocks of the switching network in the previous section. The other is the switching matrix. Switching matrices typically have a large number of input and output ports. They can typically be classified into two major groups: single-stage switching matrix and multistage switching matrix, as shown in Fig. 14.10.

Figure 14.8
Switching element with output queues.

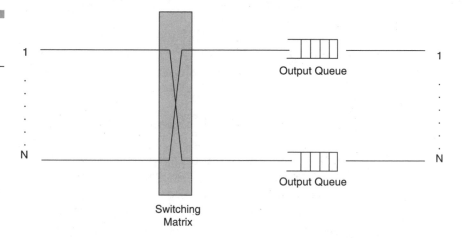

Figure 14.9
Switching element with central queuing.

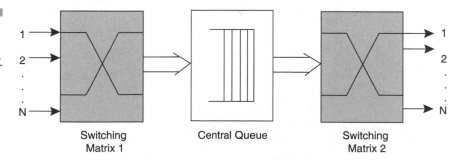

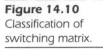

Figure 14.10
Classification of
switching matrix.

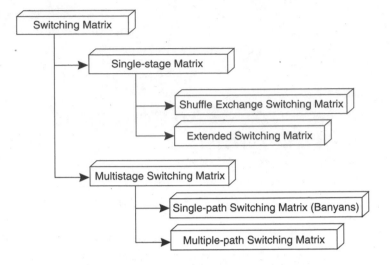

14.7.1　Single-Stage Switching Matrix

A single-stage matrix is characterized by a single stage of switching elements connected to the input and outputs of the matrix. Two types of
single-stage networks are described in this chapter: shuffle exchange and
extended.

14.7.1.1　Shuffle-Exchange Switching Matrix.　The shuffle-
exchange switching matrix is based on a perfect shuffle permutation,
which is connected to a stage of switching elements. Figure 14.11 shows
an example of a shuffle-exchange network. In this matrix, a feedback
mechanism is used to reach an arbitrary output from a given input.
Thus, a typical cell can pass through the matrix several times before
reaching its proper destination. This switching matrix is also called a
recirculating switching matrix. This matrix requires only a small number
of switching elements, but the performance is very poor because of the
feedback mechanism.

14.7.1.2　Extended Switching Matrix.　A switching network with
$k \infty k$ switching elements is shown in Fig. 14.12. In this matrix, any size
switching matrix can be implemented. The advantage of this type is that it
has a negligible cross-delay because the cells are buffered only once while
crossing the network. The cross-delay is dependent on the location of the
input. It is possible to form a single-stage network as large as $128 \infty 128$. For
large systems, however, multistage networks are preferred.

14.7.2 Multistage Switching Matrix

Multistage switching matrices were created to avoid the drawbacks of the single-stage switching matrix. They are built of several stages interconnected in a specific link pattern, according to the number of paths

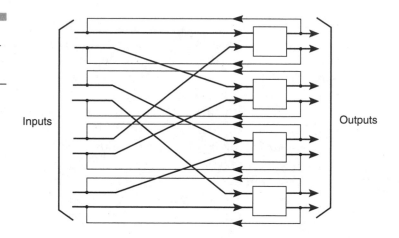

Figure 14.11
Example of a shuffle-exchange switching matrix.

Inputs

Outputs

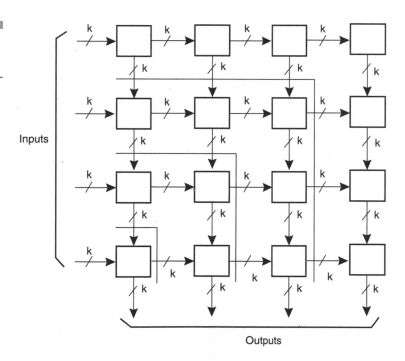

Figure 14.12
Extended switching matrix.

Inputs

Outputs

available to reach the destination output from a given input. These matrices are classified into two types: single-path and multiple-path.

14.7.2.1   Single-Path Switching Matrix.

Figure 14.12 shows an example of a single-path switching matrix with four stages. In a single-path switching matrix, only one path exists to reach the destination from a given input. These networks are sometimes called *Banyan networks*. Routing is very simple because only one path exists to reach the proper output. Delta networks are a special type of Banyan networks. Here, each output port is identified by a unique destination address that allows for simple routing of the cells to the destination. Hence, this network is sometimes called the *self-routing network*. The matrix in Fig. 14.13 is called a Delta-2 switching matrix.

The Delta-2 switching matrix with four stages has the topology of a baseline switching matrix. The thick lines indicate the path from input 5 to output 13 (binary destination address 1101). The switching element in each stage processes one bit of the 4-bit address. Each bit can have one of two values, 0 or 1. The switching element routes the cells in each stage depending on the value of the bit. In this example, the bit is 1 in the first stage. On arriving at the first stage, the switching element

Figure 14.13
Delta-2 switching matrix with four stages.

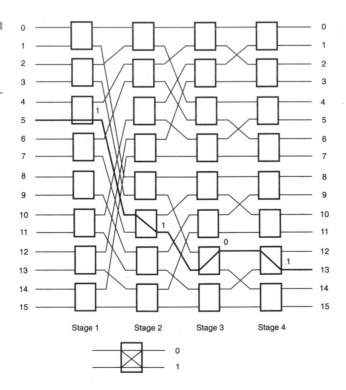

reads the value of the first bit if the bit is 1, as is the case in this example. The cells are routed via the downlink. If the value of the bit is 0, as in the case of the second bit, the switching element routes the traffic via the uplink. In this way, each cell is routed to its destination point.

14.7.2.2 Multiple-Path Switching Matrix. In a multiple-path switching matrix, many alternate paths exist for the destination output from a given input. This type of matrix has the advantage of reducing or avoiding internal blocking. The internal path is determined in most cases during the connection setup phase, and all the cells of that connection use the same internal path set at the time of connection. If FIFO is provided at each switching element, cell sequence integrity can be guaranteed, and no resequencing is necessary. There are two types of multiple-path networks: folded and unfolded. In folded networks, all inputs and outputs are located on the same side of the switching network, and the network's internal links are operated in a bidirectional manner. In unfolded networks, the inputs are located on one side and the outputs on the opposite side of the network. The internal links are unidirectional, and all cells must pass through the same number of switching elements.

Figure 14.14 shows an example of a multipath interconnection (MIN) switching matrix. This switching matrix is realized by adding a baseline switching matrix with reversed topology. The baseline switching matrix topology is shown in Fig. 14.13.

14.8　ATM Cell Processing in a Switch

The main functions of an ATM switching node are VPI/VCI translation and cell transport from the input to the appropriate output. Earlier, we showed cell processing using a table-controlled principle. There are actually two principles to address these tasks: self-routing or table-controlled.

14.8.1　Self-routing Principle

In self-routing, the VPI/VCI translation must be performed at the input of the switching element, as shown in Fig. 14.15. After translation, an internal identifier that precedes the cell header extends the cell. A cell header extension requires an increased internal matrix speed. Once the internal identifier is attached to the cell, it is routed via the self-routing principle described in Sec. 14.7. Each connection (incoming to outgoing) has a specific switching matrix internal identifier. This identifier is unique to that switching matrix and cannot be reused at another switching matrix. In a point-to-multipoint connection input, VPI/VCI is

Figure 14.14
Example of a multi-path interconnection switching matrix.

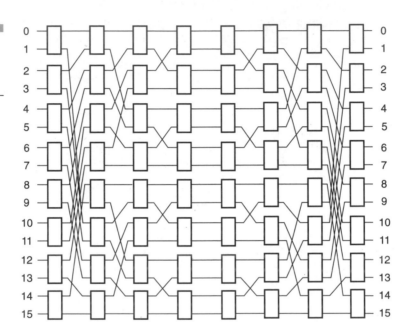

Figure 14.15
Self-routing switching elements.

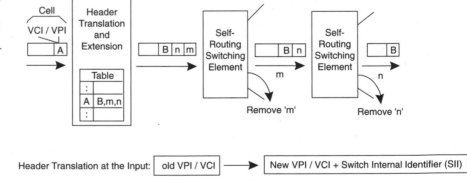

Header Translation at the Input: old VPI / VCI ⟶ New VPI / VCI + Switch Internal Identifier (SII)

VCI Virtual Channel Identifier
VPI Virtual Path Identifier
SII Switch Internal Identfier

Figure 14.16
Table-controlled
switching elements.

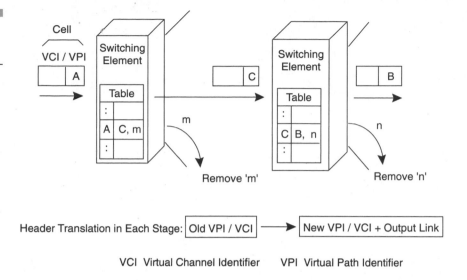

Header Translation in Each Stage: Old VPI / VCI ⟶ New VPI / VCI + Output Link

VCI Virtual Channel Identifier   VPI Virtual Path Identifier

assigned a multiple-switch internal identifier, thus enabling cells to be copied and routed to different destinations, depending on the identifier.

14.8.2 Table-Controlled Principle

In table-controlled switching, the VPI/VCI cell header is translated in each switching element into a new header. Figure 14.16 shows this type of cell translation. During the connection setup phase, the contents of the tables are updated. Each table entry consists of the new VPI/VCI and the number of the appropriate output port or link.

14.9 Summary

In this chapter, we covered broadband ATM switching. We addressed the requirements and building blocks, such as different types of queues and switching matrices. Among the different queuing mechanisms, central queuing requires the lowest memory capacity because of buffer sharing.

Among the switching matrices, multistage networks have better performance compared to single-stage networks. With respect to cell processing principles for large multistage switching networks, the self-routing principle is preferred because it is superior in terms of controlling complex connections and failure behavior.

CHAPTER 15

Broadband Transmission Network

15.1   Overview

In this chapter, we address how information is carried in a broadband transmission network. In the ATM switching environment, it is assumed that all information is placed into the payload of ATM cells. However, not all information is in the form of ATM cells in a broadband transmission network. The broadband transmission network should be designed in such a way that the traffic from the existing digital asynchronous network can be carried along with the new ATM traffic. The basic function of a transmission network is to transport information from the originating point to the destination without loss of information or delay. In addition to these responsibilities, other transmission network responsibilities include:

- Generation of cell (packetizer)

- Transmission of cells and existing isochronous traffic

- Multiplexing and demultiplexing of cells and other existing isochronous traffic

- Cross-connecting of cells and existing isochronous traffic

- Switching of cells and existing isochronous traffic

To meet these functions, ITU-T has selected SONET/SDH as the transmission protocol. SONET/SDH, however, is not the only protocol that can transport existing ATM cell. Traditional protocols do support ATM cells.

To deploy any successful network, including a broadband one, the most critical component of the whole network is the transmission system, which includes the physical cable. Unless the transmission systems are in place, no switching or any other system in the network can be used. Many technological advances in areas such as switching, intelligent networks, etc., were possible because of the advances made in transmission systems, such as fiber optics, fiber-terminals, etc. Fiber technology and equipment are available and being deployed around the world.

In this chapter we examine the transmission system for the broadband network and address its components and their functions. We also study the broadband reference architecture that brings together the different components. Both local and trunk network architectures are also explained in this chapter.

15.2 Broadband Transmission Functional Components

A transmission system consists of many components, each having a function to perform related to the transport of the information from one point to another. Here, we look into some of the functional components of SONET/SDH and ATM, the transmission and switching technologies for future BISDN.

15.2.1 SONET Multiplexer

A SONET multiplexer has p inputs and one output, as shown in Fig. 15.1a. An input tributary operates at the STS-3nc/OC3nc rate, which depends on the individual tributary. The SONET multiplexer synchronously multiplexes the input tributaries into an output stream operating at the STS-3m rate. This output rate is equal to the sum of the input tributary rates. SONET multiplexers can also be cascaded back-to-back. It is not necessary that the input be STS-3nc/OC3nc (frame-carrying concatenated ATM cells); in fact, the input can carry existing digital signals such as DS1 or DS3, mapped alongside ATM cells. DS3 is mapped directly onto an STS-1 payload, where DS1 is mapped onto a VT-1.5. Thus, within an STS-1 payload, 28 VT-1.5s can be accommodated in an STS-1 frame. In this multiplexer, inputs i to p can be STS-1, DS1, or DS3; all can be present as part of the input. Thus, the output STS-3nc/OC3nc frame consists of the combined payload of DS3, DS1, and ATM cells, enabling all the different traffic to be carried on one transmission network.

15.2.2 SONET Demultiplexer

The SONET demultiplexer performs the inverse function of the SONET multiplexer, as illustrated in Fig. 15.1b. The SONET demultiplexer synchronously demultiplexes the single input stream into p output streams, which corresponds to the input stream of the associated SONET multiplexer. Thus, if the input consists of a combination of STS-3nc, DS1, and DS3, the output consists of exactly the same elements. Figure 15.2 shows a cascade of multiplexers, where lower-speed inputs are multiplexed back-to-back to a higher speed in a cascade. With today's equipment, the

Figure 15.1*a*
SONET multiplexer.

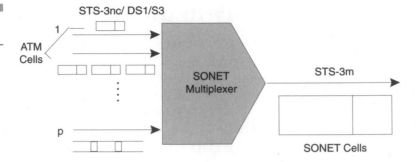

Figure 15.1 *b*
SONET demultiplexer.

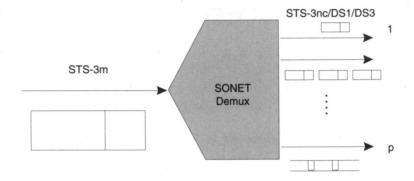

Figure 15.2
Example of cascaded
multiplexers.

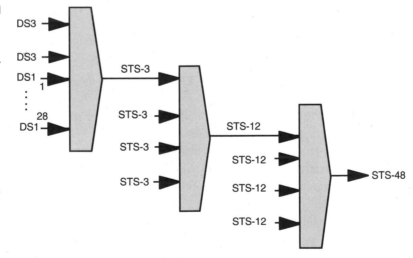

users do not need to buy multiple multiplexers because one piece of equipment can be configured with any combination of input and output interfaces. For example, one can combine four DS1s, two DS3s, and one OC3 as input and one OC48 as output. In this case, the output frame might not be fully packed because of its very high speed, but adding an additional input interface can easily incorporate future expansion. In a typical transmission terminal, a SONET multiplexer and demultiplexer are packaged together.

15.2.3 STS-3nc Cross-Connect

An STS-3nc has p inputs and q outputs, as shown in Fig. 15.3, where all of them operate at the same rate. An STS-3nc can connect any input to zero, one, or more outputs, thereby duplicating the input signal at those outputs. The relative timing between STS-3nc streams might or might not be preserved as the streams pass through the cross-connect. The basic function of this cross-connect is to regroup different VTs and STS-3nc to the appropriate port, which is destined for a single location.

15.2.4 ATM Concentrator

An ATM concentrator has p inputs and one output. Each input tributary operates at the STS-3nc or DS3 rate. The ATM concentrator receives incoming ATM cells at a variable bit rate at each input. Cells designated as unoccupied are deleted. Occupied cells are buffered at the input until they can be merged with other cells into the output stream. The output stream operates at the STS-3mc rate, illustrated in Fig. 15.4. The output rate depends on the ATM traffic characteristics within the input tributaries and on the degree of concentration desired. This concentration of ATM

Figure 15.3
STS-3c SONET cross-connect.

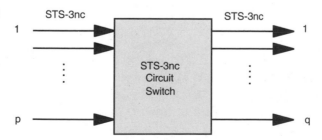

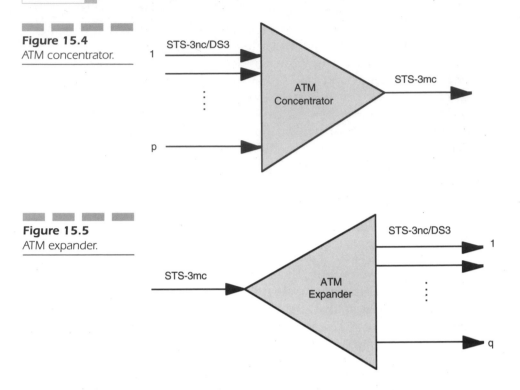

Figure 15.4
ATM concentrator.

Figure 15.5
ATM expander.

cells is called *statistical multiplexing*. This concentration of cells can be standalone or integrated with others, such as the ATM switch, as part of an ATM switching node.

15.2.5   ATM Expander

The ATM expander performs the inverse function of the ATM concentrator, as shown in Fig. 15.5. An incoming STS-3mc stream of cells is put on the appropriate output port with appropriate empty cells to pad the output variable information rate. Usually, an ATM concentrator is cascaded with an ATM expander to perform the bidirectional function for the ATM cells.

15.2.6   ATM Switch

An ATM switch typically consists of a concentrator, expander, multiplexer, and demultiplexer to adapt the different rates at the input ports of the ATM switch. As shown in Fig. 15.6, an ATM switch has p input ports and q output ports, where $p > q$. Input and output ports operate at various rates, ranging from DS1 to STS-3mc. The header of the incoming ATM cell is examined to determine the output port to which the cell must be routed. Information in the header is used as an index into a table that contains routing and translation information. The details of the ATM switch were discussed in Chap. 14.

15.2.7 Service Module

A service module is part of the network, but performs its function at a layer higher than the ATM layer (Fig. 15.7). For BISDN protocols, these layers are the adaptation, management, and control layers. Examples of service modules are the following:

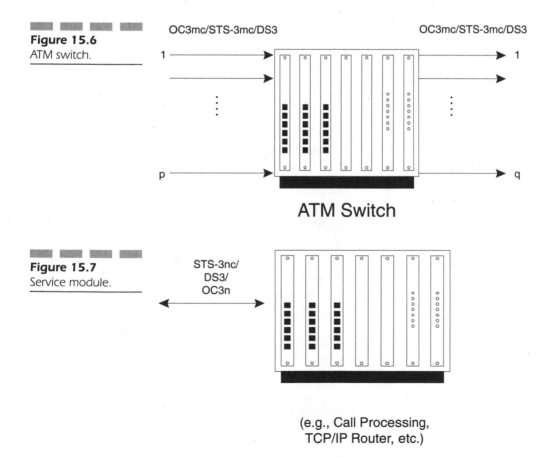

Figure 15.6
ATM switch.

OC3mc/STS-3mc/DS3   OC3mc/STS-3mc/DS3

1 ──────────→ ──────────→ 1

p ──────────→ ──────────→ q

ATM Switch

Figure 15.7
Service module.

STS-3nc/
DS3/
OC3n

(e.g., Call Processing,
TCP/IP Router, etc.)

■ A service module that receives user-network signaling messages, performs call processing functions, and controls the switching matrix table

■ A service module that receives multimegabit connectionless data, possibly performs the segmentation and reassembly functions, examines the level 3 header, and routes the datagram to the destination or to another connectionless data service module

■ A multicast bridge that receives incoming cells, copies the cells, and routes the copies of the cell to multiple destinations.

15.2.8   Interworking Units

Interworking units provide the adaptation functionality from narrowband to broadband. The existing digital asynchronous transmission system maps to a synchronous transmission system. A typical example is the mapping of DS3 to STS-1 payload or OCI payload or DSI to V1.5 payload in the SONET frame, as shown in Fig. 15.8.

15.3   Broadband Transmission Functions

One of the basic functions provided by any transmission network is the transfer of information from the source to the destination without error. Because of the high speed and usage of fiber optics to transfer information in broadband networks, very stringent performance requirements in terms of bit-error rate become necessary. In broadband transmission networks, ATM cells carry the information in their payload. It is not necessary, however, that information be carried in the

Figure 15.8
Interworking unit.

STS-3nc/
OC3nc

Internetworking unit

Interface to Narrowband Network
(e.g., DS-3, DS1)

ATM cells. The standards bodies have defined standards such that information from different existing transmission systems, such as digital asynchronous system (DS1, DS3, E1, and E3), can carry ATM cells. Of course, ATM cells can also be carried in a SONET/SDH network. The broadband transmission network typically uses some or all of the functional components mentioned in Sec. 15.2. The transmission functions related to transfer of ATM cells are

- Generation of cells
- Transmission of cells
- Multiplexing and demultiplexing of cells
- Cross-connecting of cells
- Switching of cells

Functions related to the switching of ATM cells have been studied in Chap. 13. The other functions are addressed in this chapter.

15.3.1 Generation of Cells

Cell generation in a broadband network can occur in two ways:

- In a broadband/ATM customer premises equipment, which is a broadband terminal that has the capability to generate ATM cells.
- If the CPE is a nonbroadband terminal, the network must convert the information into ATM cells and vice versa.

In the case of a broadband/ATM terminal, the CPE has an adapter card that segments the information into 53-byte ATM cells with appropriate VPI/VCI values. The adapter card generates speeds from 1.5 to 155 Mbps, enabling the end-to-end services to have the same protocol (including the intermediate nodes). There are numerous advantages to broadband terminals: reduced delay due to protocol conversion from one network to another, ease of operations, administration, and maintenance (OAM), etc. Figure 15.9 shows a typical broadband terminal.

In the case of a conventional or non-ATM terminal, the adaptation of information must be performed in the network. The network component that performs this function is called an ATM packetizer/depacketizer. The principle here is as simple as cutting a long ribbon into evenly sized pieces. Figure 15.10 depicts this concept.

This function will initially be located in the backbone network due

Figure 15.9
Broadband terminal.

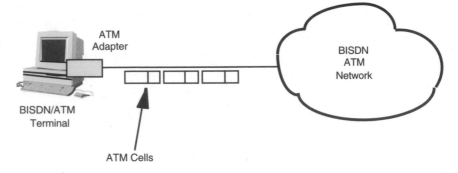

to economics, and will later move to the customer's premises to realize a complete ATM-based broadband network.

15.3.2   Transmission of Cells

In principle, ATM cells can be transported on any transmission system. The only requirement is guaranteed bit independence so that there are no restrictions on cell information contents. To accommodate the transport of ATM cells in existing systems, standards must be developed that enable the user to transmit ATM cells. In fact, the ATM Forum's main objective is to develop a user-network interface and network-network interface for existing systems, in addition to the proposed BISDN standards by ITU-T. To achieve network synchronization on a synchronous transmission network, care must be taken that clocks are synchronized throughout the system. Bellcore, in its technical reference TR-NWT-000253, Issue 2 ("SONET Transport System Common Generic Criteria"), has detailed the requirement of the clock so that synchronization can be maintained in a SONET environment. Figure 15.11 shows how synchronization is maintained in a BISDN network.

In BISDN, network synchronization is obtained from a reliable, stable clock source, which has an accuracy of stratum 2 or 1.[1] All the elements in the network are directly synchronized to the single clock. Because it is not possible to have a direct link from a single clock to all the network elements, the timing information is usually extracted from the neighboring node (the node that has a direct connection) in the network. This node then transfers that timing to the next node in the line. All nodes in the network are thus synchronized. Because timing is an important element in a synchronous network, care must be taken to

---

[1] The stratum 1 clock is the most accurate clock, whose oscillation remains constant over a long period of time. The source for this clock is usually from an atomic clock.

Figure 15.10
ATM packetizer/
depacketizer.

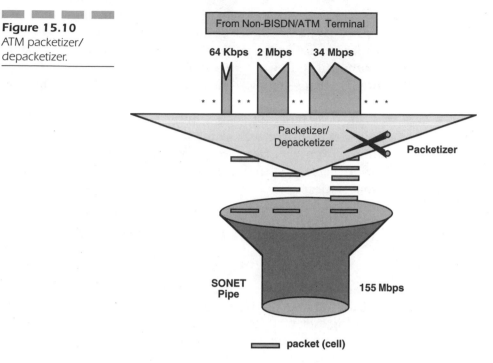

Figure 15.11
Example of clock syn-
chronization.

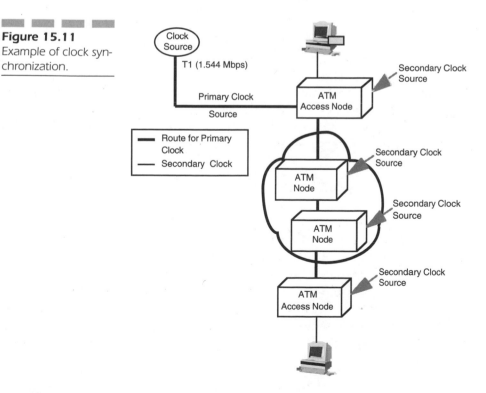

have a backup. Thus, in a BISDN network, each node must be able to fall back on the secondary clock, if the primary clock fails or loses synchronization for a short period. Typically, the secondary source is internal to a node. In some cases, however, it might be another external clock source. Timing is one of the more important features required by synchronous transmission system equipment. In general, no equipment can be sold without incorporating good timing features, such as primary and secondary clocks. In the real world, large pubic networks get their reference timing from a nuclear source, which is supposed to be the most stable and reliable. All other timing clocks are always in exact accordance with that nuclear source.

15.3.3   Multiplexing and Demultiplexing of Cells

A typical multiplexer multiplexes several signals that originate from different BISDN customers on to a single access line. Usually, the signal sources in a multiplexer vary from DS1 to OC3, which operate at various line speeds. For example, the input signal can be asynchronous or synchronous, and the output can be SONET, but on the input side, asynchronous traffic is mapped onto synchronous traffic (SONET), which might be OC1/STS-1. These input signals are multiplexed together to form higher SONET rates (OC48/STS-48).

In an ATM multiplexer, all incoming idle cells are sorted out. Thus, the ATM traffic can be concentrated, and it is performed by an ATM concentrator. The achievable degree of concentration depends on the traffic characteristics and the requested quality of services. The device that performs the reverse of the ATM concentrator is called the *ATM expander,* and this type of multiplexing is statistical.

15.3.4   Cross-Connecting of Cells

An ATM cross-connect is a VP switch that can flexibly map incoming VPs onto the outgoing VPs and thus enable establishment of VPCs through the ATM network. The cross-connect can also concentrate ATM traffic and perform management functions of the physical and ATM layer of BISDN. A typical use of this cross-connect is to access the ATM switching backbone network. A typical ATM switch can be configured as a regular switch or a cross-connect. In ATM terminology, an ATM switch can be configured as a VC switch or a VP switch.

15.4 Broadband Reference Network Architecture

A reference architecture model for the broadband network is a conceptual division of functions that must be performed to transport user information through the network. It is a basic tool for studying alternate network architectures in both local and trunk segments of the network. In many instances, some of these functions can be merged together or completely ignored. The reference architecture is just a logical segmentation of functions; the functions can be in any part of the network. The reference architecture model that is depicted in Fig. 15.12 consists of the following layers:

- Customer premises node (CPN)
- Distribution/drop plant
- Remote multiplexer node (RMN)
- Subfeeder plant

Figure 15.12
Broadband reference network architecture.

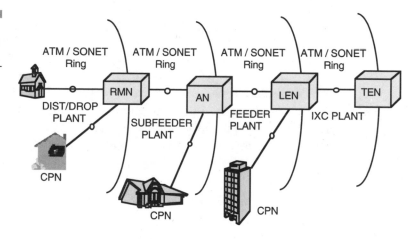

CPN	Customer Premises Node
RMN	Remote Multiplexer Node
AN	Access Node
LEN	Local Exchange Node
TEN	Transit Exchange Node
IXC	Interexchange Carrier

- Access node (AN)
- Feeder plant
- Local exchange node (LEN)
- Interexchange plant
- Transit exchange node (TEN)

A set of functions corresponding to each layer is performed. Depending on individual architecture realizations, some functions in a particular layer might not be implemented, or, in some cases, an entire layer can be eliminated.

CPN provides conversion between the various service interfaces and the integrated user-network interface. It is assumed that single-mode fiber/multimode fiber in the distribution/drop plant carries information to and from a single user. Fibers used in the subfeeder, feeder, and interexchange plant carry information to and from many users.

RMN and AN guarantee that only information destined for a single customer flows downstream over a distribution fiber. Upstream, the RMN and AN prevent information from one customer adversely affecting information of another. The LEN provides interconnections among the customers served by that LEN by performing switching. The TEN provides interconnections and switching among the LENs served by that TEN. Because narrowband networks will continue to exist for many years, internetworking units are necessary at the local exchange and at transit exchange nodes to provide the necessary conversions and adaptations for interconnecting the narrowband networks. The IWUs can be separate modules connected to the broadband switching systems or integrated into broadband switching systems. Table 15.1 shows the different functions performed by each network layer.

15.4.1   Local Network Architecture

Conceptually, the simplest realization of a BISDN local network is the star topology, where one access line per customer exists. This topology is used in today's telecommunications networks. The local network is part of the broadband reference network architecture. Figure 15.13 shows the local network topologies in the BISDN reference network architecture. Other topologies, such as rings and double stars, are also recommended. For broadband networks, ring topologies are considered because of the need for survivability in the local network.

Network Layer	Functions
Customer premises node	ATM and SONET multiplexing, NT2 functions
Distribution/drop plant	Physical layer functions (transmission) (uses technologies discussed in Chap. 9)
Remote multiplexer node	SONET/ATM multiplexing/demultiplexing and ATM concentrator and expander
Subfeeder plant	Physical layer functions (transmission) (uses technologies discussed in Chap. 8)
Access node	STS-3nc cross-connect, ATM concentration/expansion, traffic segregation, ATM switching, SONET multiplexing/demultiplexing
Feeder plant	Physical layer functions (transmission) (uses technologies discussed in Chap. 8)
Local exchange node	STS-3nc cross-connect, ATM concentration/expansion, traffic segregation, ATM switching, SONET multiplexing/demultiplexing, higher-layer functions, internetworking with other networks
Interexchange plant	Physical layer functions (transmission) (uses technologies discussed in Chap. 8)
Transit exchange node	STS-3nc cross-connect, ATM concentration/ expansion, traffic segregation, ATM switching, SONET multiplexing/demultiplexing, higher-layer functions, internetworking with other networks

Figure 15.13
Example of local network topologies.

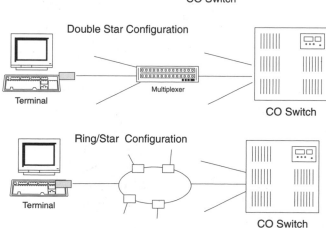
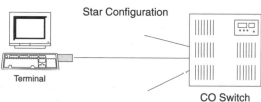

15.4.2   Trunk Network Architecture

Figure 15.14 shows a typical trunk network architecture. The cross-connect is connected to an ATM switch on one side and a SONET fiber linear terminal (point-to-point terminal) on the trunk side in each location. SONET transmission and ATM switching combine to form the typical BISDN trunk network. The cross-connect or multiplexer might be the interface between the BISDN/ATM switch, which switches ATM cells, and the SONET terminal, which multiplexes the ATM and conventional traffic in that location into a common fiber-based technology.

In the second example, shown in Fig. 15.15, the linear fiber terminal is replaced by a ring terminal. There are many advantages in using the

Figure 15.14

Example of typical trunk network.

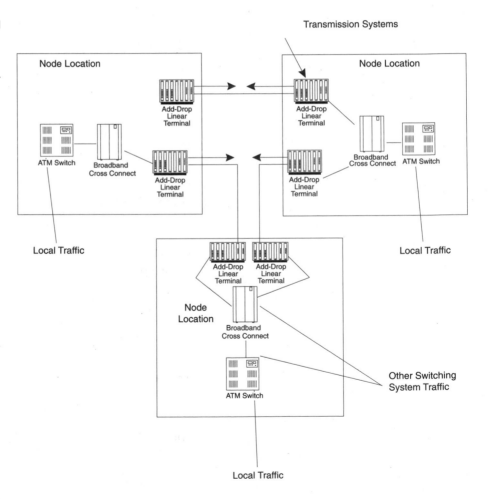

Figure 15.15
Example of trunk network with linear fiber terminal replaced by ring terminal.

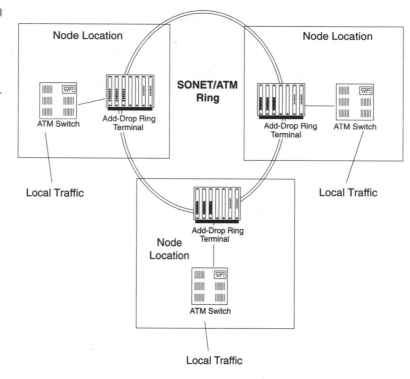

ring terminal. Foremost among them is the survivability of the traffic between two locations; there is always an alternate route. Alternate routes are very valuable in the case of a long-distance backbone network, where a huge amount of traffic is carried on each trunk between two points. In this network, if a link fails, the traffic is automatically routed via another route to its destination. The only traffic lost is the local traffic near the failure. It is expected that ring trunk architecture will be preferred in broadband transmission networks.

15.5 Summary

In this chapter, we addressed the broadband transmission network, its different components, and their functions. The transmission network plays an important part in the success of BISDN deployment. Unless the transmission network is successfully implemented, the overall success of the network is questionable. In fact, any service provider who is in the business of providing communication services spends a lot of time and money to ensure that the transmission network is fail-proof.

For example, service providers are deploying SONET rings instead of SONET linear terminals. In the former, if any link fails, the network automatically reroutes the traffic, thus providing 100 percent survivability, whereas in the latter, human intervention is required to reroute the traffic. In the United States today, most of the backbone networks are fiber-based, and some are already migrating toward SONET ring-based transmission networks.

16

Broadband
Intelligent
Network

16.1   Overview

The objective of this chapter is to discuss the intelligent network architecture in an ATM-based broadband environment. There has been a lot of discussion on broadband transport and switching with very little discussion on the IN aspect. Before we propose a new broadband intelligent architecture, we need to understand the current IN architecture and its limitation with respect to support services in a broadband environment. Then, based on those limitations, we discuss several options. There is no right architecture to recommend; it is up to the service provider to migrate to an architecture that will support the service they plan to offer.

IN is not a technology or a set of services but rather a concept for a new approach to the development and deployment of telecommunications and information services. An IN permits functionality and capability to be distributed flexibly at a variety of network entities and allows the service to be provided via service-independent control architecture. IN was developed with the following objectives in mind: rapid development and deployment of services; ubiquitous service access; multimedia services support, i.e., integrating voice, data, and video; vendor independence; cost-effective service delivery environment; and compatibility with existing networks.

As public carriers plan to offer new broadband services and consolidate different types of networks into a single ATM-based broadband network platform, the question of supporting the future services on existing IN platform has been raised. It has become very clear that the current IN cannot support some of the objectives mentioned previously. Thus, the issue of how to evolve the existing IN architecture to support the objectives needs to be addressed.

This chapter outlines some of the options being considered for broadband IN along with some background on the current IN architecture and its limitations.

16.2   Current IN Architecture

Figure 16.1 shows a high-level view of the current IN architecture and how the different components interact with each other.

The following elements are part of the IN network:

- Service management system (SMS)
- Service control point (SCP)
- Signal transfer point (STP)
- Service switching point (SSP)
- Intelligent peripheral (IP)

Figure 16.1
Current IN architecture. STP=Signal transfer point. SCP=Service central point. SSP=Switch service point.

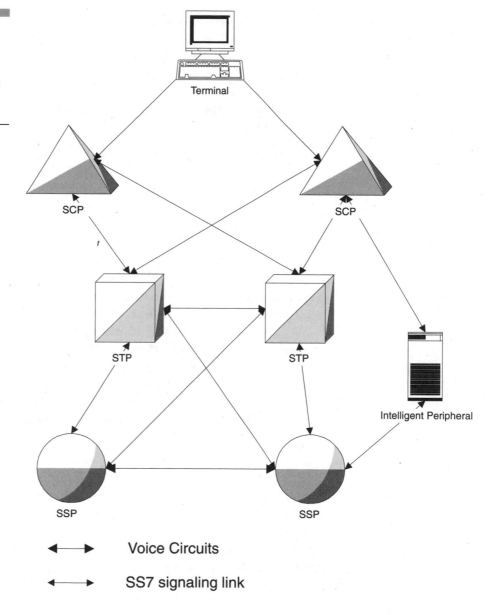

The functions of these IN network elements are described in the following subsection.

SSP: SSP serves as an access point for service users and executes heavily used services. It is basically the software that is present in the switch. The basic function of this software is to identify the IN-based call and initiate a trigger and hold the call till a reply is received from SCP or IP which contains the instruction on next steps for the call.

STP: STP is part of the common channel signaling 7 network, or simply SS7. SS7 is a standardized communication interface through which the goal of the multivendor SCP and SSP can be achieved. STP switches SS7 messages to different SS7 nodes. The use of standalone or integrated STP depends on specific network configurations. STP is normally developed by traditional switch manufacturers such as Northern Telecom or AT&T.

SCP: SCP is used when new IN services are introduced into the network and activated. If a service is based on functional components, the functional components are elected using a service logic interpreter. Some SCP services require large amounts of data that must reside on direct-access storage devices such as disks. The service programs and data are updated from the SMS. SCP is a commercial database stored on a fully redundant computer. It should be able to access databases efficiently and reliably and provide a software platform for rapid service creation.

SMS: The network operators usually own the SMS. It updates the SCPs with new data or programs and collects statistics from them. SMS also enables the service subscriber to control his or her own service parameters via a terminal linked to the SMS. For example, the subscriber can define the day and time when a number should be routed to a specific path. This modification is filtered or validated by the network operator. SMS is a commercial computer, usually a mainframe, which provides a development environment for new services.

IP: IP provides enhanced services usually controlled by an SCP or SSP. It is more economical for several users to share an IP because the capabilities in IP are either not in SSP or too expensive to put in all SSPs. Typical examples of IP functions are customized announcements, speech synthesizing, voice messaging, speech recognition, or database information that is made accessible to the end user. By making IP physically separate from SSP but connected via a standard interface enables any vendor to own and operate an IP, thus giving the IP provider an opportunity to provide value-added services to its users.

16.2.1 Limitation of IN Architecture

We briefly described the current IN architecture in the previous section. This architecture has some limitations in supporting broadband services. Current IN uses 56-kbps links to transport the signaling information via specialized systems. This link speed is sufficient for today's service requirement, but is unacceptable for the response time and volume required in a broadband environment, particularly for services requiring long paths and extensive user-network or SCP-to-SCP interaction. Thus higher-speed links are needed to alleviate the delay and meet the response time requirements. This has also become a big issue with recent deregulation and requirement of local number portability and new wireless services such as PCS.

Another issue in today's IN systems is multiple generations of signaling systems being used to handle SS6, SS7, and DTMF (digital touchtone multifrequency). These systems are managed to interoperate.

16.3 ATM-Based Broadband IN Architecture

There are several approaches being proposed to alleviate the potential limitations of today's IN architecture. Here, we will look at three of them: ATM-based quasi-associated broadband IN architecture and ATM-based associated broadband IN architecture. A third approach is a combination of these two approaches.

16.3.1 ATM-Based Quasi-Associated Broadband IN Architecture

Figure 16.2 depicts an example of ATM-based quasi-associated broadband IN architecture. In Fig. 16.2, the messages related to a call control between two BB-SSP are transported over links directly connected via the virtual paths through the BB-STP's. Figure 16.3 shows the protocol stack of the network elements involved in the architecture.

This architecture follows today's IN architecture concept with enhanced STP and SCP capabilities for broadband service needs. In this architecture, BB-SSP communicates with BB-SCP through BB-STP as today's IN network does. But the basic difference is that the BB-STP is an

Figure 16.2
ATM-based quasi-
associated broad-
band IN architecture.
BB=Broadband.

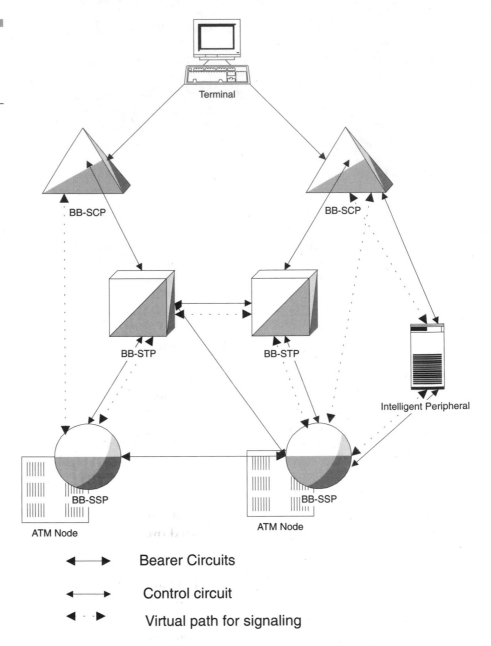

Bearer Circuits

Control circuit

Virtual path for signaling

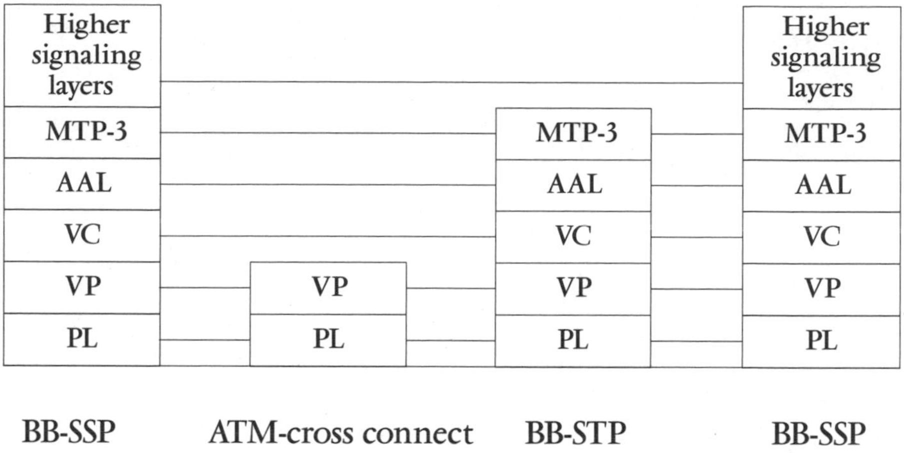

Figure 16.3
Protocol stack for
quasi-associated
broadband IN
architecture.

Higher signaling layers				Higher signaling layers
MTP-3			MTP-3	MTP-3
AAL			AAL	AAL
VC			VC	VC
VP	VP		VP	VP
PL	PL		PL	PL

BB-SSP	ATM-cross connect	BB-STP	BB-SSP

ATM-based switching system with an MTP-3 controller, which performs the signaling functions.

In a quasi-associated architecture, ATM transport is used in place of today's one-to-one dedicated transport. This architecture requires a significant upgrade in SCP capacity from today's SCP, in addition to an increase in capacity of the links between BB-STP and BB-SCP. This eventually could make the broadband IN difficult to grow beyond certain capacity for economic and operational reasons.

16.3.2 ATM-Based Associated Broadband IN Architecture

Figure 16.4 depicts an example of ATM-based associated broadband IN architecture. In Fig. 16.4, the messages related to a call control between two BB-SSP are transported over links directly connected via the virtual paths between the BB-SSP and BB-STP. Figure 16.5 shows the protocol stack of the network elements involved in the architecture.

In the associated mode architecture, each ATM node with BB-SSP capability has direct access to BB-SCP, which may be placed in a centralized or distributed manner. In Fig. 16.4 the BB-SCPs are centralized with full protection. This architecture eliminates the potential scalability limitation in the existing architecture. In this architecture, the BB-SCPs are partitioned and replicated for higher throughput and reliability in a cost-effective manner. The distributed BB-SCP placement scenario can be more cost-effective in an ATM-based IN architecture because it requires fewer links to BB-SCP.

Figure 16.4
ATM-based associated broadband IN architecture.

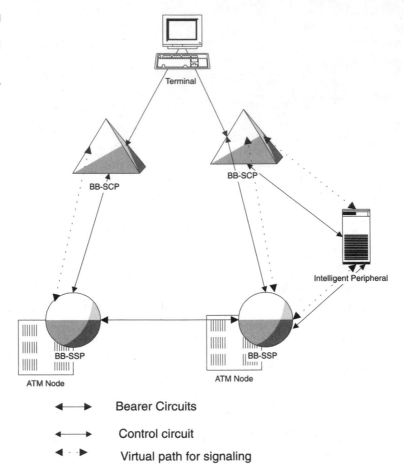

Terminal

BB-SCP

BB-SCP

Intelligent Peripheral

BB-SSP

ATM Node

BB-SSP

ATM Node

←——→   Bearer Circuits

←——→   Control circuit

◄ ‥ ►   Virtual path for signaling

Figure 16.5
Protocol stack for associated broadband IN architecture.

Higher signaling layers			Higher signaling layers
MTP-3			MTP-3
AAL			AAL
VC			VC
VP	VP	VP	VP
PL	PL	PL	PL

BB-SSP   ATM-XC   ATM-XC   BB-SSP

16.4 Comparison of ATM-Based Broadband IN Architecture

Both architectures have advantages and disadvantages. The basic difference is in the routing of signaling information. Table 16.1 shows the comparison of two ATM-based IN architecture options. The reason the routing is different is the use of BB-STP in quasi-associated architecture. The benefit of using BB-STP is an easy evolution path from current IN architecture. Even in an associated architecture, there is a need to interface with other existing IN architecture deployed by other service providers, so a need arises for the two architectures to co-exist with each other. Options are being considered so that a combination of these two will be the solution to fill the gap between today's IN and broadband IN architecture.

TABLE 16.1

Comparison of ATM-Based Broadband IN Architecture

Functions	Quasi-Associated Architecture	Associated Architecture
Functional layer	Network layer	ATM virtual path layer
Routing method	MTP-3-based rerouting	VP-based path restoration
Routing information	Signaling link selection/ origination and destination	VPI
Redundancy	Preplanned routes	Preplanned or dynamic routes
Role of rerouting	Restoration against link failure/node failure	Restoration against link or node failure and also against congestion
Trigger signal	Alarms from level–2 changeover message	VP-AIS, VP-FERF or other protection messages

16.5   Summary

We have reviewed several ATM-based broadband IN network architectures that could be used to support both today's services and future broadband services. Each of these architectures has a potential role to play. Providers using today's IN architecture would prefer quasi-associated broadband IN architecture to enable a smooth interface with existing platforms, but for the new players an ATM-based associated architecture will be more favorable. However, the real implementation will depend on other factors such as cost, availability, and knowledge.

ATM
Environments

We now change our focus from broadband to ATM environments exclusively because ATM is the most important subset of broadband networks. ATM can be used as a transmission technology as well as the switching technology in broadband. This part provides an overview of the usage of ATM technology in different environments, i.e., local area networks, wide area networks, and public networks, such as local exchange carriers (LECs) and interexchange carriers (IECs).

CHAPTER 17

ATM in Local Area Networks

17.1   Overview

So far, we have seen different technologies, their architectures, and the concepts behind them, including ATM. Starting with this section, we see how ATM technology can be applied to different environments, such as local area networks, wide area networks, and public networks. In this chapter, we address the use of ATM in LANs, first by analyzing the current technology options available for LANs and the reasons why ATM has become the talk of LAN vendors as the future technology. We then address the different ways through which one can migrate to ATM in the LAN environment. Last but not the least, we see what applications are driving ATM in the LAN environment.

17.2   LAN Requirements

In today's LAN environment, the requirements are changing so rapidly that no unique solution or technology exists to address all of them. Before we talk about the different technologies, let's see what the requirements are for today's and next generation's LANs. We have classified the requirements of a LAN environment into three major categories:

- Unlimited growth path for higher speed
- Guaranteed quality of service
- Enterprise-wide uniform network management

17.2.1   Unlimited Growth Path for Higher Speed

Unlimited growth path means that the access speed of the workstations to the servers should be capable of being easily increased without modifying the network or system. Currently, access speeds of even 10 Mbps are more than sufficient. In the future, however, one might need at least a 150-Mbps access speed to provide multimedia services. If a user is replacing an existing system in order to meet immediate needs, then it has to be in such a way that it can also handle future needs for multimedia applications. If a 150-Mbps access speed link is installed now, the user could request higher-speed access when necessary to access the required multimedia information from the server with negligible response time. To achieve this capability, the network and technology should be in place *before* the need arises.

17.2.2 Guaranteed Quality of Service

The issue of QOS for each user and each service arises when a network handles different services, such as voice, data, and video. Of course, each service has a different QOS. The new technology should be designed to handle different levels of QOS based on user requirements, such as delay, response time, throughput, cost, etc.

17.2.3 Enterprise-Wide Uniform Network Management

The concept of enterprise-wide uniform network management becomes simple if everyone uses the same equipment across the entire enterprise network because the management function of all the equipment is the same and thus easy to manage. The same concept of network management becomes very complex, however, if multiple vendors supply equipment with different architectures using different management systems. The big problem then becomes system integration, which is true even in today's network environment. The new technology should therefore have good network management features to adapt to this heterogeneous network management.

17.3 Technology Options for LANs

Now that we have discussed the requirements, let's look at the different technologies available for the LAN environment. Each of the technologies has its own advantages and disadvantages, depending on its usage, such as the type of application, performance, throughput and latency requirement, geographic bound, and cost.

We analyze five different technology categories applicable for LAN environments:

- Switched Ethernet

- Fiber distributed data interface
- 100 base-VG (voice grade)
- ATM
- Gigabit Ethernet

Table 17.1 shows a comparison of these five technologies. They are further discussed in the following subsections.

17.3.1   Switched Ethernet

Switched Ethernet is available today and used primarily for data, but it has limited multimedia support. The performance of the switched Ethernet is higher than that of the shared Ethernet, and it has a low latency because of the dedicated bandwidth. This technology is used only in the LAN environment. One of the factors favoring switched Ethernet is the cost. Switched Ethernet is preferred to shared Ethernet because of

TABLE 17.1

Comparison of LAN Technologies

	Switched Ethernet	Shared FDDI	100 Base-VG	ATM	Gigabit Ethernet
Product availability	1992—1993	Since 1990	1994	1994	1997
Application drivers	Client-servers Working Group	LAN backbone	Client-servers Working Group	Backbone, interconnect	LAN backbone
End-user performance	Higher than shared Ethernet	Higher than shared Ethernet	Higher than shared Ethernet	Very high	Very high
Geographic scalability	Limited to Working Group	Working Group, building	Limited to Working Group	LAN-MAN-WAN	LAN
Bandwidth scalability	Limited per user, high for aggregation	None	None	Very high per user, high for aggregation	Very high per user, high for aggregation
Cost	Lowest	High	Same as switched Ethernet	Initially higher than FDDI, expected to drop to same cost as switched Ethernet	Less than ATM
Standards maturity	NA	Stable	Just starting	Evolving	Evolving

the requirement of dedicated access. The drawback is, of course, the dedicated access to the workstation or terminal.

17.3.2   FDDI

FDDI is used only for data in very high-performance workgroup communities. Currently, a number of vendors offer FDDI products. The performance of FDDI is much better than that of Ethernet and token ring-based networks, but its disadvantage is that it is limited to shared media only. Again, this is a LAN-only application with very limited use in WAN. Currently, the cost of FDDI is extremely high but is expected to come down as newer technologies enter the market.

We discussed the FDDI technology in detail in Chap. 3. As the name indicates, it is a fiber-based network. Currently, a more cost-effective coaxial-based network has been developed as an alternative to FDDI called CDDI (coaxial distributed data interface). Many developments have occurred in FDDI, such as FDDI II, which is capable of handling isochronous traffic (voice). FDDI II was developed to compete against a growing number of new technologies entering the LAN arena and is capable of handling all types of traffic, including ATM.

17.3.3   100 Base-VG

100 base-VG is a relatively new technology. It was standardized in 1992, but with limited product availability. This technology is primarily used for data application and some multimedia. Its performance is superior to FDDI. Again, this is a LAN-only technology, and its cost is expected to be comparable to switched Ethernet or higher.

17.3.4   ATM

At present, ATM has proved itself as a viable LAN option. Although lots of vendors have announced the introduction of ATM in their product lines, it has not performed as expected. The biggest advantage of this technology is that it is suitable for the transmission of data, voice, video, and image. However, vendors have come up with creative ways to bring life to existing LAN technologies such as Ethernet to meet the service needs. The method of transportation of these was mentioned in Chap. 8. This technology has the highest performance, unlimited bandwidth, and lowest latency. It is available in LAN, MAN, and WAN environments. It is currently expensive, but the cost is expected to decrease to the level

Part 5: ATM Environments

of currently available technologies. A detailed review of ATM technology was also discussed in Chap. 7.

17.3.5 Gigabit Ethernet

Gigabit Ethernet is the latest extension to IEEE 802.3, the standard that defines 10- and 100-Mbps Ethernet. Billed primarily as a backbone switch-to-switch and switch-to-server application, it furnishes 1 Gbps of raw bandwidth over coaxial cable runs of up to 25 m. There are specs for Gigabit Ethernet to operate over Category 5 UTP (unshielded twisted pair).

In other areas, it retains many of the same features as Ethernet, from the CSMA/CD access method to the Ethernet packet format. One difference is the physical signaling scheme, which is borrowed from ANSI's Fiber Channel spec. While the basic requirements for Gigabit Ethernet are set out in IEEE 802.3, the 802.3z Task Force has been charged with hammering out the spec specifics to standardize it.

17.4   LAN Environment

LAN environments can be categorized based on the following:

- Topology of network
- Media type used in network
- Access method to network
- Technology used

Each is discussed in the following subsections.

17.4.1   Topology of the Network

Topology addresses how the nodes or terminals are connected with each other. Currently, most LANs are in either a bus or ring topology, as shown in Figs. 17.1 and 17.2, respectively. The reason these two topologies are used predominantly in the LAN environment is that both operate on the principle of sharing the transmission medium. In the early years of LANs, the objective was to connect multiple users located within a building. Today, a growing need exists for dedicated bandwidth to access new applications (such as multimedia) where voice, video, and data are integrated. In this environment, the bandwidths to each user can no longer be shared, but must be dedicated. New technology is therefore needed to provide a dedicated bandwidth to each user, enabling the user to access information at a high speed. The topology that offers such dedicated bandwidth is already in use in the telecommunication environment and is called a *star topology*. Figure 17.3 shows a simple star topology.

Figure 17.1
Bus-based LAN topology.

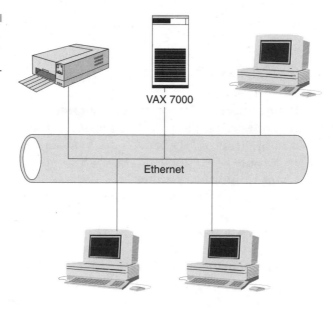

Figure 17.2
Ring-based LAN topology.

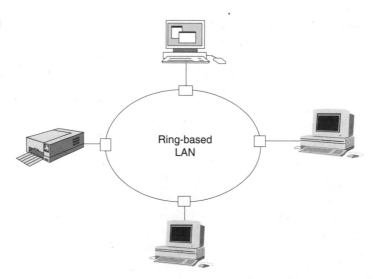

Figure 17.3
Star-based LAN topology.

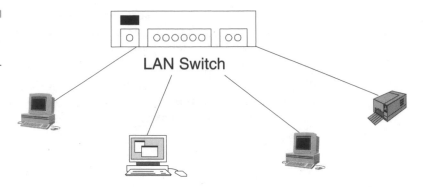

17.4.2 Media Type Used in the Network

In the past, copper cables connected computers. Today, coaxial cables are used instead because of the reduction in cost and the ability to carry more data in terms of bits per second. Fiber optics has recently become popular because of its ability to carry high-speed data with negligible loss or error in information over long distances and because of its small physical size. The future usage of fiber-optic cables in a LAN environment is expected to be very high.

There are two types of fiber optics: multimode and single-mode fibers. Multimode fibers are made of plastic, whereas single-mode fibers are made of glass. In a LAN environment, the plastic fibers that operate in multimode are cheaper than single-mode fibers. Multimode fibers are also designed to carry information error-free over a distance considered sufficient for the LAN environment. A typical multimode fiber can carry information error-free for a distance of 3 miles, whereas a single-mode fiber can carry information error-free for 25 miles; a LAN usually covers less than 3 miles. Thus, multimode is the choice of LAN users. Today, multimode fibers are comparable in cost to coaxial cable, making them even more attractive in LANs.

17.4.3 Access Method to Network

In LAN environments, two types of access methods are used: carrier sense multiple-access/collision detection and token passing.

CSMA/CD is an enhanced version of the Aloha protocol developed by the University of Hawaii. CSMA/CD is a technique where all the stations listen on the transmission line. A station that wishes to transmit does so only if it detects the channel is idle. This procedure is called *carrier sensing,* and the access strategy used is termed a *CSMA scheme.* Collisions can still occur because stations are physically displaced from one another, and two or more stations might sense that the channel is idle and start transmitting, causing a collision. Once stations detect collision, they transmit a special jam signal to notify all other stations about the collision on the link. In other words, think of CSMA/CD as two polite people who start to talk at the same time. Each politely backs off and waits a random amount of time before starting to speak again.

Another access method is token passing. Here, each device on a LAN receives and passes the token. The device with the token has the right to use the single channel on the LAN. The key to remember is that a token-passing or token-ring LAN has only one channel, which is a high-speed channel that can move a lot of data. It can, however, move only one conversation at a time. In other words, it is like a musical ball game, where a ball is passed from one person to another until the music stops. Then, whoever has the ball must pick an instruction card and act accordingly. In a token-ring LAN, the ball is the token, and whoever gets the token can transmit data on the ring.

The disadvantage of these access methods is that only one terminal can access the network to communicate at one time. Hence, these methods are not suitable when more than one user tries to access the network. Thus, dedicated access comes into play, where each terminal has a dedicated line connected to a LAN hub, as shown in Fig. 17.3. To evolve from the existing bus or ring-based LAN environment into something completely different, such as a switched hub-based network (e.g., telephone public network), however, is a daunting task. Careful planning is needed before such a migration. Numerous problems exist with the current architecture and topology. At the time of deployment users did not have much choice, so they had to use what was available. Today, there are about 15 million LAN ports installed, and the original designer of this technology did not expect this amount of usage. The difficulty arises when one must rearrange the network so that when people move from one place to another, they do not see any change in their networking environment (same user name but different domain name).

17.4.4 Technology Used

In addition to previous categories, technology plays an important role in deciding the migration and extending the life of the LAN environment.

For instance, with 10-Mbps Ethernet, it is easier to migrate to 100-Mbps Ethernet than to ATM-based LAN architecture. Thus, the type of technology used plays a critical part in extending the future of LAN architecture, especially in the consideration of migration to ATM-based LAN architecture.

17.5 Architecture Alternatives

ATMs in LAN environments are basically implemented in existing products, such as routers and hubs. Figure 17.4 shows a typical ATM-based router. The functionality of such a product is basically multiprotocol routing plus ATM, especially for traffic management. The interfaces to the router include all the LAN interfaces, such as HSSI, DSI, DXI, etc.

Different architecture alternatives are available with ATM in a LAN:

- Router-centric view
- ATM-centric view
- Balanced view
- LAN emulation

Each is discussed in the subsections below.

Figure 17.4
ATM as backbone.

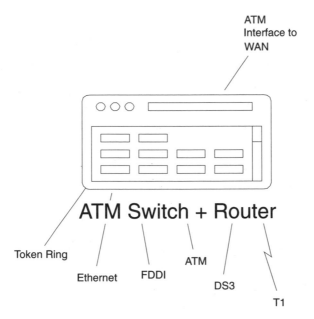

17.5.1 Router-Centric View

In the router-centric view architecture, as shown in Fig. 17.5, the backbone network is router-based, and the ATM is an access vehicle. In this architecture, the router performs the backbone routing function between IP domains, and the ATM switch in the network performs the local switching functions.

17.5.2 ATM-Centric View

In an ATM-centric view architecture, as shown in Fig. 17.6, the ATM nodes serve as the backbone, and the router becomes the access vehicle to the network. The ATM-centric view is a typical view of the future architecture, if ATM is deployed in the public network.

17.5.3 Balanced View

The balanced view architecture, as shown in Fig. 17.7, is a combination of router and ATM-backbone architecture. This architecture usually occurs in a transition phase, i.e., from a router-based to an ATM-based

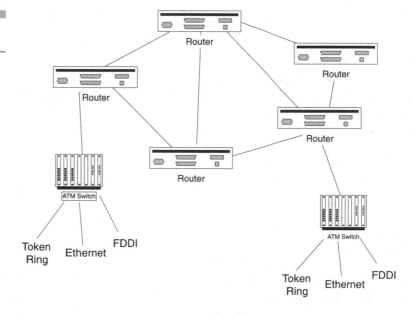

Figure 17.5
Router-centric view.

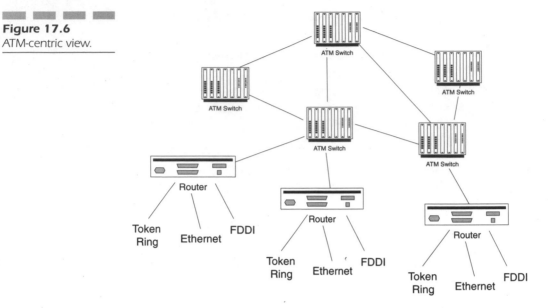

Figure 17.6
ATM-centric view.

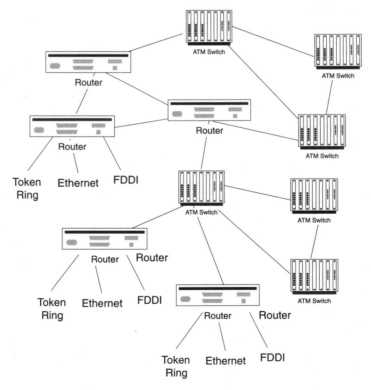

Figure 17.7
Balanced view.

backbone architecture. Typically, these architectures are used in larger companies with multiple locations.

17.5.4 LAN Emulation

The LAN emulation architecture, as shown in Fig. 17.8, uses ATM to provide virtual LAN interconnect where the intelligent peripheral address encapsulation occurs. Here, the router-generated IP addresses are mapped onto ATM cells and transported across the ATM network using one of the ATM virtual channel connecting networks, thus enabling LAN connectivity.

Recent developments in standards activity by ATM Forum and IETF (Internet Engineering Technical Forum) have identified a smooth migration to ATM from native legacy environments. The standards that enable such a smooth migration are MPOA (multiprotocol over ATM) and LANE (LAN emulation) standards. These two standards have enabled network managers and operators to build multivendor multiprotocol networks. MPOA is designed to offer significant scalability using the techniques mentioned in this chapter.

17.6 Transition to ATM-Based LAN

Today, the whole industry is excited about ATM, especially the LAN industry. What is the reason for all the interest? The answer is Internet/Intranet applications. Internet/Intranet has put bandwidth-hungry applications within the reach of every desktop. This has driven network managers to evaluate all their network plans for long-term scalability and cost-effectiveness. ATM stands very close to the top. During the past 5 years, the basic technology for bridges and routers has changed drastically. Simple bridges gave way to learning bridges and then to routing bridges. Single-protocol routers have been replaced by multiprotocol routers that offer both bridging and routing. The latest trend includes the migration of these to ATM-based systems.

One of the most difficult decisions for a company or individual to make is whether or not to migrate from an existing technology to a new one, such as ATM. Many questions arise when addressing such a migration. If we assume the new technology is ATM, then the following questions should be answered:

Figure 17.8
LAN emulation.

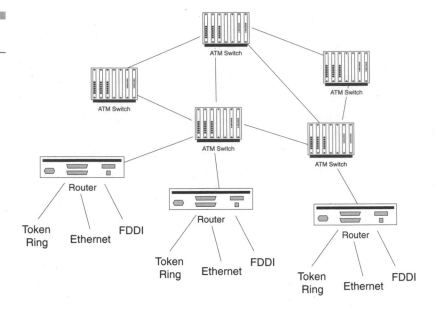

- How will the new ATM feature work in LANs?
- What is the best way to evolve to ATM from today's Ethernet, token ring, and FDDI?
- How will ATM interface with existing LANs and WANs?
- What happens to the existing hubs and routers now in use?

Some of these questions have been addressed in recent developments in the standards organizations. As far as the first question is concerned, the new features of switched virtual circuits will enhance the existing LAN features. To address the rest of the questions, we propose a three-phase evolution path from the current environment. These phases are based on customer input such as the following:

- Existing equipment should be replaced only when it can be written off, which often results in extending the life of the existing technology.
- The new technology should be a more cost-effective alternative and easy to migrate.
- The new technology should have an evolution strategy to handle additional developments.

Figure 17.9 shows today's LAN environment. This environment is typical in a corporate network, where FDDI serves as the backbone connection between many departmental LANs based on Ethernet, token ring, etc., with varying speeds. This to be the starting point for our transition. Figure 17.9 also shows the typical interface speed to the different networks, which ranges from 1.544 to 100 Mbps.

Figure 17.10 shows phase 1 of the transition to ATM-based LANs. Here, an ATM switch is used to provide a switched environment, compared to FDDI's bus-based shared architecture, to replace the FDDI. The purpose of a switched environment is to provide a dedicated connection between LANs on demand. Here, the routers are used to communicate with the outside world. In some instances, FDDI will become one of the access networks to the ATM switch, either as a new LAN or as a replacement for one of the existing LANs, such as Ethernet or token ring.

Figure 17.11 shows phase 2 of the transition. Here, an ATM switch is used to connect to the outside world at the interface. The results of ATM deployment in this phase are the following:

- Improved performance, scalability, and management of multiple LAN environments

- Cell switching used in the backbone network

- ATM backbone becomes a competitive alternative to FDDI in similar networking environment.

Figure 17.9
Today's LAN environment.

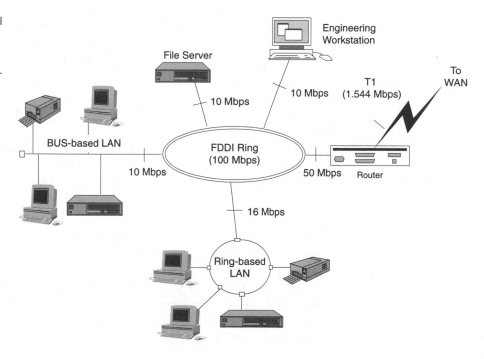

Figure 17.10
Phase 1 of transition
to ATM-based LAN.

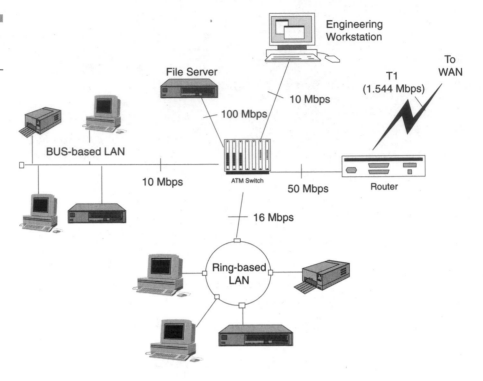

This phase is typically applied in a university campus environment, where the LANs are scattered all around the campus. Figure 17.11 also shows the typical interface speed at which different LANs interact. In this phase, the ATM adapters become increasingly cost-effective, enabling workstations to be connected directly to the ATM switch via a 100-Mbps interface. New applications start to proliferate as ATM migrates to the desktop.

Figure 17.12 shows phase 3 of the ATM deployment in LAN. Here, the token-ring or bus LANs disappear, and all the terminals or workstations are connected directly to the ATM switch. The LAN environment is completely cell-based, with switched architecture. In this environment, the interface runs 100 Mbps and higher, thus opening a window of opportunity in terms of new applications, especially video-based applications, to the desktop. By this time, not only is the LAN environment mature for widespread ATM deployment, but ATM availability in WANs and in the public network also becomes widespread, thus enabling ATM-based WANs to be set up to connect remote LAN sites or servers.

These three phases are not the only ways to evolve to an ATM-based LAN. Networks at different locations have different needs and demands.

Thus, users can skip a phase or adopt a different architecture than the one discussed here. The transition suggested here is more of an example than a real deployment scenario. Usually, a deployment strategy is based on many factors, such as cost, technology maturity, applicability, and current LAN environment.

17.7   Applications Driving ATM in LAN

So far, we have seen the requirements for LAN users and the technology to meet those requirements. We have also seen a possible evolution scenario from an existing LAN to an ATM-based LAN and different architecture alternatives to provide a smooth transition. All these are fine, but what applications will users need to evolve to an ATM-based LAN?

The application that is driving the LAN to increase bandwidth is Internet/Intranet, and the main application for an ATM LAN is also Internet/Intranet, which is reinvention of internetworking. Although

Figure 17.11
Phase 2 of transition to ATM-based LAN.

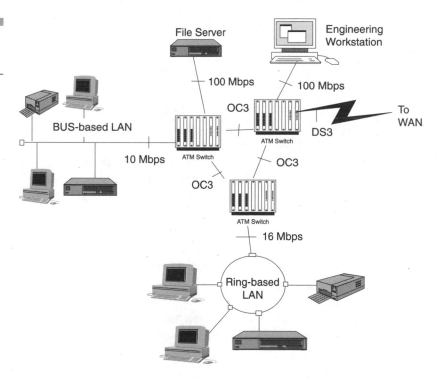

Figure 17.12
Phase 3 of transition
to ATM-based LAN.

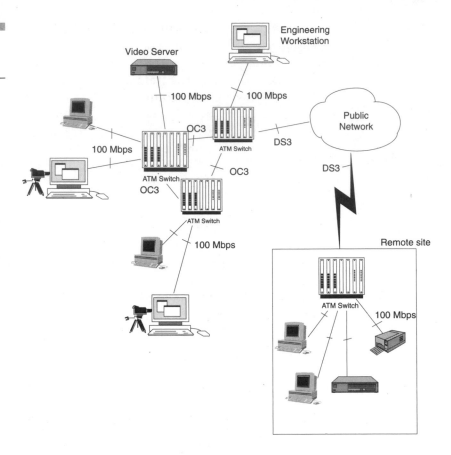

internetworking is not an application, it consists of LAN applications such as file transfer, e-mail, remote database access, and other applications that do not belong to this category. Today, we build router-based internets that are too big, too complex, and too diverse to be well managed because internetworking is out of control. As mentioned in the evolution of an existing LAN to an ATM-based LAN, the best place to start is with the routers, and then reposition these routers step-by-step as traffic fades at the periphery of an ATM network. The reason for starting with the routers is that they are the biggest market segment and the most profitable from an equipment vendor's perspective. Other areas do not seem to be as good a starting point for ATM-based LANs. Standards development, such as MPOA and LANE, have enabled this migration in a more cost-effective manner.

Compared to router-based internetworking, ATM networking offers many advantages over today's internet:

■ Local ATM nodes perform switching better than today's LAN hubs because LAN hubs broadcast information to all LAN ports. In a star-wired configuration, broadcasting is unnecessary and a waste of resources. In ATM, the traffic is routed only to the required nodes, thus saving the resources for other uses.

■ ATM switches offer the promise of multiple "virtual LANs" in a single switch, making moves, additions, and changes a simple matter of adjusting workgroup membership routers at a network management console. These virtual LANs can be extended across several switches to provide access to remote servers with almost the same throughput and delay as if they were local.

In short, the need for reinventing internetworking will be the crucial application for ATM LANs, but careful analysis and planning are needed before making such a change. In fact, it is essential that ATM become a standard and that it be scalable to large sizes, operate at high speed, and meet diverse requirements.

17.8   Summary

In this chapter, we saw the technology options available for LAN environments today. We looked into different architecture alternatives and addressed how one could evolve from today's environment to an ATM-based LAN environment. We also clarified the misconception of the "killer" application for ATM, which had been considered to be multimedia because of the hype created by the public. In reality, the killer application is simply reinventing LAN internetworking via Internet/Intranet. In other words, reinventing the LAN to redesign it in such a way that it can handle the traffic growth in a manageable manner by using the latest advances in many areas of technology.

CHAPTER 18

ATM in Wide Area Networks

18.1 Overview

Before we address the role of ATM in wide area networks, we need to define a WAN and its aliases. WAN is also known as a *corporate network, enterprise network,* or *private network.* It is typically an extension of a LAN outside the building or campus over the public or private links to other LANs in remote buildings or cities. A basic difference between a WAN and a LAN is that a WAN uses common carrier lines or private lines and a LAN does not. The connection from a LAN to a WAN is typically made through a device called a channel service unit/data service unit, which is connected to a router on the LAN side. The CSU/DSU connects the digital line (T1) to a data communication device, such as a router. The basic function of a CSU/DSU is to convert the LAN protocol to a public network digital protocol, such as T1 or T3.

As we address the role of ATM in a WAN, we look into some of the technology requirements demanded by a WAN. Typically, more than one technology can meet the requirements of WANs, such as a router, frame relay, SMDS, and ATM, as described in Part 2 of this book. Because ATM has been selected as the future broadband switching technology, we address the transition from today's TDM- (router-) based environment to an ATM-based one. Here the transition is only an example of how today's WAN can be evolved. In reality, the evolution path depends on various factors, such as optimum cost (which can vary from business to business), technology availability, etc. It is speculated that early ATM services will appear in the WAN environment for private network applications. In effect, corporations will use ATM to connect scattered LANs together into a large corporate network. Initial applications expected in ATM-based WAN are data, and later, video and voice.

18.2 ATM-Based Hubs

Before we address ATM in a hub environment, we must first understand what a hub means. A *hub* is typically an interface point for different LANs within a building or a campus that connects the LANs. The hubs typically consist of routers that handle the function of routing between the LANs within a building and remote LANs via the WAN. Figure 18.1 shows a typical router-based hub backbone environment, where the router enables interaction between the LAN switch in a campus or to the outside world via a WAN. The connection to the outside

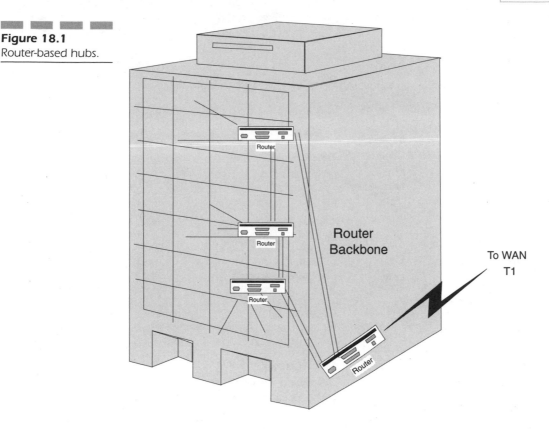

Figure 18.1
Router-based hubs.

world is via the CSU/DSU, which performs protocol conversion (i.e., from LAN protocol to TDM-based public network protocol). The equipment is currently designed for data traffic only, however. To handle voice and video, additional equipment, such as a PBX and video codec, are required to be connected to a TDM device. Additional WAN lines are also required because effective sharing is not possible. Thus, with TDM technology, the inherent disadvantage is the waste of bandwidth, or the ineffective use of bandwidth. In a WAN environment, effective bandwidth utilization as compared to a LAN environment is essential because while the bandwidth in LANs is free, the bandwidth in WANs is very expensive. Thus, every effort is made to use available bandwidth effectively.

Figure 18.2 illustrates this concept. ATM in the WAN environment is the only technology that fulfills the requirement of effective bandwidth utilization. Replacing the routers in Fig. 18.3 by an ATM switch allows migration to an ATM-based hub environment, thus enabling the network to migrate to a switched environment.

Figure 18.2
LAN and WAN
bandwidth cost.

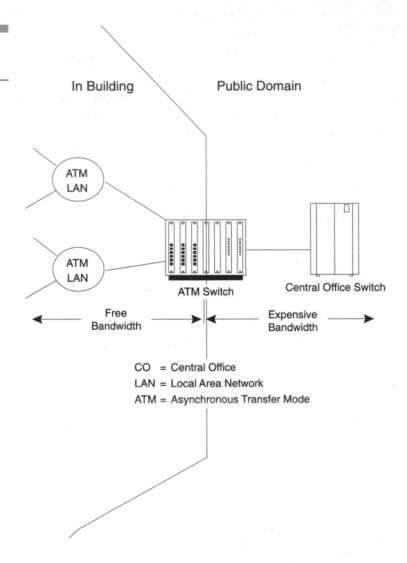

In Building   Public Domain

ATM
LAN

ATM
LAN

ATM Switch

Central Office Switch

← Free
Bandwidth →|← Expensive
Bandwidth →

CO = Central Office
LAN = Local Area Network
ATM = Asynchronous Transfer Mode

In addition to efficient bandwidth utilization, ATM enables users to integrate voice, data, and video on the same network, thus creating a more efficient shared use of the available bandwidth. With ATM in the WAN network, other benefits also arise, such as easy evolution to higher-speed bandwidth on demand, conformance with global standards, etc. Figure 18.4 shows the savings in bandwidth that can be achieved by migrating from today's TDM-based WAN environment to an ATM-based WAN environment. The percentage of utilization shown in Fig. 18.4 for the TDM environment is based on today's router-based private WAN network. The reason for such resource wasting is that the network is designed based on busy-hour (BH) utilization, which is usually only 30 percent of a day's traffic. With this type of calculation, a corporation usually ends up having much more bandwidth than typically used.

Thus, ATM in a WAN environment uses resources effectively, which is why experts predict that WAN is the first place where ATM can be tested and deployed. Numerous vendors are currently manufacturing ATM products applicable for the WAN environment.

Figure 18.3
ATM-based hubs.

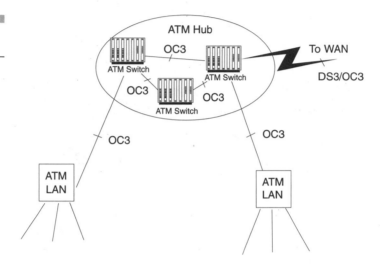

Figure 18.4
Bandwidth efficiency.

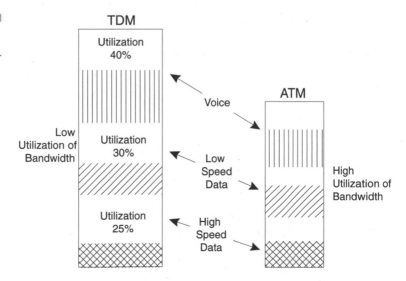

18.3 WAN Technology Requirements

A WAN typically is a network that covers a large geographical area. It thus creates certain technical requirements, some of which are

- Standards compliance
- Switching/routing capability
- Performance
  - Throughput
  - Nodal and link delay
  - Nodal reliability/availability
- Protocol handling support
- Relative cost of technology
- Network management support

Each is discussed in the following subsections .

18.3.1 Standards Compliance

Standards compliance allows the WAN to carry multiprotocol traffic easily and to potentially construct a network from multivendor equipment. It also allows vendor equipment with different internal designs to interact as if all had the same protocol and were from the same vendor. Compliance helps service providers and large corporations get competitively priced equipment from different vendors, and they do not have to depend on one vendor who then controls their network by controlling the cost. Thus, providers and corporations actively participate in the standards-making process both at national and international levels. Standards compliance is one reason ATM is a reality around the world.

18.3.2 Switching/Routing Capability

All traffic must be routed or switched to arrive at its destination. Without switching, connectivity would be impossible. Switching and routing thus allow a very robust and fault-tolerant network. This capability enables the network to effectively utilize its resources with many users. Switching, along with transmission, is a very important component of the network. In a WAN environment, however, the transmission systems are usually leased from public service providers, depending on the routes required for connectivity. Switching, on the other hand, can be publicly or privately owned, and each has its own pros and cons. If the public carrier controls the switching, then the public carrier also manages the network because the details of usage, such as billing, are available only in the switch itself. In this case, the public carrier knows the traffic characteristics. If the corporation controls the switching, the traffic information remains within the corporation. The problem here is that the corporations need additional personnel to run and manage the network, which becomes difficult if the corporation's primary area of business is not related to telecommunications or data communications. There is a point with respect to the size of the network where companies can cost effectively manage their own internal network. Usually this could be justified for large corporations, where everything from having and running the network require special skills. If the company's primary business is other telecom or datacom, it becomes difficult to justify the cost of running the network to someone who has the least understanding of its value to the company's management.

In case of small organizations it becomes obvious to have specialized personnel to run networks which can be cost effectively out-sourced.

18.3.3   Performance

Performance is another key driver in any network architecture. It is the only indication that a network is healthy or that it is running out of capacity. The network operator must monitor the network's performance to determine when it is time to upgrade the network capacity to handle additional users or traffic. This type of information is available through certain parameters that help the network operator to monitor the network status. The most commonly used parameters are throughput, delay through the node and link, and nodal reliability/availability.

18.3.3.1   Throughput.   Throughput is the key criterion that affects the performance of any network. The network's aggregate throughput is dependent on the individual nodal throughput; hence, it is important to monitor and measure this parameter constantly. Throughput is one of the performance parameters that end users are aware of and often complain about in their network. *Throughput* is the total amount of traffic that can be carried in a unit of time; it is usually measured per second during the busy hour. The higher the throughput, the higher the performance. In a typical network, the throughput is equal to 70 percent of the node or link capacity. Nodes and links are designed to do exactly that as a precautionary measure to prevent the node or link from going down in case of overload. The throughput determines the amount of traffic that can pass through a node or a link in any given unit of time. In a broadband network, the switch node throughput runs about 20 to 100 Gbps.

18.3.3.2 Nodal and Link Delay. Network delay is probably the single most important parameter for end users. Once a WAN is put in place and users try to access a service at a remote LAN, they don't understand why it takes so long to access the information. What they forget or don't care about is that the server is at a remote location and the interconnection is at a low speed.

One alternative to lower user complaints is to increase the bandwidth to interconnect nodes, but this is obviously very expensive. A second alternative is for technology to support a larger bandwidth. The third way is to select a nodal technology that matches the application environment with minimal delays through the nodal equipment.

Nodal equipment delays are a major contributing factor to nodal delays in the WAN. Nodal delay occurs because the users cause more traffic than the node can handle, with the result that the node has to queue the traffic. If the queue limit is exceeded, traffic is lost (cells are discarded). The delay seen by the user is really the queuing delay at each node. The other delay is the link delay.

One delay no one can prevent is the transmission propagation delay caused by natural phenomena. It is the time taken for an electrical signal to propagate from point *A* to point *B*—usually about 10 to 20 µs. In a broadband network, even a microsecond is a large delay. With fiber optics and information traveling at light speed, this delay is reduced, but this delay is critical in a WAN network design. When delays add up, the lack of performance becomes significant.

18.3.3.3 Node and Link Reliability/Availability. The nodes and links are the fundamental building blocks of any network. Their unavailability negatively impacts productivity. When designing a WAN, one must ensure that the individual transmission and nodal components provide a fairly high degree of availability (usually 99.9 percent). In a WAN environment, redundancies have usually been built into the switch by the vendors because of the market needs. The node, otherwise known as a switch, must be up and running all the time. Equipment vendors, especially for broadband equipment, provide one-to-one, hard-swap backups, including the power source to the node. In addition to availability, reliability is critical. Every interface to the switch has a backup interface to meet the strict standards set forth for switching nodes. Link availability and reliability are critical, because the links are often leased from the public carriers. The carrier usually guarantees the link availability as part of the lease agreement. Today's public network providers guarantee the availability of transmission at all times.

18.3.4 Protocol Handling Support

Most WAN applications require protocol support of varying degrees. Eventually, the network and the transport-level protocols must be supported if the application is to successfully run on the network. Since a proliferation of protocols exist in any network, a wide variety must be accommodated. Typically, a careful balance between the native protocol support and the use of a gateway for other protocols is required. In a LAN environment, there are many nonstandard protocols. In a public environment, however, most of the protocols are as per the specifications defined by the standards body at the national or international level. This connection of LAN via public leased lines requires additional equipment to accomplish protocol conversion. The problem with protocol conversion is the additional overhead involved, which in turn reduces the effective throughput or utilization of expensive WAN bandwidth.

18.3.5 Relative Cost of Technology

When implementing any new technology, the "mother of all evil" is the relative cost of the technology. Cost is always a key consideration for any network design and it has many components—typically a fixed and variable cost. The biggest cost factor is usually the variable cost, which is where most of the users look for savings from a new technology. In today's WANs the transmission links are leased. The lease agreement is usually on a yearly basis. Thus, the user agrees to pay for the leased line regardless of the use of those facilities. With new technology, the links can be used on demand with varying bandwidth, and the user pays for the usage only, enabling the users to access the expensive transmission link only when needed. Thus, new technologies such as ATM look cost-effective in spite of the initial fixed cost of the technology.

18.3.6   Network Management Support

As mentioned earlier, a WAN is a network covering a vast geographical area, which is where the network management feature offered by the equipment vendors plays a key role. Network management is the ease with which the network can be operated on a daily basis by a small staff, resulting in savings in overall operations. With the advent of network management standards, such as simple network management protocol (SNMP), service providers can manage different network equipment from different vendors using common network management systems. These network management systems enable the network operator to manage the network from a remote location. The network management software also provides a large amount of statistical information about the network, including performance, usage, traffic patterns, and growth in traffic. In some cases, most of the network problems, such as isolating the faulty device, can be accomplished from the network control center.

18.4   Technology Option for a WAN Network

Now that we have discussed the WAN requirements, let's look at the different technology options available for the WAN environment. This book covers most of the technology options available for a WAN environment. These technology options are the same for the public network environment. But usually some of these technologies will be deployed in a corporate environment earlier than public network. Each of the technologies has its own advantages and disadvantages, depending on its usage, such as the type of application, performance, throughput and latency requirement, geographic bound, and cost.

	Frame Relay	DQDB	SMDS	ATM
Standard organization	ITU-T	IEEE	Bellcore	ITU-T
Year of standard	1992	1991	1990	1992
Targeted services	Data	Data, voice, and video	Data	Broadband services (voice, data, video, and multimedia)
Main application	High-speed data communications	LAN interconnect	High-speed data communications	Broadband communications network
Operation	Public Network	Public Network	Public Network	Public/private
Network	IEEE 802 LAN	IEEE 802	IEEE 802	BISDN
Interworking with	BISDN	BISDN	BISDN	
Transmission rates, Mbps	1.544, 2.048	150	Up to 50	Up to 2.4 Gbps
Distance (range)	No limit	No limit	No limit	No limit
Transmission medium	Copper wire	Optical fiber	Copper, optical fiber	Optical fiber
Start of transmission	Contention	Slot reservation, BW reservation	Slot reservation	All options considered
Number of priorities	2	3	4	4
End of transmission	Frame unit	Slot unit	Slot unit	Slot unit
Addressing	16-bit	20-bit VCI or preassigned	Fixed (20∞1)	8/12-bit VPI+16-bit VCI
Error check	16-bit CRC	8-bit HCS10-bit CRC	8-bit HCS10-bit CRC	8-bit HCS10-bit CRC
Data removal	Not required	Not required	Not required	Under study

TABLE 18.1 Comparison of WAN Technologies

We will address four different technology categories applicable for WAN environments: frame relay, DQDB, SMDS, and ATM. This is in addition to the traditional TDM technology used today. Table 18.1 compares these four technologies and gives a high-level view of the pros and cons of these technologies.

18.5   Transition to ATM-based WAN

In this section, we address what the best step-by-step migration path is from today's router/TDM-based WAN to an ATM-based WAN. The reasons for migrating to ATM in a WAN environment are

■ Need for more aggregate bandwidth

■ Need for on-demand bandwidth

■ Need for efficient use of available resources, especially the expensive ones, such as lease facilities

■ Single network management system to manage all the network elements

We assume the target WAN is an ATM-based solution from today's router/TDM-based solution. It is not necessary that an ATM-based solution be the target WAN solution, however; it depends on the current and future user requirements. In fact, the end users can migrate from any existing technology to any target technology as long as the technology meets their objectives. For example, a user who has currently deployed frame relay technology can evolve to an ATM-based network if a need exists for higher bandwidth applications. In this case, the evolution path might or might not be the same as the one proposed here. The transition to ATM is thus an example of a typical WAN environment transition to an ATM-based WAN environment.

The evolution is based on the assumption that frame relay and SMDS are still in the early stages in terms of widespread deployment as the backbone in corporate networks. Also, frame relay and SMDS cannot handle isochronous (voice) traffic.

We propose a three-phase transition from a router/TDM environment to an ATM-based WAN environment. Figure 18.5 shows a typical router/TDM-based WAN environment. This example assumes that there are three locations in two different cities connected via routers at each location. The different locations are connected via leased T1 private lines whose bandwidths are 1.544 Mbps. In one of the links, there is more than one T1 leased line. The topology of the links is as follows:

■ Two T1 leased lines between city A, location 2 and city B campus

■ One T1 leased line between city A, location 2 and city A, location 1

■ One T1 leased line between city A, location 1 and city B campus

Figure 18.5
Typical WAN
environment.

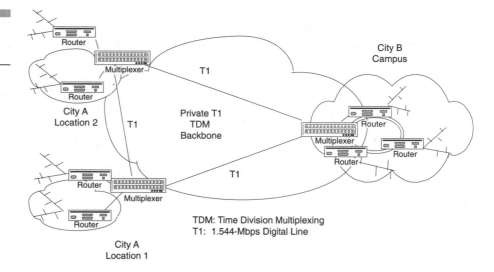

The link capacities are decided based on the usage between the two points during a busy period. Thus, during a nonbusy period, the capacities are not utilized or are underutilized. This network is only for data traffic; a separate network exists for voice. If the need for data traffic is less than T1, some voice can be multiplexed at the TDM box. With ISDN technology, some sharing occurs between data and voice traffic, but not to the extent where one gets real cost savings due to integration.

Some of the limitations of this network are due to limited backbone bandwidth (limited to T3), low bandwidth utilization (average), and no network management facilities. Each phase of the evolution should address these limitations.

18.5.1   Phase 1

Figure 18.6 shows phase 1 of the proposed evolution. The connection to the WAN is via an ATM switch situated at different locations; dedicated lines of various capacities are required between the locations. Initially, these lines are expected to be T1. All traffic within a premise terminates through a router at the ATM switch, which switches the traffic between the routers for both intrapremise and interpremise traffic.

The benefits of migrating to phase 1 are as follows:

Figure 18.6
Phase 1 of transition.

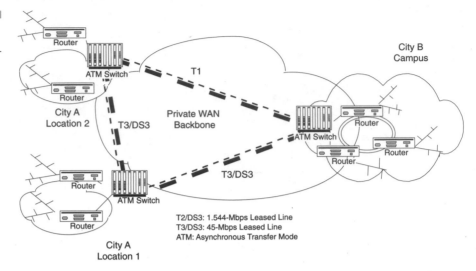

- Premise traffic consolidation. All the traffic (data) is consolidated at the ATM hub, which does intra- and interpremise switching.
- Backbone upgrade (depending on traffic demand) from T1 to T3. Once the ATM hub is developed, the backbone network can be easily upgraded from T1 to T3 when the demand arises because the ATM hub already has the capability.
- WAN traffic consolidation (voice, data, and video) via ATM switch. With the help of the ATM hub, integrating different traffic becomes easy.

18.5.2 Phase 2

Figure 18.7 shows phase 2 of the WAN network evolution. In this phase, the backbone network speed is upgraded from T3 to OC3. Not only is the capacity of the link increased, but it is also moved from the electrical to the optical domain. At the same time, public ATM service becomes available from service providers. ATM also impacts other traffic, such as voice, where the PBX will be connected to ATM switches, which is where the initial cost savings begin to appear from traffic integration.

As mentioned earlier, backbone link sizes are designed based on the busy period usage. In this phase, network capacities are not used during the nonbusy period because, with ATM, the user sets up a connection when the traffic needs to be transmitted. The customer is billed only for the usage period. This benefit is in addition to the others obtained by consolidating the voice, data, and video traffic. The following are the overall benefits of migrating to this phase:

- Total ATM solution in the WAN environment
- Benefits from the consolidation of data, voice, and video
- Easy link-speed upgrade and migration to a more reliable optical domain

18.5.3 Phase 3

Figure 18.8 shows phase 3 of the WAN evolution to a complete broad-band/ATM-based solution. In this phase, the public network has evolved considerably to provide true BISDN services. The BISDN network becomes available, i.e., SONET, ATM, IN, and all the AAL layers (for adaptation of

Figure 18.7
Phase 2 of transition.

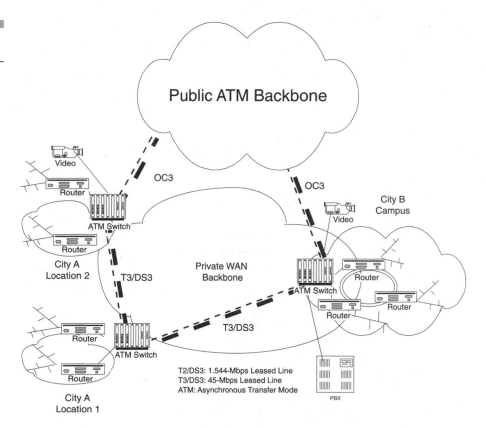

Public ATM Backbone

Video
Router
ATM Switch
OC3
OC3
City B
Campus
Video
Router
ATM Switch
Router
Router
City A
Location 2
T3/DS3
Private WAN
Backbone
Router
Router
T3/DS3
ATM Switch
Router
T2/DS3: 1.544-Mbps Leased Line
T3/DS3: 45-Mbps Leased Line
ATM: Asynchronous Transfer Mode
PBX
City A
Location 1

Figure 18.8
Phase 3 of transition.

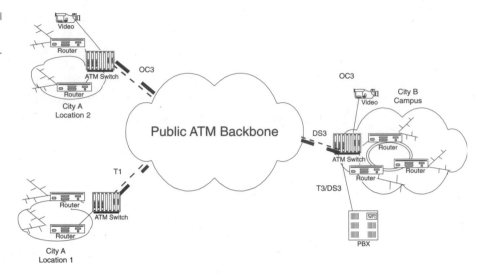

existing services) are deployed in the network. The backbone network is fully optical and has 100 percent redundancy. The real benefits of traffic consolidation are achieved. Users in the environment access the expensive WAN facilities in the most cost-effective manner. New services can be added without restriction from the technology or available facilities. Video becomes a way to communicate, e.g., desktop video, video mail box, etc.

18.6   Summary

No other network uses ATM more effectively than WAN/enterprise/ corporate networks. One of the main driving forces is the need for more bandwidth and better utilization of the same link to boost performance of the network while protecting the current investment. The driving force behind ATM in a WAN is the need to access scarce resources at remote locations that are beyond reach. In this chapter, we addressed the transition from existing router-based WAN technology to ATM-based technology, taking into account the issues such as throughput, performance, standards, etc.

ATM in
Public Networks

19.1 Overview

The most visible area for ATM technology is in public networks. Most of the major networks around the world *are* public (available to anyone who needs service, and controlled by government in some way) and their objective is to provide unbiased communications service to anyone. In the United States, these networks are categorized by regulatory bodies into local exchange carriers and interexchange carriers. (This is changing since the Telecom Act of 1996.) LECs provide the local access services, whereas IECs provide long-distance services (interstate/inter-LATA). LATA is an acronym for local access transport area. In most other countries, telecommunication networks are controlled by the government under the department of post, telegraph, and telephones (PTTs). Some of these countries have already followed the footsteps of public network environments in the United States in terms of opening up the networks for competition and private ownership, which leads to the deployment of new technologies to meet market needs.

In this chapter, we address the role of ATM in public local access and backbone environments. In the United States, the public telephone network is segmented into local exchange networks, otherwise known as LECs, owned and operated by the regional Bell operating companies and independents. These carriers are monopolistic in the areas they serve and hence they are regulated by the government. For example, in the United States, the LECs are regulated by the Federal Communications Commission. (This has changed with the Telecom Act of 1996.) The IEC is simply the long-distance carrier network, which is where many carriers compete with each other for market share in long-distance services.

Each of these carriers has its own traffic share, network, switching, and transmission requirements. Because these carriers carry all types of traffic (voice, video, and data), they want to evolve their networks so that one network can handle all types of traffic. To carry all types of traffic on a single network, the carriers need switching and transmission systems that can handle such demands in terms of different bit rates and characteristics, which is where ATM and SONET come into play. Here ATM provides switching and SONET provides transmission systems. Thus in this chapter we look into the role that ATM plays in these network environments. We then propose a strategy for the public backbone network's transition from today's network to an ATM-based one.

19.2   Public Network Requirements

For ATM to be deployed in public networks for voice, video, or data, it must meet all requirements put forward by the regulatory bodies, such as the FCC in the United States. In a competitive environment like the United States, the carriers usually not only meet the basic requirements but also go further with their own requirements, which are more stringent than those imposed by the regulatory bodies in order to differentiate themselves from other service providers in terms of features offered. This act, in turn, puts the burden on the switch manufacturers to design network equipment (switching and transmission) that can meet these higher requirements.

In addition to the WAN requirements mentioned in Chap. 16 [standards compliance, switching/routing capability, performance (i.e., throughput, delay through the node, and nodal reliability/availability) protocol handling support, relative cost of the technology, and network management support], the public network has the following additional requirements:

- Ubiquitous access
- Bit-error rate (BER) of 10^{-9} or better
- Blocking probability of 0.01 or better
- Survivability
- Redundancy and protection
- Downtime as specified by regulatory bodies
- Economic efficiency compared to existing technologies
- Flexibility for growth, higher speed, switch size, etc.

In this section we describe these requirements. Not all of these requirements can be achieved from day one, but an evolution plan is necessary to meet those requested by the carriers and customers.

19.2.1   Ubiquitous Access

The public carrier must provide nationwide coverage for the backbone network. In the United States, a long-distance carrier must have a point of presence (POP) in every local access transport area (LATA). In the case of a local access provider (regulated service provider), every carrier must provide a uniform fixed basic cost of service to anyone who wants telephone service. Additional costs are subsidized through a complex process.

19.2.2   Bit-Error Rate

With today's fiber-optic technology, carriers not only carry huge amounts of data at the speed of light but the data is error free. In fact, at one time the carrier that deployed the first fiber-optic network advertised that it could guarantee data integrity 99.999999 percent of the time. Accurate data is all related to what is called bit-error rate (BER):

BER = (number of bits received in error/total number of bits received) × 100

where BER is defined as the percentage of bits received in error compared to the total number of bits received. It is usually expressed as a number to the power of 10. Currently, the BER requirement for a public network is 10^{-9} or better, which means that there should be only 1 bit error for every 1 billion bits or less.

19.2.3   Blocking Probability

In a telephone environment, if a telephone call cannot be completed, it is said to have been blocked. Blocking is a fancy way to say that the caller received a busy signal. A call can be blocked at many different locations in the network. It can be blocked because of the unavailability of the network ports or lines or because the receiver is using the line. As far as the service provider is concerned, blocking probability refers to the former. A *blocking probability* is a unit that measures the number of calls blocked or measures the network's ability to handle the offered traffic. It is defined as the probability that a call can be blocked in a given period of time, usually during the busy hour. In the public network, blocking probability is 0.01 (1 percent) or less. Thus, less than 1 percent of the calls made during the busy hour are blocked. For example, if there are 100 calls in a busy hour and the blocking probability is 1 percent, one call is blocked and 99 calls get through the network. A 1 percent blocking probability is one of the main requirements for a voice-based network. Therefore, regardless of the type of network, this requirement must be met for voice applications. In the case of data, no real-time transfer is required; thus, data needs a completely different set of requirements. Blocking probability is used to measure the grade of service provided by the carrier. GOS varies for the different types of networks: data, voice, or video.

19.2.4   Survivability

Survivability simply means that every node and link has a standby backup. If a node fails, the traffic is rerouted via other nodes. If a link fails, all the traffic on that link is rerouted. It is very complex and expensive to design and deploy such a system because the carrier must decide how much (capacity) backup is required.

One can achieve survivability in many ways, such as using rings in the transmission network. In broadband communications using SONET as the transmission standard, SONET rings provide automatic restoration if a cable is cut, thus providing survivability. For switching nodes, redundancy is provided by having a completely redundant interface, switching matrix, and power source for the switches.

19.3   ATM in Local Access Networks

Public local access technologies were discussed in Chap. 9 and public local access architecture options were discussed in Chap. 13. In addition, we mentioned the BISDN reference architecture along with local access networks. The voice-based telephone architecture is usually star or double-star, and the data-based packet network is also usually star or bus. Figures 19.1 and 19.2 show typical local access architectures for telecommunications networks and computer networks, respectively. This is the most dominant access architecture used today.

In Figs. 19.1 and 19.2, the ATM switch is a potential candidate for the central office, or access tandem switches in the telecommunications network and a packet switch in the public computer network. To deploy the ATM switch and take advantage of the services ATM is capable of providing, however, the existing local loop infrastructure must be upgraded from twisted-pair to either enhanced copper technologies, coaxial, or fiber as discussed in Chap. 9. In the trunk network, however, ATM can be deployed immediately because fiber is already commonly in use. Standards have been defined for mapping ATM at DS3 and higher speeds that can be used as an ATM interface directly into the ATM switch.

The use of ATM locally varies, depending on the type of customer served. In a telecommunications environment, customers are typically categorized as residential or business. The respective networks are referred to as residential and business networks. Each of these addresses a different set of applications. Although ATM can be deployed in any of these logical segments of the public local access network, it is generally deployed in the business network to provide service to those customers. The reason is service providers could make a business case to provide services to business customers.

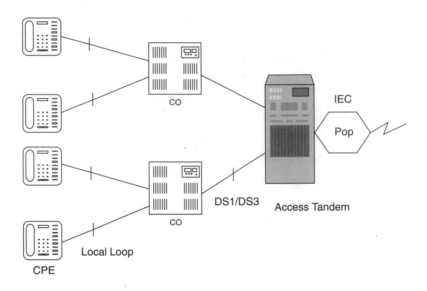

CO	Central Office
CPE	Customer Premise Equipment
IEC	Inter Exchange Carrier

Figure 19.1
Telecommunications network access architecture.

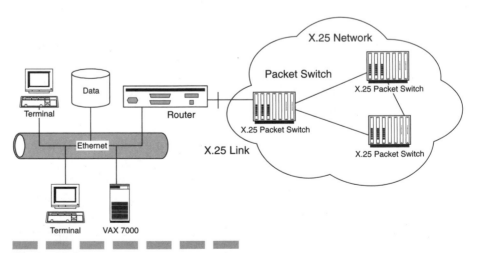

Figure 19.2
Computer network access architecture.

Deploying ATM as an access platform for residential customers is not currently justifiable because of a lack of traffic demand capacity that ATM can handle. Recently, new service providers and Internet service providers will probably justify deploying ATM in the residential network due to the high demand in internet access services. To provide such a service, the existing telephone network must first be upgraded with new compression technologies, such as asymmetrical digital subscriber loop (ADSL or other x-DSL). Then by using ATM/Ethernet technologies at level 2 on top of the x-DSL technology, services such as high-speed internet access can be provided. Of course, these are dependent on the loop length, which is the portion between the customer location and the CO, and it is identified to be about 18 ft or less. Several studies have been conducted on architecture alternatives for deploying fiber optics in the residential broadband network, but the conclusion is that there is no business case to justify fiber in the loop plant for the mass market.

In terms of opportunities, however, no other segment of the network has more opportunity for ATM switches than the local access network. Currently, many trials are being conducted to evaluate the potential for ATM services in public local access networks combined with some recent broadband access technologies. The initial services targeted are for data service such as high-speed internet access; voice is expected to be carried as traditional circuit-switched networks. For voice to be carried on ATM networks, ATM technology must prove it can provide the quality of service available today in a circuit-switched network, which will happen over time as the ATM service matures.

19.4   ATM in Backbone Networks

Backbone networks are also called long-haul or long-distance networks, either at the national or international level, and they connect subnetworks. They consist mostly of long-haul transmission systems and large switching systems carrying large amounts of traffic. The U.S. IECs came into existence in 1984 after the breakup of AT&T. These telecommunications networks provide a wide range of voice services across interstate, inter-LATA boundaries (LATA is a logical division of regions). However, in the 1960s, funded by the U.S. Department of Defense (DOD), the first data network, called ARPANET, was introduced, and today it has evolved to what is called NSFNET (National Science Foundation Network) or, more popularly, the Internet. Initially, the Internet was a research network connecting universities across the United States and in other countries. Recently, however, this network has opened up for commercial purposes so that anyone can subscribe to it or access it. This has created a huge paradigm shift in the way businesses and consumers interact. The Internet traffic, which has been growing at a rate of about 30 percent per month, has shown no evidence of slowing down.

As global businesses expand, the need for reliable high-speed communication for voice, data, and video increases. As a result, an upgrade of the existing network then becomes necessary. ATM as a technology meets the characteristics required to support the new traffic demand for now and in the future.

ATM's initial application is to provide large businesses with wide area LAN connectivity. Here, the IECs can bypass the local carrier and connect directly to the backbone network. With the telecommunications deregulation, where competition is open to all players in all markets (with some restrictions), all the major players are positioning themselves to take advantage of the regulatory environment.

Figure 19.3 shows a typical backbone network. The network consists of two layers: the backbone switching system and the concentrator or multiplexer. The concentration layer is where the traffic from the access networks is collected and passed to the backbone. Initial deployment of ATM is an overlay onto the switching layer.

This backbone can be compared to any backbone network in the world and is usually controlled by the PTT, as referred to in other countries. In the United States, the voice network consists of two layers: the access layer (called POP), which is present in every LATA, and the backbone switching layer. The equipment present at each POP is simply a concentrator or multiplexer. The traffic collected from the local access network is offered to the switching layer, which performs the switching and other value-added services.

The public data network (also known as the Internet) also has a similar hierarchy where the POP is replaced by a regional network connecting the universities and other networks such as America-Online (AOL), etc. The traffic from the universities is then offered to the regional networks, which, in turn, offer the traffic to the backbone Internet, to be switched to other regional networks or to the international network. This network is pure data based on packet-switching technology using routers. Recently, this network was contracted to MCI and Sprint. MCI has deployed ATM switches with an OC-12 interface and it is called vBNS.

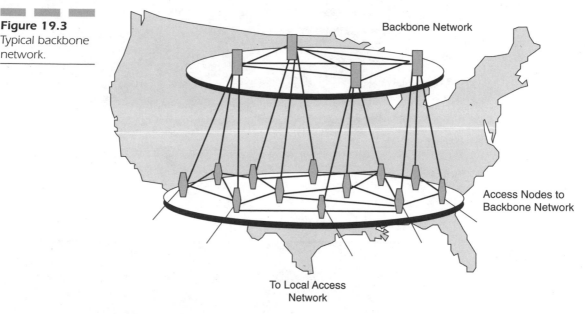

Figure 19.3
Typical backbone
network.

Backbone Network

Access Nodes to
Backbone Network

To Local Access
Network

19.5 Public Network Trends

The public network is becoming the "mother of all networks"—one of
the most important networks around the world. With privatization
occurring around the world, the latest battleground has become deployment of the latest technology in transmission and switching, service
that can be accessed anywhere. In this section, we see the trends in
the public network in the areas of traffic, technology, and the international public network.

As mentioned before, current public networks are dominated primarily
by voice traffic. Although data traffic is carried on a separate network, its
traffic has come close to voice traffic. Figure 19.4 shows traffic trends; it
shows that traffic is shifting from voice to nonvoice (video and data) traffic. It is speculated that, by the end of the decade, data traffic will dominate. But the biggest question for service providers is whether the revenue
will match the traffic growth.

No other industry has seen more changes in technology than
telecommunications. Figure 19.5 shows the trend in technology over
time. The initial technology that dominated the public network
was analog, followed by digital. The next generation is ATM. Figure
19.5 shows how the new technology is slowly replacing the older
technology.

Figure 19.4
Public network traffic
trends.

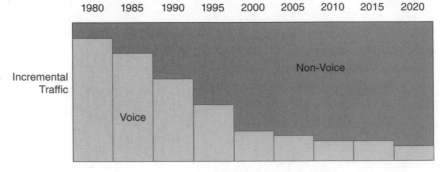

Source: Stephen Flemming, Northern Telecom

Figure 19.4
Public network traffic
trends.

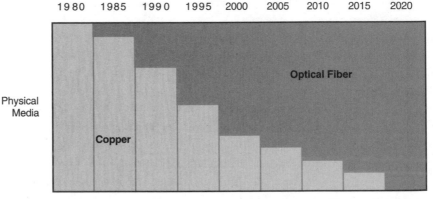

Source: Stephen Flemming, Northern Telecom

Figure 19.5
Public network tech-
nology trends.

Before broadband can be deployed in the public network, the back-bone technologies must be deployed. The two most important technologies for broadband are SONET for transmission and ATM for switching and access functions, as illustrated in Fig. 19.6. The first technology to be deployed in the network is SONET/SDH. The next step is to provide ATM backbone switching (first as cross-connect, then upgraded to switched), and the last is to deploy ATM at the access switches.

Once SONET and ATM are deployed in the public network, the next stage is to deploy broadband services, currently perceived as the ultimate in the telecommunications and data communications environment. Figure 19.7 shows a pyramid of technologies that need to be deployed before BISDN is realized. The bottom of the pyramid is the common transport infrastructure. For broadband communications, SONET/SDH fiber-based transmission technology has been selected and is currently being deployed around the world. The next layer of the pyramid is the broadband switching infrastructure with ATM, which is in the early stages of trial and deployment. (It is expected to be deployed in the late 1990s.) The next level to provide public network services used the available network equipment. The topmost layer, which is the target, is the deployment of the intelligent network. IN is the third component of the broadband to be deployed with international standards compliance. It is expected to happen by the beginning of the next century. Chapter 16 discusses

Figure 19.6
BISDN capability deployment in embedded base.

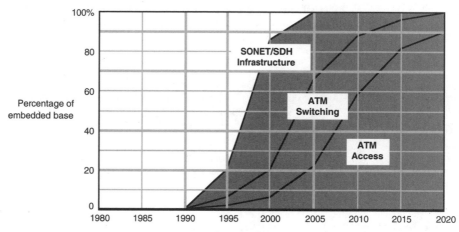

Source: Stephen Flemming, Northern Telecom

Figure 19.7
Public network deployment of BISDN.

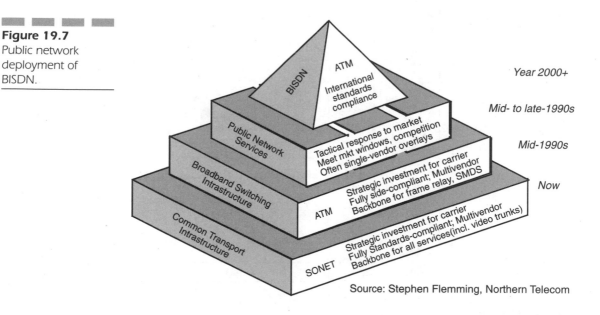

Source: Stephen Flemming, Northern Telecom

some to the issues with current IN architecture and proposes some potential options for broadband IN architecture.

With a true broadband network deployed across all segments of the public network, the public network view will be drastically changed. Figure 19.8 shows one such view. Here, the user plane consists of most of the existing customer premises equipment used in residential and business environments. The access part brings the user traffic to the public network through any means available today. Then, depending on the user community of interest (COI), the traffic is divided into different segments. All traffic will be connected via the communication plane, however, where the broadband technologies and existing technology will be present.

19.6   Transition to ATM-Based Public Networks

Since public networks are categorized into local and long distance, as far as the initial deployment of ATM is concerned, we will focus mainly on

Figure 19.8
A public network view.

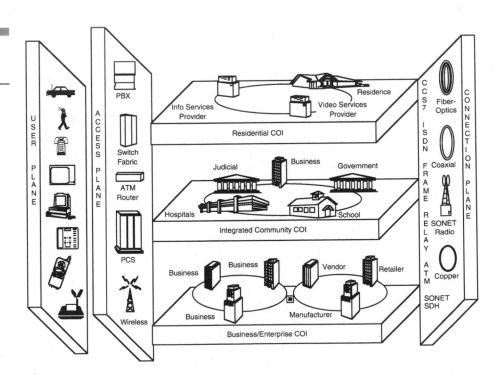

backbone networks. Broadband/ATM in the backbone network offers numerous immediate advantages:

- Broadband bandwidth
- Scalable bandwidth
- Improved network response time
- High quality of service
- Easy provision of services because of unified network management
- Efficient utilization of network resources
- Increased economics by aggregation of voice, data, and video
- Reduction in operating costs
- Maximum flexibility

Since we mentioned that the initial services provided by an ATM-based network will be data, let's assume the path to true ATM/broadband will evolve from today's IP-based network, similar to the Internet in the United States. In other words, the ATM network will initially be deployed in a data network, and voice will be carried on the conventional telecommunications network. The assumption here is that traditional service providers will deploy ATM-based overlay networks that complement their voice networks. The assumption in this scenario is well suited for new providers who are planning to build an optimum network and interconnect with traditional service providers for call completion.

The transition to a broadband/ATM-based network is proposed to take place in four phases from today's X.25/frame-relay-based packet-switched network to the SONET/ATM-based broadband network. Before describing the four phases, let's look at today's environment of public networks.

19.6.1 Today's Environment

Figure 19.9 shows a typical X.25/frame-relay packet-switched network with a LAN interface via routers carrying IP-based internet traffic. The X.25 network is designed to carry data with 100 percent data integrity. To meet this objective, the X.25 network performs error correction and detection for every packet at every node. Numerous disadvantages exist with this system, such as the very slow transmission speed and unnecessary processing. For example, the X.25 network processing of a packet is

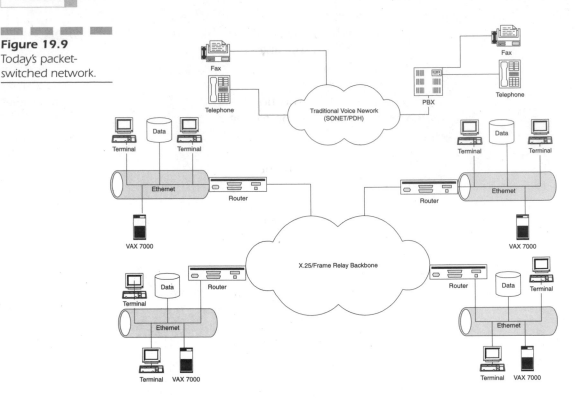

Figure 19.9
Today's packet-
switched network.

performed by as many as three layers of the OSI protocol: the physical, data link, and network layers. The reason for such processing overhead is that when the X.25 network was designed, the transmission system was not reliable, and the objective was to deliver the information error-free regardless of the time to deliver. This need has changed; today, the information must not only be delivered error-free but it also must be delivered fast (depending on the user's request). This IP-based data network has been recently upgraded to a frame-relay network in some portions, but the majority still use an X.25-based IP network.

19.6.2 Phase 1 of the Evolution

Figure 19.10 shows phase 1 of the evolution of the packet-switched network. Here, the X.25 switches are replaced with frame-relay switches completely, and they become extensions of X.25 switches. This replacement meets the need for data services of less than T1 speed.

The frame relay operates in an X.25 mode called virtual circuit mode, where the connection must be set up before data can be transmitted. In the frame-relay network, access speeds up to 1.544 Mbps (T1) and 2.048 Mbps (E1) are possible. Here only two layers of the OSI protocol stack are used. The functions of the network layer are done at the CPE itself, which has the intelligence to process the packets. In the initial design of X.25, the CPE was not assumed to be as intelligent as it is today. The details of frame-relay protocol were covered in Chaps. 4 and 5.

The other network, SMDS, is the first public broadband service proposed by Bellcore for RBOCS. It provides data services up to T3, or 45 Mbps. In SMDS service, all network interfaces, such as customer interface, switching interface, and internetwork interfaces are defined. Here, the frame-relay network interconnected to the regional SMDS network is usually operated by the RBOCS in the United States. The details of SMDS architecture were discussed in Chap. 6.

19.6.3   Phase 2 of the Evolution

The second phase of the evolution is shown in Fig. 19.11. In this phase, the ATM switches are upgraded from frame-relay switches, which act as

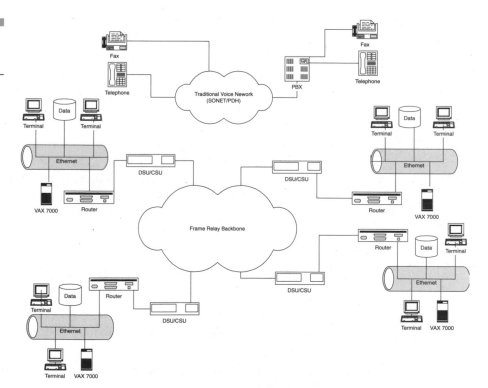

Figure 19.10
Fast packet-switched network—phase 1.

Figure 19.11
Fast packet-switched
network—phase 2.

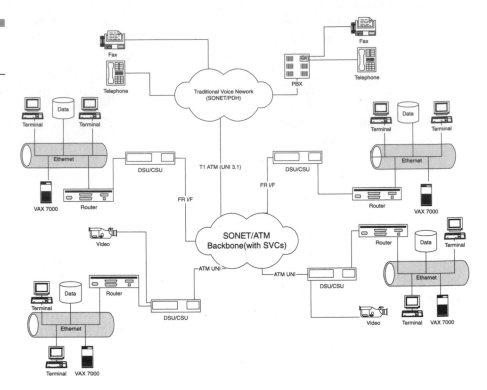

a backbone to the switched network. The ATM network provides a similar virtual circuit but with bandwidth ranging from 1.544 Mbps (T1) to 622 Mbps (OC12), enabling a wide range of services to be accommodated. The X.25 frame-relay networks, and the SMDS networks become access networks to the ATM backbone at various speeds. Here, for the first time, voice traffic at T1 or higher speeds can be tested on the ATM backbone. Most of the traffic, however, will still be on an existing circuit-switched network. In this environment, voice traffic may be carried in one of the following ways:

1. As CBR. In the ATM world and in the traditional voice world it is called circuit emulation. This option maintains the existing quality of service provided by traditional service providers.

2. As IP-voice over Internet. If it is transported over ATM, it will be carried as AAL-5 protocol. This option is considered to have the lower quality of service when compared to traditional voice service.

3. As VBR-rt (real-time variable bit rate). This option is native to the ATM world and is considered to have the quality of service

sufficient to meet most user requirements. In reality, though, it is a notch below compared to traditional voice quality.

So carrying voice in these options with varying quality of service will depend on the service provider and user acceptance. Some service providers are offering as many as 10 levels of quality service to customers.

19.6.4 Phase 3 of the Evolution

The third phase of the evolution is shown in Fig. 19.12. The broadband switching is introduced (ATM switching with SONET transmission), and the access is provided by X.25, frame-relay, and SMDS network-based services. Some switches do not have SONET capability but do have ATM switches with standard digital interfaces (DS1, DS3) as in the case of ATM-based LANs or hubs. The information in the backbone, however, is carried in ATM cells, which are switched by the ATM/broadband switch. These cells ride on the SONET transmission system facilities. Most carriers will, in fact, evolve to this phase in the very near future (depending on the availability, maturity, and cost of technology) and will remain at this stage for a long time until true broadband is justified across the network.

Figure 19.12
Initial BISDN network—phase 3.

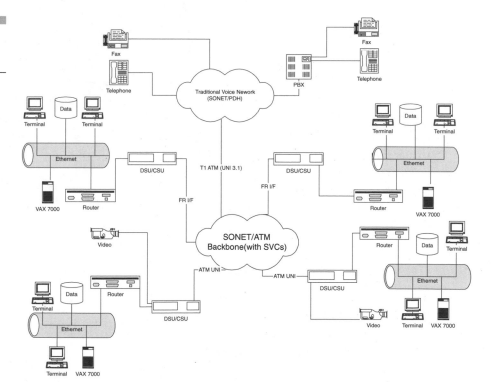

19.6.5 Phase 4 of the Evolution

In phase 4, the complete or true broadband network comes into existence, as illustrated in Fig, 19.13. All the switches in the network adopt the BISDN protocol, and the interfaces are in ATM/SONET. No protocol conversion or adaptation is necessary because the whole network is based on one protocol, i.e., ATM/SONET BISDN. This network takes advantage of all the benefits defined for broadband networks, and it has the capability of proving that all present and future services can be provided without any protocol conversion. At this time, IN will be mature and deployed to utilize the underlying network infrastructure.

In fact, many long-distance carriers are already on the verge of migrating from phase 1 to phase 2. The most realistic architecture is phase 3; hence, the final stage of most networks will be phase 3. To achieve true integrated voice, video, and data, we propose phase 4, the true broadband network, where voice, data, and video become one with all the intelligent network features. Although Phase 4 is far from reality in most cases, it should not be ignored as a desirable goal. Phase 4 is a viable option for a new service provider planning to take advantage of the deregulated environment, a possibility more likely in countries outside the United States.

Figure 19.13
BISDN network—
phase 4.

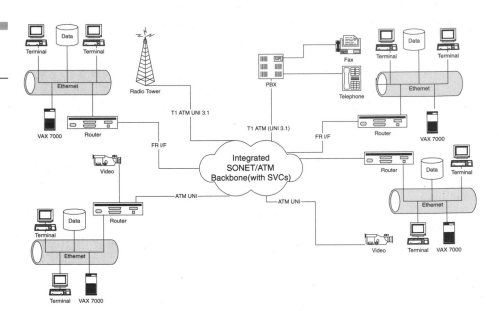

19.7 Summary

In this chapter, we addressed the role of ATM in public networks. One of the early deployments of ATM will be in the backbone network as a transport, with some local-access exceptions where technologies described in Chap. 9 and architecture described in Chap. 13. will dominate. ATM/broadband will be used initially as an overlay network to the existing voice network. ATM's initial traffic is expected to be data. If ATM proves itself for voice traffic, a slow migration of voice will occur. In the transition section, we mentioned the different phases of transition. It is not necessary that all public networks go through this transition; some networks could bypass some of the phases. The transition shown here is only an example evolution of an existing network to an ATM/SONET-based broadband network. But in order for ATM-based broadband to be successful, other provider services, such as network management, and other business support systems, such as billing, need to be developed before real advantage can be achieved from this broadband vision.

Broadband
Network Design

So far, we have looked at different ATM technologies and environments. We have also looked into ATM switching and transmission networks. Now that we have seen all these pieces, we need to know how these technologies all fit together in a network. Next, we look into how to design a broadband network or how to upgrade an existing telephone network to handle integrated broadband traffic. We discuss the issues related to broadband network design.

In theory, the access network should be completed before the backbone network. In the real world, however, the backbone network is usually built or upgraded first, because this is the most cost-effective way since this portion of the network is shared by many users. The access network is then designed in phases, spread out over time, based on cost justification and traffic demand.

Remember that broadband network design is completely different from conventional telecommunications or computer network design because broadband must handle various types of traffic from narrowband to integrated broadband traffic (voice, video, and data), each with different characteristics, such as holding time, bit rate, peakedness, and average bit rate. This part of the book addresses the access network design and backbone network design at a very high level without going into detailed performance analyses. Another important aspect of the design not considered here is the business aspect. Usually engineering and design of a network are driven by the business goal and objective of a service provider. These business issues will drastically impact the design aspects.

CHAPTER 20

Broadband Access Network Design

20.1 Overview

In this chapter, the design of the access portion of the public network is covered. Figure 20.1 shows the reference access network in the United States, which is used to access the public backbone network. The access network is where all traffic originates and terminates. Without the access portion, no traffic could exist in the backbone. This network is so critical to backbone network providers that they pay up to 40 percent of their revenue to the providers of local access networks.

This chapter addresses the design issues of estimating traffic, link (transmission system) sizing, and node (switching system) sizing in the access network. The different components in a network are

■ CPE, which means the network is owned by the public carrier located at the customer premises

■ Local loop, which is the link connecting the CPE and the central office (CO) and is the first interface to the public network

Figure 20.1
Reference access network.

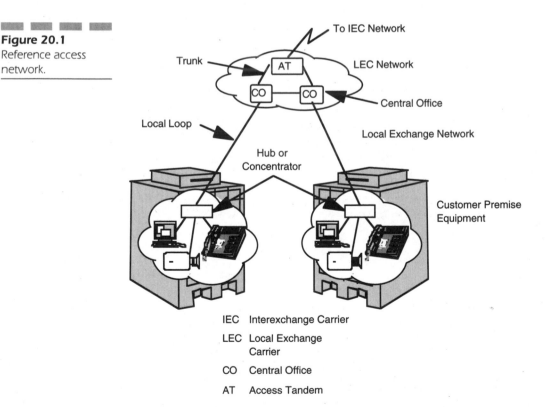

IEC	Interexchange Carrier
LEC	Local Exchange Carrier
CO	Central Office
AT	Access Tandem

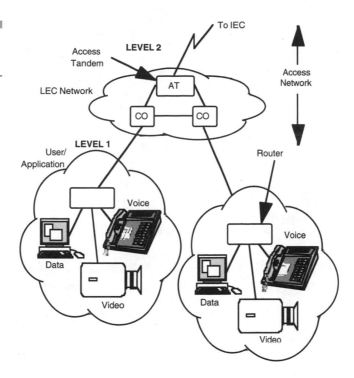

- Trunk links, which are the links connecting different COs
- Access tandem, which is the second level of switching providing traffic consolidation.

Each of these components must be considered in designing the access network.

20.2 Broadband Access Network Definition

Before listing the requirements, let's define an access network. An *access network* can be categorized into two possible access levels: the user or application level and the public network level. Figure 20.2 depicts these two levels.

The user level defines the access required to the public network resources. The link between the customer's hub and the central office is the access interface to the public network. The user level provides the greatest diversity in interfaces, protocols, architecture, technologies, and standards compared to any other level in the network hierarchy. Some of these were described in Chap. 15. User network design is based on the amount of traffic generated from different sources, such as voice from PBX, data from LANs, and video from desktop or a videoconferencing center within the user's premises. All this traffic must be identified during the design at the user/application level. This information is usually available within the company.

The next level is the access interface to the backbone network. This is usually connected to a router, bridge, PBX, switch, customer service unit/data service unit, or any other device that has a standard interface related to the public networks and capable of performing protocol conversion at the customer premises. These access devices are sometimes called hubs or access nodes. In the broadband environment, this device should be able to handle all types of traffic (voice, video, and data). For simplicity, assume one interface exists, through which all traffic leaves the user's premises. This traffic can be connected directly to the backbone network, bypassing the local exchange network; however, it is connected via the LEC. Thus, the network from the customer's premises interface point to the backbone network forms the access network.

20.3 Network Design Requirements for Broadband Access

In a broadband environment, design of the access network is based primarily on existing traffic projections for each customer or user. The most difficult part here is to identify a customer's traffic requirements. Customers can design their own private networks; they have all the traffic and usage pattern information. For a public network provider, however, it is difficult to project the exact traffic that might be generated from the many user applications, especially if the traffic projections are nonexistent, such as broadband traffic. Network requirements are set in such a way as to meet these uncertainties, allowing for expansion if the projections are not accurate. As a result, it is difficult to design a public network. In this section, we divide the public access network requirements into the following general categories:

- Traffic
- Protocol
- Architecture
- Services, features, and functions
- Access route diversity (redundancy)

20.3.1 Traffic

One of the most important aspects of the network design is to estimate traffic. In a broadband network, traffic from the user comes from various applications, each with varying characteristics and usage patterns. All these parameters are used to estimate traffic, but it is difficult to estimate broadband traffic, because no such traffic currently exists. In Sec. 20.4, we look into the details of this traffic engineering problem.

20.3.2 Protocol

In order to interface to the public network, the interface protocol should meet the public network specifications, such as Bellcore, ANSI, IEEE, etc., set by the standards committees. For a broadband network, the protocol should be capable of handling integrated voice, video, and data traffic in addition to the published standards. In some instances, the user might initially use a protocol to handle only data or voice, but later, when the need arises, the user might be required to integrate all the traffic at the hub level. When that need arises, the user might prefer to use the same protocols to avoid unnecessary protocol conversion, but that choice results in inefficient utilization of public network bandwidth.

20.3.3 Architecture

Once the protocol has been chosen, the architecture that will interact with the selected protocol needs to be determined. Usually, certain protocols and technologies go together. Many standard architectures exist, such as star and double-star, which are used in public telecommunications networks. There are also logical-ring, physical ring, and bus architecture for local area networks. These architectures vary, depending on the technologies. The logical-ring architecture is typically used with fiber technology. In the design of access networks, the architecture should be selected so that it provides both short- and long-term benefits in terms of handling current and future traffic and user growth. For example, in a star topology, as shown in Fig. 20.3, a dedicated line and port must be added in order to add a new user.

In the case of the ring topology, shown in Fig. 20.4, no additional link or port needs to be added to the hub. Here, the link capacities are already in place for existing users who share the facilities. In this topology, adding a new user is easy, but new users reduce the bandwidth available to the other users because of sharing. Thus, a limitation on the number of users that can be added must be set if reasonable performance is to be maintained. In a ring topology, the transmission rate is inversely proportional to the capacity of the ring. It is therefore impor-

Figure 20.3
Addition of a terminal in a star topology.

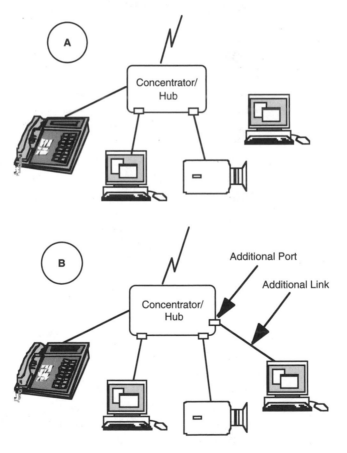

Figure 20.4
Addition of a terminal
in a ring topology.

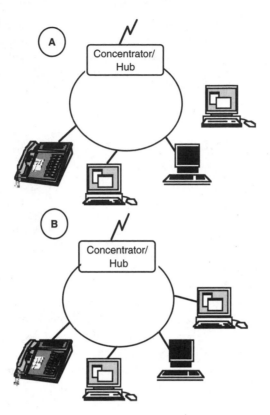

tant to select the right architecture for broadband networks, and each one of the architectures has advantages and disadvantages.

20.3.4 Services, Features, and Functions Required

When a user interfaces to the public network through an access device, certain features, functions, and services are required for standard interface and protocol support. The services, features, and functions vary with the protocol used. For example, the VPI- and VCI-based services are dependent on the ATM protocol. Because these services are protocol-dependent, if the ATM protocol is changed, the services also change. It is thus necessary to decide on the protocol, based on the services it provides. The services, features, and functions provided with the protocols must be considered in the design of the access network. Today, service providers

Figure 20.5
Access route diversity.

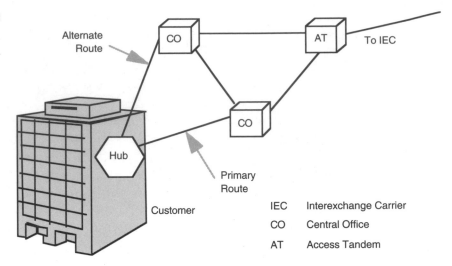

can provide service transparency, i.e., the user service characteristics are preserved regardless of the access protocol, and this is achieved by service mapping. The disadvantage with service mapping is that the overhead involved in each protocol consumes additional bandwidth, which is an inefficient use of the system resources. The user should therefore consider all services offered when deciding on a particular protocol.

20.3.5   Access Route Diversity

Integrated broadband networks are unique in that all traffic going outside the premises exits via a single very high-speed interface. Thus, the customer's only communications interface to the outside world is via that one interface. Any damage or failure to this interface means that the customer is vulnerable to being cut off from outside communication. It is therefore necessary to provide a completely diverse, redundant access route to each interface point in the network, as shown in Fig. 20.5.

20.4   Broadband Access Network Design

In this section, we look at a high-level process for designing a broadband access network and explain the steps involved in the design of the access network. Like other networks, there are many ways to approach the design of a broadband network. Let us assume a bottom-up approach, as illustrated in Fig. 20.6.

As mentioned earlier, designing a broadband network is a lot more complicated than designing a conventional circuit-switched telephone network or a packet-switched computer network because broadband networks are designed for specific applications. For example, the telephone network is designed to carry voice and is optimized for voice traffic, and, although data can be carried, it is not transmitted efficiently. Likewise, a computer network is designed to transfer data, with requirements that are quite different, and full-duplex communication is necessary. Voice transmission is not possible at all in a computer network.

In broadband networks, integrating the different types of traffic onto a single network so that its resources are used efficiently is a formidable task.

We mentioned in Chap. 1 that a typical network consists of nodes (switching centers) and links (transmission lines). Broadband networks are no exception. For the design of a broadband access network, we need a reference network architecture. Figure 20.7 shows the reference access architecture for a broadband network.

To design a broadband access network, the traffic from each customer (business or residential) needs to be estimated, and these traffic patterns

Figure 20.6
Bottom-up approach for design.

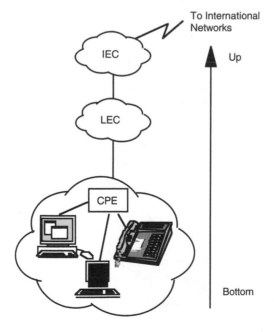

Figure 20.7
Reference access net-
work architecture.

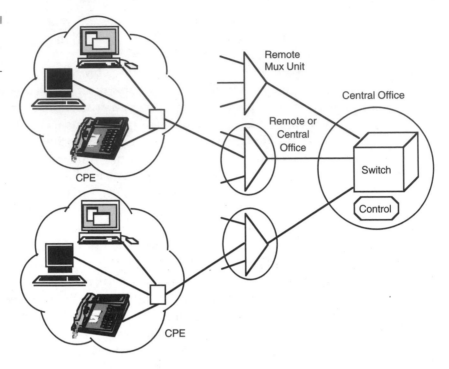

and usage characteristics during peak periods need to be analyzed and understood. For example, residential customers' telephone usage peaks between 4 and 6 p.m. In broadband network, video traffic is included, which peaks between 7 and 10 p.m. (prime time). Figure 20.8 shows approximate traffic patterns for different traffic types.

We can see from the chart that each type of traffic has a different usage pattern. In designing a network, the peak period for each pattern should be considered when designing the network. For example, peak traffic is around 11 a.m. Thus, the network should be designed to handle that traffic.

The following design issues should be addressed in designing a broad-band access network:

- Traffic engineering
- Access technology selections
- Link or transmission network design
- Broadband access node design

Each is described in the following subsections.

20.4.1 Traffic Engineering

The most important component when designing a network is estimating the network traffic. Traffic that does not yet exist (e.g., switched video, personal communication service, etc.) are difficult to estimate. While data is available for existing traffic, new traffic sources make traffic projection more guesswork than concrete engineering. Here, we propose a simplified way to estimate different types of traffic.

In traffic analysis, the basic assumption is that all traffic can be categorized into voice continuous bit rate or data variable bit rate.

Assume that video traffic belongs to one of the two categories. If video traffic is packetized, it is VBR; if not, it is CBR of high bandwidth and large holding time (compared to voice traffic holding time). Voice traffic can also be packetized to become VBR traffic. At this time, packetized voice traffic on a broadband network is far from a reality, so we can assume that most of the voice traffic is CBR.

Usually, each traffic type has its own measurement units. Voice traffic is measured in CCS (hundred call seconds, where the first C represents the roman symbol for hundred) or erlangs, depending on the country of origin. Data traffic is usually measured in packets, messages, frames,

Figure 20.8
Example of traffic patterns for different traffic on a peak day.

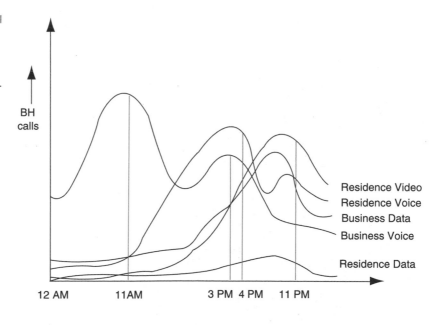

or cells. For simplicity, assume all types of traffic are converted to bits per second. Data traffic units are usually expressed in packets per second or bits per second. Video traffic units are usually expressed in bits per second.

The first step is to convert all the traffic into bits per second. Usually, the available information on traffic is in bytes per day, but the networks are designed based on busy hour traffic. It is customary to assume BH traffic to be 25 percent of the day's traffic, depending on the country. Figure 20.9 shows a typical traffic source for a business customer. Figure 20.10 shows typical traffic sources for a residential customer.

From Figs. 20.9 and 20.10, the following conversion can be derived. Note that the busy hours for voice, video, and data might be different.

Total traffic offered to the network

$$= \sum_{i=1}^{n} (\text{total residential traffic})_{i \text{ BH}} + \sum_{i=1}^{m} (\text{total business traffic})_{i \text{ BH}}$$

Figure 20.9
Business access traffic. Traffic_b = business traffic.

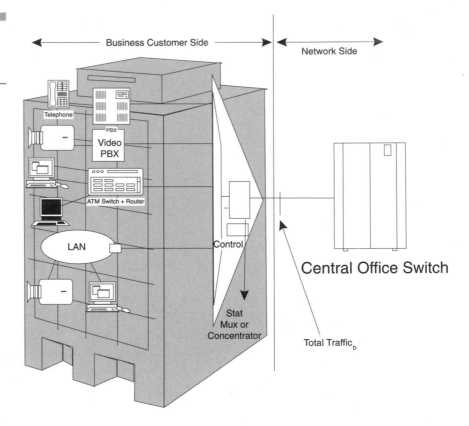

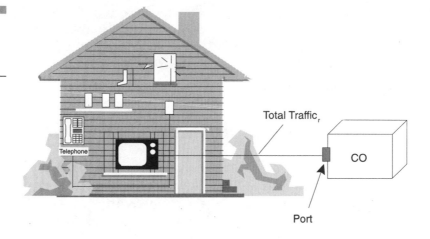

Figure 20.10
Residential access traffic. $Traffic_r$ = residential traffic.

where n = total number of residential customers
m = total number of business customers
BH = busy hour

$$Residential\ traffic|_{BH}$$

$$= \sum voice\ traffic|_{res\ BH} + \sum data\ traffic|_{res\ BH} + \sum video\ traffic|_{res\ BH}$$

where res BH = residential busy hour.

$$Business\ traffic|_{BH}$$

$$= \sum voice\ traffic|_{bus\ BH} + \sum data\ traffic|_{bus\ BH} + \sum video\ traffic|_{bus\ BH}$$

where bus BH = business busy hour.

Once traffic is estimated, all the traffic in the BH is summed to estimate total traffic expected on the network. This estimate is based on extremes, such as the peak data traffic period. The expected traffic varies with the usage pattern. Because the effective traffic changes with time, it is important to keep the user traffic information up to date.

Typical voice/data traffic distribution is as follows. Note that these are approximate distributions; distribution varies from application to application, customer to customer.

- Expected traffic = 100 percent
- Intrapremises = 70 percent
- Extrapremises = 30 percent

Of the extrapremises traffic, 80 percent is intra-LATA and 20 percent is inter-LATA. For instance, switched video traffic for residential customers is usually intra-LATA (93 percent), where the traffic originates from the local video store server. These traffic distribution patterns can be used while designing the links and nodes in the public access network.

20.4.2   Access Technology Selection

After the traffic has been estimated, the customer must decide on the most suitable technology to access the public network. Many factors are involved in selecting the right technology. For the sake of simplicity, assume the selection is based on technology capability. Table 20.1 shows the appropriate technologies based on different types of customer traffic. The appropriate technology can then be selected after reviewing Table 20.1.

20.4.3   Link or Transmission Network Design

As mentioned in Chap. 1, one of the components of the network is the physical link connection between the different switches or nodes in the network. In a broadband network, these links operate at very high speed and carry huge amounts of information. These links are part of the transmission system of a network. The transmission system carries the traffic from point *A* to point *B* error-free, as shown in Fig. 20.11.

TABLE 20.1

Access Technology for Different Traffic Rates

Traffic Type	Effective BH Traffic, bps, in the Access Line*	Access Speed Required	Appropriate Technology
Voice only	<64 kbps	DS0, ISDN	ISDN, POTS
Voice+data	<1.544 Mbps	T1, FT1, PRI	HDSL, T1, PRI-ISDN
Data	≤1.544 Mbps	T1, FT1	FR, ATM, T1, PRI, x-DSL
Data	>1.544 – ≤45 Mbps	FT3, T3	ATM DS3, DS3, STS-1
Voice+data	>1.544 Mbps	FT3, T3, OC3	ATM
Voice+data+video	>1.544 Mbps	FT3, T3, OC3	ATM

*Traffic includes allocation for uncertainties.

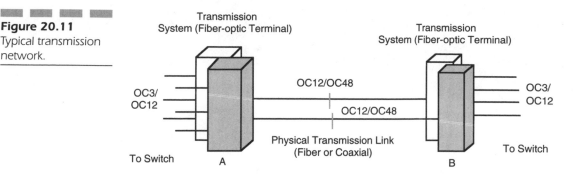

Figure 20.11
Typical transmission
network.

It is easy to estimate the traffic on the link if the traffic originates at point *A* and terminates at point *B.* Because points *A* and *B* are usually several hundred miles apart in an access network, care must be taken that the link is reliable and error-free. In a real-world network, not all nodes are fully connected as direct links. Usually, each node is connected to two or three adjacent nodes. To reach other nodes, the traffic must traverse the intermediate nodes that connect the source and destination node. Thus, to estimate the size of the intermediate link, all traffic passing through the link in the BH must be taken into consideration. (The link design between the switches or nodes in the access networks is discussed in Chap. 21). The most critical portion of the access network is the link between the customer and the network. As this portion is more relevant to the backbone network design, it is also covered in Chap. 21.

Because only one link exists from the customer premises carrying all the traffic to the network, the capacity of the link should be designed based on the effective sum of all the traffic. Care must be taken to consider the utilization of the link caused by each type of traffic. Figures 20.9 and 20.10 showed typical sources of traffic from a business and residential customer, respectively, in a broadband network environment. Table 20.2 shows the typical traffic characterization required in designing the access network.

Assume that each device at the customer premises generates x_1 to x_n Mbps $|_{BH}$ traffic, which is calculated based on the traffic characteristics in Table 20.2.

Therefore, total expected traffic is

$$\sum_{i=1}^{n} x_i \text{ Mbps} \,|_{BH} = K$$

TABLE 20.2

Broadband Traffic
Characteristics

Service	Peak Rate	Duration, hr	Burstiness	BH call attempts
NTSC video	45 Mbps	0.25	1.70	4
HDTV	150 Mbps	0.25	1.35	4
Voice	64 kbps	0.05	1	2
Video conferencing	1.5 Mbps	0.67	1	2
Imaging	1 Mbps	0.25	15.60	3
File transfer	1.5 Mbps	0.0056	15	6
Transaction data	100 kbps	0.0083	200	20

Source: J.Burgin, "BISDN Resource Management," North Holland, 1990, Netherlands.

where n = total number of traffic sources
i = traffic source
K = total expected traffic

Of these, a certain percentage of the traffic usually remains within the premises. The total traffic leaving the premises is calculated as follows. Let A be the percentage of traffic leaving the premises.

$$\text{Total traffic leaving the premises} = K \times A = Z\,\text{Mbps}\,|_{BH}$$

Use of the traffic value in conjunction with Table 20.1 makes it possible to determine the appropriate technology for the expected traffic. Keep in mind though, that it is necessary to predict the customer's traffic over the next 5 to 10 years. Then, using the traffic numbers, the required access technology can be determined from Table 20.1. These calculations enable the carrier/customer to select the appropriate access technology and speed required by the traffic at the end of the study period. The speed is the link access speed required from the customer premises to the network node.

To design the rest of the links in the public access network, the effective utilization of each access link (customer link) must be calculated. Summing the traffic of all customers provides the effective trunk-side link size. Usually, the trunk-side links are connected to more than one node, typically two or three. In that case, the traffic must be distributed to reach its destination via the shortest path, which is based on either distance or link utilization. Figure 20.12 shows the relation between access side and trunk side and its traffic distribution.

Figure 20.12 shows how the trunk traffic is calculated in the network.

$$\text{Total traffic} = x_1 + x_2 + x_3 = K \text{ Mbps}$$

Of these, $x'_1 + x'_2 + x'_3$ Mbps $= M$ terminate within the CO-A switch. Total trunk traffic on node is

$$\text{CO-A} = y_1 + y_2 = N \text{ traffic units}$$

or

$$\text{CO-A} = K - M = N \text{ traffic units}$$

The calculation of y_1 and y_2 trunk traffic is similar to the calculation of traffic between nodes in the backbone network, which is addressed in Chap. 21.

Figure 20.12
Trunk-side traffic on the access network.

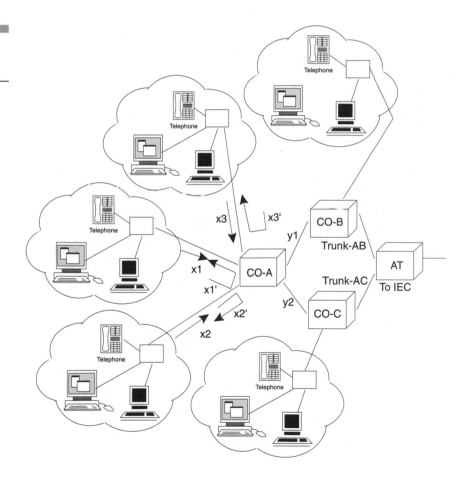

On the trunk side, the effective utilization of the link is usually 70 to 80 percent of link capacity including overhead. On the access side, the utilization is less than 10 percent on average.

20.4.4   Broadband Access Node Design

Figure 20.13 shows a typical broadband access node, including the access side, access ports, trunk side, and trunk ports.

The broadband access node design is based on three main factors:

■ Total access ports required (access links)

■ Total trunk ports required (trunk links)

■ Total traffic offered to the switch, i.e., the sum of all the port speeds (total ports)

Thus, the access node size is determined by its traffic-handling capability and number of ports. These parameters can be calculated in the following way:

Figure 20.13
Broadband access node.

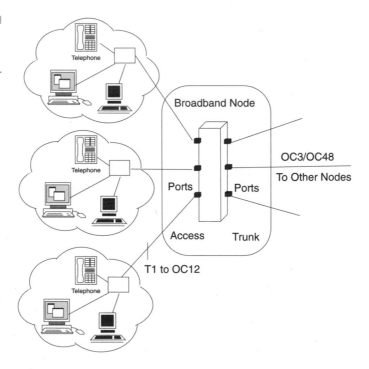

Total broadband access node size, in Mbps

$= S$ traffic per port (access and trunk)$|_{BH}$

Broadband access node size in number of ports

$= S$ access link $+ S$ trunk links

The number of access ports is usually higher than the number of trunk ports because of the higher utilization of the link on the access side compared to the trunk side. Trunk-side links are more effectively utilized, and the link speed on the access side is usually less than that of the trunk side. Typically, the ratio of the number of access ports to the number of trunk ports is 10:1. In designing the node, plans for future expansion in terms of switch capacity and additional ports must be considered.

20.5 Broadband Access Network Topologies

Typical topology for a telecommunications or computer network is a star or double star, as shown in Fig. 20.14.

Because of the requirements set forth in the design of broadband communications, along with the availability of new technologies such as fiber for higher capacity, numerous topologies are under consideration for access networks. Some of these topologies are the following:

- Physical star/logical star
- Physical ring topology
- Logical star/physical ring
- Physical ring/logical ring
- Bus/star and bus/bus

We describe the most popular architectures in the following subsections.

20.5.1 Physical Star/Logical Star Topology

Figure 20.15 illustrates physical star/logical star topology. This topology offers the maximum potential bandwidth to each customer and hence

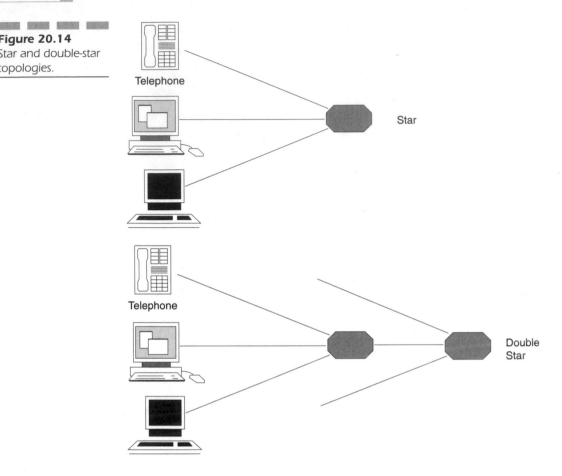

Figure 20.14
Star and double-star topologies.

provides maximum flexibility in providing service and future upgrades. This architecture simplifies the administration of bandwidth requirements for individual customers and the diagnosis and partitioning of faults, so the life cycle operational costs are low. The dedicated facilities of this architecture provide a high degree of security and limit unauthorized access, but these advantages can result in a higher initial cost. This topology should be considered when potential demand exists for a full range of services, when high reliability/security is required, or when the distances are short and initial cost is not a sensitive parameter.

20.5.2 Physical Ring/Logical Star Topology

This topology is physically interconnected as a ring, but a wavelength or time slot is allocated for each node. The initial cost for this architecture might be lower than that for a physical star because of the sharing of fiber, but the electronics cost can be higher because of the higher bandwidth requirements. This architecture takes advantage of the logical-star topology by providing security and privacy.

20.5.3 Physical Star/Logical Ring Topology

This topology has the same physical layout as the physical star/logical star, as shown in Fig. 20.16. At the central node, however, the receive fiber from each node is connected to the transmit fiber of another node. Because information passes through all nodes and links on the ring, bandwidth is more difficult to administer, higher-speed interfaces are required, and fault partitioning is more difficult.

In this topology, the number of switch ports can be reduced. For example, the nodes at either end are connected to the switch directly, and the other nodes are connected to a patch panel (cheap manual connector board) and looped back. In the case of broadcast video type, the signal can be broadcast to one CPE and can flow to other CPEs without utilizing switch resources.

Figure 20.15
Example of physical star/logical star topology.

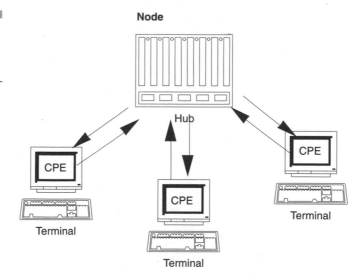

Physical star/logical star

Figure 20.16
Example of physical
star/logical ring
topology.

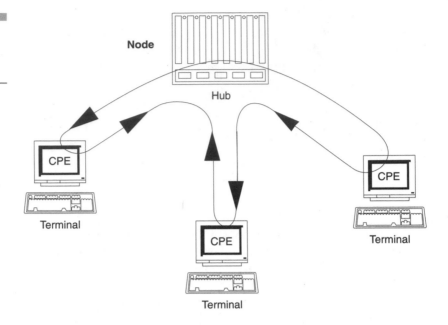

20.6   Summary

Design of the broadband access network poses interesting design issues
mainly because all types of traffic are carried on the network without
differentiation. Because each type of traffic has its own characteristics, it
must be treated separately. To meet these requirements, the issues of
traffic, link, and node must also be considered separately and designed
with care. In addition, the appropriate access topology must be selected
to meet both short- and long-term requirements.

21

Broadband
Backbone
Network Design

21.1 Overview

Once the access design is complete for the broadband network, it becomes necessary to decide how to connect it. It is not possible to connect all the access nodes together because of the network's complexity. For example, there are about 25,000 central office switches at the local exchange level in the United States; the local exchange carriers have a second level, called the access tandem, which does traffic aggregation, to connect them together. There are about 1200 access tandem nodes. Thus, on average, the ratio of central office locations to access tandem locations is 10:1 (more than one CO can exist in a location). These central office and access tandem nodes form the switching portion of the local access network. These networks were part of AT&T until 1984, and the nodes were part of the hierarchical network. Today, local exchange carriers have two levels, the central office switches and access tandem switches, as shown in Fig. 21.1.

This network is called the access network for the backbone network. The next level above this access network is called the backbone network or interexchange carrier network, which, according to a U.S. Modified Final Judgment court ruling, can carry only inter-LATA and interstate traffic. Thus, this network forms the backbone, and the local exchange carrier becomes the access network for the interexchange carrier, also called the long-distance network. Figure 21.2 shows a typical backbone network with access networks subtending these backbone network switches.

Now that we have defined the backbone network, let's design one. One of the main purposes of this network is to transport the traffic across the geographical borders while the access network originates and terminates a connection.

21.2 Broadband Backbone Network Design Requirements

In broadband communication networks, the backbone network should be 100 percent perfect in all ways, i.e., the network should have zero downtime, zero percent blocking, and unlimited bandwidth to handle all of the traffic all of the time. Users expect these requirements from

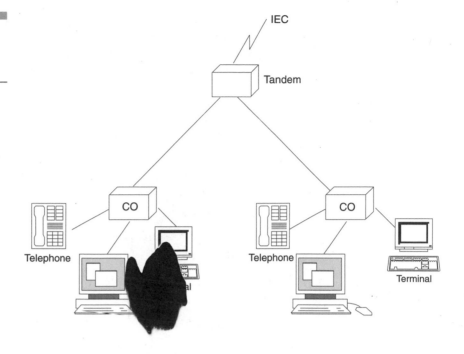

Figure 21.1
Two levels of local exchange carrier network.

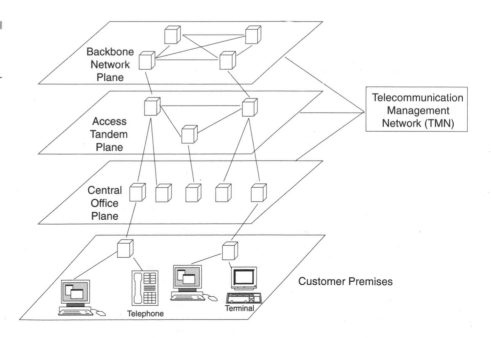

Figure 21.2
Backbone, access, and CPE plane.

the backbone network. Of course, it can be costly to design such a perfect network, so the objective of the network designer is to find a balance between cost and perfection. When compared to access networks, backbone networks are far more efficient and cost-effective because of the higher rate of shared services by users. The backbone network can therefore provide more services than the access network. Some of the services provided include the following:

- Intelligent network services
- Dynamic bandwidth allocation
- Distributed network management
- Redundant network for protection
- Efficient utilization of resources
- Efficient economics of scale
- Advanced technology-based services

For a customer with multiple locations connected via a private network, the public network itself usually acts as a virtual backbone network that connects the different sites. Figure 21.3 illustrates a typical public network, and Fig. 21.4 shows a private network.

Figure 21.3
Public switched
network.

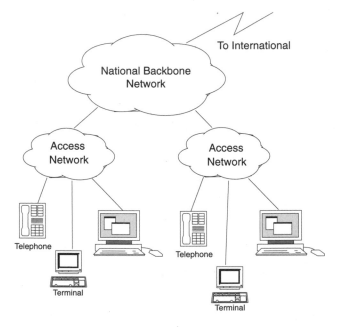

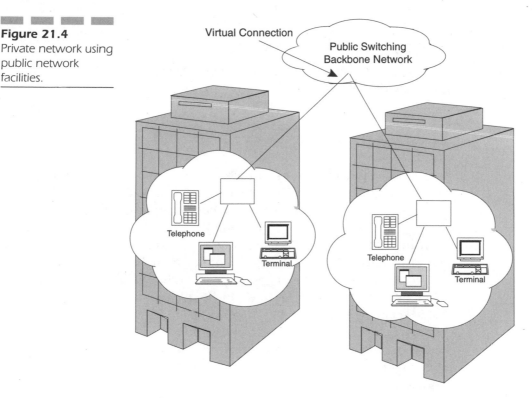

Figure 21.4
Private network using
public network
facilities.

In most cases, customers are connected via the local public network, but sometimes they can be directly connected to the public backbone network and bypass the local access network in a private network. Sometimes private network customers use their own facilities for the access portion of the network, enabling customers to avoid paying access charges to the local access provider. Sometimes customers bypass the public network completely and use private facilities managed end-to-end. This trend is no longer popular with large customers because of changing technology and the cost involved in managing a network, especially if their core business is not in telecommunications. Thus, most customers prefer to bypass the local access network to get to the backbone network because of the advanced services provided by backbone network providers.

In Chap. 20, we defined network requirements under four categories:

■ Interfaces
■ Protocols

■ Architectures

■ Features, functions, and services

In addition to these requirements, other requirements for these categories are described in the following sections.

21.2.1   Interfaces

Interfaces to public networks always follow the standards. Certain interfaces are required for voice and data traffic, with varying speeds depending on the traffic requirements of the customer or the serving access node in the local exchange network. In a broadband network, a common interface exists for transporting voice, data, and video. The typical access interfaces to a broadband backbone are shown in Table 21.1.

A variety of protocols can be mapped to DS1 and DS3. Protocols such as ISDN PRI, 24 DS0, or 1.544 Mbps can be mapped to DS1. About 40 Mbps of SMDS or ATM cells or 28 DS1 cells can be mapped to a DS3 protocol. The traffic in the network is transported at DS1 or DS3 speed regardless of how the traffic is mapped and transported. It becomes the function of the switching equipment and termination equipment in the transmission network to identify the appropriate protocol to convert the traffic.

21.2.2   Protocol

Although access to the backbone network consists of various protocols, such as frame relay, SMDS, X.25, and ATM, all must be mapped to a common backbone protocol. The current trend in the public network is to use SONET/SDH for transmission and frame relay, SMDS, or ATM

TABLE 21.1

Broadband
Interfaces

Interface Terminology	Interface Speed	Domain Type
T1	1.544 Mbps	Electrical
DS3	45.76 Mbps	Electrical
OC3	155 Mbps	Optical
OC12	622 Mbps	Optical
OC48	2.4 Gbps	Optical
OC96	9.6 Gbps	Optical

for data traffic switching. Voice traffic is still handled by conventional voice switches. Although ATM can handle voice, it will be a while before voice traffic goes on the ATM backbone. In the case of a data network, the current protocol is TCP/IP. Most of today's video traffic is carried via CATV in a broadcast mode using traditional AM/FM analog technology.

21.2.3   Architecture

Backbone architecture is always ahead of access architecture in terms of technology, features, and services provided to the end user because of the requirements set forth by end users and regulatory bodies. Only service providers with effective service operate the backbone networks due to the presence of competition. Because broadband networks should provide numerous advantages to the end user at minimal cost, the backbone architecture must always improve and look for additional cost-cutting alternatives. The usual backbone architecture is almost fully meshed and is expected to be in the form of rings.

21.2.4   Features, Functions, and Services

The features, functions, and services in a backbone network vary with the type of technology being supported. If the backbone network is SMDS, it can support DQDB or SMDS interfaces. If ATM is used, it can support all types of interfaces, ranging from X.25 to ATM. Thus, the type of technology selected dictates the services, features, and functions, which vary from technology to technology.

21.3   Broadband Backbone Network Design

Three major components exist in the design of a broadband backbone network, and they are similar to the ones in the access network:

- Traffic engineering
- Link design
- Node design

Before addressing these areas, let's look at the backbone network in the United States. Currently, the United States has both a public telephone network and a computer network, each designed and optimized for its specific applications—the public telephone network for voice traffic and the public computer network for data. The traffic pattern and characteristics of the applications for each network are different and therefore must be engineered differently, which, in turn, affects the design of the nodes and links in the networks. In a broadband communications network, the backbone network needs to handle all the traffic, where the network optimization is transparent to each user who requests the service. The user can be a local access carrier who provides the access function of originating and terminating the traffic or an end user such as a business or residential customer.

21.3.1   Traffic Engineering

Traffic engineering in the backbone network is as complicated as in the access network. In the backbone network, the access speeds are very high; a failure in the link can cause problems for many customers. Thus, as a part of design, traffic is usually split between two backbone nodes to prevent any traffic loss in case of a link failure. Before we go into traffic segmentation, let's look at the traffic source. For a backbone network, most of the traffic comes from the access networks, as shown in Fig. 21.5. In some cases, it bypasses the local access network.

The traffic is generated from the access network via the access node, which provides all traffic to the backbone network. The problem is in the difficulty of identifying the destination of the traffic. Voice, video, and data each have a separate pattern of traffic distribution, which can vary depending on industry and business. To simplify the network design, engineers use the gravity method. The principle behind the gravity method is that each node receives the same amount of traffic it gave to the network. This theory might not be an accurate measurement, but it is sufficient to design the network. The formula for calculating the traffic to different destination nodes is as follows:

$$t_{m,n} = \frac{T_{m,i} \times T_{n,i}}{T_{L,i}}$$

$$t_{m,i} = \sum_{j=1}^{n} t_{L,i}^{\ j}$$

$$T_{L,i} = \sum_{l=1}^{L} \sum_{j=1}^{n} t_{l,i}^{\ j}$$

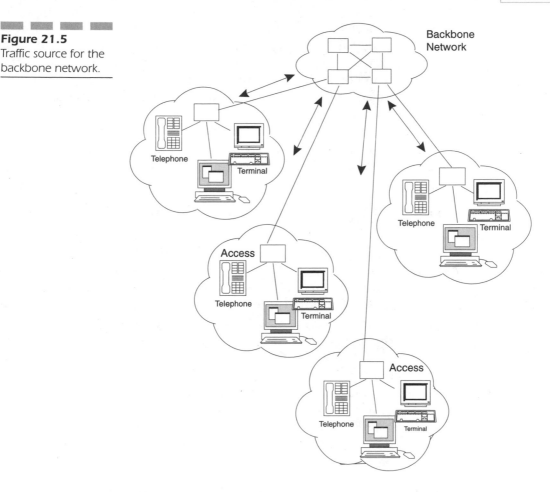

Figure 21.5
Traffic source for the backbone network.

where m = originating node
$\quad\quad\quad n$ = destination node
$\quad\quad\quad i$ = year
$\quad\quad\quad L$ = total number of nodes
$\quad\quad\quad t_{m,n}$ = traffic between m and n in the ith year
$\quad\quad\quad T_{m,i}$ = traffic from m in the ith year
$\quad\quad\quad T_{n,i}$ = traffic from n in the ith year
$\quad\quad\quad T_{L,i}$ = total traffic from all nodes in the ith year

The gravity model gives the traffic between each pair of nodes in the network. Once the amount of traffic is known, the next step is to decide how the traffic is to be routed. Traffic can be routed in many ways, but the most popular one uses the shortest path. Several new algorithms have been developed for this routing pattern, and one of them uses the concept of a virtual pipe between a pair of nodes via different routes, which can be varied in real time, depending on the traffic. Before the network can be designed, the traffic must be represented. The traffic between pairs of nodes is usually represented by a matrix, where the x-axis represents the source nodes, and the y-axis represents the destination nodes, as shown in Table 21.2.

Each box is filled with the traffic from the source to the destination. The traffic matrix contains very important data, which is used in the link and node design of a backbone network.

21.3.2 Link or Transmission Network Design

Once the traffic is known, especially the traffic between each node pair, the traffic on the link between the pair can be estimated. This calculation is simple if a direct link exists between the two nodes because the traffic that passes through the link is the same as the traffic between the node pair. In the real world, however, no network is fully connected, even in the broadband backbone network. Thus, the traffic must pass through many nodes via links to reach its destination. For example, Fig. 21.6 shows a typical four-node network. Assume that the traffic from A to D is given, and the network is connected as shown in Fig. 21.6.

The network consists of four nodes: A, B, C, and D and three links l_1, l_2, and l_3. For the traffic from node A to reach node D and vice versa, it must pass through nodes B and C via links l_1, l_2, and l_3 before reaching destination node D. The traffic of link l_1 is

$$\text{Traffic in one direction} = \text{traffic } (AD)$$

$$\text{Traffic in other direction} = \text{traffic } (DA) + \text{traffic } (BA) + \text{traffic } (CA)$$

Thus, the size of link l_1 should be based on the maximum of two directions. Similarly, for links l_2 and l_3, the total traffic in both directions

TABLE 21.2	Source/Destination	Node 1	Node 2	Node 3	Node 4
Traffic Matrix	Node 1	✓			
	Node 2		✓		
	Node 3			✓	
	Node 4				✓

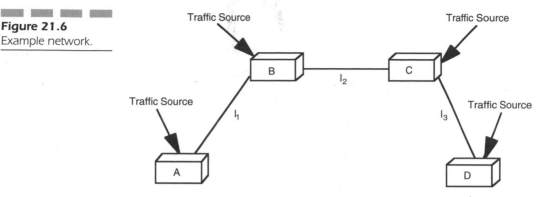

Figure 21.6
Example network.

of each link must be estimated, and the link size should be the maximum traffic in two directions. When designing the link, all the intermediate traffic must be taken into consideration. There should be sufficient room for unforseen situations—e.g., some extra capacity must be allocated for each link. This variable is simple if the network is small, but in today's complex broadband network, link sizes must be optimized without incurring additional cost and while taking every possible uncertainty into consideration. Link size depends on how much traffic is routed via that link, and routing depends on the type of algorithm used. Many algorithms are based on distance, cost, or a combination of both. For broadband networks, the routing algorithm must be dynamic and should be adjustable, depending on the situation of the traffic at the time of routing.

In most cases, carriers use existing routing methods unless carriers are convinced that a new algorithm is easy to use and cost-effective. Broadband networks require dynamic routing algorithms because of the bandwidth-on-demand type of traffic. In dynamic routing algorithms, routing decisions reflect changes in the traffic pattern. Because we do not know the exact broadband traffic between each pair of nodes, it is crucial to estimate the traffic correctly. Without knowing the traffic between the nodes, it is difficult to perform routing. In the case of broadband networks, because of the uncertain traffic patterns, the best algorithm to use is the distributed routing algorithm, which uses dynamic routing. In distributed routing, each node periodically exchanges explicit routing information with each of its neighbors.

Once the traffic between the node pair is available, we can find the route taken by the traffic under various conditions using any routing algorithm. It is possible to estimate the link size from the results of the routing algorithm. The link can be sized using the loading factors during the peak periods. Usually, it is assumed that the peak-hour traffic is 80 percent of the link capacity. In other words, almost 80 percent of the link is utilized at any given time. Thus, the link bandwidth in one direction (we can assume the same bandwidth in the opposite direction) can be given as

$$\text{Link bandwidth } (l_{ij}) = \sum_{j=1;\, i=1}^{j=m;\, i=n} \text{point-to-point traffic from } i \text{ to } j$$

$$+ \text{ transit traffic between } i \text{ and } j + 20\% \text{ loading factor}$$

where i, j = nodes on the network
$\quad\ l_{ij}$ = link between nodes i and j

Total link capacities are obtained by summing all the individual link capacities. Link capacity does not mean the total traffic traversing the network. Sufficient bandwidth is reserved in the link to handle the uncertainties so that almost all traffic can be rerouted without bringing down the network. In addition to designing the link capacity to handle existing traffic, it should be designed to handle future traffic whose characteristics are not very predictable. All traffic calculations are currently based on trials and theoretical research work. The traffic can be estimated by use of these theories and extrapolation of existing traffic by the public carriers.

Thus, to summarize the steps in designing the broadband backbone link:

1. Calculate the total access traffic on a per-node basis.
2. If node-to-node traffic is not available, use the gravity method to estimate node-to-node traffic.
3. Use a routing algorithm to route the traffic in the given network topology.
4. Sum all the traffic on a link-by-link basis to calculate link traffic.
5. Add "fudge factors" for uncertainties, such as 20 percent of additional bandwidth to provide an estimated link capacity.

21.3.3   Node Design

After calculating traffic and link capacity, we can now design the size of the backbone node. Typically, four parameters define the design and size of a broadband node:

- Total traffic-handling capacity of the node, which is typically the size of the backbone switching matrix.
- Total number of access ports and their capacities.
- Total number of trunk ports and their capacities.
- Total number of ports on the node (access+trunk).

Figure 21.7 shows these parameters in a typical node, such as switch or cross-connect system.

Determination of these parameters can result in a good estimate of the size of a broadband node. The size (speed) of each port and the number of ports (access and trunk) depend on the traffic arriving and leaving the node and the number of traffic sources. In backbone networks in the United States, the traffic comes from different LATAs, as shown in Fig. 21.8. The carrier that owns the backbone network should have a presence in each LATA. All traffic is collected at a point in the LATA and offered to the backbone network on a single port to the backbone node. If the traffic exceeds the capacity of the port, the carrier decides whether to add another port or put a concentrator at the interface point in the LATA. This decision depends on many factors, such as the distance between the LATA and backbone node, the cost of that distance in dollar per circuit, and the cost of the port in the backbone node. These factors are illustrated in Fig. 21.9.

Once the approximate traffic is calculated from each LATA, the number of ports required from the LATA can be determined. Justification to

Figure 21.7
Typical node.

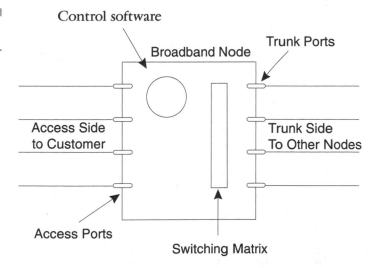

Figure 21.8
Backbone network
interface at LATAs
network.

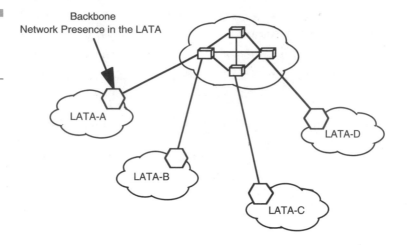

Figure 21.9
Backhaul cost.

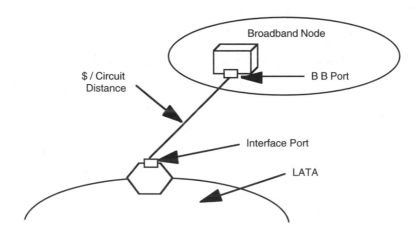

deploy an ATM port (stat mux) or conventional port (mux) is based on a comparison of the cost of the port to the backhaul cost of the traffic to the backbone node. The backhaul is illustrated in Fig. 21.9. Based on the number of ports per LATA to each node, the number of access ports required for the backbone node can then be calculated.

The number of access ports for each broadband node is

$$\text{Number of access ports } I_{\text{node}} = \sum_{i=1}^{n} \frac{\text{traffic from LATA } i}{\text{port speed on the broadband node}}$$

where n = total number of LATAs homing to the node.

Note that port speed is the effective speed multiplied by 80 percent. For example, if the effective speed is 155 Mbps, the port speed is 155 × 0.8, or 124 Mbps.

$$\text{Total number of access ports} = \sum_{j=1}^{m} \text{number of access ports for node } j$$

where m = total number of nodes.

Now that we have calculated the total number of access ports, let's address the size of the switching matrix. The size is basically twice the effective traffic offered plus sufficient capacity (an extra 20 percent) to handle traffic growth for the next 5 to 10 years.

$$\text{Total switch size}$$
$$= (\text{total traffic offered} \times 2) \times 1.2$$
$$+ \text{projected traffic for the next 10 years}$$

The next step is to calculate the number of trunk ports. Usually, the number of trunk ports in a node is the same as the number of adjacent nodes to that node. If the traffic to a node exceeds port capacity, an additional port to the same node can be added. In either case, one still needs to estimate the traffic on the trunk at each node. In addition to handling the traffic at each node, the trunk should have the capacity to handle almost all the traffic being carried on the other trunks. This type of backup is required because of the amount of traffic being carried and the reliability the carriers have guaranteed to their customers.

To calculate the number of trunk ports and their speeds, we use the gravity method to distribute the traffic between the nodes and route them using one of the routing algorithms such as shortest-path algorithm. This algorithm provides the traffic at each node on the trunk side and the speed of the trunk ports from which an estimated number of trunk ports can be found. The number of trunk-side ports used as a backup to provide for redundancy are then added to the traffic number. For simplicity, assume the ports have a one-to-one backup. The number of trunk ports is then exactly twice the trunks required to handle the traffic.

To summarize:

$$\text{Total trunk ports required} = \sum_{i=1}^{n} \frac{\text{traffic from/to adjacent node } i}{\text{port speed}}$$

where n = number of adjacent nodes.

Note that we use the maximum of the two directions of traffic between a node pair.

$$\text{Total trunk ports with backup added}$$
$$= \sum_{j=1}^{m} (\text{number of trunk ports for traffic} + \text{number of trunk ports for backup})_j$$

where m = number of broadband nodes.

The network design proposed here is for a typical real-world public network, where the network, along with the number of nodes and nodal locations, already exists. This network design does not suggest how many locations are required or the location for the nodes. To determine this information, a completely different methodology must be used. Usually, nodal location is decided when designing a private network.

The network design can become complicated with dual homing and the distribution of traffic to various nodes depending on the conditions set by the carrier to distribute the traffic pattern.

21.4   Broadband Backbone Network Topologies

Certain topologies are being proposed that can effectively use broadband technologies, such as SONET transmission systems and ATM switching, for a broadband network. Backbone network topologies for a broadband backbone network are either a ring or meshed topology.

The topologies for access to the broadband backbone network are

- Star topology
- Ring topology
- Dual-homing ring topology
- Dual-homing star topology

The topologies for the backbone and access networks vary, depending on the type of technologies used in those networks. Figure 21.10 shows the ring/star topology combination.

Figure 21.11 shows a topology with multiple rings, which is the proposed topology for the broadband network environment. This architecture provides all the features, services, and functions required for broadband network.

Figure 21.10
Combination of star and ring topologies.

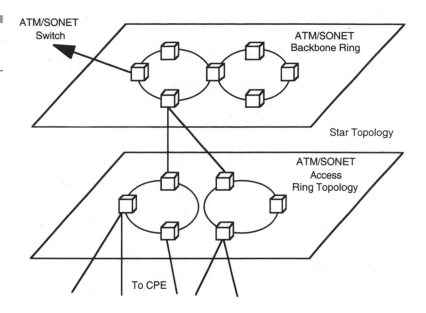

Figure 21.11
Combination of ring topologies.

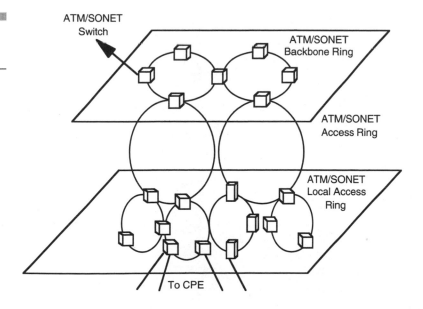

The topology for a network is selected based on the ability to add links and nodes when necessary, so that the traffic is shared evenly and the existing links or nodes are not overloaded. Of course, a link or node is added only when no other alternative exists, such as rerouting the traffic on a fully utilized link.

21.5 Summary

This chapter presented the design issues related to the broadband backbone network and its requirements. Although some of the requirements are similar to those of the access network, the requirements are more stringent in terms of failures in the backbone network. Three categories are related to the design:

- The traffic offered from the access network

- The link capacity design

- The broadband backbone node design

The different topologies and architectures used in the broadband network environment were discussed. For a SONET/ATM environment, ring topology is recommended because of the advantages offered by a SONET ring network, such as an alternate route if one ring is cut off.

PART 7

Miscellaneous

Here we address issues that do not fit in any of the previous sections of the book. There are four chapters in this part. Chapter 22 discusses broadband/ATM deployment activities around the world. Chapter 23 discusses the worldwide telecommunications regulatory bodies that are involved in deciding telecommunications standards and policies related to global communications. Chapter 24 discusses the different opportunities for broadband equipment vendors in the telecommunication network. Finally, Chapter 25 discusses the future of broadband communications and potential future directions of broadband technologies, which may very soon be a topic for a new book.

22

Broadband around the World

22.1   Overview

In the previous chapters, we discussed the various broadband technologies and protocols. We then looked into the different environments where ATM/broadband is applicable. Then, we discussed how to design a broadband network (access and broadband networks). We mentioned that the most important element of design is estimating customer traffic based on the applications used. The best way to determine an application's characteristics is to test it out with real customers running real applications. This chapter gives a tour of different trial efforts under way around the world. These trial activities can offer service providers insight into potential traffic characteristics. Early trials on broadband ATM were focused on the ATM technology itself. Also, trials are conducted to understand the technology, market, and the service delivery. Since writing the first edition of this book, the broadband trials have moved on to validate the service over ATM-based broadband networks. Thus the aspect of end-to-end broadband network trials began gaining more attention. In some cases, such as video broadband trials, numerous trials were conducted and shut down. The lessons learned pointed out that the trials had to be conducted in a real-time environment and be applicable to needs of users. In general, though, ATM-based broadband trials have been very successful. However, in spite of the early success of some trials, some questions users still ask are:

■ Is ATM hype or real? If so, for what application?

■ Is ATM a universally accepted technology (in terms of geography and ability to support a variety of services)?

■ What proof is there that ATM will deliver the advantages promised?

■ What applications are suitable for ATM/broadband?

■ What is the "killer" application for broadband?

A simple answer to these questions is that ATM is for real, it is a universal standard, and proof is available from completed trials and commitments made by service and equipment providers around the world. Some of these trials are mentioned in this chapter. In recent years, internet access has become the killer application that drives the need for broadband.

The answer to suitable applications for ATM/broadband is given in Chap. 2. Specific applications with respect to trials are mentioned in Chap. 2. Tests and trials answer these questions and help in understanding the real-world broadband communication environment.

To obtain more recent information readers are requested to check out *http://www.cefriel.it/~scalisi/atm.html,* a web site that provides a comprehensive list of all of the research activities on ATM and broadband network.

22.2 ATM/Broadband Trials in North America

No other country has more broadband trial activities and commitments than the United States. In all segments of the network—voice, data, and video—some activity related to trial, testing, or deployment of broadband is under way. In terms of deployment of service, however, the United States is a bit cautious, especially in the public LEC network, with some exceptions. Some of the ATM/broadband test beds and trials are mentioned along with the applications being tested. In general, the applications fall into one of the three major categories: voice, video, or data.

Canada, along with the United States, has currently deployed an ATM-based broadband as their backbone network for internet access.

22.2.1 United States

Contrary to the popular belief that the average researcher is a single professor with a group of students, most of the research in broadband networks is being conducted by large teams of senior researchers from large organizations. In some cases, the research involves multiple organizations. The best known broadband networking test beds are called gigabit-networking test beds, because the transmission systems are in gigabits. They are funded by the government agencies, such as National Science Foundation (NSF), Advanced Research Projects Agency (ARPA) of the Department of Defense, and others. Funding from other government agencies and industries also contributes to these gigabit test beds. The initial work on test beds was created in 1989 and coordinated by the Corporation for National Research Initiative (CNRI). The current gigabit networking test beds are

- Blanca test bed (*http://choices.cs.uiuc.edu/blanca/*)
- Aurora test bed
- Nectar test bed
- CASA test bed
- VISTA test bed
- MAGIC test bed (*www.magic.net/*)
- BAGNET test bed (*george.lbl.gov/BAGNET.html*)
- NCGN test bed (*http://www.ncgni.org/*)

Figure 22.1 shows a gigabit test bed coordinated by CNRI.

The goal of the gigabit trials was to study and understand the broadband network parameters by simulating throughput conditions and determining the effect of delay with different combinations of applications. In addition to these test beds, the U.S. IECs have deployed their own nationwide ATM network to provide ATM-based services. Some of the carriers are Sprint, Worldcom, AT&T, and MCI. In the following subsections, we give an overview of some of the gigabit test beds and their objectives.

22.2.1.1 Aurora Test Bed. This is one of the gigabit test beds sponsored by ARPA/NSF grants. Figure 22.2 shows an Aurora transmission

Figure 22.1
CNRI gigabit test beds.

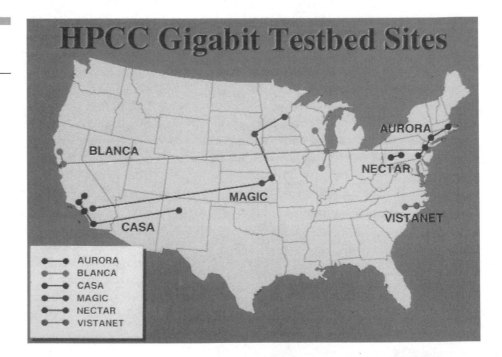

Figure 22.2
Aurora network.

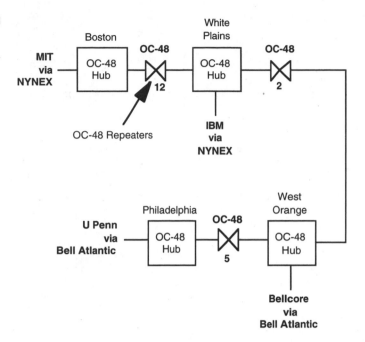

network spanning from Boston (Massachusetts Institute of Technology) to Philadelphia (University of Pennsylvania). The transmission networks are SONET OC-48 systems from Northern Telecom; the ATM switches are from Bellcore and IBM. This network was deployed in three phases:

- Phase 1: White Plains, N.Y., to West Orange, N.J., in 4Q92
- Phase 2: West Orange, N.J., to Philadelphia Pa. (University of Pennsylvania), in 2Q93
- Phase 3: White Plains, N.Y., to Boston Mass. (Massachusetts Institute of Technology), in 4Q93

Based on the research conducted on this network, numerous papers have been published. The research was conducted in many areas, including switches, architecture, flow control, congestion control, and ATM protocol. In addition to these areas, this project is now used for conducting experiments in interfaces between different protocols with ATM/SONET.

22.2.1.2   CASA Network Test Bed.   Figure 22.3 shows the CASA network topology. The network was designed to experiment on applications of distributed computing. This network is in California and funded by

Figure 22.3
CASA network.

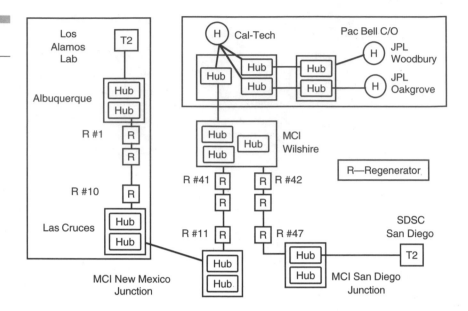

ARPA/NSF. The network was established in 1990 to link research centers such as the Jet Propulsion Laboratory, Los Alamos Laboratory, and Cal-tech. The public carriers involved in the projects are Pacific Bell and MCI. The transmission network consists of OC48 terminals from Northern Telecom. The network consists of supercomputer centers in the previously mentioned laboratories. All the supercomputer centers are connected via high-performance parallel interface (HIPPI) to a SONET backbone. ATM switches will be added to the network later.

22.2.1.3 MAGIC Test Bed. The MAGIC (Multidimensional Applications and Gigabit Internetwork Consortium) research network is one of the newest test beds, funded by ARPA in early 1992. Its web site can be found at (*http://www.magic.net/*). It is a SONET/ATM-based network in the midwestern United States. The participants in this test bed are: Sprint, Minnesota Supercomputer Center, U.S. Army Battle Laboratory, U.S. Earth Resources Observation Systems Data Center, University of Kansas, SRI International, U.S. Army Command Battle Laboratory, DEC, Southwestern Bell Telephone, and Northern Telecom.

The second phase of the MAGIC test bed is called MAGIC II. MAGIC II is a 3-year, collaborative project involving 10 principal organizations, including carriers; the project began in August 1996. The connectivity of MAGIC to other networks will enable organizations on those networks to participate in application experiments, in tests and use of the distributed processing/distributed storage systems, and in the development and evaluation of networking technology.

Figure 22.4 shows the MAGIC network test bed. The original MAGIC project (MAGIC I) demonstrated a high-speed wide area IP/ATM network that supported a real-time terrain visualization application and a high-speed distributed storage system. MAGIC II was the extension of the MAGIC I test bed to develop new networking technology and a large-scale distributed information system. The MAGIC II information system is based on a very general paradigm in which high-performance computing, storage, and communications are used to provide rapid access to data that have to be processed expeditiously and delivered quickly in order to provide value to end users. Applications that use this paradigm arise in a variety of situations, including military operations, intelligence imagery analysis, and natural disasters. These applications share a requirement for access to real-time data sources and to large volumes of stored data, the existence and locations of which may not be known in advance. They also require a large amount of processing to transform the data into useful information, and they may have high performance, lower speed, and mobile end users.

Figure 22.4
MAGIC network test bed.

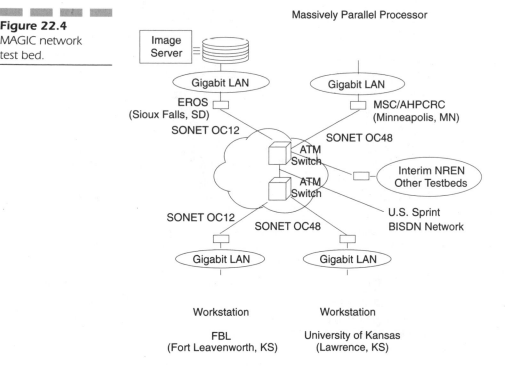

In order to develop the information system described here, the proof of concept system of MAGIC I must be scaled in several dimensions:

- Managing extremely large (~terabyte) data sets
- Processing real-time data
- Fusing multiple types of data
- Creating a large-scale IP/ATM internetwork
- Supporting very high (~1-Gbps) network throughput
- Enabling a wide range of end-user access speeds (tens of kilobits per second to hundreds of Megabits per second) and host capabilities (laptops to high-end workstations)

The objective of MAGIC II is to build on the work and facilities of MAGIC I to solve these problems of scale in the context of an application that uses georeferenced data sets and image browsing for interactive data fusion and 3-D visualization. The result will be an information system with much functionality, great extensibility, and wide applicability.

The core of the MAGIC II network is the MAGIC I facilities, a switched ATM internetwork comprised of SONET OC-48 trunks with links to ATM LANs at five sites. This internetwork, augmented with wireless sites, will continue to be the development environment for MAGIC II. The core facilities will be interconnected with other networks to create a large-scale ATM internetwork, which is the MAGIC II test environment. The designs and implementations of the networking technology, the distributed processing and storage systems, and the applications will first be tested in the development environment. Then, operation and performance will be verified in a much larger test environment.

22.2.1.4 BAGNET. The Bay Area Gigabit Network (BAGNET) is the largest ATM network in the United States. Its web site can be found at (*http://george.lbl.gov/BAGNet.html*). In this network, Fujitsu provided the ATM switches. This network consists of two FETEX-150 ATM switches. The participants in this network include firms from Silicon Valley such as Xerox, Hewlett Packard, DEC, NASA, and Pacific Bell. Pacific Bell provided the transmission system for the network. Figure 22.5 shows the proposed BAGNET test bed.

BAGNET was disbanded in May 1996 when the test bed's intended period of operation was completed. This network investigated the computer multimedia network infrastructure needed to support a diverse set of distributed applications in such an environment. The featured

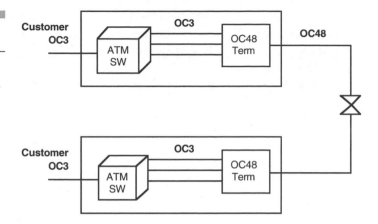

Figure 22.5
BAGNET test bed.

application for the ATM network is a generalized teleseminar capability. This network and its applications created an information highway within the Bay Area that will serve as a model for the national "information superhighway."

22.2.1.5 NCGN. The North Carolina GigaNet (NCGN) was established in May 1996 by Duke University, North Carolina State University, University of North Carolina at Chapel Hill, MCNC (Microelectronics Center of North Carolina), Cisco, IBM, and Time Warner Communications. Although the NCGN will be part of the emerging Internet 2 program, it is also being designed as a self-sustaining regional operation. An NCGN Steering Committee has been established to help develop the program into a regional operation and to provide advice on its direction and component programs.

22.2.1.6 Other Broadband Activities. In addition to the test beds described, the carriers made numerous broadband deployment plans and ATM/broadband service announcements public since 1993. These carriers have announced the first ATM-based T1 service. In addition, they are conducting international trials to provide ATM services across the Pacific and Atlantic Oceans. Some of these are addressed in the intercontinental trial section. Among the LECs, most of the RBOCs have made some sort of broadband plans or have positioned themselves for eventually providing ATM/broadband services.

In addition to public carrier plans, the U.S. Government is leading the effort to set up a National Information Infrastructure Test Bed (NIIT).

The customers in this network are distributed across various industries in the country. NIIT is led by a group of corporations, universities, and governments who will jointly test real-world applications (some of these are described in Chap. 2).

Because it is difficult to provide up-to-date information on all ongoing activities on ATM/broadband service, additional information on the trials can be obtained from magazines such as *Network World, Communication Week,* etc. A detailed list of magazines is provided in App. C.

22.2.2   Canada

OCRInet (*http://www.ocrinet.ca/*) is a federally incorporated not-for-profit corporation formed in the Ottawa-Carleton region to provide and manage the first ATM broadband network in Canada dedicated to research and development. The network is a partnership between industry, government, and education institutions. It provides a development and testing ground for new ATM network equipment, services, and applications. The backbone ring (network) includes ATM switching technology from both NORTEL and Newbridge, and the service has been provided by Bell Canada.

OCRInet began with an initial 12 research nodes. Other nodes are being, and will continue to be, connected as research needs and interests develop. The network is a "closed" network for access by and to approved members of OCRInet Inc. Membership in OCRInet is, however, "open" to any organization with a legitimate research need related to the mission and objectives of OCRInet Inc. Although OCRInet is for research purposes, precommercial applications and service development activities are permitted. The founding partners for OCRInet are Algonquin College, Bell Canada, NORTEL, Carleton University, Communication Research Centre of Canada, Gandalf Technologies, Mitel Corporation, National Research Council of Canada, Newbridge Networks, Ottawa Carleton Research Institute (OCRI), Stentor Resource Centre, Telecommunications Research Institute of Ontario (TRIO), Telesat Canada, and University of Ottawa.

22.3   ATM/Broadband Trials in Europe

Before we discuss the different countries, let's address the ATM/broadband trials in Europe. It is more difficult to deploy a single uniform standard network in Europe than in any other part of the world. To realize a single network by putting the required infrastructure in place, service providers such as British Telecom, United Kingdom, will not only have to invest a combined $270 billion, but will also have to enter cooperative ventures for the development of a new network architecture. To achieve such a goal, the European Commission (EC) did some background work, such as starting the Special Telecommunication Action for Regional Development (STAR), whose function is to help in the construction of a telecommunications infrastructure by using large strong carriers. The EC has formulated the measures for telecommunication public policy in the EC Green Paper, 1987. The policy pursues the dual goal of providing Europe with high-quality telecommunications service while strengthening the European telecommunications industry for international competition.

To achieve such a network, European carriers must extensively adopt European standards such as ETSI (European Telecommunication Standards Institute), as well as standards developed by the international standards bodies. In fact, some of the standards they have agreed upon are SDH for transmission and ATM for switching. Based on these standards, the European carriers have developed a network called Global European Network (GEN), consisting of carriers like German Telecom (DB Telecom), British Telecom, France Telecom, Telephonica of Spain, and STET of Italy, who have agreed to construct a fiber-optic transmission network. Figure 22.6 shows the GEN network.

Figure 22.6
GEN network.

GEN is a Europeanwide digital network. This network will evolve into METRAN (Managed European Transmission Network), which, beginning in 1995, will provide fast and flexible transparent transmission links up to 155 Mbps. METRAN is based on SDH standards, enabling it to support ATM switching that can be used for future BISDN services. 25 European carriers are involved in METRAN.

22.3.1   Germany

In Germany (formerly West Germany), the BISDN/ATM pilot project of DB Telecom, based on the internationally standardized ATM, went into service in 1994.

Figure 22.7 shows the German BISDN network configuration. The network consists of three BISDN exchanges in Berlin, Hamburg, and Cologne. The network initially provided ATM-based permanent virtual circuit by the end of 1994. Beginning in 1995, ATM-based SVC services were offered. The ATM switches are based on the Siemens ESWD™ platform, along with other Siemens broadband solutions. Each broadband node in the network consists of two remote ATM units with terminals, terminal adapters, and connectionless servers. Each exchange has 32 ATM

Figure 22.7
BISDN network connectivity in Germany.

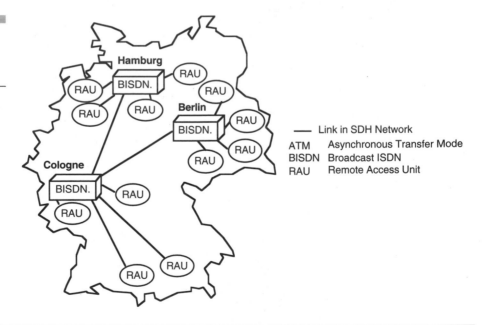

— Link in SDH Network
ATM   Asynchronous Transfer Mode
BISDN Broadcast ISDN
RAU   Remote Access Unit

---

*ESWD is a switching trademark of Siemens.

ports. Apart from testing the technical features of broadband, the following applications or services were tested:

■ Data services via LAN connections

■ Multimedia services including videoconferencing

■ Incorporation of existing voice services

22.3.2 England

As in the United States, there are multiple long-distance carriers in the United Kingdom, and each one is conducting its own ATM trials in addition to the government-sponsored SuperJanet. Two of the most popular carriers are Mercury Communication and British Telecom. In this section, we address the ATM trials planned by these carriers.

Mercury Communication is one of the largest public network operators in the United Kingdom. Its ATM trials began in October 1993. The objective of the trial was

■ To test ATM technology related to ATM switching and it's interface with router and other equipment

■ To look at practical interfaces with frame-relay and SMDS networks along with the SDH transmission system

■ To identify broadband applications that help customers

In addition to ATM trials, Mercury has conducted SMDS trials, but it has no plans to offer frame-relay service. Based on the trials, Mercury has identified that LAN interconnect will be the driving force for broadband wide area networks.

British Telecom, the largest public carrier in the United Kingdom, was awarded a contract worth £18 million over 4 years to develop a high-speed fiber-optic network for the country's higher education community. The pilot network is called SuperJanet (Joint Academic Network). The initial contract was awarded in November 1992. Figure 22.8 shows the SuperJanet network configuration.

The core network will operate at plesiochronous digital hierarchy speed ranging from 34 to 140 Mbps. The initial network consists of six sites: Cambridge; Edinburgh; the Manchester Universities; Imperial College of Science, Technology and Medicine; University College, London; and SERC Rutherford Appleton Laboratory. Six additional sites are to be added: the Universities of Wales, Birmingham, Nottingham, Newcastle,

Figure 22.8
SuperJanet network in the United Kingdom.

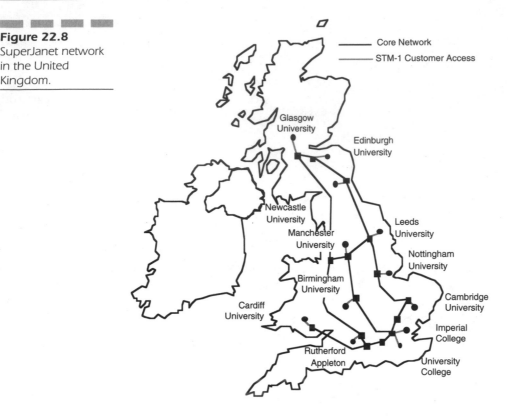

Glasgow, and Leeds. The advisory board is planning to add 40 more universities later using BT broadband network.

SuperJanet is a complement to existing Janet networks that constitute an X.25 packet network. The initial contract included the introduction of synchronous digital hierarchy in the backbone by the end of 1993. Along with SDH, ATM services are to be introduced based on ITU-T recommendations.

Leading ATM switch manufacturers have been selected for SuperJanet. The initial application of SuperJanet will be data-oriented, and most applications are currently associated with it. The following are the new applications proposed for SuperJanet:

- Distance learning
- Experimental electronic journal test bed
- Information services, such as library document distribution
- High-quality medical imaging
- Distributed group communications
- Advanced data visualization

22.3.3 Finland

Telecom Finland, the telecommunications side of Posti ja Tele (P&T) launched a pilot ATM network in May 1993, connecting sites in the Helsinki and Tampere metropolitan areas. The trial ran for 1 year, and full commercial ATM service is planned. Funding for the project came mainly from the Technology Development Center of Finland.

The core network consists of four ATM switches, two of which are based at the Tampere University of Technology. The other two switches are based at Telecom Finland headquarters in Helsinki. The two locations are connected using PDHs at 34 Mbps. The workstations used in the trial are fitted with adapter cards from the Fore switch, which implements ATM AAL 3/4 and 5 layers. The main objective of this trial is to provide the Finnish industry with up-to-date knowledge of, and experience with, the latest ATM technology.

22.3.4 France

The public carrier of France, France Telecom, has provided backbone ATM service since 1994. The initial public service will be for LAN interconnect services based on the ETSI standard. Initial access speeds for ATM service are 2, 10, 16, 25, and 34 Mbps.

France Telecom has installed two international and 15 national ATM nodes. The ATM switches are provided by Alcatel, Siemens, and Matra. The service can be accessed via LAN interfaces such as 802.3, 802.5 and FDDI using IP as well as via other interfaces, such as SMDS (SNI) and frame relay UNI (FRI).

France Telecom's launched commercial ATM service in 1995. Prior to that it conducted the following experiement:

- BREHAT ATM project, 1Q94
- BETEL (broadband exchange trans-European links)
  project
- Successor to BETEL, European ATM pilot project of virtual path-based services.

Each is described in the following subsections.

22.3.4.1 BREHAT ATM Project. The applications of the BREHAT project include audiovisual transport services, multimedia information retrieval services, and downloading of multimedia applications. The network, built in collaboration with Alcatel and TRT, consists of three ATM cross-connects located at the Centre National d'Etudes des Telecommunications (CNET) Laboratory at Rennes in Brittany and Lannion and several sites in Paris. The application areas are categorized as

- LAN interconnect
- Videoconferencing
- Video transmission
- Circuit emulation

22.3.4.2 BETEL Project. The BETEL project is actually a cooperative ATM project between France and Switzerland. As two of the sites are in France, we listed this project under France instead of Switzerland.

This phase of the project includes two applications:

- Sharing of supercomputers for scientific computing tasks
- Distance learning using videoconferencing.

In this trial, two sites (one in France and another in Geneva, Switzerland) are connected via 34-Mbps links using the ATM switch provided by Alcatel. The user sites are equipped with FDDI LAN via Cisco AGS+ and Cisco 7000 routers. Figure 22.9 shows the BETEL test bed network.

Figure 22.9
BETEL test bed network.

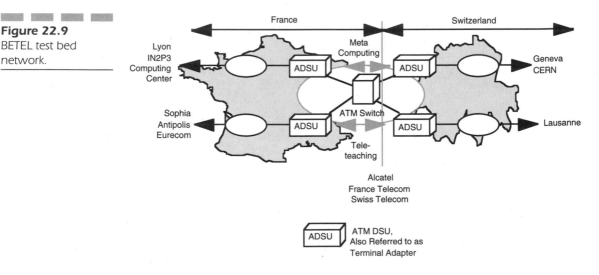

22.3.5 Switzerland

The largest ATM test bed in Europe was completed in Basel, Switzerland. The R1022 ATM Technology Test Bed (RATT) covers 800 mi^2 and is a culmination of 6 years' work under the EC backed by the Research and Development in Advanced Communications Technologies in Europe (RACE) program.

The key objective of RACE was "the introduction of Integrated Broadband Communications, considering the evolving ISDN and national introduction strategies, progressing toward community-wide services by 1995." Basel was selected because of its proximity to German and French networks and because it was the site where a 140-Mbps SDH pilot trial called BASKOM was held.

Three ATM switch prototypes were tested in the RATT network, each working at 155 Mbps at both UNI and NNI. The two main exchanges were from Alcatel Bell Telephone in Belgium and Philips Kommunikations Industrie (PKI) from Germany. A remote exchange from AT&T was hooked up via a 622-Mbps SDH link. Other subsystems include five ATM terminal adapters, two NT-2s, and one NT-1. The applications in this test bed were AAL 1, AAL 3/4, and AAL 5.

The RATT network is intended to be hooked up to other broadband networks in Belgium, Germany, France, Holland, Spain, Portugal, and Denmark. Numerous other countries are also in the process of being linked.

22.4 ATM/Broadband Trials in Asia

Asia is the largest continent with the world's largest population. With the exception of certain countries, such as Japan and Singapore, Asia lags far behind the rest of the world with regard to telephone systems. Broadband in Asia is *far* from reality. Some carriers are planning to pursue a broadband network, however, and we address two: China and Japan.

22.4.1 China

SCM/Book Telecommunication LP and China's Galaxy New Technology Co. have joined forces to design, build, and operate a commercial and civilian broadband network in one of China's most affluent areas. The initial prototype is anticipated to be a $20 million project, and it was deployed in January 1994. The network was being deployed at Gvangzhov and was operational by January 1995.

Gvangzhov is located less than 200 miles northwest of Hong Kong and has a population of 70 million, roughly equal to that of former West Germany. The China America Telecom company is working with the Gvangzhov Government to build and operate the network, which will provide foreign cable links for television programming, as well as telephone, cellular, and data services.

22.4.2 Japan

As American and European companies continue to jump on the broadband bandwagon, companies in the Asia Pacific region are also moving as quickly as possible. NTT Corp., Japan's largest public carrier, is performing extensive evaluation of BISDN services. These evaluations incorporate voice, data, and video transmission in an optical network. NTT was one of the first service providers in the world to aggressively pursue broadband network based on fiber and ATM technology as envisioned by the BISDN concept.

In Japan, the first phase of the experiments was centered on the expansion of NTT-INS (integrated network services), new broadband corporate network services based on ATM technology, and an optical transmission system for subscribers.

In phase 2, experiments were aimed at incorporating ATM, intelligent network, and a radio access system into the BISDN trial.

22.4.3 Other Asian Countries

Some countries, such as Singapore, Taiwan, and Korea, have some form of broadband trial under way, while other countries need to go a long way to build the basic infrastructure to provide any form of telecommunication service. With the opening of telecommunications to private industries, these countries have the potential to get on the broadband bandwagon when the ATM/broadband standards are mature enough and provided no political barriers stand in the way of telecom services.

22.5 Intercontinental ATM/Broadband Trials

This section discusses two intercontinental ATM trials: one across the Pacific and the other across the Atlantic.

22.5.1 Transpacific ATM Trial

KDD of Japan and AT&T of the United States have linked the two nations via the world's longest intercontinental ATM network, spanning 9000 miles. The ATM trial began operating in July 1993. The link was set up between Shinjuku, Japan, and Holmdel, N.J. This network examines the performance and quality levels of the ATM infrastructure, and it carries traditional data and emerging multimedia traffic. Network operation issues are also examined.

The ATM trial network will evolve over 3 years in three phases. Phase 1 will include the characterization of performance of its DS3 facilities and the different types of cabling that exist in the 9000-mile span. Phase 2 began operation in the second quarter of 1994 and included testing of applications such as voice, data, and videoconferencing over the ATM network. Phase 3 included a thorough evaluation of the operation and network management features, and it began in 1995.

The ATM trial network consists of AT&T GCNS-2000 ATM switches at both Shinjuku and Holmdel. Initially, 45 Mbps was be used. Figure 22.10 shows the network between Japan and the United States.

Figure 22.10
Transpacific ATM trial.

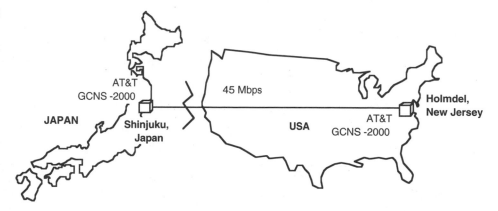

22.5.2   Transatlantic ATM Trial

France Telecom demonstrated the feasibility of ATM over intercontinental distances. The test used connectionless broadband data service
technology over ATM virtual paths for high-speed interconnection of
conventional Ethernet LANs located in New York and Paris.

The ATM switches were supplied by Thompson, which does both VP
cross-connections and constant bit rate data service (CBDS) switching.
The test demonstrated how ATM technology could be implemented in
the design of an international private enterprise network. The transatlantic lines used were the recently available TAT-11, which was provided
by Sprint International, and the access line in New York, provided by
Teleport Communications Group. Figure 22.11 shows the transatlantic
connectivity for the ATM trial.

22.6   Broadband Access Technology Trials

One of the areas that has gained lots of attention in recent years is in
the access area. It has become very clear that the current public access
network is not capable of supporting the increased demand generated
by the Internet. Of all the different network elements, the access has
clearly been identified as the bottleneck for providing broadband services. Some of the access technologies discussed in Chap. 9 have been

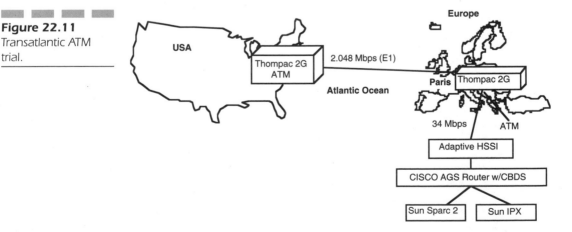

Figure 22.11
Transatlantic ATM
trial.

identified as potential candidates for alleviating the bottleneck. Most of the trials currently target high-speed Internet access applications. From the service provider point of view, their interests lie in telecommuting and in remote corporate LAN access. One of the reasons the interest is worldwide is because some of the broadband technologies are capable of taking advantage of existing infrastructures, i.e., the twisted pair used in the traditional telephone network worldwide.

The list in Table 22.1 shows some of the broadband access trials and service deployment plans announced by various service providers worldwide. The list includes trials as of July 1997.

22.7   Summary

The objective of this chapter was to show that ATM/broadband is no longer a hype or a technology only for researchers at universities. It exists now, and many lesson have been learned from the trials. In the United States, long-distance carriers have already announced a tariff for ATM-based service, which is comparable in cost with frame-relay and private-line services. This tariff is another positive indication that ATM services will be comparable in price with existing services. The demand for ATM-based services has increased drastically in recent years due to the growth of Internet/Intranet (corporate network). In fact most of the networks built are designed to support IP and ATM/SONET.

Company	Location	Speed	Applications	Trial Dates	Service Deployment
United States					
ALLTEL (CLEC and ISP)	Dalton, Ga. and Hudson Ohio	Down: 1.5 Mbps; up: 64 kbps	Internet/LAN access	Technical/marketing trial: September 1996 to February 1996. Phase 2 begins 2nd Quarter 1997—ongoing	
Ameritech (RBOC) and IBM	Wheaton, Ill. (Chicago)	Down: 1.5 Mbps; up: 64 kbps	Internet/LAN access	Concept trial: October 1996 to April 1997.	Wide-scale deployment by mid-1998 with ADSL service up to 6 Mbps planned.
AUSNet Services (ISP)	Portland, Ore.	Down:* 26—7 Mbps; up: 92—972 kbps	Internet/LAN access		February 1997.
Bell Atlantic (RBOC)	Northern Virginia Fairfax County, Virginia	Down: 1.5 Mbps; up: 64 kbps Down: 1.5 Mbps; up: 64 kbps	Internet access Video on demand	Marketing trial: September 1996—ongoing. Marketing trial: May 1995—late 1996.	Rollout in mid-1998 of RADSL services up to 7 Mbps downstream.
BellSouth (RBOC)	Atlanta, Ga.	Down: 6 Mbps; up: 64 kbps	Internet/LAN access	Technical trial: October 95—ongoing.	Wide-scale deployment in 1998.
Cincinnati Bell (ILEC/ISP "Fuse")	Cincinnati, Ohio	Down:* 1.5 Mbps—6 Mbps; up: 150 kbps—400 kbps	Internet/LAN access	January 1997—ongoing.	
GTE (ILEC)	Irving, Tex. (Dallas—Fort Worth)	Down: up to 4 Mbps; up: up to 500 kbps	Internet access	Marketing trial: February 1996, expanded April 1996—ongoing.	Not yet announced.
GTE and Microsoft Note: Duke University and Purdue University were added in May 1997	Redmond, Wash. Durham, NC. and West Lafayette, Ind.	Down: up to 6 Mbps; up: 384 kbps Down: up to 4 Mbps; up: up to 384 kbps	Telecommuting/Internet access Internet access	August 1996—ongoing	

Table 22.1 Broadband Access Trials and Service Deployment Plans of Various Worldwide Service Providers

Company	Location	Speed	Applications	Trial Dates	Service Deployment
Intelecom Data Systems (ISP)	Rhode Island	Down:* 640 kbps—2.5 Mbps; up:* 275 kbps—1.08 Mbps	Internet/LAN access		March 1997 in Rhode Island; plans to expand to other northeast areas.
InterAccess (ISP)	Chicago, Ill.	Down:* 1.5 Mbps; up: 64 kbps	Internet access	N/A	September 1996.
ioNET Inc. (NSP)	Oklahoma City and Tulsa, Okla.	Down: 7 Mbps	Internet/LAN access	N/A	Mid-summer 1997 in Oklahoma City, and Tulsa, Kansas City, Little Rock, Austin, Dallas, Houston, and San Antonio soon thereafter.
MCI (IXC), with partners NW Iowa Tele. and NW Iowa Power	Iowa, New York, and Detroit, Mich.; overseas w/BT	Down: 1.5—6 Mbps; up: 64 kbps Down: 7 Mbps; up: 640 kbps	Internet/LAN access Internet/LAN access	October 1996—ongoing April 1997—ongoing	August 1997 in Iowa; 1999 deployment.
Network Access Solutions (CLEC)	Mid-Atlantic region	Down: up to 6 Mbps	Services to ISPs		February 1997; rolling out to other regional markets throughout 1997.
NYNEX (RBOC) and Lotus	Boston, Mass.	Down: 1.5 Mbps; up: 64 kbps	Internet/LAN access	August 1996—ongoing	1999
Northland Communications (CLEC and ISP), through affiliate Oneida County Tele.	New York (Holland-Patent Central Schools)	Down: 1.5 Mbps; up: 64 kbps	Internet/LAN access	Technical trial: February 1997.	Plans to offer service to greater Utica/Rome and Syracuse areas later this year.

Table 22.1 (Continued)

Company	Location	Speed	Applications	Trial Dates	Service Deployment
Pacific Bell (RBOC)	San Ramon, Calif.	Down: 6 Mbps; up: 640 kbps	Internet access/VOD	August 1996—ongoing	Los Angeles, Silicon Valley, and Southeast Bay Area in September 1997; regionwide by end of 1998.
SBC Communications (RBOC) and Shell Oil	Houston, Tex.	Down: 6 Mbps; up: 640 kbps	Internet/LAN access	Technical trial: May 1996—ongoing; Marketing trial: July 1996.	Fourth quarter 1997.
Signet Partners (ISP)	Austin, Tex.	Down: up to 6 Mbps	Internet/LAN access		Austin in January 1997; Houston and San Antonio by June 1997.
Transport Logic (ISP), in conjunction with Advanced Corporate Solutions	Portland, Ore.	Down: 640 kbps—2.5 Mbps; up: 275 kbps—1.08 Mbps	Internet/LAN access	N/A	April 1997 for Portland; four more Washington and Oregon cities by end of May.
Canada					
BC Tel (CLEC)	Greater Vancouver and Victoria, BC	Down: 1.5—7 Mbps; up: 64—640 kbps	Internet/LAN access	Technical/marketing trial: November 1996.	September 1997.
Bell Canada (RBOC)	Kanata, Ontario, and St. Bruno, Quebec	Down: 22 Mbps; up: 1 Mbps	Internet/LAN access	Customer trial: September 1996—ongoing.	Fall of 1997.
CADVision (ISP)	Calgary, Alberta	Down: up to 6 Mbps	Internet access		Limited service launched January 1997.

Table 22.1 (Continued)

Company	Location	Speed	Applications	Trial Dates	Service Deployment
Canada (Continued)					
SaskTel (CLEC)	Regina and Saskatoon	Down: 1.5 Mbps; up: 64 kbps	Internet access	N/A	Limited services launched November 1996.
Stentor (CLEC)	St. John, Fredericton, and Moncton, NB Winnipeg, Manitoba	Down: 1.5 Mbps; up: 64 kbps Down: 1.5 Mbps; up: 64 kbps	Internet access Internet access	Technical trial: December 1996—ongoing Technical trial: November 1996—ongoing	Second quarter 1997. Third quarter 1997.
Telus Communications (formerly EdTel-CLEC)	Edmonton, Alberta	Down: 1.5 Mbps; up: 64 kbps	Internet/LAN access	Marketing trial: March 1996—ongoing.	1997.
UUNet (ISP)	Toronto, Ontario	Down: 1.5 Mbps; up: 64 kbps	Internet access	Marketing trial: June 1996—December 1996	First quarter 1997.
Europe					
AMUSE†	Milan, Italy (Telecom Italia)	Down 8.2 Mbps; up: 640 kbps	VOD/internet access	Technical trial began early 1997.	
Belgacom (Belgium)			VOD	Technical trial: September 1995.	
British Telecom (UK)	Colchester and Ipswich	Down: 2 Mbps; up: 9.6 kbps	VOD/internet access	Marketing trial: June 1995—ongoing; technical trial: September to June 1996.	Not announced; widespread availability expected 1999.

Table 22.1 (Continued)

Europe (Continued)

Company	Location	Speed	Applications	Trial Dates	Service Deployment
Deutsche Telekom AG (Germany)					
France Telecom (France)	Brittany	Down: 8 Mbps; up: 640 kbps	VOD		Marketing trial: November 1996.
Helsinki Telephone Co. (Finland)	Helsinki	Down: 2 Mbps; up: 9.6 kbps	VOD	August 1995—March 1996	Began limited roll-out in February 1997 in Helsinki. Will offer remote work, media meeting points, fast Internet access, 3D virtual city, "Net phone," and live video.
Kingston Comm-Hull (UK)	Hull		VOD	Technical trial: March 1996; Marketing trial: Fall 1996.	Sometime in 1997.
Swiss Telecom PTT (Switzerland)	Grenchen	Down: 2 Mbps; up: 9.6 kbps	VOD/internet access	September 1995—ongoing.	
Telecom Eireann (Ireland)		Down/up: 2 Mbps (HDSL)	Internet/LAN access		
Telecom Finland (Finland)			Internet/LAN access	ADSL trials to start soon.	
Telecom Italia (Italy)	See AMUSET	Down: 8.2 Mbps; up: 640 kbps	VOD	Technical trial: began early 1997.	

Table 22.1 (Continued)

Company	Location	Speed	Applications	Trial Dates	Service Deployment
			Europe (Continued)		
Telefónica España (Spain)				ADSL trials to be conducted in 1997.	
Telnor (Norway)			VOD	January 1996.	
Telia AB (Sweden)	Stockholm		VOD/internet access	September 1995.	Spring/summer 1997.
			Middle East/Africa		
Bezeq (Israel Telecom)	Tel Aviv and Jerusalem	Down: 2 Mbps; up: 9.6 kbps	VOD	Technical trial: April 1996—ongoing.	
			Asia/Pacific		
Chunghwa Telecom (Taiwan)	Central Taipei	Down: 1.5 Mbps; up: 9.6 kbps	Near VOD/remote access	Marketing trial: December 1996—ongoing.	
Hong Kong Telecom (Hong Kong)		Down:* 51 Mbps; up: 1.5 Mbps	VOD	VOD: summer 1996.	Commercial rollout in July 1997.
Korea Telecom (Korea)	Six cities		VOD/internet/ distance learning/ shopping	Marketing trial: August 1996.	Commercial rollout year-end 1997
Singapore Telecom (Singapore)	5000 homes by year-end 1997		VOD/internet	Technical trial: February 1996; Commercial trial began June 1997.	Islandwide rollout by the end of 1998.
Telstra (Australia)	Melbourne	Down: 2 and 6 Mbps	Broadcast/VOD	Marketing pilot: April—October 1996.	Second half of 1997.

*Rate-adaptive ADSL.
†AMUSE is the European Commission's Advanced Multimedia Services to Residential Users (AMUSE) cooperative program.

Table 22.1 (Continued)

CHAPTER 23

Telecommunications Standards

23.1 Overview

Standards are a set of specifications that groups of people from different countries and regions (continents) or from within a country agree to follow. Standards are especially important in the telecommunications industry because of the need for different groups of people to be able to interface. Telecommunications is a major industrial sector for two reasons:

- It is vast in terms of revenue generated per year
- It affects all aspects of commercial and domestic life

Standardization within telecommunications is intended to perform three basic functions:

- Facilitate interconnection between different users
- Facilitate the portability of equipment within different applications and regions
- Ensure that equipment bought from one vendor can interface with that from another

In this chapter, we provide an overview of the standards-making process and of the different standards organizations at national and international levels around the world. Almost every organization has some sort of involvement in the broadband communications standards-making process. Study groups or working groups within the standards organizations address the needs and issues of broadband communications.

23.2 Standards-Making Process

The most difficult process in the standards arena is at the global level. Historically, each country has had its own postal, telephone, and telegraph authority. Countries have set standards and monopolized local manufacturing and service providers. There has been little interest in standardization. Even when standards bodies were set up, they produced recommendations rather than requirements (hence not enforceable) containing many country-specific exceptions.

While producing standards is not an easy task, it is important to understand that standards formulation does not hold back technological progress. At the same time, once a technology becomes established and companies have invested in rival systems, each player is eager to promote its methodology as the international standard. Furthermore, leaders in any field are reluctant to slow down and agree to standards that can eventually help their rivals.

Standards-making is an expensive business. It is estimated that hundreds of millions of dollars per year are spent on worldwide telecommunication standardization activities. The standards-making process is one of cooperation at many levels, nationally and internationally. Cooperation exists between industrial concerns within a country, between these concerns and their national governments, and between nations at the international level. User groups and trade organizations usually have members from several countries. Figure 23.1 shows an example of a standards-making process in the United States.

Many industrial organizations have multinational operations, and their revenues exceed the gross national product of some countries. Cooperation is important to obtain agreement on standards, but a danger exists that the many separate groups and interests can result in different standards being prepared for the same item. This fact has resulted in the world being divided into two transmission standards, 2.048 Mbps (A-law codec) in Europe and 1.544 Mbps (μ-law codec) in the United States and Japan.

To accommodate the many conflicting interests, the international standards-making organizations often concentrate on producing base standards, which contain variants or alternative methods to allow flexibility for the implementers. By adopting one of the variants it simply means that the implementers will be compliant with the standard; however, there is no guarantee that equipment based on separate variants

Figure 23.1
Example of standards-making process in the United States.

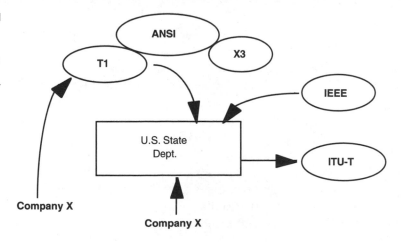

will interface successfully. It is the responsibility of the implementers to ensure that different equipment is interoperable.

The interface problem is being tackled by regional and national standards bodies, often consisting of trade organizations and users groups with well-defined requirements. These groups might be manufacturers or users. They adopt internationally based standards as functional standards or profiles, which contain only a limited subset of the permissible variants. Agreed-upon test specifications and methods are also developed to ensure that equipment designed to the different variants permitted within the functional standards can interface. Independent test houses such as Bellcore or Cable Labs then conduct conformance tests against the selected profiles and certify products that meet these requirements. The standards-making process can be categorized into three stages, as shown in Fig. 23.2. The three stages are base standards, functional standards, and conformance standards. Each of the standards down the ladder is more specific in order to meet the needs of a smaller group, such as within a country. These multiple levels of standards have led to several problems:

■ Standards take too long to develop, primarily due to the need to reach a consensus between rival factions. Thus, the de facto standards, based on proprietary solutions, are available ahead of international standards. The standards-making bodies then must

Figure 23.2
Standards-making process.

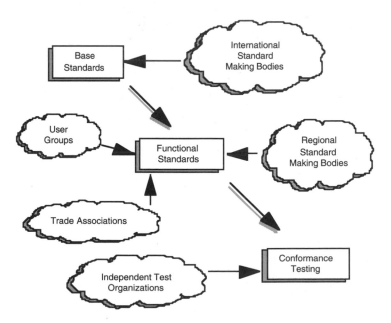

either accept the de facto standard and abandon their own, or accepting the existence of two standards. If standards are developed too early, the technology might change, making the standards obsolete.

■ Standards must often cover every aspect of the intended application, usually resulting in overlap and duplication. The alternative is to avoid duplication by allowing de facto standards in areas not yet covered.

23.3   Standards Architecture

Figure 23.3 shows today's information/telecommunications standards-making architecture. This architecture gives an idea of the complexity of telecommunications standards-making. The arrows show the direction of the information flow and the interface required for that organization to reach a consensus. One can see that there are different levels of standards-making, including national, regional, and global/international. In Fig. 23.3, the central circles represent ITU-T and JTC1, which are international organizations. Other organizations deal with the issues at a regional level and contribute their methods or ideas to the international organization to influence the decision in their favor. These regional organizations are formed by user-interest groups or other specialized organizations, which hope to have their ideas and technology adopted as standards at a national level. These organizations are shown in the periphery.

Each worldwide region is controlled by certain standards bodies. Some standards bodies and regions where they have jurisdiction are:

T1	North America
ETSI	Europe
TTC	Japan
TTA	Korea
AOTC	Australia
CITEL	Latin America

Figure 23.4 shows these standards bodies. They have the ultimate say in their region. These organizations also represent their regions in international organizations such as ITU and JTC (Joint Telecommunications Committee).

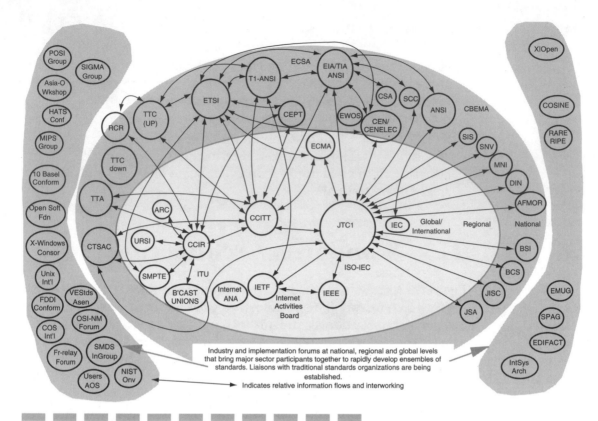

Industry and implementation forums at national, regional and global levels that bring major sector participants together to rapidly develop ensembles of standards. Liaisons with traditional standards organizations are being established.

Indicates relative information flows and interworking

Figure 23.3 Global telecommunication standards architecture.

Figure 23.4 Regional standards bodies worldwide.

TSACC	Telecommunications Standards Advisory Council of Canada
CITEL	Telecommunication Commission
ETSI	European Telecommunication Standards Institute
TTC	Telecommunication Technology Committee
TTA	Telecommunication Technology Association
ACC	Australian CCITT Committee
ATSC	Australian Telecommunications Standardization Committee

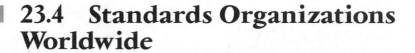

23.4 Standards Organizations Worldwide

The foremost international standards-making body for telecommunications is the International Telecommunications Union; the International Standards Organization for information technology standards. With the blurring of lines between telecommunications and information technology, however, the activities of the ITU and the ISO often overlap.

23.4.1 The ITU

The ITU was founded in 1865 as the Union Telegraphique, with the primary goal of developing standards in telecommunications. In 1947, it became a specialized agency for the United Nations telecommunications, under UN Charter Articles 57 to 63, when it was renamed the ITU. Figure 23.5 shows the new structure of ITU. ITU currently has three main functions:

■ To encourage the interconnectivity of telecommunications equipment and services by promoting and establishing technical standards in these areas.

■ To promote the best use of scarce telecommunications resources by the implementation of international regulations. This task is especially important in the use of the radio frequency spectrum, which the ITU controls via the ITU-T, ITU-R, and the International

Figure 23.5
Structure of ITU.

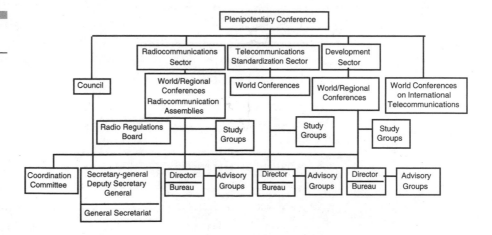

Frequency Registration Board (IFRB), and conferences such as WARC and ITC.

■ To encourage the growth of telecommunications in developing countries via the Technical Cooperation Department (TCD) and the Telecommunications Development Bureau (TDB).

In addition, the ITU carries out other ancillary functions for its members, such as organizing telecommunications exhibitions to keep members informed of the latest advances in technology. The best known exhibition is the Telecom Exhibition, which is held every 4 years.

At the end of 1993, the ITU had 173 countries as members, each with equal voting rights. Recently formed countries, such as Lithuania, have also become members of ITU. Only administrative bodies, or government departments concerned with telecommunications, can be ITU members. The United Kingdom is thus represented by the Department of Trade and Industry. Most other countries are represented by state-owned PTTs. For the United States, representation is by a complex mix of government agencies and suppliers, but the interface is only through the State Department. In addition, other organizational groups are recognized and can attend meetings of the ITU and its organizations but cannot vote. Some of these organizations are the following:

■ *Recognized Private Operating Agencies (RPOAs)*. Over 80 of these have been recognized by the ITU and consist of telecommunications operators. Examples of these are BT and Mercury in the United Kingdom and Nippon Telephone and Telegraph Corporation (NTT) in Japan.

■ *Scientific and Industrial Organizations (SIOs)*. There are over 150 of these, including IBM, Northern Telecom, Siemens, etc.

■ *International Organizations (IOs)*. There are over 50 IOs recognized so far. These are mainly trade organizations and user groups, such as the International Telecommunications User Group (INTUG).

RPOAs can be members of ITU-T and ITU-R and have voting rights, although SIOs and IOs can only be advisory members.

23.4.2   The ITU-T

The Comite Consultatif Internationale Telephonique et Telegraphic (CCITT), recently changed to ITU-T, is the primary vehicle for developing technical standards in the telecommunications field. Throughout this book, the new terminology ITU-T has been used. In the 1989 Plenipotentiary, the ITU-T and ITU-R were directed to conduct their activities with due consideration for the work of national and regional standardization bodies, keeping in mind that the ITU must maintain its preeminent position in the field of worldwide standardization for telecommunications. The two ITUs (ITU-T and ITU-R) were given a mandate to coordinate global standards activities, with the ITU-R developing standards in the radio field, which is the opposite of those of the ITU-T.

The International Frequency Registration Board (IFRB) comprises five specialists elected by the Plenipotentiary Conference. The IFRB acts as the custodian of an international public trust. Its main duty is to decide whether new frequencies assigned to radio users are in line with the conventional radio regulations. It also provides advice on improving the utilization of the radio spectrum and on the preparation and organization of the Administrative Radio Conferences.

The World Administrative Radio Conference (WARC), the World Administrative Telephone and Telegraph Conference (WATTC), and the Regional Administrative Radio Conference (RARC) are held at irregular intervals as required. These conferences approve changes to the regulations in their respective fields. The WATTC establishes principles relating to the operation of international telecommunications public services. The WARC revises regulations governing the use of radio frequency spectrum and geostationary satellite orbits. The RARC deals with specific radio communication questions of a regional nature.

The task of the ITU-T is vast and almost doubles with every Plenary. Because of the problems of producing standards in a timely fashion, the ITU-T, at its 1988 IX Plenary held in Melbourne, Australia, agreed to an accelerated procedure for issuing standards. Recommendations are now adopted as soon as they have been stabilized, rather than by full ratification of the Plenary Assembly. Thus, standards could be ready within 1 year of starting work.

The ITU-T has also adopted more of a coordinating role between the various national and regional standards-making authorities. Key among these are the U.S. T1 committees, the Japanese TTC, and the European ETSI. The ideas and work from these organizations, in addition to those from R&D organizations, manufacturers, users, and service providers, flow in and out of the ITU-T until they are stable and become accepted as standards.

An area of contention in ITU-T standards-making activities is the work carried out by Study Group III, which produces recommendations covering pricing and supply conditions, especially for international leased circuits. The European community has stated in a Green Paper that this work conflicts with the communities' competitive laws.

Table 23.1 shows the ITU-T study groups, where each study group is responsible for a certain area. For example, Study Group XVIII is responsible for broadband-related activities. The table summarizes the function performed by each study group.

TABLE 23.1

ITU-T Study Groups

Study Group	Services
Study group I	MHS, fax, directory services, UPT service descriptions. GVNS, PCS/UPT, ICCN.
Study group II	Network operation, numbering/routing country codes, fax quality.
Study group III	Tariff and accounting principles, accounting rates, data accounting.
Study group IV	Maintenance.
Study group V	Protection against electromagnetic effects.
Study group VI	Outside plant.
Study group VII	Data communications networks MHS, data communications, X.25 for ICCN.
Study group VIII	Terminals for telematic services.
Study group IX	Telegraph networks and telegraph terminal equipment.
Study group X	Languages for telecommunication applications.
Study group XI	Switching and signaling; SS7, UPT, IN, ICCN, network outage; ISDN services.
Study group XII	Transmission performance of telephone networks and terminals.
Study group XV	Transmission systems and equipment.
Study group XVII	Data transmission over the telephone network.
Study group XVIII	ISDN, broadband, CBDS, UPT network terminology

*Most of the broadband-related standards come out of this study group.

23.4.3   The ISO

Based in Geneva, the ISO is a nontreaty organization and body of the United Nations. The ISO's primary aim is to promote the development of international standardization to facilitate international trade in goods and services. The ISO mainly works in the information technology area, while the International Electrotechnical Commission is involved in standards for electrical and electronics engineering. All standards developed by ISO are published as international standards. It is the responsibility of the individual national standards organizations to promote and distribute these standards within their own countries.

The ISO's members are primarily national standards-making bodies, such as ANSI (United States), BSI (United Kingdom), and DIN (Germany). Members can be active or participating, designated as P members, or they can be corresponding members or observers, designated as O members. P members lead technical committees or subcommittees.

The ISO and the ITU-T work closely together in areas of common interest. For example, all ISDN activities within ISO are conducted in Technical Committee TC97, which is responsible for information-processing systems. This committee has two subcommittees. SC6 is involved with telecommunications and information exchange between systems. This subcommittee is working with the ITU-T on common channel signaling (CCS) and the relationship of ISDN to the open system interconnect model. SC21 is responsible for developing the seven-layer OSI model on which the ITU-T has modeled ISDN.

The ISO and the IEC work together in many areas through their joint technical programming committee (JTPC). This committee ensures that the two bodies avoid working on overlapping items. The ISO and the IEC have also set up a Joint Technical Committee on Information Technology, called JTC1, to develop generic information technology standards. This committee incorporates ISO TC97 and IEC TC93. JTC1 is responsible for producing international standards profiles (ISPs). Other organizations conduct conformance testing, such as the standards promotion and application group (SPAG) in Europe and the corporation for open systems (COS) in the United States. All these organizations cooperate in the Feeders Forum, set up in 1987, which unifies the technical work and provides a forum for liaison with ISO and IEC.

23.4.4 International Trade and User Groups (INTUG)

INTUG was formed in 1974 to represent the telecommunications user organizations from several countries, including the United States, the United Kingdom, Australia, and Japan. It is active in promoting the interests of its members and lobbying associations, such as the ITU, CEPT, PTTs, and ITU-T. Any person or group can join except PTTs and manufacturers, who need to be represented directly as individual members.

23.4.5 European Standards

The largest group of countries is in Europe, and the one that shows the greatest integration is the European Community (EC). Within the EC, Directorate General XIII (DGXIII) is responsible for telecommunications, information industry, and innovation. Its aims are

- To assist in the development of the general economy by building a sound telecommunications infrastructure throughout Europe
- To foster growth of the telecommunications service sector so that it is effective and economically viable
- To develop the telecommunications industry within Europe so that it can compete effectively on the world stage.

DGXIII has six directorates and contacts with the senior officials group on telecommunications (SOGT), which comprises ministers of telecommunications and industry. They meet every 6 weeks under the chairmanship of the director general. A subcommittee of SOGT is the analysis and forecasting group (GAP), which studies industrial developments in selected areas such as ISDN, broadband, cellular, etc. GAP organizes meetings that member countries attend and provides opinions. The output is the recommendations that can be made mandatory within the EC.

One of the major aims of the single European market is to ensure the free movement of goods and services, which requires the coordination of standards activities. A 1990 Green Paper proposed setting up the European Standardization Organization (ESO) to oversee the activities of the European standards-making bodies like CEN, CENELEC, and ETSI.

23.4.5.1 CEPT. The Conference European des Administrations des Postes et des Telecommunications (CEPT) was formed in 1958 by the

PTTs to provide harmony within standards groups. It presently consists of 31 members, covering all the countries of the European Community and the European Free Trade Association (EFTA), plus PTTs from other European countries.

CEPT is a sister organization to CEN/CENELEC and participates in many of its work programs. This organization is administered by a member nation for 2 years, and meetings of the plenary body are held every 2 years.

Historically, CEPT has been noted for its restrictive bureaucratic policies rather than its commercial outlook, an image it is anxious to change. In the past, most of the PTTs paid only lip service to standardization. Because CEPT issued recommendations that were not enforceable and contained many country-specific exceptions, the standardization effort was largely ineffectual.

A 1987 European Commission Green Paper on competition in Europe within telecommunications markets clearly defined the PTTs as commercial undertakings (rather than monopolistic telecommunications administrations) that were subject to competition and with separate regulatory and operational activities. As a result of this paper, in January 1988 CEPT set up an independent body, called the European Telecommunication Standard Institute (ETSI), to carry out all the standards activities on its behalf. CEPT still maintained the Technical Recommendations Application Committee (TRAC), formed in 1986, to approve standards for connection of equipment to public networks.

23.4.5.2 ETSI. ETSI is an independent organization funded by its members, who decide on its work program. The EC and EFTA, however, can fund ETSI to produce specific standards of interest to the community. ETSI's main interest is in telecommunications, although it also has interests in information technology, for which it cooperates with CEN/CENELEC, and in broadcasting, where it works with the European Broadcasting Union (EBU). The following are ETSI's main aims:

■ To complete worldwide standards, in line with Europe's needs, and to choose a single option where many are allowed in international standards

■ To anticipate the worldwide standards scene by adopting European standards and proposing these to international standards-making bodies

- To prepare a common European position for input to worldwide standards bodies such as ITU-T, ITU-R, IEC, and ISO and support these bodies in their work

ETSI membership is open to a wide spectrum of organizations of which there are six types:

- Administrations that are part of the administration of a country
- Public network operators
- Manufacturers
- Users and user organizations
- Private service providers
- Research organizations

It is this diverse range of membership that is the prime strength of ETSI, as it ensures a healthy interchange of views. In June 1997, there were 582 members of ETSI, of which manufacturers accounted for 42 percent; public network operators, 21 percent; national administrations, 7.1 percent; and users/service providers, 30 percent. Twenty three countries were represented from the EC and EFTA, Turkey, Malta, Cyprus, Czechoslovakia, and Poland.

There are currently 12 technical committees within ETSI:

- Radio, equipment, and systems (RES)
- Groupe speciale mobile (GSM)
- Paging systems
- Satellite earth stations
- Network aspects
- Business telecommunications
- Signaling protocols and switching
- Transmission and multiplexing
- Terminal equipment
- Equipment engineering
- Advanced testing methods
- Human factors

Figure 23.6 shows the relationship of ETSI with international organizations such as ITU, and Fig. 23.7 shows the ETSI relationship with European standards organizations such as CEN.

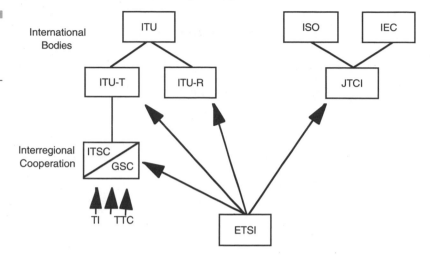

Figure 23.6
ETSI relationship with international organizations.

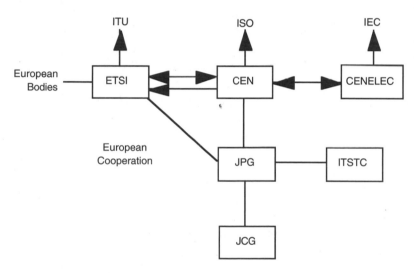

Figure 23.7
ETSI relationship with European organizations.

23.4.6 American Standards Organization

In the United States, the T1 committee addresses telecommunications standards issues. Committee T1 currently has approximately 125 member companies, agencies, and other participants. To carry out its work program of 140 projects, Committee T1 has established six primarily function-oriented technical subcommittees with subtending working groups and subworking groups, as illustrated in Fig. 23.8.

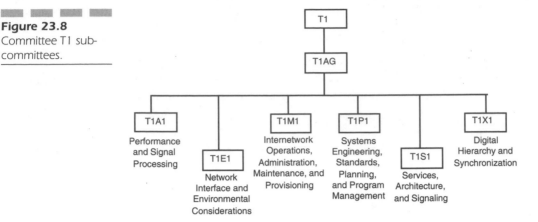

Figure 23.8
Committee T1 sub-committees.

Committee T1 also has an advisory group (T1AG) comprising elected representatives from each of the four interest groups to carry out T1 directives and develop proposals for consideration by the T1 membership. Committee T1 is open to participants all around the world. The T1 committee comes under the ANSI standards organization, which deals with standards such as telecommunications, information technology, and electrical and electronics standards. It provides input to the Telecom Group in the State Department, which in turn provides input to international standards organizations such as ITU-T, ITU-R, etc.

23.5   ITU-T Related BISDN Standards

ITU-T began the standards activities on BISDN in 1985 in its Study Group 18. The focus was on the next generation of network concepts, architectures, technologies, and services for high-speed flexible communications. The basic recommendation was completed in 1990. Since then, the BISDN recommendations have evolved to meet the immediate needs of the telecommunications industry.

The detailed protocol specifications are being released in three steps. Release 1 recommendations were for the ATM adaptation layer, which does the adaptation for various data rate types such as frame relay, TCP/IP, etc. These recommendations include functions such as point-to-point, constant bit-rate services. The first set of signaling recommendations corresponding to release 1 was released in 1994. This set is compatible with existing Q.931 (BISDN-UNI signaling) and B-ISUP (BISDN-NNI signaling). The recommendation for release 2 (1994-1995) will support VBR capability for voice and video, point-to-multipoint connection, and QOS. The release 3 recommendation (1997) covered enhanced connection configuration for multimedia. The recommendations related to the current stage of BISDN are shown in Fig. 23.9.

23.6 Summary

In this chapter, we gave an overview of standards bodies involved in the telecommunications industry. We covered the process involved in standards making. Many standards organizations are present both at national and international level. Every organization has some broadband-related activity as a part of its subgroup. Among the international standards-making

Figure 23.9
BISDN-related ITU-T recommendation.

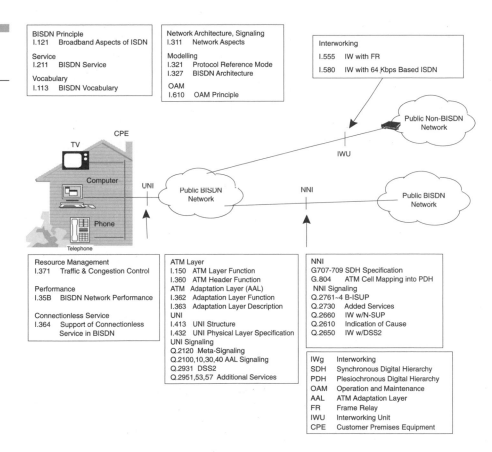

bodies for telecommunications, the foremost is the International Telecommunication Union (ITU), which has specialized organizations to address different areas of standards. There are numerous special interest groups formed by vendor and user proponents of technology to agree on technology options and provide coherent representation to standards organization around the world.

With the advent of broadband and other technologies, the lines between the telecommunications and information technology activities often overlap, forcing different organizations to work very closely with each other.

24

Broadband
Equipment
Vendors

24.1 Overview

As mentioned earlier, ATM is the switching technology that will be used for future broadband communications, and it is a technology expected to span all the different segments of the network worldwide. In this chapter, we list some of the equipment vendors who provide ATM-based equipment.

As far as ATM equipment vendors are concerned, it is not difficult for anyone to guess who is developing ATM-based products. In fact, it is difficult to tell which vendor has not made plans for ATM products. Everyone from chip manufacturers, such as Texas Instruments, to telecommunications switch manufacturers, such as AT&T, has put forward plans for ATM in their respective fields of expertise.

This chapter identifies the various components of the network that use different ATM functions. This enables the reader to understand the different portions of the network where equipment vendors are positioning their ATM products. Figure 24.1 shows a generic network that identifies the opportunities for ATM products. Since it has become impossible to track all the functions featured in each vendor's products, this chapter has listed the potential ATM vendors along with their web addresses. These vendors develop products that address the various network elements identified in this chapter.

24.2 Reference ATM Network Configuration

Based on Fig. 24.1, some of the areas of opportunity for ATM equipment manufacturers in hardware, software, and firmware are

1. VLSI chipsets

2. Adapter interfaces

3. LAN switches

4. Hub or campus backbone switches

5. Access multiplexer and switches

6. ATM backbone

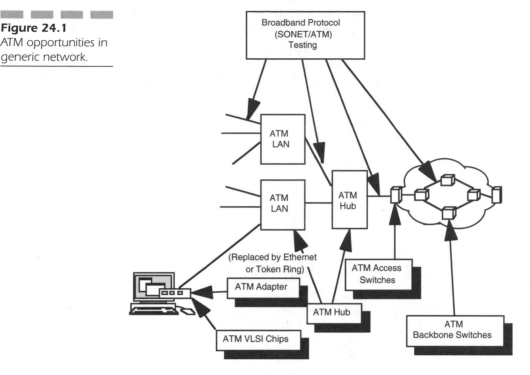

Figure 24.1
ATM opportunities in
generic network.

7. ATM test equipment to test the equipment and interfaces for standards compliance

Although ATM is the common technology throughout the network, the environment and requirements for each of the ATM products are different. An equipment vendor can design a product to be positioned in more than one market by packaging the product accordingly, which is how equipment vendors differentiate their products and position themselves for a particular market. For example, backbone ATM switches must meet the government and regulatory bodies' standards requirements in terms of downtime, redundancy, etc., whereas an ATM LAN switch has to satisfy the customer whose needs might include the ability to connect the existing LAN networks to an ATM LAN switch.

In this chapter, we provide an overview of the products of some of the vendors in each segment of the market. Again, this discussion is only to show the commitment made by different vendors with respect to ATM products at the time of this writing.

24.3   ATM Equipment Vendors for LAN Products

No other area provides more opportunity for equipment vendors than LANs. Equipment manufacturers of all segments have developed some sort of ATM equipment, including

- Chips
- Adapters
- LAN switches

Each is discussed in the following subsections.

24.3.1   ATM Chips

All of the semiconductor manufacturers have positioned themselves to provide ATM chips, and most of them are already ATM Forum members. Some of the manufacturers are Applied Micro Circuit Corp., Base2 Systems, National Semiconductor, QPSX, Saturn Synoptics Chip Development, Texas Instruments, Transwitch, and Vitesse G-Taxi chip.

The ATM chip functions as the broadband protocol layer, including the mapping of cells to the SONET OC3 interface payload, the DS3 PLCP ATM adaptation layer functions, and other protocol functions of varying interface speeds. These chips are used in the development of ATM products such as ATM adapters, ATM access switches, backbone switches, etc. They are also used in all ATM equipment that performs standard functions.

24.3.2   ATM Adapters

ATM adapters are the interface cards plugged into a computer typically in a workstation or PC bus. The information from the computer is transferred to external devices via the ATM interface card. The function of the ATM adapter is to adapt the data to the ATM format (cells for routing through the ATM network without any additional protocol conversion delay). This interface card puts in appropriate virtual path identifier and virtual channel identifier values in the ATM cell.

Currently, workstation adapters are available from Adaptive and Fore Systems for many of the popular workstations, including Sun, Silicon Graphics, DEC, Next, and Hewlett Packard. These adapters operate at a speed of 100 Mbps, using the AAL 3/4 or AAL 5 ATM adaptation layer.

Other manufacturers have developed lower-speed adapters. For instance, Newbridge has developed a 51-Mbps adapter for unshielded twisted-pair category 3 adapters for SBUS, NUBUS, Microchannel, ISA, EISA, VME, and Futurebus-based systems. Today a wide range of cost-effective adapters for various systems are available from various vendors.

24.3.3 Local ATM Switches

Local ATM switches connect computers or workstations in a star topology as shown in Fig. 24.2. These switches have interfaces to workstations at 100 or 140 Mbps and Ethernet interfaces at 16 Mbps. Currently, 100-Mbps (TAXI), 45-Mbps (DS3 ATM UNI with PLCP), and 155-Mbps (SONET-OC3c) interfaces for the workstations are available. These switches can be used as

Figure 24.2
Typical local ATM switch environment.

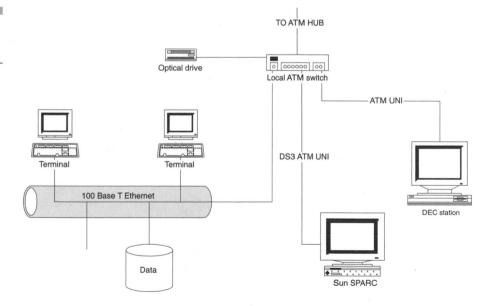

hubs, depending on the type of interface available for the switch. In fact, these vendors manufacture ATM-based hubs.

24.4   ATM Hub or Campus Backbone

Hubs are used to connect multiple LANs; usually there is a LAN for each department in a building. These shared LANs use the broadcast method, where the end stations in the LAN accept all the frames transmitted, discarding the ones that are not addressed specifically to them. The conventional technique for an oversubscribed shared LAN is to split the LAN into two and connect the segments with a bridge or router. This type of optimization leads to numerous LANs with very few users, which becomes difficult to manage. To help users set up small LANs, smart hubs came into existence. These hubs allow any equipment (bridge, router, or LAN) to reside in any segment. Sometimes they are called switching hubs, because specific small groups of ports are assigned to a LAN segment for switching between the ports. Currently, most of the smart hubs are connected via fiber-optic cables, enabling the hubs to be linked to high-speed LANs such as FDDI. As interfacing became more and more complex, these smart hubs started directly connecting to desktop PCs with a single hub to connect multiple hubs back-to-back. These hubs will be upgraded to ATM modules and continue to have Ethernet and token-ring interfaces while switching is performed on the ATM backbone between them. These ATM hubs will have more ATM ports and fewer other LAN interface ports such as Ethernet, FDDI, etc.

Currently, over a dozen vendors are in the hub market. These ATM hubs have aggregate bandwidths ranging from 2 to 10 Gbps, with interface port speeds ranging from 1.5 to 155 Mbps. The switch architecture might vary from vendor to vendor, but the basic cell switching is done in the hardware (VLSI chips perform the switching in all of them). In simple terms, the function of these hubs is to convert LAN frames into ATM cells from different interfaces. This equipment is sometimes called the *cell slicer.*

ATM has clearly hit its stride, and products will be rolling out en masse throughout the year. In addition to local area and workgroup switches, a raft of component products (e.g., ATM chipsets, ATM interfaces, and ATM LAN analyzers) will enable users to deploy enterprisewide ATM-based networks.

24.5 ATM Equipment Vendors in WAN

In this section, we address the products of ATM vendors designed to connect remote sites. Figure 24.3 shows a typical ATM switch (ATM hub used in WAN applications).

We described the requirements for a typical product in a WAN environment in Chap. 18. This product can be an ATM switch or an ATM concentrator. Vendors targeting this market are T1/T3 multiplexer or mux and X.25 packet-switch equipment vendors.

Figure 24.3
ATM switch as WAN interface.

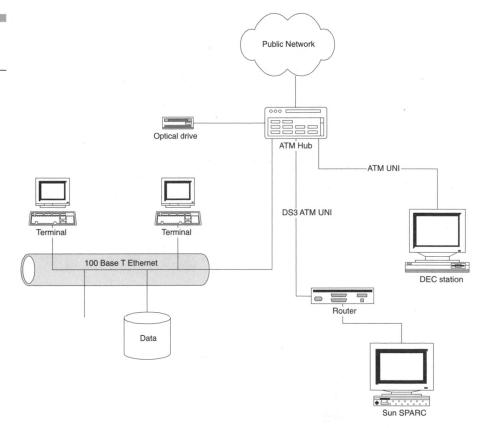

24.6   ATM Vendors' Strategy in Public Networks

This market segment is the one where only a very few large players exist, and they operate on a global basis. They are telecommunication switch and transmission equipment manufacturers whose annual revenue exceed $1 billion. As mentioned in Chap. 19, the requirements for equipment in a public network are more stringent than in any other segment. The largest market for ATM switches in the public network is those used either as a central office or an end-office switch.

24.7   Equipment Vendors in ATM/Broadband Testing

It is interesting that so many equipment manufacturers are addressing the different ATM environments. When the customer needs to know the features and how they operate or needs to verify their compliance with standards requirements, however, testing equipment is needed. Currently, only a few vendors have come up with ATM/broadband testing equipment. They are Hewlett Packard, ADTech, Network General, Wandel, and Goltermann.

Testing products are used for testing the broadband equipment functionality and protocol according to the specification. For instance, SONET and ATM are testing according to the ITU specification. Vendors take a layered approach to test the various broadband protocol. For example, Hewlett Packard has taken a structured layer-by-layer approach, i.e., testing each layer of the BISDN protocol independently. Figure 24.4 shows the BISDN protocol used by Hewlett Packard to test different layers.

24.8   Summary

In this chapter, we discussed ATM products in different environments that were addressed in Part 5. The different environments where ATM vendors are focusing are ATM chips, ATM adapters, ATM LANs, ATM hubs, ATM access switches, and ATM backbone switches. Some vendors package their products in such a way that they can address more

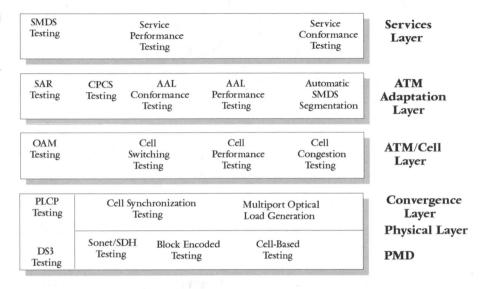

Figure 24.4
HP BISDN protocol stack for testing.

than one market. Table 24.1 lists some of the potential vendors, their core products, and their web address where up-to-date information on the products is available.

TABLE 24.1

ATM Product Vendor List

Vendors	Company Product Description	Internet Web Address
3Com	Global data networking solutions, including routers, hubs, remote access servers, switches, and adapters for Ethernet, token ring, and high-speed networks.	*http://www.3com.com/*
Adaptec	Desktops and high-performance SCSI, RAID, and ATM products for enterprisewide computing and networked environments.	*http://www.adaptec.com/*
ADC Kentrox	Manufactures ATM, switching, and network management products.	*http://www.kentrox.com/*
ADC Telecommunications	End-to-end networking solutions for telecoms, cable, wireless, and corporate networks.	*http://www.ps-mpls.com/ADC/*
Adtech, Inc.	Manufacturer of ATM test systems and data link simulators.	*http://www.adtech-inc.com/*
Advanced Computer Communications	LAN, WAN, and mainframe connectivity, bridges, routers etc.	*http://www.acc.com/*

Vendors	Company Product Description	Internet Web Address
ADTRAN	Designs, develops, and manufactures ADvanced TRANsmission products for high-speed digital communications, including ISDN, DDS, switched digital, T1, and HDSL.	*http:// www.adtran.com/*
Agile Networks	Manufacturer of ATM backbone networks for building and campus area environments.	*http://www.agile.com/*
Alcatel	Leading worldwide supplier of communications systems, equipment, and cable for public and private networks and business communications.	*http://www.alcatel.com/*
Alcatel Bell	Belgian-based manufacturer of a wide range of telecoms equipment—site showcases multimedia networks and their applications.	*http://www.alcatel.com/*
Amati Communications Corporation	Develops and markets advanced telecommunications products—ADSL.	*http://www.alcatel.com/*
Ascend Communications	Remote networking products for corporate communications, telecommunications operators, internet service providers etc.	*http://www.alcatel.com/*
Ascom Timeplex	ATM products and other telecommunications equipment.	*http://www.alcatel.com/*
Astarté Fiber Networks, Inc.	Design and manufacture of a line of optical-fiber switches.	*http://www.starswitch.com/*
ATM Ltd.	Low-cost ATM products supporting video conferencing, video mail, and other multimedia.	*http://www.atml.co.uk/atml.htm*
Bay Networks	Switched internetworking solutions for corporate information systems—Ethernet, FDDI, ATM etc.	*http://www.baynetworks.com/*
Bell Laboratories	Research arm of Lucent Technologies.	*http://www.bell-labs.com/*
Breeze Wireless Communications Inc.	Wireless ATM LANs, wireless bridges, and wireless E1/T1 links.	*http://www.breezecom.com/*
BroadBand Technologies	U.S.-based manufacturer of broadband optical access networks.	*http://www.bbt.com/*
Broadband Telephony Buyer's Guide	Directory with links to suppliers of equipment, applications, technologies, and products for voice data and video transmissions.	*http://www.broadband-guide.com/*

TABLE 24.1

(Continued)

Vendors	Company Product Description	Internet Web Address
Cabletron	Networking solutions management, networking, transceivers, and connectivity solutions.	http://www.ctron.com/
CACI Products Company	Develops and distributes simulation software for capacity planning and performance prediction of LANs and WANs.	http://www.caciasl.com/
CallWare Technologies Inc.	Intranet/LAN/WAN computer telephony development house.	http://www.callware.com/
Cellware GmbH	ATM products for networking, SMDS, FDDI, video on demand etc.	http://www.cellware.de/
Com21	ATM-based, high-speed products bringing internet and interactive multimedia into residential, educational, and commercial use.	http://www.com21.com/
Compression Technologies Inc.	Manufacturer of wide area network optimization and security equipment.	http://compression.com/
Compusource	Listing of computer companies, including large manufacturers URL list.	http://www.cuhp.co.uk/
Comverse Technology Inc.	Multimedia communications processing technology and products.	http://www.comverse.com/
Consultronics	A globally operating telecommunications test equipment manufacturer.	http://www.consultronics.on.ca/
Continental Resources	Complex systems and networking solutions, test equipment etc.	http://www.conres.com
Control Data	Designs and implements systems for LAN management, electronic commerce, network reengineering, and distributed systems management.	http://www.cdc.com/
Controls Inc.	Manufactures digital control equipment including remote monitoring via phone or wireless modem.	http://www.controlsinc.com/
Controlware Communications Systems	ISDN solutions for worldwide telecommunications, including terminal adapters for dial backup systems and inverse multiplexers.	http://www.cware.de/
CTEL Profile	Vendor of telecommunications monitoring equipment.	http://www.ctel.com/Profile.htm

TABLE 24.1

(Continued)

Vendors	Company Product Description	Internet Web Address
Crystal Group Inc.	Manufacturer of industrial PC tailored for the computer telephony market.	*http://www.crystalpc.com/*
Dash Open Phone Systems	Manufactures a TAPI-compliant PC-based telephone system; voice mail, automated attend, and ACD capable.	*http://www.dashops.com/*
Data Comm for Business Inc.	A diverse range of data communications products, including LAN/WAN, frame-relay, multiplexor, switching, and wireless communications products.	*http://www.dcbnet.com/*
DeskNet Systems	ATM test equipment and network analyzers.	*http://frame-relay.indiana.edu/ vendors/desknet/*
Digi International	Hardware and software products delivering seamless connectivity solutions for multiuser environments, remote access, and LAN connection.	*http://www.digibd.com/*
Digital Equipment Corporation	Manufacturer of gigabit ATM switches.	*http://www.digital.com/*
Digital Link Corporation	High-speed digital access products for WANs.	*http://www.dl.com/*
Digital Technics Inc.	Generic digital switching platform for use from PBX to central office switching.	*http://www.access.digex.net/~dti/*
DSC Communications Corporation	Digital switching, transmission, access, and private network system products for the worldwide telecommunications marketplace.	*http://www.dsccc.com/*
Efficient Networks	ATM adapter and ATM software for CPE devices.	*http://www.efficient.com/*
Ericsson	Digital switching, transmission, access, and private network system products for the worldwide telecommunications marketplace.	*http://www.ericsson.se/*
FastComm Communications	Data communications and ATM access products, frame-relay switches.	*http://www.fastcomm.com/*
Fibronics International	Product range includes ATM, FDDI, Ethernet, and token-ring hubs and switches.	*http://www.fibronics.co.il/*
FORE Systems Inc.	ATM switches, LAN access products, software, network, and video adapters.	*http://www.fore.com/*
Fujitsu products	Maker of ATM and other telecommunications equipment.	*http://www.fujitsu.com/*

TABLE 24.1

(Continued)

Vendors	Company Product Description	Internet Web Address
General DataComm Inc.	Network ATM products and solutions.	*http://www.gdc.com/*
General Signal Networks	Ethernet, WAN, and token-ring solutions, testing and diagnostic applications.	*http://www.gsnetworks.com./*
GL Communications Inc.	Manufactures PC-based telecommunications test equipment.	*http://www2.ari.net/glcomm/*
GTE Laboratories	Manufactures edge ATM switches.	*http://info.gte.com/*
Harris Communications Systems and Services	Voice and data switching, microwave radio, wireless telephony, network testing and support, integrated systems and services.	*http://www.harris.com/*
Hekimian Laboratories	Leading independent supplier of automated test systems for telecommunications networks in the United States.	*http://www.hekimian.com/*
Hewlett Packard	Maker of broadband test equipment.	*http://www.hp.com/*
IBM	Maker of ATM-based adapter cards and broadband network management systems.	*http://www.ibm.com/*
Inficom-Wireless Data Transfer	ATM wireless modems and wireless networking products.	*http://www.inficom.com/*
Intecom	Multimedia solutions: advanced PBX, CTI, call center and video communications.	*http://www.intecom.com/*
Integrated Telecom Technology	IgT system-level ATM semiconductor devices and software drivers.	*http://www.igt.com/*
Intel	ATM-based chipset.	*http://www.intel.com/*
Interphase Corporation	ATM adapter cards.	*http://www.iphase.com/*
Ipsilon Networks Inc.	IP switching products.	*http://www.ipsilon.com/*
ISD Communications Inc.	Digital communications products utilizing time-shift keying—TSK digital modulation techniques	*http://www.tricon.net/ Comm/isd/isdcomm/*
.ISR Global Telecom	Network management tools.	*http://www.isrglobal.com/*
Italtel	Italian telecoms manufacturer: public switching, transmission, radio and business systems.	*http://www.italtel.it/index.html*

TABLE 24.1

(Continued)

Vendors	Company Product Description	Internet Web Address
JM Fiber Optics	Fiber-optics products for LANs, multimedia, telephony, and data communications.	*http://www.jmfiberoptics.com/*
Jupiter Technology Inc.	Low-cost, feature-rich frame-relay access products.	*http://www.jti.com/*
K-Net	Manufacturers of ATM video products and distributers of ATM networking equipment.	*http://www.k-net.co.uk/*
Language Systems Design	Lossless data compression ICs for communications applications.	*http://lossless.com/*
Laser Communications Inc.	High-speed infrared wireless communication equipment.	*http://www.lasercomm.com/lasercomm/*
Lucent Technologies	Advanced telecommunications equipment for public and corporate network and consumers.	*http://www.lucent.com/*
MICOM Communications Corp.	Networking solutions for integrated voice and data.	*http://www.micom.com/*
MicroLegend Telecom Systems	SS7 network control and monitoring systems for intelligent network services.	*http://www.microlegend.com/*
Microsoft	Leading manufacturer of broadband application software.	*http://www.microsoft.com/*
Motorola	Maker of broadband ATM interface cards, VLSI chips.	*http://www.mot.com/*
Network Communications Corporation	Network analysis instruments for LAN, WAN, and enterprise network environments.	*http://probe.netcommcorp.com/*
Network Equipment Technologies Inc. (N.E.T.)	WAN backbone solutions for integrating voice, data, and video frame relay, LAN internetworking and ISDN capable.	*http://www.net.com/*
nCUBE	Produces video or media servers for large video on demand applications delivering MPEG-2 over ATM interfaces.	*http://www.ncube.com/*
Netrix	Complete office connectivity solutions including LAN, WAN, frame relay, voice/ fax, and video.	*http://www.netrix.com/*

TABLE 24.1

(Continued)

Vendors	Company Product Description	Internet Web Address
NEC	Fiber optic, cellular, PBX, public switching, satellite earth station, and other equipment.	*http://www.nec.com/*
Net2Net Corporation	Management and analysis systems for the ATM market.	*http://www.net2net.com/*
NetSpan	Networking and internetworking solutions for personal computer and workstation networks.	*http://www.netspan.com/*
NetStar	High performance computer networking products.	*http://www.netstar.com/*
Network Systems	ATM products, network management, data security, routing, HIPPI, and other products.	*http://www.network.com/*
Newbridge Networks	Produces and services a comprehensive family of networking products and systems delivering multimedia communications.	*http://www.newbridge.com/*
Nortel	Global provider of communications solutions and a full range of communications products for both public and private networks.	*http://www.nortel.com/*
Optical Data Systems Inc. (ODS)	Networking solutions for Ethernet, token-ring, fiber distributed data interface, and ATM networks.	*http://www.ods.com/*
Performance Telecommunications	Provides digital subscriber loop, xDSL, products.	*http://www.perftel.com/*
Phoenix Datacom	Testing and diagnostic products for communications and telecommunications, particularly ATM and ISDN.	*http://www.phoenixdata.co.uk/*
PMC-Sierra Inc. (Subsidiary of Sierra Semiconductor)	Networking component solutions focusing on broadband ATM, SONET/SDH and subT1/E1 applications.	*http://www.pmc-sierra.com/*
Positron Fiber Systems	Advanced broadband access network systems for local telecommunications carriers—SONET/SDH.	*http://www.positronfiber.com/*
PP-COM Telecommunication+ Networking GmbH	Supplies store and forward communication systems.	*http://www.ppcom.de/*
Progressive Communication Supply Inc. (ProComm)	Supplier of telecommunications and data communications copper, fiber cable, connectors, outlets, installation tools, and testers	*http://www.csiworld.com/pro comm/procomp2.htm*

TABLE 24.1

(Continued)

Vendors	Company Product Description	Internet Web Address
Promptus Communications	Network access products for high-speed digital networks, e.g., remote LAN and Internet access.	*http://www.promptus.com/*
Racal-Datacom	Digital access, LANs, WANs, and network management.	*http://www.racal.com/*
RAD Data Communications	Manufactures LAN/WAN access solutions: high-speed multiplexers, modems, rate and interface converters for token-ring and Ethernet access.	*http://www.rad.co.il/*
RADCOM	Manufactures LAN/WAN/ATM protocol analyzers.	*http://www.radcom.co.il/*
SAGEM (SAT networks and telecommunications division)	Telecommunications equipment supplier.	*http://www.sagem-sat.co.uk/*
Sattel Communications Company	Leading manufacturer of digital switching systems for public and private telecommunications network products.	*http://www.sattelcom.com/*
Shiva Corporation	Provides analog and digital remote access WAN and internet equipment.	*http://www.shiva.com/*
Siemens Network Systems Division	Network solutions for LANs, interworking, cabling systems, multiplexers, X.25, frame-relay, SMDS, ATM network management.	*http://www.siemens.de/vs/*
Standard Microsystems Corporation	LAN adapters, hubs, and switches.	*http://www.smc.com/*
Sun Microsystems	Workstations, multimedia, networking, ATM, and fast Ethernet software, etc.	*http://www.sun.com/*
SVEC Computer Corporation	Full line of Ethernet LAN products, including network interface cards, hubs, repeaters, print servers, concentrators, bridges, and routers.	*http://www.svec.com/*
TDK Semiconductor Corp.	Manufacturer of chips for modem, Ethernet, ATM, transceivers, etc.	*http://www.tsc.tdk.com/*
Tekelec	Network diagnostic, switching, and IN products.	*http://www.tekelec.com/*
Tektronix	Test solutions for broadband, video, and wireless networks and other products.	*http://www.tek.com/*

TABLE 24.1

(Continued)

Vendors	Company Product Description	Internet Web Address
Telco Systems Inc.	Network access products, including optical multiplexers, broadband multimedia systems, and internetworking equipment.	*http://www.telco.com/*
Telecommunications Techniques Corporation (TTC)	Manufactures state-of-the-art telecommunications test equipment	*http://www.ttc.com/*
Telefonica Sistemas Ingeniera De Productos (TSIP)	Network architecture and management systems engineering.	*http://tsip.tsai.es/tsip/itsip.htm*
Texas Instruments' Digital Light Processing Site	Enhanced video images using digital technology.	*http://www.ti.com/dlp*
TranSwitch Corporation	VLSI semiconductor products for advanced telecommunications products—ATM, SONET/SDH.	*http://www.txc.com/*
Tut Systems	Cost-effective high-bandwidth connectivity products: 155 Mbit ATM copper transceivers.	*http://www.tutsys.com/*
Universal Networks	LAN, WAN systems integration.	*http://www.uninet.com/*
Visual Networks	Family of management access products for wide area data services, e.g., frame relay, ATM, and internet.	*http://www.visualnetworks.com/*
Wandel & Goltermann	Test equipment for telecommunications and data communications.	*http://www.wg.com/*
Westell Technologies	Broad range of analog, digital, and fiber systems for local access networks.	*http://www.westell.com/*
Whitetree Network Technologies	High-performance networking solutions based on ATM technology.	*http://ftp.whitetree.com/*
Xylan Corporation	Switches for high-bandwidth networks—Ethernet, token ring, FDDI/CDDI, Fast Ethernet, ATM.	*http://www.xylan.com/*

TABLE 24.1

(Continued)

CHAPTER **25**

The Future of Broadband Communications

25.1 Overview

The previous 24 chapters covered broadband communications and how various technologies come together, especially ATM and SONET. Broadband communications with ATM is still in its infancy; much progress has been made since the first edition of this book, but many issues are still pending. The focus of this chapter is to go further into the evolution of broadband communications and see what the future will be. Some issues that have delayed the deployment of broadband will be addressed.

In addition, we look into some of the future broadband technologies in the areas of access, switching and transmission technology. Access, switching and transmission technologies are currently a combination of electrical and optical domain in the network systems. In these systems, the signal regeneration, add/drop, switching, etc., is accomplished in the electrical domain, while the long-haul transport is accomplished in the optical domain. In this case, the electrical domain becomes a bottleneck for speeds greater than 100 Gbps.

To achieve speeds greater than 100 Gbps, the electrical bottleneck must be replaced with optical-domain regeneration, switching, and add/drop functionality. Optical amplifier and switches are already available on a limited basis from the research labs around the world. Here we will address some of them.

25.2 B-ISDN and ATM-Based Broadband Networks

It is expected that broadband network infrastructure will be constructed using B-ISDN framework and ATM as the switching core technology. We will briefly examine some of advantages and disadvantages of ATM-based broadband networks, and the reasons it will succeed as the underlying technology for the broadband communications infrastructure on a global basis.

25.2.1 Advantages of ATM-Based Broadband Network

There are a number advantages of ATM-based cell switching technology. The network permits an arbitrary mesh topology of point-to-point links between switches, which allows the network to be flexible, scalable, and fault tolerant. The switches can be designed to be highly scalable, and network growth consists of scaling the switches and corresponding links without the constraints of shared medium networks, such as rings or buses. We can use an arbitrary topology to construct broadband networks using the hierarchical organizations required to reasonably address and manage ATM-based broadband networks, which are connection-oriented, allowing quality of service guarantees. The routing overhead is performed via connection setup, allowing the per cell routing to be done easily by the hardware as a simple table lookup. Finally, datagram service can be provided over a permanent connection set overlay for the purpose. A significant advantage of ATM networks is that the standards have been designed to scale (upwards) in data rates. SONET OC-3c (155 Mbps) and OC-12c (622 Mbps) are standard now, as well as OC-48c (2.4 Gbps) and beyond (OC-192c, OC-768c, etc.).

25.2.2 Disadvantages of ATM-Based Broadband Networks

In spite of the benefits, there are, however, a number of disadvantages for ATM-based broadband networks, primarily due to the current standards and real-world implementations of ATM. The biggest offender is the small cell size with a 48-octet payload. This was a compromise between two small proposed cell sizes of 32 and 64 bytes, chosen by the voice community to avoid the need for echo cancellation. Another problem is the decision to require sequenced delivery (for real-time applications such as voice) and omit a sequence number from the ATM cell header (necessary, given the small cell size; the AAL3/4 sequence number is intended only for error detection, not for resequencing). While it is possible to design switches and routing algorithms to enforce all cells in a stream to follow the same path, this restricts the design space. Also, the evolution's current technology such as IP and its next-generation version addresses the same issues as ATM has been dealing with. With IP being used widely around the world, it has become a battleground for technologies to debate the value of ATM against IP in terms of supporting data services.

25.2.3 Why ATM-Based Broadband Networks Will Succeed

In spite of the disadvantages imposed by ATM-based broadband network and BISDN standards, it seems clear that ATM and B-ISDN will be the basis of the future broadband infrastructure. In spite of certain technical problems with the BISDN and ATM standards, the fact that there is a standard that had been agreed on for the physical, link, and network layers is significant. The whole point of networking is interoperability, and this outweighs technical compromises and defects. A wide range of network component manufacturers and service providers are doing, or planning to do, BISDN and ATM, in many cases prematurely (see the manufacturer list in Chap. 24). Now that we have said this, we should note again that there is much to still be defined. The easy problems such as cell format, segmentation and reassembly, and physical layer protocols have been defined, while the difficult issues of multipoint virtual connection routing and traffic management are far from settled. We also shouldn't be surprised to see some revisions in the current standards. The problems with a small cell size can be overcome by a large cell definition, i.e., a cell size that scales with data rate or cell groups. The connection-oriented nature allows this to be a connection parameter. Similarly, a larger cell payload would allow a larger header to be used for a sequence number without further sacrificing header efficiency.

We should observe also that while differences between the connection-oriented versus datagram (connectionless) and ATM versus IP arguments have frequently taken on the proportions of a "holy war," there will eventually be peace. In a connection-oriented ATM world, datagrams will have to be supported; this is currently being pursued as ABR (available bit rate) traffic. In the IP world, bandwidth reservations will be introduced in the packet routers to provide QOS for IP traffic. Both camps are trying to solve the same problem, and the solutions will converge. The global information infrastructure will be based on a ATM broadband with much of the flavor of existing IP networks and applications.

25.3 Challenges in Deploying the Broadband Network

Even though we have general agreement on ATM cell relay as the core transport technology/switching for the emerging broadband infrastructure, there are a number of problems that have yet to be solved and worked into the standards. These technical and practical challenges pose nontrivial barriers to the deployment of a broadband global information infrastructure.

25.3.1   Technical Problems

A number of very difficult problems remain to be solved in order to deploy ATM-based broadband networks on a large scale. Virtual connection routing is one of them, and the difficulty is due to the need to find a path with available resources to meet the users requested quality of service parameters, while optimizing network resources and load balancing. The general case for dynamic multipoint-to-multipoint connections is very challenging indeed, and will require routing heuristics. There are also a number of open issues regarding signaling between switches within the network (especially with ATM and traditional switches and routers). Other problems involve mobile addressing and the associated dynamic routing and rerouting, which will be increasingly important.

Whereas using a rate or flow specification to ensure an application's compliance to the traffic contract makes it easier to design network interfaces and to engineer switches and buffer sizes, it places the burden of determining a reasonable set of parameters on the application or user. Although this may be a simple matter for some well-behaved or well-understood applications, such as voice or uncompressed video, it will be exceptionally difficult for other applications, such as for general multimedia interactive applications or distributed computing.

The available bit-rate traffic class is targeted toward solving this problem, since it provides an IP-like connectionless service over ATM networks. Unfortunately, there are a number of cases where this will be inadequate. As an example, a user requesting a file transfer using FTP may tolerate some variance in the response time it takes to get the file, and thus in the value of the average rate.

Another problem related to broadband networks is the network itself. A broadband network is an extremely complex *systems of systems*, and frequently it does not exhibit the behavior we would like. The assumption in broadband networking has been that many bursty sources would aggregate to relatively uniform traffic, with the corresponding benefits in reduced network resources. This causes complexity in terms of managing the network, which is a daunting task.

25.3.2   Practical Challenges

There are a number of additional challenges of a more practical nature, for which the technical solutions are not easy. Network management has always been a difficult problem but will become much more difficult in multiservice multirate broadband networks.

Security, privacy, and authentication services will have to be provided. This is a standard concern in networks which trades against the desire to share information. This is not a new problem, but it is of increasing concern as the number of users with access to networks (including crackers) increases, as does the desire to conduct commerce and business across an integrated network infrastructure. Electronic fund transfers will no longer have the (perceived) physical security of private networks controlled by the banks with switches controlled by telephone carriers.

The architecture of the network and switches to allow the provision of content and the deployment of new services and application, some within the network, and some by external service providers, will become an increasingly challenging problem. The current efforts in intelligent networks (see Chap. 16) targeted toward the telephone network will not be sufficient for emerging integrated broadband networks, and many pieces of the current IN architecture will be subsumed by broadband signaling and multipoint connection routing. There will be a greater need for the structural and architectural aspects of IN to determine where functions reside in the network and switches, and to allow the rapid deployment of new services and applications without replacing current infrastructures.

These practical issues are complicated by the wide range of host and terminal equipment intelligence we should expect for a long time to come. Some of this will be legacy, but a typical home may have a large HDTV set in the living room whose primary interface is not a keyboard but a voice-activated PC that also can display entertainment video and a number of relatively dumb telephone sets.

25.3.3   Compatibility, Standards, and the Seamless Network

The ability to maintain backward compatibility with existing protocols and host software is critical, but can impose technical compromises on new protocols and architectures. We will have to live in a world of multi-protocol and legacy networks for a long time to come. Existing transport protocols, such as TCP/IP and TP4 will be required to operate over new network infrastructures just to support the existing applications that use them. IP has served as a powerful unifying layer for heterogeneous subnetworks, and will also have to be supported for the foreseeable future. Any solutions will have to balance the ability to enhance the performance and services of these existing protocols, while providing the new performance and functionality needed for emerging applications.

Similarly, standards are particularly necessary in the network world, since they provide the means to allow interoperation, but the premature adoption of poor or overly rigid standards can do more harm than good. It is a very tricky business to go from research and experimentation to preliminary standards to solid standards to which products can be designed.

The B-ISDN and ATM standards originally assumed a strict and relatively simple hierarchical network structure, with a public backbone network at the top. The current internetworking in reality is far from this due to the postdivestiture structure of the U.S. telephone networks and the structure of the current internet. The vision of a seamless LAN-MAN-WAN-GAN ATM infrastructure will not be realized for some time to come. Furthermore, the need for policy-based routing complicate the original assumptions.

25.3.4   Economic Issues

There are certainly some components of the network infrastructure that are a natural monopoly, e.g., the last mile or the local loop. On the other hand, we are moving to a more competitive world in the provision of host and terminal equipment, as well as services, facilities, and network content.

The emerging network infrastructure should make it easier on the user, but it appears that delivery to the home will be available via telephone lines, CATV cable, cellular and PCS communications, satellite feeds, and possibly fiber in the power transmission lines. The question arises: how many distinct network outlets should be "in the wall"? We will have to decide if the connectivity between the various local access networks is sufficient or if multiple feeds will be required with a local gateway or switch in the home. A number of standard issues here relate to new technology, including providing reasonable incentives to deploy infrastructure, given regulatory constraints.

Billing is considerably more difficult for broadband integrated networks than for constant rate or leased-line communication. Billing for broadband networks must be based on the resources required for the network, which means that in addition to the amount of data transferred and the peak rates required, it will have to be based on traffic characteristics such as burstiness. Furthermore, for broadband networks to be a success, they will have to be affordable and the pricing will have to be nonlinear, but this means that bandwidth providers will face the reselling of fractional bandwidth. Incremental pricing of excess network capacity may be a useful concept but a difficult one to implement.

25.4   Future Broadband Technology Trends

This section addresses some of the future trends in broadband technologies in the areas of access, switching, and transmission.

25.4.1   Access Technology

Access is one of the areas where technology is backtracking due to economic and real-world implementation issues. In the early 1990s when broadband was first envisioned, network planners and designers assumed that fiber would be used in every home and business. In fact, NTT of Japan put forward a detailed rollout plan along with the cost to do so.

But the reality with respect to access is that the traditional telephone service has migrated to a wireless (fixed and mobile) domain, which has gained sufficient momentum worldwide as the preferred medium for low bandwidth services. These include traditional voice service and voice band data services such as modem and fax.

In the meantime, the traditional twisted pair was being deployed worldwide for voice service, and it gained a new life with technologies such as x-DSL (discussed in Chap. 9 along with its architecture in Chap. 13). These technologies, along with ATM as a switching technology, will keep network planners and implementers busy for the next 25 years.

25.4.2   Broadband Switching Architecture

With the current growing demand not only for traditional voice, data, and still-picture services but also for high-speed and broadband communications services, such as video phone, video conferencing, HDTV distribution, and high-speed file transfer services, the need for broadband communications networks has been increasing. ATM switching systems are flexible enough to handle a wide range of communications services. To implement broadband services nationwide, a switching system should be capable of accommodating 100 to 10,000 user network interfaces (UNIs), i.e., more than 150 Mbps per UNI. Thus, a 1-Tbps ATM switch, which can handle the traffic of hundreds or thousands of input and output ports with several gigabit-per-second bit rates, will be required.

The bottleneck with existing ATM switches handling such high speeds is the electrical switching fabric or matrix. The only way to achieve these higher speeds is to migrate to a completely optical domain. A switch that uses an optical switching fabric is called a *photonic ATM switch.* Currently, several types of photonic ATM switches have been developed. In this chapter, we address two photonic switch architectures.

Figure 25.1 shows the configuration of a typical photonic ATM switch. Although most of the present research has focused on the efficient utilization of the available bandwidth in the optical matrix switch, electronic circuits are still used to control the optical matrix switch. Thus, it is necessary to convert the optical header to an electrical header and to generate an electronic control signal for the optical matrix switch by translating the electronic header. As a result, the switching speed is limited by the electronic control circuit operating speed. Thus, for a $N \times N$ optical switching matrix, N^2 electronic control signals are required. With the increase in the number of input and output ports, the electronic control circuit becomes quite complicated because of the rapidly growing number of high-speed electronic circuits.

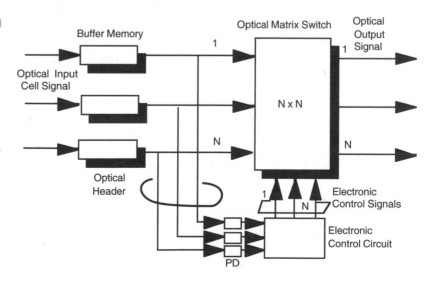

Figure 25.1
First-generation photonic ATM switch architecture. (*IEEE Communications,* April 1993, p. 63. Reprinted with permission.)

An electronic buffer memory is used for the queue in an electronic environment. In the case of an optical environment for an optical buffer, a fiber delay line is most often used in the conventional photonic ATM switch. In the case of an electronic buffer memory, the switching speed in the photonic ATM switch is limited by the electronic operating speed of the buffer memory. As for the optical-fiber delay line, it can store extremely high-speed optical signals. To increase cell signal speed, strict precision in the delay line length is required. Furthermore, the fiber delay line memory is not suitable for such integration.

Figure 25.2 shows the next-generation photonic ATM switch architecture. Here, a photonic input buffer ATM switch is depicted. This switch consists of optical first-in—first-out buffer memories and an optical $N \times N$ self-routing circuit. When the cells bound for the same output are sent to the self-routing circuit from different FIFO buffer memories at the same time, the cell with the highest priority can be self-routed, while the other cell signal is rejected to prevent cell contention. The high-speed optical buffer memory is expected to be constructed by converting serial cell signals into parallel signals and by using massively parallel optical interconnections.

25.4.3 Broadband Transmission Systems

In the 1990s, commercial broadband transmission rates were 2.4 Gbps, and regenerators are placed every 40 to 80 km along the cable path. The next-generation transmission rates can go beyond 1 Tbps and only require repeaters every 1000 km. In the next generation, the repeaters will regenerate the signal optically. In today's regenerators, the incoming optical signals must be converted to an electrical signal, and the electrical signal power must be amplified. This electrical signal is then converted back to

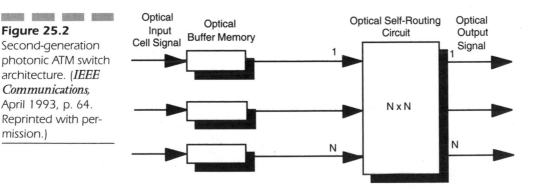

Figure 25.2
Second-generation photonic ATM switch architecture. (*IEEE Communications*, April 1993, p. 64. Reprinted with permission.)

an optical signal. In the case of optical amplifiers or regenerators, the signal remains in the optical domain, thus reducing the delay and loss incurred due to electrical-to-optical conversion. Figure 25.3 shows today's regenerators, and Figure 25.4 shows the optical regenerator.

25.5 Areas of Broadband Not Covered

Most of the chapters in this book addressed the issues related to end-to-end broadband with emphasis on ATM-based broadband networks and the related technologies. Certain areas of broadband, such as the operation support system (i.e., the network management, service management, etc.) and associated costs, are not addressed in this book. Although these

Figure 25.3
Today's electrical repeater or amplifiers.

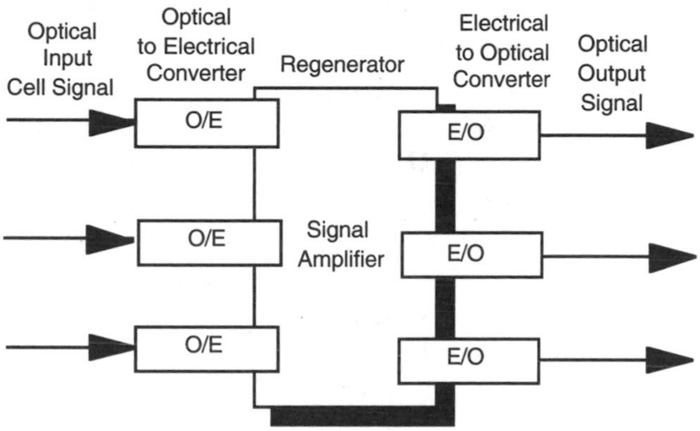

Figure 25.4
Optical repeater or amplifiers.

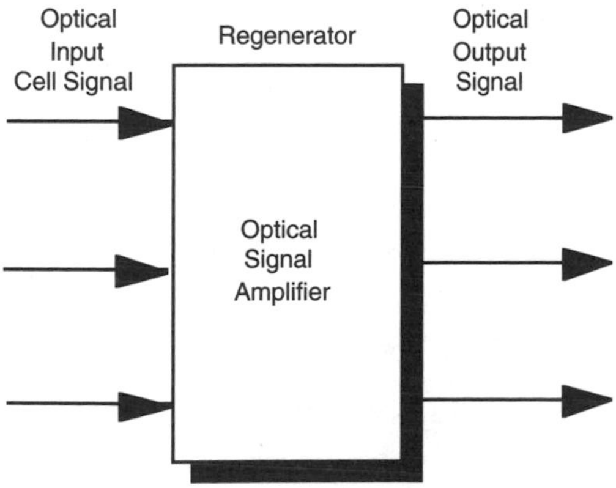

are important areas, in general, it is beyond the scope of this book. In fact, this book focuses on broadband technology aspects that are more important to service providers than end users who really don't care how the services are delivered as long as the services meet their criteria.

Another area not discussed is the implementation of true broadband because true broadband implementation is still far from a reality. Full implementation is expected to take more than 25 years and over a trillion dollar investment, provided a commitment is made and the implementation done right the first time.

25.6   Final Thoughts

Over the past few years, interest in broadband communications has grown drastically, especially with the growth and increased visibility of the Internet. It has become the "talk of the town," with many people involved in making its future a reality. Numerous issues still linger and this is to be expected. Every effort is being made to provide an understanding of the basic technology behind a broadband communications world. In my opinion, broadband communications is a reality in the near future. It is only a matter of time before everything needed for broadband communications falls into place. As this book goes to press, several enhancements in these areas have probably been made, which is always a never-ending process as technology and market dynamics keep evolving.

APPENDIX A

Appendix A

TELECOMMUNICA-
TIONS OPERATING
COMPANIES

Company Name	Internet Address	Major Service Offering
ACC Corp.	*http://www.acccorp.com/*	Long distance, international, and local service telephony provider.
American Communications Services, Inc. (ACSI)	*http://www.acsi.net/*	Competitive local exchange carrier in a variety of U.S. cities.
AGT	*http://www.agt.net/agt1/agt.home.html*	Telecommunications company operating in Alberta, Canada.
AirTouch Communications	*http://www.airtouch.com/*	Wireless service provider.
ALESTRA	*http://www.aliant.com/*	Mexico.
Aliant Communications	*http://www.aliant.com/*	Independent telecommunications operating company based in Lincoln, Nebraska.
Aliatel	*http://www.aliatel.cz/*	Czech Republic.
Americatel Corp.	*http://www.americatel.net/*	International common carrier.
Americom Long Distance	*http://www.xmission.com/-americom*	Long-distance telephony service provider.
Ameritech	*http://www.ameritech.com/*	News, people, speeches, school, current commercials.
AT&T	*http://www.att.com/*	Prototype with history and 1993 annual report.
ATU Telecommunications	*http://www.atu.com/*	Alaska.
Avantel	*http://www.avantel.com.mx/*	Mexico.
BC Telecom	*http://www.bctel.com/*	Provider of voice, data, and enhanced telecommunications to British Columbia.
BelCom	*http://www.belcom.net/*	Russia and other republics of the former Soviet Union.
Belgacom	*http://www.belgacom.be/*	Belgium.
Bell Atlantic	*http://www.ba.com/*	Legislation, archives, history, executive profiles and speeches, media.
Bezeq	*http://bezeq.macom.co.il/*	Israel.

555

Company Name	Internet Address	Major Service Offering
Bell Canada	*http://www.bell.ca/*	Ontario and Quebec, English and French language.
BellSouth	*http://www.bellsouth.com/*	U.S. RBOC serving southeastern states.
British Telecom (BT)	*http://www.bt.com/*	Largest operator in United Kingdom.
Cable & Wireless	*http://www.mercury.co.uk/ othersit.html*	Competitive long-distance service provider in United Kingdom and internationally.
Cellnet	*http://cellnet.chc.co.uk/*	U.K. mobile network operator.
Cincinnati Bell	*http://www.cinbelltel.com/*	U.S. RBOC in Cincinnati.
Citizens Telephone Cooperative	*http://www.win.bright.net/ citizens/*	U.S. RBOC in the United States.
DDI	*http://www.ddi.co.jp/*	Japanese long-distance company.
D & E Communications, Inc.	*http://www.detele.com/*	LEC, long distance, wireless, voice and data equipment, internet.
Deutsche Telekom	*http://www.dtag.de/english/ index.htm*	Germany.
ED TEL	*http://www.edtel.com/*	Telco for City of Edmonton, Alberta, Canada.
Electric Lightwave, Inc.	*http://www.eli.net/*	Vancouver, Wash.-based full-service business telecommunications provider.
EnerTel	*http://www.enertel.nl/*	Telecommunications operator in the Netherlands.
Estonian Telecom	*http://telecom.ee/*	Estonia.
Excel Telecommunications Inc.	*http://www.exceltel.com/*	Dallas, Tex.
Finnet Group	*http://www.finnet.fi/*	Finland.
France Telecom	*http://www.francetelecom. fr/*	France.
Frontier Corporation	*http://www.frontiercorp. com/*	Formerly known as Rochester Telephone; provider of telecommunications services in the United States.

Company Name	Internet Address	Major Service Offering
General Communication Inc. (GCI)	http://www.gci.com/	Alaskan telecommunications provider.
GTE Corporation	http://www.gte.com/	Largest independent local operating company. Now provides local, long-distance and other telecommunications services.
Helsinki Telephone Company	http://www.hpy.fi/	Finnish telecommunications company.
Hong Kong Telecom	http://www.hkt.net/index.shtml	Hong Kong telecommunications service provider.
Island Tel	http://www.pei.sympatico.ca/island_tel/	Prince Edward Island, Canada.
ITC Long Distance	http://www.itctelecom.com/	Preferred provider of long distance for nonprofit trade associations.
KDD	http://www.kdd.co.jp/	Long-distance provider in Japan.
Korea Telecom	http://melon.kotel.co.kr/ktrl/koreatelecom.html	Korea.
LCI International	http://www.lci.com/	Long-distance service provider in the United States.
LDDS Worldcom	http://www.wcom.com/	Long-distance carrier.
LD Exchange.com	http://www.ldexchange.com/	Wholesaler of international long-distance rates to carriers worldwide.
McLeod USA	http://www.mcleod.net/	Local phone service, long distance, voice mail, paging, Internet access, and e-mail.
Maritime Telephone & Telegraph	http://www.mtt.ca/	Nova Scotia, Canada.
MATAV	http://www.matav.hu/index_e.html	Hungary.
MAXITEL GROUP	http://www.maxitel.pt/	Portuguese private telecommunications operating company.
MCI, Inc.	http://www.mci.com/	Second largest long-distance provider in the United States.

Company Name	Internet Address	Major Service Offering
Mercury Communications	*http://www.mercury.co.uk/*	Second largest long-distance provider in the United Kingdom.
MTS NETCOM	*http://www.mts.mb.ca/*	Manitoba Telephone System, Canada.
NBTel	*http://www.nbnet.nb.ca/*	New Brunswick, Canada; English and French language.
NewTel Communications	*http://enterprise.newcomm.net/ntc/*	Newfoundland, Canada.
Nippon Telephone and Telegraph (NTT), Japan	*http://www.ntt.co.jp/*	Includes R&D information.
NorthWestel Inc.	*http://www.yukonweb.wis.net/business/nwtel/*	Northern Canada.
NYNEX	*http://www.nynex.com/*	U.S. RBOC in the United States. Now merged with Bell Atlantic.
NYNEX CableComms	*http://www.nynex.co.uk/nynex/*	U.K. telephony and cable provider.
OTE	*http://www.gsc.net/business/ote/ts.htm*	Greece.
Pacific Bell		ISDN, CalREN, PB NAP, press releases, PacBell Gopher, mailing lists.
Pac-West Telecomm, Inc.	*http://www.pacwest.com/*	Full-service telephone company serving California with special services for ISPs.
PlusNet	*http://www.plusnet.ch/*	Germany.
Portugal Telecom	*http://www.telecom.pt/*	Portugal.
PTT Telecom	*http://www.ptt-telecom.nl/*	Dutch.
Quebec Telephone	*http://www.quebectel.qc.ca/qtel/qt0000ag.htm*	Canada.
Radiotel	*http://www.radiotel.ro/*	Romania.
Rogers Communications, Inc.	*http://www.rogers.com/*	Wireless, long-distance, cable systems, and multimedia in Canada.
RSL Communications, Ltd.	*http://www.rslcom.com/*	International long-distance telephone company.

Company Name	Internet Address	Major Service Offering
SaskTel	*http://www.sasktel.com/*	Saskatchewan, Canada.
SFR	*http://www.sfr.fr/*	Société Française du Radiotélé-phone, in French.
Singapore Telecom	*http://www.singtel.com/*	
Southern New England Telephone (SNET)	*http://www.snet.com/*	(SNET)
Southwestern Bell	*http://www.swbell.com/*	U.S. RBOC serving Texas, Kansas, Arkansas, Oklahoma, and Missouri.
Sovam Teleport	*http://www.sovam.com/*	Russia.
Sprint Communications Company	*http://www.sprint.com/*	
Sprint/United Telephone—Florida	*http://www.utelfla.com/*	
SPT Telecom	*http://www.spt.cz/html/indexa.htm*	Czech Republic.
Stentor	*http://www.stentor.ca/*	Alliance of Canadian operating companies.
Swiss PTT	*http://www.vptt.ch/*	
Tampere Telephone	*http://www.tpo.fi/*	Finland.
Tele2	*http://www.tele2.se/*	Sweden.
Telebec	*http://www.telebec.qc.ca/*	Quebec, Canada.
Teleboss (Pty Ltd.)	*http://www.teleboss.co.za/*	Telephony solution provider in South Africa.
Tele Danmark	*http://www.teledanmark.dk/*	Danish and English.
Telecom Argentina	*http://www.telecom.com.ar/*	Argentina.
Telecom Eireann	*http://www.telecom.ie/*	
Telecom Eireann (Ireland)	*http://www.broadcom.ie/telecom/dupjmc/teprofile.html*	Ireland.
Telecom Finland	*http://www.tele.fi/*	Finland.
Telecom Italia	*http://www.telecomitalia.interbusiness.it/*	Italy.

Company Name	Internet Address	Major Service Offering
Telecom Malaysia	http://www.telekom.com.my/	Malaysia.
Telecom New Zealand	http://www.telecom.co.nz/index.html	New Zealand.
Telecom Poland	http://www.tpsa.pl/	Poland.
Telecom Portugal	http://www.telecom.pt/uk_pages/uk_index_pt.htm	Portugal.
Telecom UK	http://telecom.co.uk/	U.K. telecommunications and phone card company.
Telefonica de Argentina	http://www.telefonica.com.ar/	Argentina.
Telefonica de Espana	http://www.telefonica.es/	Spanish PTT.
Telefonica del Peru	http://www.telefonica.com.pe/	Peru.
Teleglobe Canada (English language)	http://www.teleglobe.ca/	International telecommunications carrier.
Telenor	http://www.telenor.no/	Local, long-distance, satellite, and cellular provider in Norway. Norwegian only.
Telenordia	http://www.telenordia.se/	Sweden.
Teleport Communications Group	http://www.tcg.com/	Competitive local exchange carrier.
Telepost (Norway)	http://web.telepost.no/	Norwegian only.
Telesat Canada	http://www.telesat.ca/	
Televerket Research Institute (Norway)	http://www.nta.no/xtf/xtf.html	Norwegian only.
Telfort	http://www.telfort.com/	Dutch long-distance operator.
Telia	http://www.telia.se/	Swedish "national" telephony company.
Telkom Indonesia	http://www.telkom.co.id/	Indonesia telecommunications company.
Telkom SA	http://www.telkom.co.za/	South Africa.

| TELMEX | *http://www.telmex.com.mx/* | Mexico. |

Company Name	Internet Address	Major Service Offering
Telstra Corporation Ltd.	*http://www.telstra.com.au/*	Australia.
Turku Telephone	*http://www.ttl.fi/*	Finland.
US WEST	*http://www.uswest.com/*	U.S. RBOC serving midwestern states.

APPENDIX B

Appendix B

REGULATORS

Regulator Name	Area Served	Internet Address
Australian Telecommunications Authority	Australian telecommunications regulator	*http://www.austel.gov.au/*
BAKOM - OFCOM	Swiss telecoms regulator	*http://www.admin.ch/eved/m/bakom/main.html*
(BAPT)	Bundesamt für Post und Telekommunikation	*http://www.bapt.de/English/default.htm*
Bundesministerium für öffentliche Wirtschaft und Verkehr	Austrian Ministry of public works and communications.	*http://iis.joanneum.ac.at/BMWV/Telekom/*
Bundesministerium für Post und Telekommunikation	German regulator for telecommunications.	*http://www.government.de/inland/ministerien/post.html*
Canadian Radio-television and Telecommunications Commission (CRTC)	Canadian regulatory body for telecommunications	*http://www.crtc.gc.ca/*
Deparpostel	Department of Tourism, Post, and Telecommunications in Indonesia.	*http://www.telkom.go.id/postel.htm*
Department of Trade and Industry	U.K. regulatory responsibility in conjunction with OFTEL.	*http://www.dti.gov.uk/*
Federal Communications Commission	U.S. telecommunications regulatory commission.	*http://www.fcc.gov/*
Hoofddirectie Telecommunicatie en Post	Dutch telecommunications and post regulator.	*http://www.minvenw.nl/hdtp/home.html*
Industry Canada— Telecommunications/ Spectrum Management	Canada	*http://info.ic.gc.ca/ic-data/telecom/telecom-e.html*
Ministère francais poste, telecommunication, espace	French telecommunications regulator.	*http://www.telecom.gouv.fr/*
Ministry of Information and Communication	Republic of Korea.	*http://www.mic.go.kr/*
Ministry of Posts and Telecommunications	Japan.	*http://www.mpt.go.jp/*

Regulator Name	Internet Address	Area Served
ISPO	The Information Society Project Office of the European Commission	*http://www.ispo.cec.be/*
I'M Europe	General information from EC Telecommunications and Information Industries DGXIII.	
New Zealand Ministry of Commerce	Includes information on communications policy, spectrum management, and IT usage statistics.	*http://www.echo.lu/*
Office of the telecommunications authority (OFTA)	Hong Kong regulator	*http://www.ofta.gov.hk/*
OFTEL	U.K. telecommunications regulator.	*http://www.oftel.gov.uk/*
Post & Telestyrelsen	Swedish telecommunications regulator.	*http://www.pts.se/*
Secretaria de Communicaciones y Transportes	Mexico's telecommunications regulator.	*http://www.sct.gob.mx/*
Telehallintokeskus-Telecommunications Administration Centre	Finnish regulatory agency under the Ministry of Transport and Communications.	*http://www.thk.fi/*
Telestyrelsen-National Telecom Agency Denmark	Denmark	*http://www.tst.dk/*
WTO Protocol on World Trade in Telecoms	New Zealand government summary of WTO agreed protocol on world trade in telecommunications.	*http://www.mft.govt.nz/Business/File/vol3no1.htm*

APPENDIX C

TELECOMMUNICATIONS
JOURNALS
AND MAGAZINES

Access (monthly)
Telecommunications Research
P.O. Box 12038
Washington, DC 20005

ACM—Transactions on
  Information Systems (quarterly)
Association for Computing
  Machinery
11 West 42d St.
New York, NY 10036

Advances in Telematics (irregular)
Ablex Publishing
355 Chestnut St.
Norwood, NJ 07648

*AES—Journal of the Audio
  Engineering Society* (monthly)
AES
60 East 42d St.
New York, NY 101165-0075

At the LATA Level (weekly)
CCMI/McGraw Hill
50 S. Franklin Tpk.
Ramsey, NJ 07446

AT&T Technical Journal
  (bimonthly)
AT&T
550 Madison Ave.
New York, NY 10022

AT&T Technology (quarterly)
Richard A. O'Donnell
550 Madison Ave.
New York, NY 10022

British Telecom Journal (quarterly)
British Telecom
81 Newgate St. Fl.
A2 London EC1A 7AJ
England

Budavox Telecommunications Review
  (quarterly)
Telecommunication Foreign
  Trading Co. Ltd.
Budafoki tu 79, H-1392
Budapest X1, Hungary

*Bulletin Signaletique des
  Telecommunications* (monthly)
Centre National d'Etudes des Tell
Service of Documentation
Interministerielle
38-40 Rue de General LeClerk
92131 Issy-Les-Moulineaux
France

Business Communications Review
  (monthly)
BCR Enterprises, Inc.
950 York Rd.
Hinsdale, IL 60521

COMSAT Technical Review
(semiannually)
COMSAT Corp.
22300 COMSAT Dr.
Clarksburg, MD 20871

Cable TV Law and Finance
(monthly)
New York Publishing Co.
111 Eighth Ave.
New York, NY 10011

Canadian Communications
(semimonthly)
MACLEAN-Hunter Ltd.
Business Publication Div.
MACLEAN-Hunter Bldg.
777 Bay St.
M5W 1A7 Toronto,
Ontario
Canada

Communication (weekly)
NTIS
5285 Port Royal Rd.
Springfield, VA 22161

Communications Consultant
(monthly)
Jobson Publishing Corp.
352 Park Ave. S., 16th floor
New York, NY 10010

Communications News
(monthly)
Edgell Communications
7500 Old Oak Blvd.
Cleveland, OH 44130

Communications Week (weekly)
CMP Publications
600 Community Dr.
Manhasset, NY 11030

*Congressional Report on
Communications* (semimonthly)
New Media Publishing
1117 N. 19th, #200
Arlington, VA 22209

Data Communications (monthly)
McGraw-Hill
1221 Ave. of the Americas
New York, NY 10020

Data Communications Management
(bimonthly)
Auerbach Publishers
1 Penn Plaza
New York, NY 10119

Datamation (monthly)
Reed Publishing Co.
44 Cook St.
Denver, CO 80206

*Datapro Reports on
Telecommunications* (monthly)
Datapro Research Corp.
600 Delran Pkwy.
Delran, NJ 08075

European Telecommunications
(semimonthly)
Probe Research Inc.
3 Wing, #240
Cedar Knolls, NJ 07927

FCC Rulemaking Reports (biweekly)
Commerce Clearing House
4025 W. Peterson Ave.
Chicago, IL 60601

FCC Week (weekly)
Capital Publications
1101 King St., #444
Alexandria, VA 22314

Fiber Optic Sensor (monthly)
Information Gatekeepers Inc.
214 Harvard Ave.
Boston, MA 02134

Fiber Optics (monthly)
Taylor and Francis
3 East 44th St.
New York, NY 10017

Fiber Optics and Communication News (weekly)
Information Gatekeepers Inc.
214 Harvard Ave.
Boston, MA 02134

Fiber Optics News (weekly)
Phillips Publishing Inc.
RD #2, Box 486, Saw Mill Rd.
Red Hook, NY 12571

Fiber to Home (biweekly)
Information Gatekeepers Inc.
214 Harvard Ave.
Boston, MA 02134

Fiber and Integrated Optics (quarterly)
Taylor and Francis, Inc.
79 Madison Ave. #1110
New York, NY 10016

Focus on Communications (monthly)
Business Communications
3190 Miraloma Ave.
Anaheim, CA 92806

Global Communications (monthly)
Cardiff Publishing Co.
6300 South Syracuse Way
Englewood, CO 80111

Globe Communications IEEE (annually)
IEEE
345 East 47th St.
New York, NY 10017

GTE Telenet Packet (monthly)
GTE Telenet Communication Corp.
12490 Sunrise Valley
Reston, VA 22096

IEEE Communications Magazine (monthly)
Institute of Electrical and Electronics Engineers
345 E. 47th St.
New York, NY 10017

IEEE Journal on Selected Areas in Communications (bimonthly)
Institute of Electrical and Electronics Engineers
345 E. 47th St.
New York, NY 10017

IEEE Network (bimonthly)
Institute of Electrical and Electronics Engineers
345 E. 47th St.
New York, NY 10017

IEEE Spectrum (monthly)
Institute of Electrical and Electronics Engineers
345 E. 47th St.
New York, NY 10017

IEEE Transactions on Communications (monthly)
Institute of Electrical and Electronics Engineers
345 E. 47th St.
New York, NY 10017

*International Telecommunications
  Union Operational Bulletin*
  (monthly)
International
  Telecommunications Union
Place de Nation, CH1211
Geneva 20, Switzerland

ISDN Report (semimonthly)
Probe Research Inc.
3 Wing Dr. #240
Cedar Knolls, NJ 07927

ISDN User (bimonthly)
Information Gatekeepers Inc.
214 Harvard Ave.
Boston, MA 02134

Japan Telecommunication Review
  (quarterly)
Telecommunications Association
Tokyo, Japan

Japan Telecommunications
  (monthly)
Ciber Inc.
International Trade Commission
  Bldg.
500 E St., SW
Washington, DC 20024

Journal of Optical Communications
  (quarterly)
Fachverlac Schiele und Schoen
GMBH
Markgrafenstrasse 11PF
610280, D-1000
Berlin 61, Germany

*Liberia Ministry of Posts and
  Telecommunications Annual Report*
  (annually)
Ministry of Posts and
  Telecommunications
Monrovia, Liberia

Lightwave (monthly)
Penn Well Publishing Co.
P.O. Box 987
1 Technology Park Dr.
Westford, MA 01886

List of International Telephone Routes
  (annually)
International
  Telecommunications Union
Place de Nation, CH1211
Geneva 20, Switzerland

Long Distance Letter (monthly)
Phillips Publishing Inc.
7811 Montrose Rd.
Potomac, MD 20854

*Military Fiber Optics
  Communications* (biweekly)
Information Gatekeepers Inc.
214 Harvard Ave.
Boston, MA 02134

Mobile Communications Business
  (monthly)
Phillips Publishing Inc.
7811 Montrose Rd.
Potomac, MD 20854

Mobile Phone News (biweekly)
Phillips Publishing Inc.
7811 Montrose Rd.
Potomac, MD 20854

Network World (weekly)
IDG Communications
161 Worcester Rd.
Framingham, MA 01701

Networking Management
  (monthly)
Penn Well Publishing Co.
P.O. Box 987
1 Technology Park Dr.
Westford, MA 01886

NTT Topics (quarterly)
Ruder, Finn, and Rotman
110 E. 59th St.
New York, NY 10022

Pay Phone News (monthly)
Telestrategies Publishing
1355 Beverly Dr., Box 1218
McLean, VA 22101

Perspective on AT&T and BCR
Products and Marketing
(monthly)
BCR Enterprises, Inc.
950 York Rd.
Hinsdale, IL 60521

Planning Guide 1 Inter-LATA
Telecommunications Rates and
Services (monthly)
McGraw-Hill
50 S. Franklin Tpk.
Ramsey, NJ 07446

Planning Guide 2 Inter-LATA
Telecommunications Rates and
Services (monthly)
McGraw-Hill
50 S. Franklin Tpk.
Ramsey, NJ 07446

Planning Guide 3 Value Added
Networks and Data Private
Line Telecommunications
Rates and Services
(monthly)
McGraw-Hill
50 S. Franklin Tpk.
Ramsey, NJ 07446

Postel (monthly)
National Press for the
Department of P&T
Pretoria, South Africa

Regulation News (monthly)
Interconnections Pub. Inc.
P.O. Box 128
Rhinebeck, NY 12572

Revue Francais des
Telecommunications
(quarterly)
Ministere des PTT
Paris, France

Saskatchewan Telecommunications
Annual Report (annually)
Saskatchewan
Telecommunications
Saskatchewan, Canada

Sasktel News (monthly)
Saskatchewan
Telecommunications
Saskatchewan, Canada

Soviet Journal of Communications
Technology and Electronics
(16 per year)
John Wiley/Scripta
Technica
7961 Eastern Ave.
Silver Spring, MD 20910

Swedish Telecom Annual Report
(annually)
Televerket
Farsta, Sweden

Telecom (English Edition)
(semiannually)
Televerket
Farsta, Sweden

Telecom Bulletin
(semiannually)
Fleural Management Co.
Ottawa, Ontario
Canada

Telecom Australia Annual Report
(annually)
Telecom Australia
Melbourne, Australia

Telecom Insider (monthly)
International Data Corp.
Framingham, MA 01701

Telecom Today (monthly)
British Telecommunications
London, England

Telecommunication Journal
(monthly)
International
Telecommunications Union
Place de Nation, CH1211
Geneva 20, Switzerland

Telecommunications
(monthly)
Horizon House—
Microwave Inc.
685 Canton St.
Norwood, MA 02062

Telecommunications Abstracts
(10 per year)
R.R. Bowker, EIC
New York, NY

Telecommunications Alert
(monthly)
Management
Telecommunications Pub
New York, NY

*Telecommunications Authority of
Singapore Telecoms Annual Report*
(annually)
Telecommunications Authority
of Singapore
Singapore

*Telecommunications Journal of
Australia* (3 per year)
Telecommunications Society of
Australia
Melbourne, Australia

Telecommunications (Norwood)
(monthly)
Horizon House
Norwood, MA 01105

Telecommunications (Potomac)
(quarterly)
Phillips Publishing Inc.
7811 Montrose Rd.
Potomac, MD 20854

Telecommunications Policy
(quarterly)
Butterworth Science
Guildford, England

*Telecommunications Product
plus Technology*
(monthly)
Penn Well Publishing Co.
P.O. Box 987 1 Technology Park
Dr.
Westford, MA 01886

Telecommunications Product Review
(monthly)
Marketing Programs and Services
Group
1350 Piccard Dr.
Rockville, MD 20850

Telecommunications Reports
(weekly)
Telecommunications
Reports
1036 National Press Bldg.
Washington, DC 20045

*Telecommunications Technology
Dianxin Jishu* (monthly)
Guoji Shudian
Beijing, China

Telecommunications Sourcebook
(annually)
North American
Telecommunications
Association
1036 National Press Bldg.
Washington, DC 20045

Telecommunications Swedish Edition
(quarterly)
Televerket
Farsta, Sweden

*Telecommunications Systems and
Services Directory* (irregular)
Gale Research Inc.
835 Penobscott Bldg.
Detroit, MI 48226

Telecommunications Week (weekly)
Telecommunications Reports
1036 National Press Bldg.
Washington, DC 20045

Telecommunicazioni (quarterly)
Societa Italiana
Telecommunicazioni
Milan, Italy

Telecoms International (monthly)
Computer World
Communications
Neuilly Sur Seine cedex
France

Telecoms Technical Quarterly
(quarterly)
Directorate General of
Telecommunications
Taiwan, Republic of China

Teleconnect (monthly)
Telecom Library Inc.
12 West 21st St.
New York, NY 10010

Telektronikk
(quarterly)
Elektrotechniek
Teledirektoratet
Oslo, Norway

Telematica (5 per year)
Etas Kompass S.P.A
Milan, Italy

Telematics and Informatics
(6 per year)
Pergamon Press Inc.
Journal Division
Maxwell House
Fairview Park
Elmsford, NY 10523

Telephony (weekly)
Intertec Publishing Co.
55 East Jackson Blvd.
Chicago, IL 60604

U.S. Telecom Digest
(23 per year)
Capitol Publishers, Inc.
1101 King St. #444
Alexandria, VA 22314

Journals and Other Electronic Media

ATM Component Review. A quarterly publication which contains detailed technical information on components available for use in ATM products.

Bellcore's DIGEST of Technical Information.

Business Communications Review (http://www.bcr.com/).Cable World (http://www.mediacentral.com/index/CableWorld).

Communications Standards Review (http://www.csrstds.com/). Publishes journals reporting on formal telecommunications standards in the ITU, ETSI, and TIA.

Communications Standards Review. ITU, TIA wireline, wireless, and fiber-optic work-in-progress.

Communications Week Interactive (http://www.emap.com/cwi/).

Communications Week Interactive. The page for corporate network managers.

Computer Telephony. The magazine for computer and telephone integration.

d.Comm (http://www.d-comm.com/). Daily news and features for information and communications workers, published by *The Economist*.

Data Communications Magazine (http://www.data.com/).

Dataquest. Covers developments in infotech industry, trade, company information of relevance to the Indian and Asia/Pacific infotech industry.

DBS Online.

ICB Toll Free News (http://www.icbtollfree.com/). Regulatory and telecommunications industry reporting.

IEEE Communications Magazine.

IEEE Internet Computing. Bimonthly magazine covering internet-based computer applications and technologies.

Indepth Magazine (http://www.eclipse.net/~indepth/index.html). Coverage of the global telecommunications market.

Indian Techonomist. Newsletter on India's information industry: computers, communications, and broadcasting.

Interactive Age (*http://www.wais.com/techweb/ia/current/off-the-pages.html*).

Internet Australasia.

Internet Telephony. Online home of *Telephony* magazine.

Network World Magazine.

NII Scan. Journal from Singapore devoted to "Tracking NII Policies Worldwide."

NSF Network News. Official newsletter on the evolution of the NSFNET and the Internet.

Satellite Journal International.

Technology In Government. Information systems and telecommunications.

Technology Online. Technology CyberMagazine.

Technology Review. MIT's magazine.

Tech Web. Entry point to all CMP publications (e.g., *Communications Week,* and *Information Week.*

tele.com. Focuses and analyzes the new common business and technology issues.

tele.com (*http://www.teledotcom.com/*). Publication for telecommunications service providers.

Telecom A.M. Daily telecommunications information resource covering all aspects of the telecommunications industry: mobile data, local competition, regulation, online activities, and interactive markets.

Telecom Digest (*WWW interface*). One of the oldest mailing lists covering telecommunications topics. Also appears as newsgroup comp.dcom. telecom.

Telecom Information Clearinghouse.

Telecom Market Monitor. Daily telecommunications newsletter featuring market column and company news.

Telecom Publishing Group (*http://www.cappubs.com/tpg*). Produces a range of titles in telecommunications.

Telecom Regulation (*WWW interface*). Mailing list on regulation of telecommunications (includes searchable archives).

Telecom Reseller Opportunities Magazine. Information for companies that buy, sell, resell, and bundle telecommunications products and services.

Telecom Tribune. English language publication dealing with Japan's telecommunications industry.

Telecom Tribune (http://teltrib.techjapan.co.jp/yearmap.html). News, information, and statistics on Japanese telecommunications.

Telecom Update. Weekly summary of telecommunications news with the focus on Canada.

TELECOM-CITIES Discussion List. Practical and theoretical aspects of the changes advanced telecommunications and telematics are rendering on our urban centers.

TelecomEuropa (http://www.telecoms.com/text/te-pubs.htm). Produces newsletters for the telecommunications industry.

Telecommunications Magazine.

TELECOMMUNICATIONS Magazine (http://www.telecoms-mag.com/tcs.html).

Telecommunications Policy. Journal on economics, politics, regulation of telecommunications, and information systems.

Telecommunications Reports International, Inc. (TRI) (http://www.tr.com/). News and information services for the communications, multimedia, and electric utility industries.

Tele-Consumer Hotline. Information to help consumers better understand the broad new array of communications products and services.

TeleGeography Home Page (http://www.telegeography.com/).

Telektronikk magazine (Norway).

Telemanagement. Monthly review of telecommunications management issues in Canada.

Telephony (http://www.internettelephony.com/).

TELE-Satellit News. Continuous newsfeed.

Televak Uitgeverij. Trade magazine for cable, telecommunications, and media.

The Technology Reporter. Resource for those interested in computers, technology, the Internet, and telecommunications.

The Telecom Virtual Storefront. Computer telephony, voice and fax processing, internet telephony, and speech recognition.

Total Telecom (http://www.totaltele.com/). Daily news and information service for telecommunications professionals. *Total Telecom.* News and information about the global telecommunications business.

Voice & Data (http://www.voicendata.com/). Indian communications magazine.

Washington Telecom Newswire (http://wtn.com/wtn/wtn.html).

World Telephone Numbering Guide Links and news regarding telephone numbering in various countries and regions.

World Wide Web Journal.

World Wide Web, WWW. An international, archival, peer-reviewed journal which covers all aspects of the world wide web.

ZD Internet Life. Web-based magazine from Ziff-Davis Publishing.

ZD Internet Magazine MegaSite. Internet and Intranet computing.

Ziff-Davis Interactive. Gateway to all Ziff-Davis online publications, including *PC Magazine, PC Week,* and *Inter@ctive Week.*

Znews.com. E-zine covering the latest net and tech issues.

BIBLIOGRAPHY

Aceveres, J. J.: "A New Minimum Hop Routing Algorithm," INFOCOM '87, 1987.

Ahmadi, H., and W. E. Denzel: "A Survey of Modern High-Performance Switching Techniques," *IEEE Journal on Selected Areas of Communication,* vol. 7, no. 87, September 1989.

Ahmadi, H., R. Guerin, and K. Sohraby: "Analysis of Leaky Bucket Access Control Mechanism with Batch Arrival Process," GLOBECOM, 1990.

Akhtar, S.: "Congestion Control in a Fast Packet Switching Network," master's thesis, Washington University, St. Louis, Missouri, December 1987.

Akinpelu, J. M.: "The Overload Performance of Engineered Networks with Nonhierarchal and Hierarchal Routing," *BSTJ**, vol. 63, no. 71, 1984.

Albanese, A., H. E. Bussey, S. B. Weinstein, and R. S. Wolf: "A Multi-Network Research Testbed for Multimedia Communication Services," *ICC '91,* 1991. IEEE, Denver, Colo.

Anagnostou, M. E., et al.: "Quality of Service Requirements in ATM Based B-ISDNs," *Computer Communications,* vol. 14, no. 4, 1991.

Andrade, J., W. Burakowski, and M. Villen-Altamirano: "Characterization of Cell Traffic Generated by an ATM Source," ITC-13[†], 1991.

Ang, P. H., P. A. Ruetz, and D. Auld: "Video Compression Makes Big Gains," *IEEE Spectrum,* October 1991.

ANSI[‡]: ANSI T1.105-1988, "American National Standard for Telecommunications—Digital Hierarchy—Optical Interface Rates and Formats Specifications," 1988.

ANSI: ANSI T1.105-1991, "Digital Hierarchy—Optical Interface Rates and Formats Specifications (SONET)," 1991.

ANSI: ANSI T1.105a-1991, "Supplement to T1.105," 1991.

---

*BSTJ = *Bell South Technical Journal.*
[†]ITC = International Telecommunications Conference.
[‡]ANSI is in New York, New York.

577

ANSI: ANSI T1.106-1988, "American National Standard for Telecommunications—Digital Hierarchy—Optical Interface Specifications (Single Mode)," 1988.

ANSI: ANSI T1.117, "Digital Hierarchy—Optical Interface Specifications (SONET)."

ANSI: ANSI T1.606 add, "Addendum to T1.606," (T1X1/90-175), 1990.

ANSI: ANSI T1.606-1990, "Telecommunication—Frame Relay Bearer Service—Architectural Framework and Service Description," 1990.

ANSI: ANSI T1.6ca, "Core Aspects of Frame Protocol for Use With Frame Relay Bearer Service," (T1S1/ 90-214), 1990.

ANSI: ANSI X3.139 (Draft), "Fiber Distributed Data Interface (FDDI)—Media Access Control (MAC-2)," Draft Maintenance Revision 4.0, October 1990.

ANSI: ANSI X3.139-1987, "Fiber Distributed Data Interface (FDDI)—Token Ring Media Access Control (MAC)," 1987.

ANSI: ANSI X3.148 (Draft): "Fiber Distributed Data Interface (FDDI)—Physical Layer Protocol (PHY-2)," Draft Maintenance Revision 4.0, October 1990.

ANSI: ANSI X3.148-1988, "Fiber Distributed Data Interface (FDDI)—Token Ring Physical Layer Protocol (PHY)," 1988.

ANSI: ANSI X3.166-1990, "Fiber Distributed Data Interface (FDDI)—Physical Layer Medium Dependent (PMD)," 1990.

ANSI: ANSI X3.184-199X (Draft): "Fiber Distributed Data Interface (FDDI)—Single Mode Fiber Physical Layer Medium Dependent (SMF-PMD)," Rev. 4.2, May 1990.

ANSI: ANSI X3.186-199X (Draft), "Fiber Distributed Data Interface (FDDI)—Hybrid Ring Control (HRC)," Rev. 6.2, May 1991.

ANSI: ANSI X3T9.5/84-49, "Fiber Distributed Data Interface (FDDI)—Station Management (SMT)," Rev. 6.2, May 1990.

Ash, G. R., A. H. Kafker, and K. R. Khrishnan: "Servicing and Real Time Control of Networks with Dynamic Routing," *BSTJ,* vol. 60, no. 8, 1981.

Ash, G. R., R. H. Cardwell, and R. P. Murray: "Design and Optimization of Networks with Dynamic Routing," *BSTJ,* vol. 60, no. 8, 1981.

ATM Forum: "Network Compatible ATM for Local Network Applications," phase 1, version 1.0, 1992.

ATM Forum: "ATM UNI specification," version 3.1, June 1995, ATM Forum Technical Committee.

Banwell, T. C., et al.: "Physical Design Issues for Very Large ATM Switching Systems," *IEEE Journal on Selected Areas of Communication,* vol. 9, no. 8, 1991.

Bar-Noy, A., and M. Gopal: "Topology Distribution Cost vs. Efficient Routing in Large Networks," Proceedings of SIGCOMM '90, 1990, IEEE.

Bell, T., and K. Pawlikowski: "The Effect of Data Compression on Packet Sizes in Data Communication Systems," ITC-13, 1991.

Bellcore: Bellcore Framework Advisory, FA-TSV-001109, "BISDN Transport Network Framework Generic Criteria."

Bellcore: Bellcore Technical Advisory, TA-TSV-001059, "Generic Requirements for SMDS Networking," issue 2, August 1992.

Bellcore: Bellcore Technical Advisory, TA-TSV-001061, "Operations Technology Network Element Generic Requirements in Support of Interswitch and Exchange Access SMDS," May 1991.

Bellcore: Bellcore Technical Advisory, TA-TSV-001210, "Generic Requirements for High-Bit-Rate Digital Subscriber Lines," 1989.

Bellcore: Bellcore Technical Advisory, TA-TSV-001235, "SMDS Generic Criteria on Operations Interface—Information Model Supporting Intercarrier SMDS," issue 1, April 1993.

Bellcore: Bellcore Technical Advisory, TA-TSV-001237, "SMDS Generic Requirements for Initial Operations Management Capabilities in Support of Exchange Access and Intercompany Serving Arrangements," issue 1, June 1993.

Bellcore: Bellcore Technical Advisory, TA-TSV-001238, "SMDS Generic Requirements for SMDS on the 155.52 Mbps Multi-Services Broadband ISDN Intercarrier Interface (B-ICI)," issue 1, December 1992.

Bellcore: Bellcore Technical Advisory, TA-TSV-001239, "Generic Requirements for Low Speed SMDS Access," issue 1, June 1993.

Bellcore: Bellcore Technical Advisory, TA-TSV-001240, "Generic Requirements for Frame Relay Access to SMD," issue 4, June 1993.

Bellcore: Bellcore Technical Reference, TR-TSV-000772, "Generic System Requirement in Support of SMDS," issue 1, May 1991.

Bellcore: Bellcore Technical Reference, TR-TSV-000773, "Local Access System Generic Requirements, Objectives, and Interfaces in Support of Switched Multimegabit Data Service," issue 1, June 1991; rev., January 1993.

Bellcore: Bellcore Technical Reference, TR-TSV-000774, "SMDS Operations Technology Network Element Generic Requirement," issue 1, March 1992; supp. 1, March 1993.

Bellcore: Bellcore Technical Reference, TR-TSV-000775, "Usage Measurement Generic Requirement in Support of Billing for Switched Multimegabit Data Service," issue 1, June 1991.

Bellcore: Bellcore Technical Reference, TR-TSV-001060, "Switched Multimegabit Data Services Generic Requirements for Exchange Access and Intercompany Serving Arrangements (SMDS)," issue 1, December 1991; rev. 1, August 1992; rev. 2, March 1993.

Bellcore: Bellcore Technical Reference, TR-TSV-001062, "Generic Requirements for Phase 1 SMDS Customer Network Management Service," issue 1, March 1993.

Bellcore: Bellcore Technical Reference, TR-TSV-001063, "Operations Technology Generic Criteria in Support of Exchange Access SMDS and Intercompany Serving Arrangements," issue 1, December 1992; Rev. 1, March 1993.

Bellcore: Bellcore Technical Reference, TR-TSV-001064, "SMDS Generic Criteria on Operations Interfaces—SMDS Information Model and Usage," issue 1, December 1992.

Bellcore: Bellcore TR-NWT-000909, "Generic Requirements and Objectives for Fiber-in-the-Loop Systems," 1991.

Bellcore: Bellcore TR-NWT-001209, "Generic Requirements for Fiber Optic Branching Components," 1991.

Bellcore: Bellcore SR-NWT-001756, "Automatic Protection Switching for SONET," issue 1, 1990. Bellcore: Bellcore SR-NWT-002076 "Report on the Broadband ISDN Protocols for Providing SMDS and Exchange Access SMDS," issue 1, September 1991.

Bellcore: Bellcore SR-NWT-002224, "SONET Synchronization Planning Guidelines," issue 1, 1992.

Bellcore: Bellcore SR-TSV-002198 "Support of Intercarrier Aspects of SMDS in a BCC Multiswitch Network," issue 1, March 1992.

Bellcore: Bellcore SR-TSV-002395, "Switched Multimegabit Data Service First Phase for Exchange Access SMDS and Intercompany Serving Arrangements," issue 1, July 1991.

Bellcore: Bellcore SR-TSV-002422, "Phasing of Service Capabilities and Information for SMDS Customer Network Management Service," issue 1, September 1992.

Bellcore: Bellcore TA-NWT-001042, "Generic Requirements for Operations Interfaces Using OSI Tools: SONET Path Switched Ring Information Model," issues 1 and 3, 1992.

Bellcore: Bellcore TA-NWT-001250, "Generic Requirements for Synchronous Optical Network (SONET) File Transfer," issue 2, 1992.

Bellcore: Bellcore TR-NWT-000253, "Synchronous Optical Network (SONET) Transport Systems: Common Generic," issue 2, 1991.

Bellcore: Bellcore TR-NWT-001230, "SONET Bidirectional Line Switched Ring Equipment Generic Criteria," issue 2, 1992.

Bellcore: Bellcore TR-TSP-000496, "SONET Add/Drop Multiplex Equipment (SONET ADM) Generic Criteria," issue 3, 1992.

Bellcore: Bellcore TR-TSY-00023, "Wideband and Broadband Digital Cross-Connect Generic Requirements and Objectives," issue 2, 1989.

Bellcore: Bellcore TR-TSY-000303, "Integrated Digital Loop Carrier System Generic Requirements, Objectives, and Interface," issue 1, rev. 3, 1990.

Bermejo, L., P. Parmentier, and G. H. Petit: "Service Characteristics and Traffic Models in a Broadband ISDN," *Electrical Communication,* vol. 64, no. 2/3, 1990.

Bertsekas, D., and R. Gallager: *Data Networks,* 2d ed., Prentice-Hall, Inc., Englewood Cliffs, N.J., 1991.

Biocca, A., G. Freeschi, et. al.: "Architectural Issues in the Interoperability between MANs and ATM Network," *Proceedings of XIII ISS,* Stockholm, Sweden, 1990.

Boiocchi, G., L. Fratta, et. al.: "ATM Connectionless Server: Performance Evaluation," *Proceedings Modeling and Performance Evaluation of ATM Technology,* Perros, Pujolle, and Takahashi (eds.), North Holland, 1993.

Bonomi, F., K. Fendick, and N. Giroux: "The Available Bit Rate Service," *The ATM Forum Newsletter,* October 1995 (*http://www.atmforum.com/atmforum/53bytes-1095-2.html*).

Borelli, V. R. and H. Gysel: "Fiber-Optic Super Trunking: A Comparison of Performance & Topologies Using Analog and/or Digital Technologies," NCTA (National Cable Television Association) Technical Papers, 1990.

Boyer, G., and W. Pugh: "Broadband Access: Comparing Alternatives," *IEEE Communications Magazine,* August 1995, pp. 34 ff.

Boyer, P. F.: "Congestion Control for the ATM," 7th International Teletraffic Congress Seminar, Morristown N.J., October 9—11, 1990.

Brightman, J.: "Hybrid Fiber/Coax: Front Runner in the Broadband Transmission Race," *Telephony,* November 28, 1994, pp. 43 ff.

Bubenik, R., and J. Tuner: "Performance of Broadcast Switch," *IEEE Transactions Communications,* vol. 37, no. 1, 1989.

Burgin, J.: "BISN Resource Management," North Holland, Netherlands, 1990.

Burgin, J., and D. Dorman: "Broadband ISDN Resource Management: The Role of Virtual Paths," *IEEE Communications Magazine*, September 1991.

Catlett, C. E.: "In Search of Gigabit Applications," *IEEE Communications Magazine*, vol. 30, no. 5, April 1992.

Catlin, B. J.: "Wireless Cable Television—Frequently Asked Questions (FAQ)," *Colorado State University Homepage*, April 1995 (*http://www.cs.colostate.edu/~catlin/wireless-cable.html*).

Chao, H. J.: "Design of Leaky Bucket Access Control Schemes in ATM Networks," ICC '91, 1991, pp. 180–187, IEEE, Denver, Colo.

Chemouil, P., M. Lebourges, and P. Gauthier: "Performance Evaluation of Adaptive Traffic Routing in a Metropolitan Network: A Case Study," GLOBECOM '89, 1989.

Chen, W-T., H-J. Liu, and Y-T. Tsay: "High-Throughput Cell Scheduling for Broadband Switching Systems," *IEEE Journal. Selected Areas in Communications*, vol. 9, no. 9, December 1991.

Chiddix, J. A.: "Fiber Backbone—Multichannel AM-Video Trunking," NCTA Technical Papers, 1989.

Cicora, W. S.: "Cables' Excellent Position in HDTV," ATC, 1990.

Cisneros, A., and C. A. Brackett: "A Large ATM Switch Based on Memory Switches and Optical Star Couplers," *IEEE Journal of Selected Areas in Communications*, vol. 9, no. 8, October 1991.

"Computer Based Training (CBT)," ATM Forum Technical Committee, 1995.

Cosmas, J. P., and A. Odinma-Okafor: "Characterization of Variable Rate Video Codecs in ATM to Geometrically Modulated Deterministic Process Model," ITC-13, 1991.

Cox, J. R., M. E. Gaddis, and J. S. Turner: "Project Zeus," *IEEE Network Magazine*, vol. 7, no. 2, March 1993.

Crocetti, P., L. Fratta, et. al.: "ATM Based SMDS for LANs/MANs Interconnection," *Proceedings of XIV ISS*, Yokohama, 1992.

D'Ambrosio, M., and R. Melen: "Performance Analysis of ATM Switching: A Review," *CSELT Tech. Rep.*, vol. 20, no. 3.

Darcie, T.: "Subcarrier Multiplexing for Lightwave Networks and Video Distribution Systems," *IEEE Journal on Selected Areas in Communications,*, vol. 8, no. 7, September 1990, pp. 1240—1248.

Data Communication Magazine, all 1993 issues.

Datapro's Broadband Networking, 1992.

Davie, B. S., J. M. Smith, and C. B. S. Traw: "Host Interfaces for ATM Networks," *High Performance Communications,* Kluwer Academic Publishers, The Netherlands.

DePrycker, M.: *Asynchronous Transfer Mode: Solution for Broadband ISDN* (2nd ed.), Ellis Horwood, Chichester, England, 1992.

DePrycker, M., and J. Bauwens: "A Switching Exchange for an Asynchronous Time Division Based Network," ICC '87, Seattle, Wash., 1987.

DEC: Northern Telecom, Stratacom, Cisco, "Frame Relay Specification with Extensions," revision 1.0, 1990.

Decina, M., P. Giacomazzi, and A. Pattavina: "Shuffle Interconnection Networks with Deflection Routing for ATM Switching: the Open-Loop Shuffleout," ITC-13, 1991.

"Digital MMDS Looks Good," *Video Information Provider Newsletter,* September 1995.

Dittmann, L., and S. B. Jacobsen: "Statical Multiplexing of Identical Bursty Sources in an ATM Network," GLOBECOM '88, 1988 p. 97, IEEE, Denver, Colo.

Dixit, S., and P. Skelly: "MPEG-2 over ATM for Video Dial Tone Networks: Issues and Strategies," *IEEE Network,* September/October 1995, pp. 30 ff.

Doshi, B. T., S. Dravida, P. K. Johri, and G. Ramamurthy: "Memory, Bandwidth, Processing and Fairness Considerations in Real Time Congestion Controls for Broadband Networks," ITC-13, 1991.

Doshi, B. T., and S. Dravida: "Congestion Controls for Bursty Data in High Speed Wide Area Networks: In Call Parameter Negotiations," ITC Seventh Specialist Seminar on Broadband Technology, 1990.

Dron, L. G., G. Ramamurthy, and B. Sengupta: "Delay Analysis of Continuous Bit-Rate Traffic over an ATM Network," *IEEE Journal on Selected Areas of Communication,* vol. 9, no. 3, April 1991.

Dziong, Z., et al.: "Bandwidth Management in ATM Networks," ITC-13, 1991.

Dziong, Z., K. Q. Liao, and L. Mason: "Flow Control Models for Multi-Service Networks with Delayed Call Set Up," INFOCOM '90, 1990.

Eckberg, A. E.: "Generalized Peakedness of Teletraffic Processes," ITC-10, 1983.

Eng, K., M. Hluchyj, and Y. Yeh: "Multicast and Broadcast Services in a Knockout Packet Switch," INFOCOM '88, 1A.4, 1988.

Fitzpatrick, G. J., et. al: "Analysis of Large Scale Three Stage Networks Serving Multirate Traffic," ITC '13, 1991.

Frederick, J.: "Future-Proofing with Hybrid Fiber/Coax," *CED: Communications Engineering & Design,* September 1995, pp. 52 ff.

Fujimoto, N., T. Ishihara, and K. Yamaguchi: "Broadband Subscriber Loop System Using Multi-Gigabit Intelligent Optical Shuttle Nodes," *Proceedings of GLOBECOM '87,* paper 37.3.1.

Fujiyama, Y., et. al: "ATM Switching System Evolution and Implementation for B-ISDN," ICC '90, 1990, IEEE, Atlanta, Georgia.

Galassi, G., G. Rigolio, and L. Verri: "Resource Management and Dimensioning in ATM Networks," *IEEE Network Magazine,* May 1990.

Gallassi, G., G. Rigolio, and L. Fratta: "ATM: Bandwidth Assignment and Bandwidth Enforcement Policies," GLOBECOM '89, 1989, IEEE, Dallas, Tex.

Gerla, M., J. A. S. Monteiro, and R. Pazos: "Topology Design and Bandwidth Allocation in ATM Nets," *IEEE Journal on Selected Areas of Communication,* vol. 7, no. 8, October 1989.

Ghanbari, M.: "Two-Layer Coding of Video Signals for VBR Networks," *IEEE Journal on Selected Areas of Communication,* vol. 7, no. 5, June 1989.

Giacopelli, J. N., J. J. Hickey, W. S. Marcus, W. D. Sincoskie, and M. Littlewood: "Sunshine : A High-Performance Self-Routing Broadband Packet Switch Architecture," *IEEE Journal of Selected Areas in Communications,* vol. 9, no. 8, October 1991.

Gopal, I. S., I. Cidon, and H. Meleis: "PARIS: An Approach to Integrated Private Networks," ICC '87, 1987.

Griffin, J. T.: "Cost and Performance Comparison of Fiber-Optic CATV Super Trunks Utilizing FM and Digital Techniques," Jerrold Applied Media Lab, *NCTA Technical Papers,* 1989.

Gruber, J. G.: "Delay Related Issues in Integrated Voice and Data Networks," *IEEE Journal on Selected Communication,* June 1981.

Gruber, J. G., and N. H. Le: "Performance Requirements for Integrated Voice and Data Networks," *IEEE Journal on Selected Areas of Communication,* December 1983.

Hajikano, K., et al.: "Asynchronous Transfer Mode Switching Architecture for Broadband ISDN-Multistage Self Routing Switching," ICC '88, 1988, IEEE, Philadelphia, Penn.

Handel, R., and M. N. Huber: *Integrated Broadband Networks; An Introduction to ATM-Based Networks,* Addison-Wesley, Reading, Mass, 1991.

Hart, G. and N. H. Piercy: "Rogers Fiber Architecture, Rogers Engineering," *NCTA Technical Papers, 1989.*

Heldman, R.: Global Telecommunications—Layered Networks Layered Services, McGraw-Hill, Inc., New York, N.Y., 1992.

Henrion, M., et al.: "Switching Network Architecture for ATM Based Broadband Communications," ISS '90, Stockholm, 1990.

Hirano, M., and N. Watanabi: "Characteristics of a Cell Multiplexer for Bursty ATM Traffic," ICC '89, 1989, IEEE, Boston, Mass.

"History of Wireless Cable," *Heartland Wireless Communications Inc. Homepage,* November 1995 (*http://www.onramp.net:80/heartland/histca/histca.htm*).

Hluchyj, M. G., et al.: "The Knockout Switch: a Simple Modular Architecture for High Performance Packet Switching," ISS '87, 1987.

Hodge, W. W.: *Interactive Television,* McGraw-Hill, Inc., New York, N.Y., 1994.

Huang, A., and S. Knauer: "Starlite, a Wideband Digital Switch," GLOBECOM '84, Atlanta, Ga., 1984, IEEE, Atlanta, Ga.

Hui, J. Y.: "Resource Allocation for Broadband Networks," *IEEE Journal on Selected Areas of Communication,* vol. 6, no. 9, December 1989.

Hui, J. Y.: *Switching and Traffic Theory for Integrated Broadband Networks,* Kluwer Academic Publishers, Norwell, Mass., 1990.

Hui, J., and E. Authurs: "A Broadband Packet Switch for Integrated Transport," *IEEE Journal on Selected Areas of Communication,* vol. 5, 1991.

"IBM Announces the World's First MPEG-2 Digital Video Single-Chip Encoder," *IBM Microelectronics Homepage,* March 28, 1995 (*http://www.chips.ibm.com/news/newsmpeg.html*).

IEEE Communication Magazine, all issues 1992 to April 1994.

IEEE: "Gigabit Network Testbeds," *IEEE Computer,* vol. 23, no. 9, IEEE, September 1990.

IEEE Network Magazine, all 1992, 1993 issues.

IEEE: "DQDB Subnetwork of a Metropolitan Area Network," IEEE Standard: P802.6, 1991.

"Industry Leaders Converge to Form ADSL Forum," *Datapro Communications Analyst,* February 15, 1995.

Irvin, D. R.: "Making Broadband-ISDN Successful," *IEEE Network Magazine,* vol. 7, no. 1, January 1993.

ISO*: ISO-IEC/JTC1/CD 10918 (JPEG), "Digital Compression and Coding of Continuous-Tone Still Images," 1991.

ISO: ISO-IEC/JTC1/CD 11172 (MPEG I), "Coding of Moving Pictures and Associated Audio for Digital Storage Media at up to about 1.5 Mbps," 1990.

ISO: ISO-IEC/JTC1/SC2/WG9N 36/CD 11154 , "Progressive Bi-Level Image Compression," revision 4.1, 1992.

ISO: ISO-IEC/JTC1/SC29/WG11 (MPEG II), "Coded Presentation of Picture and Audio Information," 1992.

ITU†: ITU-R Recommendation 601, "Encoding Parameters of Digital Television for Studios," 1982.

ITU: ITU-R Recommendation 656, "Interfaces for Digital Component Video Signals in 525-Line and 625-Line Television Systems," 1982.

ITU: ITU-R Recommendation 709, "Basic Parameter Values for the HDTV Standard for the Studio and for International Programme Exchange," 1990.

ITU: ITU-R Recommendation 710, "Subjective Assessment Methods for Image Quality in High Definition Television," 1990.

ITU: ITU-R Recommendation 714, "International Exchange of Programme Electronically Produced by means of High-Definition Television," 1990.

ITU: ITU-T Draft Recommendation I.374, "Network Capability for the Support of Multimedia Services," 1992.

ITU: ITU-T Recommendation G.650, "Definition and Text Methods for the Relevant Parameters of Single Mode Fibers," 1992.

ITU: ITU-T Recommendation G.651, "Characteristics of a 50/125-mm Multimode Graded Index Optical Fiber Cable," 1992 (rev).

ITU: ITU-T Recommendation G.652, "Characteristics of a Single-Mode Optical Fiber Cable," 1992 (rev).

ITU: ITU-T Recommendation G.653, "Characteristics of a Dispersion-Shifted Single-Mode Optical Fiber Cable," 1992 (rev).

ITU: ITU-T Recommendation G.654, "Characteristics of a 1550-nm Wavelength Loss-Minimized Single-Mode Optical Fiber Cable," 1992 (Rev).

---

*ISO is in Geneva, Switzerland.
†ITU is in Geneva, Switzerland.

ITU: ITU-T Recommendation G.703, "Physical/Electrical Characteristics of Hierarchical Digital Interfaces," 1991.

ITU: ITU-T Recommendation G.707, "Synchronous Digital Hierarchy Bit Rates," 1992 (rev).

ITU: ITU-T Recommendation G.708," Network Node Interface for the Synchronous Digital Hierarchy," 1992 (rev).

ITU: ITU-T Recommendation G.709, "Synchronous Multiplexing Structure," 1992 (rev).

ITU: ITU-T Recommendation G.744, "Synchronous Digital Hierarchy (SDH) Management Information Model," 1993.

ITU: ITU-T Recommendation G.781, "Multiplexing Equipment for the SDH," 1990.

ITU: ITU-T Recommendation G.782, "Types and General Characteristics of Synchronous Digital Hierarchy (SDH) Multiplexing Equipment," 1990.

ITU: ITU-T Recommendation G.783, "Characteristics of Synchronous Digital Hierarchy (SDH) Multiplexing Equipment Functional Blocks," 1990.

ITU: ITU-T Recommendation G.784, "Synchronous Digital Hierarchy (SDH) Management," 1990.

ITU: ITU-T Recommendation G.7xx, "ATM Cell Mapping into Plesiochronous Digital Hierarchy (PDH)," 1992.

ITU: ITU-T Recommendation G.803, "Architecture of Transport Networks Based on the SDH," 1992.

ITU: ITU-T Recommendation G.825, "The Control of Jitter and Wander within Digital Network, Which are Based on Synchronous Digital Hierarchy (SDH)," 1993.

ITU: ITU-T Recommendation G.831, "Performance and Management Capabilities of Transport Networks Based on the SDH," 1992.

ITU: ITU-T Recommendation G.957, "Optical Interfaces for Equipments and Relating to the Synchronous Digital Hierarchy," 1992.

ITU: ITU-T Recommendation G.958, "Digital Line Systems Based on the Synchronous Digital Hierarchy for Use on Optical Fiber Cables," 1990.

ITU: ITU-T Recommendation H.221, "Frame Structure for 64 to 1920 kbps Channel in Audiovisual Teleservices," 1990.

ITU: ITU-T Recommendation H.230, "Frame Synchronous Control and Indication Signals for Audiovisual Systems," 1990.

ITU: ITU-T Recommendation H.242, "System for Establishing Communication Between Audiovisual Terminals using Digital Channels up to 2 Mbps," 1990.

ITU: ITU-T Recommendation H.261, "Video Codec for Audiovisual Services at p∞64 kbps," 1990.

ITU: ITU-T Recommendation H.320, "Narrowband Visual Telephone Systems and Terminal Equipment," 1990.

ITU: ITU-T Recommendation H.32x, "Audiovisual Communication Terminal for BISDN," 1992.

ITU: ITU-T Recommendation I.113, "Vocabulary Terms for Broadband Aspects of ISDN," 1992 (rev).

ITU: ITU-T Recommendation I.120, "Integrated Services Digital Network (ISDN)," 1992 (rev).

ITU: ITU-T Recommendation I.121, "Broadband Aspects of ISDN," 1990.

ITU: ITU-T Recommendation I.122, "Framework for Providing Additional Packet Mode Bearer Service," 1991.

ITU: ITU-T Recommendation I.140, "Attribute Technique for the Characterization of the Telecommunication Services Supported by an ISDN and Network Capability of an ISDN," 1992 (rev).

ITU: ITU-T Recommendation I.150, "BISDN ATM Functional Characteristics," 1992 (rev).

ITU: ITU-T Recommendation I.211, "BISDN Service Aspects," 1992 (rev).

ITU: ITU-T Recommendation I.233, "Frame Mode Bearer Services," 1992.

ITU: ITU-T Recommendation I.311, "BISDN General Network Aspects," 1992 (rev).

ITU: ITU-T Recommendation I.321, "BISDN Protocol Reference Model and its Application," 1990.

ITU: ITU-T Recommendation I.327, "BISDN Functional Architecture Aspects," 1992.

ITU: ITU-T Recommendation I.35B, "BISDN ATM Cell Transfer Performance," 1992 (draft).

ITU: ITU-T Recommendation I.361, "BISDN ATM Layer Specification," 1992.

ITU: ITU-T Recommendation I.362, "BISDN ATM Adaptation Layer (AAL) Functional Description," 1992.

ITU: ITU-T Recommendation I.363, "BISDN ATM Adaptation Layer (AAL) Specification," 1992.

ITU: ITU-T Recommendation I.364, "Support of Broadband Connectionless Data Service on BISDN," 1992.

ITU: ITU-T Recommendation I.370, "Congestion Management for the ISDN Frame Relaying Bearer Service," 1991.

ITU: ITU-T Recommendation I.371, "Traffic Control and Congestion Control in BISDN," 1992.

ITU: ITU-T Recommendation I.413, "BISDN User-Network Interface," 1992.

ITU: ITU-T Recommendation I.430, "ISDN Basic Rate User Network Interface Layer 1 Specification," 1992.

ITU: ITU-T Recommendation I.431, "ISDN Primary Rate User Network Interface Layer 1 Specification," 1992 (rev).

ITU: ITU-T Recommendation I.432, "BISDN User-Network Interface—Physical Layer Specification," 1992.

ITU: ITU-T Recommendation I.610, "BISDN UNI Operations and Maintenance Principles," 1992.

ITU: ITU-T Recommendation Q921 (I.441), "ISDN User Network Interface Data Layer Specification," 1988.

ITU: ITU-T Recommendation Q922, "ISDN Data Link Layer Specification for Frame Mode Bearer Services," 1992.

ITU: ITU-T Recommendation Q933, "DSS1 Signaling Specification for Frame Mode Bearer Service," 1992.

"ITU's World Telecommunication Development Report 1995," ITU, October 1995. (*http://www.itu.ch/WTDR95/toc.htm*).

Joos, P., and W. Verbiest: "A Statistical Bandwidth Allocation and Usage Monitoring Algorithm for ATM Networks," ICC '89, 1989, IEEE, Boston, Mass..

Kanayama, Y., Y. Maeda, and H. Ueda: "Virtual Path Management Functions for Broadband ATM Networks," GLOBECOM '91, 1991, IEEE, San Diego, Calif.

Kawashima, K., and H. Saito: "Teletraffic Issues in ATM Networks," *Computer Networks and ISDN Systems,* vol. 20, 1990.

Kazovsky, L.: "Optical Signal Processing for Lightwave Communications Networks," *IEEE Journal on Selected Areas in Communication,* vol. 8, no. 6, August 1990, pp. 973—981.

Kessler, G., and D. Train: *Metropolitan Area Networks—Concepts, Standards and Services,* McGraw-Hill, Inc. New York, N.Y., 1991.

Kim, Y. M., and K. Y. Lee: "PR-Banyan: A Packet Switch with a Pseudo Randomizer for Nonuniform Traffic," ICC '91, 1991, IEEE, Denver, Colo.

Kingsley, S.: "Synchronous Optical Network (Sonet): Overview," *Datapro Communications Analyst,* July 1995.

Kishino, F., K. Manabe, Y. Hayashi, and H. Yasuda: "Variable Bit-Rate Coding of Video Signals for ATM Networks," *IEEE Journal on Selected Areas of Communication,* vol. 7, no. 5, June 1989.

Kleinrock, L.: "ISDN—The Path to Broadband Networks," *IRE Proceedings,* vol. 79, 1991.

Kleinrock, L.: Queuing Systems, *Theory,* vol. 1, John Wiley & Sons, Inc, New York, N.Y., 1975.

Kreig, A., and W. E. Vivian: "Wireless Cable Systems and MMDS," *Broadcast Engineering,* January 1995, pp. 42 ff.

Kroner, H., P. J. Kuhn, and G. Willmann. "Performance Comparison for Resource Sharing Strategies Between Lost-Call-Cleared and Reservation Traffic," ITC-13, 1991, ITU, Geneva.

Kumar, B., and N. Subramaniam: "Routing Strategies for an Hybrid Network Architecture," *Proceedings of the 1991 Symposium on Applied Computing,* Kansas City, Missouri, April 1991, IEEE.

Kuwahara, H., et al.: "Shared Buffer Memory Switch for an ATM Exchange," ICC '90, Boston, Mass., 1989, IEEE, Atlanta, Ga.

Kyees, P. J., R. C. McConnell, and K. Sistanizadeh: "ADSL: A New Twisted-Pair Access to the Information Highway," *IEEE Communications Magazine,* April 1995.

Le Gall, D. J.: "MPEG: A Video Compression Standard for Multimedia Applications," *Communications of ACM,* vol. 34-4, 1991.

Lea, C. T.: "The Load Sharing Banyan Network," *IEEE Transactions Communications,* vol. 35, no. 12, 1986.

Lee, D-S., K-H. Tzou, and S-Q. Li: "Control Analysis of Video Packet Loss in ATM Networks," *SPIE Visual Communications and Image Processing '90,* vol. 1360, 1990.

Leland, W. E.: "Window-Based Congestion Management in Broadband ATM Networks: The Performance of Three Access-Control Policies," GLOBECOM '89, 1989, IEEE, Dallas, Tex.

Leslie, I.: "Fairisle: An ATM Network for the Local Area," *Proceedings of ACM SIGCOMM '91,* Zurich, Switzerland, September 3—6, 1991.

Louviom, J. R., J. Boyer, and J. B. Gravereaux: "Statistical Multiplexing of VBR Sources in ATM Networks," 3rd IEEE CAMAD Workshop, 1990.

Maglaris, B., D. Anastassiou, P. Sen, G. Karlsson, and J. Robins: "Performance Models of Statistical Multiplexing in Packet Video Communications," *IEEE Transactions on Communications,* vol. 36, 1988.

Marketos, J.: "The Return System: A Historical Perspective," *CED: Communications Engineering & Design,* September 1995.

McCullough, D.: "SDV: Delivering Multimedia to the Home," *CED: Communications Engineering & Design,* September 1995, pp. 36 ff.

Mehmet toy, Dr.: "ATM development and applications—Selected reading," IEEE Press, 1996. (*http://www.ieee.org/eab/*)

Minoli, D.: *Video Dialtone Technology,* McGraw-Hill Inc., New York, N.Y., 1995.

Minzer, S. E.: "Broadband ISDN and Asynchronous Transfer Mode (ATM)," *IEEE Communications Magazine,* September 1989.

Miyao, Y.: "A Call Admission Control Scheme in ATM Networks," ICC '91, 1991, pp. 391–396, IEEE, Denver, Colo.

Network World, articles in 1992, 1993 issues.

Nikolaidis, I., and I. F. Akyildiz: "Source Characterization and Statistical Multiplexing in ATM Networks," *Technical Report GIT-CC-92/24,* Georgia Institute of Technology, Atlanta, Ga, 1992.

Norgaard, K.: "Evaluation of Output Traffic from an ATM Node," ITC-13, 1991, pp. 533-537.

Onvural, R. O., and I. Nikolaidis: "Routing in ATM Networks," *High Speed Networks,* H. G. Perros, ed., Plennum Publishers, New York, N.Y., 1992.

Pangrac, D. M., and L. D. Williamson: "Fiber Trunk and Feeder—The Continuing Evolution," *ATC NCTA Technical Papers,* 1990.

Personick, S. D.: *Fiber Optics: Technology and Applications,* Plenum Publishers, New York, N.Y, 1990.

Peterson, R.: "Richard Peterson's DBS Frequently Asked Questions," Version 26, October 30, 1995 (*http://www.dbs.digifix.com/DBS/dbs_faq.htmld/00.html*).

Ransom, M. N.: "The VISTAnet Gigabit Network Testbed," *Journal of High Speed Networks,* vol. 1, no. 1, 1990.

Redman, B. L.: "Moving From Local-Area Communications to Network Computing-Capable Infrastructures," *GartnerGroup,* June 30, 1995.

Rice, W. O., and H. G. Perros: "What's New in B-ISDN Standards," *High Speed Networks,* H. G. Perros, ed., Plenum Publishers, New York, N.Y., 1992.

Russell, J.: "Multimedia Networking Performance Requirements," *ATM Networks,* I. Viniotis and R. O. Onvural, eds., Plenum Publishers, New York, N.Y., 1993.

Saito, H., M. Kawarasaki, and H. Yamada: "An Analysis of Statistical Multiplexing in an ATM Transport Network," *IEEE Journal on Selected Areas of Communication*, vol. 9, no. 3, April 1991.

Schormans, J., J. Pitts, and E. Scharf: "Time Priorities in ATM Switches," ITC-13, 1991, ITU, Geneva, Switzerland.

Schulzrinne, H., J. F. Kurose, and D. Towsley: "Congestion Control for Real-Time Traffic in High-Speed Networks," INFOCOM '90, 1990.

Schwartz, M.: *Computer—Communications Network Design and Analysis*, Prentice-Hall, Inc., Englewood Cliffs, N.J., 1977.

Schwartz, M.: *Telecommunications Networks*, Addison-Wesley Publishing Co., Reading, Mass., 1987.

Sexton, M., and Reid: *Transmission Networking: SONET and the Synchronous Digital Hierarchy*, Artech House, Norwood, Mass.

SONET Interoperability Forum Homepage (*http://www.adc.com/~don/sif/remote.html*).

Spohn, D. L.: *Data Network Design*, McGraw-Hill Inc., New York, N.Y., 1993.

Sriram, K., and D. M. Lucantoni: "Traffic Smoothing Effects of Bit Dropping in a Packet Voice Multiplexer," INFOCOM '88, 1988.

Sriram, K., R. S. McKinney, and M. H. Sherif: "Voice Packetization and Compression in Broadband ATM Networks," *IEEE Journal on Selected Areas of Communication*, vol. 9, no. 3, April 1991.

Stallings, W.: *ISDN—An Introduction*, Macmillan Publishing Co., New York, N.Y., 1989.

Sutherland, J., and L. Litteral: "Residential Video Services," *IEEE Communication Magazine*, vol. 30, no. 7, 1992.

Suzuki, H., et al.: "Output Buffer Switch Architecture for Asynchronous Transfer Mode," ICC '89, Boston, Mass., 1989, IEEE, Boston, Mass.

Sweeney, T.: "Copper Loop Breaks 50-mbps Barrier," *Communications Week International*, September 1995 (*http://techweb.cmp.com/cwi/current/50n7.html*).

Tanenbaum, A. S.: *Computer Networks*, 3d ed., Prentice Hall, Inc., Englewood Cliffs, N.J., March 1996.

Telecom Data Report, all 1993 issues.

Telecom 95 Daily: "ATM Pioneers," *Communications Week International*, no. 155, December 1995 (*http://192.216.191.71/telecom95/DURING/mktp7abc.html*).

Telecommunication Magazine, all 1992, 1993 issues.

"The Telecommunications Act of 1996: A Legalized Free-for-All," *The Yankee Group,* February 1996.

Tirtaatmadja, E., and R. A. Palmer: "The Application of Virtual Paths to the Interconnection of IEEE 802.6 Metropolitan Area Networks," *Proceedings of XIII ISS,* Stockholm, Sweden, 1990.

Tseng, K. H., and M. T. Hsiao: "Admission Control of Voice/Data Integration in an ATM Network," ICC '91, 1991, IEEE, Denver, Colo.

Turner, J. S.: "Managing Bandwidth in ATM Networks with Bursty Traffic," *IEEE Network Magazine,* vol. 6, no. 5, September 1992.

van Landegem, T., and P. Peschi: "Managing a Connectionless Virtual Overlay Network on Top of ATM," Proceedings of ICC '91, IEEE Denver, Colo., 1991.

Verbeist, W., and L. Pinnoo: "A Variable Rate Video Codec for Asynchronous Transfer Mode Networks," *IEEE Journal on Selected Areas of Communication,* vol. 7, no. 5, June 1989.

Virtamo, J. T, and J. W. Roberts: "Evaluating Buffer Requirements in an ATM Multiplexer," GLOBECOM '89, 1989, IEEE, Dallas, Tex.

Wang, Q., and V. S. Frost: "Efficient Estimation of Cell Blocking Probability for ATM Systems," ICC '91, 1991, IEEE, Denver, Colo.

Wilson, L.: "Are Price Delays Costing ATM?," Interop 95, *Information Week,* September 26, 1994. 192.216.191.71/techweb/iw/interop/926cs2.htm

Wirbel, L., and R. Wilson: "Internet Access: One-Chip Wonder?," *Electronic Engineering Times,* December 4, 1995.

Woodworth, C. B., M. J. Karol, and R. D. Gillin: "A Flexible Broadband Packet Switch for a Multimedia Integrated Network," ICC '91, 1991, IEEE, Denver, Colo.

Wulleman, R., and T. van Landegem: "Comparison of ATM Switching Architectures," *International Journal of Digital and Analog Cabled Systems,* vol. 2, no. 4, 1989.

Yamada, H., and S. Sumita: "A Traffic Measurement Method and its Application for Cell Loss Probability Estimation in ATM Networks," *IEEE Journal on Selected Areas of Communication,* vol. 9, no. 3, April 1991.

Yamashita, H., H. G. Perros, and S. W. Hong: "Performance Modelling of a Shared Buffer ATM Switch Architecture," ITC-13, 1993, ITU, Geneva, Switzerland.

Yasuda, Y., H. Yasuda, N. Ohta, and F. Kishino: "Packet Video Transmission through ATM Networks," GLOBECOM '89, 1989, IEEE, Dallas, Tex.

Yates, R. K., N. Mohé, and J. Masson: *Fiber Optics and CATV Business Strategy,* Artech House, Boston, Mass., 1990.

Zimmerman, H.: "OSI Reference Model—The ISO Model of Architecture for Open Systems Interconnection," *IEEE Transactions on Communications,* vol. 28, no. 4, April 1980.

INDEX

About the Author

Balaji Kumar is Senior Manager for Local Network Strategy and Architecture at MCI. He is a frequent speaker at industry conferences such as SUPERCOM and Interop, and has written many papers for industry publications, and chaired technical conferences. Kumar's previous management and staff positions with Andersen Consulting and Bell Northern Research, Inc., have provided him with more than 15 years of experience in the broadband communications area. A graduate of the University of Dallas (MBA) and the University of Missouri (Master of Science, Computer Science), and a professional badminton player, he is currently based in Richardson, Texas. He is also a member of IEEE and AMA.